Entangled Edens

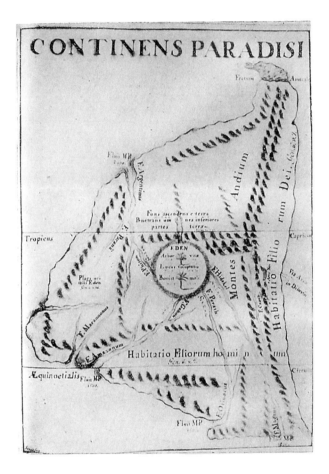

"The Continent of Paradise," a map of South America based on
Antonio de León Pinelo's book *New World Paradise (El paraíso
del Nuevo Mundo)*. First published in 1656, the map shows
Eden at the juncture of the present-day Orinoco, Amazon, and
Paraguay Rivers.

Candace Slater

Entangled Edens

VISIONS OF THE AMAZON

UNIVERSITY OF CALIFORNIA PRESS
Berkeley / Los Angeles / London

University of California Press
Berkeley and Los Angeles, California

University of California Press, Ltd.
London, England

Library of Congress Cataloging-in-Publication Data

Slater, Candace
    Entangled edens : visions of the Amazon /
Candace Slater.
        p.   cm.
    Includes bibliographical references and index.
    ISBN 0-520-22641-0 (cloth : alk. paper)
    1. Amazon River Region—Description and
travel.   2. Utopias—Amazon River Region.
3. Myth.   4. Amazon River Region—Public
opinion.   I. Title.
F2546 .S67   2002
981—dc21   2001035866

Manufactured in the United States of America
10 09 08 07 06 05 04 03 02 01
10 9 8 7 6 5 4 3 2 1

The paper used in this publication meets the
minimum requirements of ANSI/NISO Z39.48–1992
(R 1997) (Permanence of Paper). ∞

I liked the place; I liked the idea of the place.
Two rivers. Hadn't two rivers sprung
from the Garden of Eden? No, that was four
and they'd diverged. Here only two
and coming together. Even if one were tempted
to literary interpretations
such as: life / death, right / wrong, male / female
—such notions would have resolved, dissolved,
    straight off
in that watery, dazzling dialectic.

Elizabeth Bishop,
"Santarém," *Questions of Travel*

Here in the Amazon the stories spring up as fast
as trees.

Taxi driver, age eighteen,
Santarém, Brazil, 1995

Contents

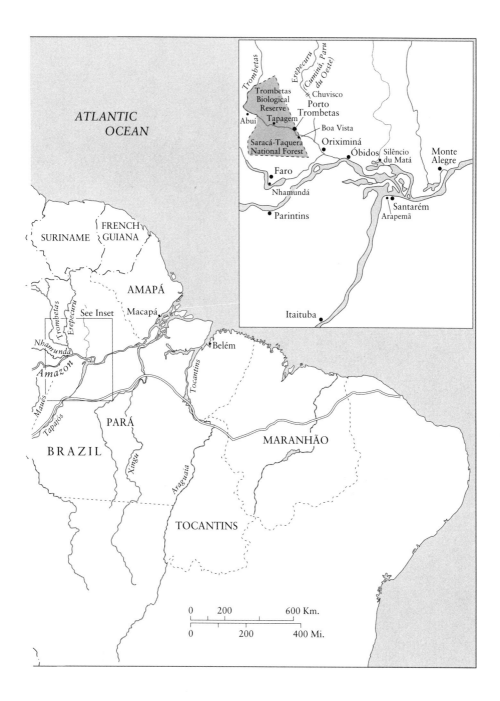

ATLANTIC
OCEAN

SURINAME FRENCH
GUIANA

AMAPÁ

Macapá

See Inset

Trombetas
Erepecuru
Nhamundá
Amazon
Maués
Tapajós

Belém

PARÁ

Tocantins

Xingu

Araguaia

BRAZIL

MARANHÃO

TOCANTINS

0   200   600 Km.

0   200   400 Mi.

Trombetas
Erepecuru
Cuminá, Paru
du Oeste

Trombetas
Biological
Reserve
Tapagem

Chuvisco
Porto
Trombetas
Boa Vista

Abuí

Saracá-Taquera
National Forest

Oriximiná

Óbidos Silêncio
du Matá

Monte
Alegre

Faro

Nhamundá

Santarém
Arapemã

Parintins

Itaituba

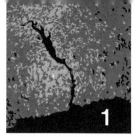

The Meeting of the Waters

Our conclusions are that a kind of aquatic alchemy takes place.

Jacques-Yves Cousteau and Mose Richards,
describing the meeting of the waters at Manaus,
in *Jacques Cousteau's Amazon Journey*

The meeting of the waters? Oh yes, there is no one here who hasn't heard the story. There is no one here who doesn't know the place.

Fisherman, age twenty-six, Araguainha, Brazil, 1988

The Amazon in Surround Sound

On a rainy March night, my childhood friend Suzanna and I find our way into seats at the back of the Natural History Museum theater in Seattle, where I have gone to visit her. "This should be interesting," says Suzanna as we lean back in the padded chairs. "I wonder what you'll think of it, after all the time you've spent in the Amazon."

The lights soon go off and then come on as pinpricks in the ceiling as an immense world of trees and waters looms before our eyes. Parrots squawk, monkeys howl, and the sun hits a wonderfully comic tree sloth,

causing several children in the audience to giggle in delight. Butterflies flit by and a snake slithers through the distant grass. The voice-over
welcomes us to the world's biggest treasure trove of biodiversity—
two thousand square miles of water, wood, and leaves. The Amazon is
the world's largest and most powerful river, the narrator tells us, dis-
charging three million cubic feet of water per second into the Atlantic
Ocean during the rainy season. The land drained by its waters covers a
full 7 percent of the earth's surface. Here, in what has become a threatened natural paradise, a typical four-square-mile patch of forest contains up to 1,500 species of flowering plants, as many as 750 species of
trees, 125 species of mammals, 400 species of birds, 100 different reptiles, 60 amphibians, and 150 butterflies.[1]

In the scenes that follow, a native healer leaves his village in the jade-
green mountains to descend into a yet greener forest in search of medicinal herbs. Along the way, he passes a group of Indians in intricately
embroidered clothing, river turtles lazing in the sun, several lithe and
handsome jaguars, and a rainbow of other plants and animals. The film
also presents the American ethnobotanist Mark Plotkin, who is investi-
gating native remedies for various ills. In a later sequence in an open-air
market, Plotkin and the healer's paths cross, and they briefly salute each
other. Once the healer finds the remedy for which he is searching, the
camera follows his return to his mountain village up the foaming river,
whose dense banks reveal myriad insects, strange-looking anteaters, and
birds.[2]

This "immense ecological machine of global importance" is full of
marvelous surprises. The crown of a single tree may host as many as five
thousand types of insect. Beneath the two-million-square-mile forest
canopy, we are told, is a timeless land far larger than the Roman empire
that spans portions of nine countries, and which is still home to hundreds of unique native cultures with rich Stone Age roots.

The healer's arrival home opens the way into a plethora of images of
an intensely lovely firmament of green and blue. As the sun sets over the
river, the camera pans over the tops of mist-shrouded trees. "Home at
last. Now it is our turn to protect and preserve all that we have seen,"
the narrator declares.

When the lights come on and people begin to leave the theater, Suzanna eyes me expectantly. "So, what did you think?" she asks. I hes-
itate, and Suzanna fixes her clear gray eyes upon me. I realize that I
can't keep what I am thinking from her any better than I could when we

were nine. "There's something you didn't like," she says, reaching for her keys.

I search for the words to express the conflicting thoughts running through my mind. I want to tell her that I both liked and didn't like the movie. The magnificent shots of the river made me feel as if I were floating once more through the flooded forest in a dugout, slapping at mosquitoes while peering up at the leafy rafters of great trees. Who watching the scenes of the sun poking through that emerald canopy could fail to be moved by the true grandeur of the forest? How could I quarrel with the message that the rain forest is a precious heritage that demands protection?

And yet, the movie struck me as a rehash of every other documentary I had ever seen in which the Amazon appeared as an exotic realm of nature. It presented all the familiar icons in the first two minutes: the snake, the jaguar, the dancing Indians in their embroidered costumes, the toucan, the big trees reflected in the even bigger river. It had the native healer and the American scientist both working to harness the forest's cures.

What bothered me most of all about the IMAX presentation, however, wasn't anything it showed. Plants and animals and native peoples fully deserve the attention that the movie gave them. Indeed, they deserve far more.[3] But where were the less-glamorous swamps and brush lands, the big and little cities that account for more than half the population of 23 million people for whom the Amazon is home?[4] Sure, there were people in the movie—the native healer, the whirling Indians in their crimson costumes, the folksy-looking people at the market. But where were the descendants of black slaves, the Sephardic Jews, the Japanese agricultural workers, the Arab merchants, and the mixed-blood rubber tappers who have helped create the rich, distinctive cultures of an immense and varied region?

Where, above all, were the ordinary people who often have a vision of nature very different from anything presented in idealized Technicolor documentaries? Where were the thorny issues of justice and injustice that scenes of a marvelous nature too often cloak? Where were the slave descendants forced off the land their great-grandparents had settled and planted, the gold miners whose genuine abuses of the land and native peoples have made them all-too-convenient scapegoats for a multitude of ills? My problem with the IMAX movie was not just that it was simplistic. It also was that the movie's presentation of exotic plants and an-

imals together with a select group of "natural" people encouraged outsiders to follow a long tradition of seeing the Amazon as a realm of nature that it was their mission or their right—and not the mission or right
of Amazonians—to protect. And this protection, no matter how well in-
tentioned, was a form of outside control, and therefore suspect.

Even as it evoked a one-dimensional world of trees and birds and giant sloths, the movie made me think back to the day that I arrived in the
Brazilian river port city of Parintins on my first trip to the Amazon in
1988. As I got off the boat, I broke the strap on my only pair of sandals. Fortunately, there turned out to be a shoemaker only a few blocks
away.[5]

"This won't be hard," the old man with bright white hair and nut-
meg-colored skin assured me. Wetting the strap with glue, he deftly rein-
serted it into the sandal, then drove in two small nails. "Your sandal will
be as good as new now," he said. "Just have a seat there by Raimundo
and wait until the glue can dry."

As I eased myself onto the splintery bench, the shoemaker's friend
Raimundo went on with the story that he had been telling when I arrived. "And so, after the third great wave broke, that man suddenly saw
his wife beside him on the beach," he said to Tô Pereira. " 'Hand over
our little boy to me so that I can take him home and rock him to sleep
in the hammock,' she said to her husband. And so, he gave the baby to
his wife. But then, when he arrived home, there was his wife alone,
preparing supper. 'Where's the baby?' she demanded, and he turned as
white as milk."

"Ah," said Tô. "So it must have been an Encantado in the wife's form
who carried off that little boy."

Raimundo nodded gravely. "It was an Encantado," he confirmed.
"Poor man! But he put too much confidence in appearances. That Encantado who appeared on the beach beside him was the spitting image
of his wife; the man didn't have the least suspicion. And so he handed
over the child. His firstborn son would grow up beneath the waves,
probably lost to him forever. So far as I know, nobody ever saw the boy
again."

Tô Pereira shook his head. "Something like that once happened to
my uncle Mané," he said. "Or at least, that is what people say. You may
already know the story. A man who looked just like my uncle's best
friend was showing up those nights when Mané was out upon the river
fishing, trying to make love to his wife. Well then, she was afraid to tell
him. But she kept getting thinner, paler. And when he finally demanded

to know what was happening, she told him everything. So then, the next morning, he went to see the friend armed with a fish knife and a revolver. Because he wasn't going to stand for anything like that, you see.

"'What do you think you're doing in my house when I'm out on the river?' he shouted at his friend, with his hand upon the gun.

"'In your house?' the friend exclaimed. 'But Mané, it's been almost two months now since my shadow has fallen on your door.' So then, of course, my uncle realized what had been happening. That man who had been visiting his wife was certainly an Enchanted Being. But look, he could have just gone and put a bullet in his best friend's head. And no one would have ever known that it was a thing of the Encante. But later, the two of them chased down the Dolphin, who plunged into the water and never appeared in those parts again."

"Why are the Enchanted Beings so attracted to humans?" I interrupted. In ethnographies of the Amazon I had seen references to folk beliefs about a wealthy underwater city peopled by shape-changing dolphins and anacondas. However, I'd never really thought about how and why these residents of the river bottom interacted with people, and listening to Raimundo's story, I found myself intensely curious.

Their absorption in the stories had made the men almost forget my presence. Both looked at me in surprise, and Tô gave an easy laugh. "The Encantados," he explained, "are a thing of nature and have no control over their own desires. They live in a city where the sidewalks are made of silver and the roofs are all of gold, but still they are attracted to human beings, because while we humans are poor, we have more liberty. And so, the woman to whom the man handed the baby was no real woman, but rather, an Encantado. And the friend who was trying to find his way into the hammock of my Uncle Mané was an Enchanted Being as well."

When I frowned in an attempt to take in what he had just told me, Tô assumed that I must doubt his story. "I don't claim these things are true," he told me crisply as he turned back to his work. "Perhaps they are, perhaps they aren't. But the point is that nature is full of mysteries that we humans will never fully understand. You who come here from the outside may find these things strange. But that is because where you live, no one spends the night upon the river. You buy fish in those little packages in the supermarket, and so, of course, you've never seen an Encantado. So these stories talk about a world you cannot know."

At the time, I didn't know exactly what to think. It was clear that the stories had a meaning far beyond exotic tall tales. But I wasn't sure what to make of a watery nature that appeared to impinge upon the lives of human beings. Although the men and women in the stories were quite capable of responding to the Encante (the husband in the second tale permanently chased away the roving Dolphin), nature was clearly something whose transformations placed it beyond human control.

Moreover, I was intrigued by Tô's barbed comments about outsiders. Was the world of the Encantados one I could not know because I did not live in the Amazon? Or was it closed to me because outsiders' overly confident vision of Amazonian nature as nothing more than a bio-diverse Rain Forest made it impossible to see the world another way? Tô's comments left me unsure about his meaning and eager to know more.

"It's these other sorts of visions that I don't find in the IMAX movie," I tell Suzanna. "Nothing in the movie makes us think about all of the very different people who live in the Amazon. Nothing makes us think that our own fascination with an idealized forest may exclude other ways of seeing—Amazonians' ways of seeing. Nothing leads us to suspect that our own focus on spectacular nature may be not only too narrow, but potentially unjust."

Entangled Edens

This book is about competing images of the Amazon. It traces back into the distant past the roots of our own notions of a dense forest realm that glimmers with possibility, and compares outsiders' present-day ideas about the Amazon to those of the people who actually live there. In so doing, it traces out a symbolic heritage every bit as complex, as precious, and as essential to the planet's future as the Amazon's much-touted biological diversity. This multifaceted heritage suggests new ways of seeing a region that is home to half of the world's living species, a fifth of its freshwater, its largest tropical forest, and a wide array of peoples whom the Rain Forest often threatens to conceal. (Capitalizing Rain Forest here and elsewhere emphasizes the iconic forest as much as the literal one, which often has no single specific geographic location.)

The accounts of the Amazon that appear in the following pages have been handed down over the centuries. A wide variety of groups and individuals have actively altered particular written texts and oral histories to fit their own needs and interests, so that what looks similar on the surface often turns out to have different meanings and different aims. The narratives that both "they" and "we" continue to recast to our own specifications underscore important differences between past and present, between a diverse collection of Amazonians and equally diverse outsiders. At the same time, the tales and their tellers are actually more interconnected than first appears, since their ideas and ours have been in constant and uneasy play for some five hundred years. The fabulously bio-diverse Rain Forest of the IMAX movie, for instance, is an heir to El Dorado, the fabled sixteenth-century city of gold. It also finds a counterpoint in the enchanted lake within a lake of slave-descendant folk tradition, whose wondrous abundance leads some storytellers to compare it to Noah's Ark. "There you have two of everything that has ever existed," one young woman in a tiny village some three hours from Parintins tells me as she shoos a stubborn fly away from her baby's chin. "Two mountain lions, two monkeys, two tambaqui fish, two stingrays, even two big, black bugs just like this one."

Inhabitants of different worlds, the scriptwriter for the IMAX movie and these Amazonian storytellers appeal to largely separate audiences, unequal in terms of money and power.[6] The stories themselves make clear the ways in which different groups and individuals use particular images to further their own interests ("These stories show how only we Amazonians truly understand the river") and make claims on nature ("And so, the river, like the land, should be ours"). In the process, the Amazon becomes significant not only as the world's biggest tropical forest, but also as a touchstone for better understanding the role of symbols in determining who gets what and in whose name.[7]

The larger story that I tell here is one of multiple and skewed encounters—between books and oral narratives, between land and water, and between different segments of an international public and different groups of Amazonians.[8] The interactions I describe here are not intended as a compendium, but rather a distillation. Although some representations of the region are more factually accurate than others, I am less concerned with stripping away layers of myth to get at something that may lie beneath than I am in better understanding the sorts of convergences and ongoing tensions evident within a rich variety of images.[9] In contrast to the IMAX movie, which sets out to portray "a timeless land where reality is more startling than myth," I argue that encounters among different myths—including that of a timeless land—have helped to shape the Amazon's myriad realities.

What I offer is not a literary or environmental history so much as an Amazon-centered poetics—by which I mean a systematic examination of words and images that can help us better understand such seemingly unpoetic concerns as deforestation and species preservation. How U.S. lawmakers vote on a foreign aid bill that will affect Amazonian countries depends much on whether they think of the region as a Green Hell or a Green Cathedral. A region billed as "the world's lungs"—and, increasingly, its "toxin-removing kidneys"—is bound to trigger different reactions than a place that appears as its heart, its brain, or its solar plexus.[10] Is the Amazon a primeval garden from which we should help exclude all or certain people in order to preserve it? Is it a source of cancer cures on which we must get patents? A jungle to be developed, or plundered for its natural resources, or cleared for agriculture? If we can identify the true source of our own desire for an unspoiled natural paradise, we may find ourselves more able to see the rich variety not just of life forms, but also of human experience, that exists within the Amazon. And in seeing this variety, we can respond in a less uniform and therefore more effective manner to a host of different people, plants, and animals. We can also better resist the tendency to dehumanize and metaphorically erase whole populations that do not share our particular environmental concerns or who voice them in very different ways.

The title *Entangled Edens* refers to the varied images of a terrestrial paradise—and of an accompanying earthly hell—that the Amazon has long evoked in both insiders and outsiders.[11] In conjuring up the original garden of delights, it confirms the central role of nature in a wide variety of portrayals of the Amazon, including a number by Amazonians.[12] The "tangle" refers to the dense labyrinth of rain forest vegetation and to the jumbled histories and geographies—north and south; European and American; local, national, and global—that lie behind competing notions such as the Green Cathedral and Green Hell.[13] Thus, while the trees and water on the cover of this book at first call to mind the vegetal universe of a hundred TV documentaries, the intertwining of the wavy forest with the uncannily treelike river hints at the many different tensions and exchanges that this larger tangle encompasses.

The initial impetus for *Entangled Edens* was my own deep sense of disjuncture. On the one hand, there were the people and the places that I, a professor of literature who had spent some fifteen years studying folk cultures in other parts of Brazil, began experiencing firsthand when I started doing fieldwork in the Amazon in 1988.[14] On the other, there were the images of the rain forest that bombarded me each time I returned to the United States. What, I wondered, could possibly be the relationship between the forest crammed with rare blue orchids and iridescent butterflies of such deep interest to my friends and students, and the mysterious underwater cities and sometimes frankly malevolent enchanted beings that kept surfacing in stories like the one I had heard while waiting for my sandal to be repaired? Was there any link at all between the people of mixed ethnic heritage whom I continued to meet on riverboats, in gold camps, and in the heart of sprawling cities, and the Indians in feathered haloes who peered out from between the giant trees on "Save the Rain Forest" posters? And why did most people back home seem wholly unaware of this multiple and very human Amazon's existence?

Too large to address directly, these questions led me to start looking at apparent convergences among a number of the most important "outside" images of the Amazon and images in the local, "inside" stories I was collecting. With time, I came to focus on a small number of recurring representations, which I present here in this book as three sets of paired chapters. In each of these cases, the initial member of the pair is from outside the Amazon, the second from within.

In thinking about how portrayals of the Amazon from outside the region have become enmeshed with others from within it, I have found it useful to think in terms of "giants" and "shape-shifters." I associate the "giants" primarily with (some) outsiders and the "shape-shifters" primarily with (some) Amazonians. However, what looks at the outset like a contrast quickly turns out to be a fluid nexus of interlacing strands. Although giants and shape-shifters have no life of their own, the varied roles and meanings that different people give them over time illuminate much larger struggles—political, economic, environmental, and symbolic. As they do so, they offer a jumping-off point into an Amazon yet more diverse and surprising than the one in the IMAX movie.

The Amazon in Space and Time

By "Amazon" or "Amazonia" I mean the entire basin drained by the Amazon River and its eleven hundred tributaries—an area approximately the size of the continental United States. Other scholars define the region differently: some include only the Amazonian portions of Brazil, Venezuela, Colombia, Ecuador, Peru, and Bolivia; some toss in Guyana, Suriname, and French Guiana. (Suriname and French Guiana are technically not part of the Amazon watershed. The first eight nations are members of the Amazon Treaty Pact of 1978, but French Guiana remains a part of France.) The region's population—which a U.N. report published in 1992 places at 23 million—is also defined in varying ways.[15] And yet, even while the Amazon's size all but guarantees its variety, it is possible to offer a capsule overview of its history.[16]

The date of the beginnings of a human presence in the Amazon—as throughout the Americas—remains open to question. Recent evidence suggests that hunters and gatherers began arriving in various corners of the Americas somewhere between ten thousand and thirty thousand—and even fifty to sixty thousand—years ago.[17]

The first waves of foragers probably entered the Amazonian interior by following river courses and picking their way through interfluvial forests. Although the repeated rise and fall in sea level during the Pleistocene era has erased any direct evidence of these earliest peoples, cave and rock-wall paintings at various sites near Monte Alegre in the Brazilian Amazon indicate a human presence dating back as early as 11,000 years ago.[18]

By the time the Europeans first laid eyes on the Amazon, the floodplain (or várzea) and its adjacent uplands (the terra firme) boasted large and prosperous chiefdoms along extensive stretches of the river. These chiefdoms were not just sizable, they were culturally sophisticated, practicing intensive agriculture, engaging in complex trade networks, and possessing artistic abilities evident in shards of intricately designed pottery. New archaeological evidence has prompted a steady rise in demographic estimates of the region. An increasing number of scholars now calculate the precontact population at as many as 15 million people.[19] A single Tapajó village on the site of present-day Santarém, for instance, extended for several kilometers and was home to more than forty thousand people.[20] These figures, together with mounting evidence that Amazonian populations inhabited not just the floodplains but parts of the terra firme, leave no doubt that various native societies of the Amazon had developed a range of techniques for successfully exploiting the resources offered by the forests and the rivers with which the land is intertwined.

The sixteenth and seventeenth centuries saw considerable European exploration of the Amazon—not just by the Spanish and Portuguese, but also by the French, the English, the Germans, and the Dutch, all eager to capitalize on a series of forest products (cinnamon, wild cacao, vanilla) and other regional items such as feathers, turtle oil, and tobacco.[21] The first European expedition to traverse the Amazon—that led by Francisco de Orellana from Ecuador in 1542—was seeking both the golden city of El Dorado and the Land of Cinnamon.[22]

These explorations, and the ensuing inroads made by missionaries, traders, and slavers, would lead to the decimation of the Indian population. Those Indians not relocated to missionary communities (the Jesuit *reducciones* or *aldeias*, which flourished throughout much of the Amazon for some 150 years) often died at the hands of government soldiers, ironically known as "rescue troops," who pressed them into slavery. Moreover, conversion to Christianity rarely proved to be a shield against imported diseases such as smallpox and measles.[23]

During this two-hundred-year period, the Europeans succeeded in reshaping existing trade patterns between the lowlands and the highlands into an export economy oriented toward the coast. At the same time, cacao, sugarcane, and cotton plantations, as well as cattle ranches, were springing up in various corners of the Amazon. This incipient plantation economy became stronger over time as a growing European taste for chocolate made cacao a prime export in Ecuador, Venezuela, and Brazil. In some portions of the Amazon, the labor for these plantations was provided primarily by African slaves, who would later join Indians and poor persons of mixed blood in popular uprisings such as the enormous Cabanagem rebellion, which convulsed the Brazilian Amazon between 1835 and 1839. Although conservative forces loyal to the Brazilian empire eventually quashed the rebels with great violence, the revolt left some thirty thousand people, or nearly a quarter of the Amazonian population, dead.[24]

Since cacao did not take up much space in the export ships that began calling at Amazonian ports to collect the harvest, there was room for a number of the previously mentioned regional commodities that otherwise might not have found their way to Europe.[25] In this sense, the growing plantation system helped rather than hindered an older extractive economy. Nonetheless, to the extent that the plantations and cattle ranches fostered reinvestment of at least a percentage of profits in the land, they held out new hope for the emergence of a regional economic network. The plantations, however, began to wane after Charles Goodyear's discovery of the process of vulcanization in 1839. The ensuing commercial viability of rubber forcibly wed the Amazon, where rubber trees were abundant, to a European industrial economy. In so doing, it squelched hopes of anything resembling regional autonomy and guaranteed that any future signs of popular rebellion would be summarily suppressed.

Europe's dependence on the Amazon for "indiarubber" helped fuel an already existing fascination with the flora and fauna that Iberian writers had been describing for at least two centuries. (The Jesuit Cristóbal de Acuña's 1641 *New Discovery of the Great River of the Amazons* contained such a wealth of detailed information about economically valuable flora and fauna that the Spaniards tried to keep it out of print.)[26] However, the great majority of later naturalists—such as Charles de la Condamine, Alexander von Humboldt, Henry Walter Bates, Richard Spruce, and Alfred Russel Wallace, who were to find an eager public—were not from Spain or Portugal, but from northern Europe and the United States. Although these "scientist-travelers" rarely had direct connections to the commercial ventures associated with the industrial expansion of the colonial powers, their studies clearly served the cause of Empire. The much cited smuggling of rubber seeds out of the Amazon to England's Kew Gardens, from which they were taken to Malaya, is part of a much broader legacy of botanical cataloguing and investigation that they helped to establish.[27]

The rubber seeds in question did so well in Malayan plantations that they quickly put the Amazonian rubber barons out of business. (Amazonian rubber trees are subject to disease when cultivated close together, and thrive only in the wild.)[28] Because so much of the wealth from rubber, or "white gold," had gone into the pockets of foreign investors or their domestic allies (often investors from Rio or Bogotá or Lima), the collapse of the rubber trade in 1910 left most Amazonians little better off than they had been before its rise. New boom-and-bust cycles—jute, gold, tin, bauxite—would replace rubber in various corners of the region.[29] However, the Amazon would continue to exist on the social and political margins of the nations that it dominates in terms of land. (The Amazonian portion of both Peru and Bolivia accounts for some three-quarters of each country's territory, yet the two are still routinely described as "Andean" nations.)

In the 1960s, a number of Amazonian nations, backed by aid from foreign banks, launched intensive development programs designed to harness the forest's riches and draw previously isolated sectors of the countries into modernization schemes. New highways were constructed, large-scale colonization projects initiated, and tax incentives given to multinational corporations that set up shop in the Amazon. In Colombia, Bolivia, Peru, and Ecuador, the construction of extensive oil and gas pipelines cut through massive tracts of land inhabited by native peoples. The resulting deforestation (and, in some cases, soil contamination) made the Amazonian Rain Forest a focal point for a new international environmental movement that assumed increasing prominence beginning in the early 1970s.

Today, the ongoing destruction of massive chunks of forest that add up to an area at least as big as France or Germany has exacerbated global fears about the loss of plant and animal species.[30] At the same time, the emergence of new populist organizations formed by Indians, rubber tappers, or black slave descendants has given a region long portrayed as a realm of nature a selectively human face. The appearance of Chico Mendes, head of the Brazilian Rubber Tappers' Union, before the U.S. Congress in 1988, and his subsequent murder the next year, drew new attention to the people within Amazonia.[31] So did the appearance of Indians in full traditional attire before the assembly charged with hammering out a new constitution for Brazil in 1988, and the massive marches of indigenous peoples demanding land rights in Bolivia and Ecuador in the early 1990s.[32]

Despite the new importance of people in portrayals of the Amazon, its wealth of cultures and its powerful and varied legacy of symbols still do not command the attention they deserve. For most nonspecialists today, the Amazon remains the marvelous, threatened natural paradise that appears in the IMAX movie. Moreover, despite growing scholarly attention to particular groups of Amazonians, the ongoing stress on the Amazon as a repository of flora and fauna whose importance dwarfs all other aspects of the region is by no means limited to a general public.

The Amazon as "Giant"

The dizzying statistics with which the IMAX movie bombards its viewers reinforce a long-standing sense of the Amazon's enormous size and vast importance. ("It's so big!" exclaimed the small boy seated in front of Suzanna, and it would be hard to disagree.) However, when I speak of "giants" in the following pages, I am referring less to these numbers or to particular gigantic entities (the world's biggest moth or fish or snake, the world's tallest tree or longest river) than to a narrative process in which one part comes to stand in for a larger whole.[33]

Giants, in the sense in which I use the word, are selective icons such as that of the Rain Forest in the IMAX movie. Like any icon—be it the symbol on which one clicks to open one's electronic mail or the gilt-encrusted images of Russian saints—a giant possesses a concentrated force. The Rain Forest is a powerful symbol because of the immediacy with which it evokes not just vivid images but a whole array of cherished beliefs about the natural world. Giants' ability to summon up these larger beliefs makes them a potent catalyst for thought and action. At the same time, however, they may also conceal or skew a larger whole to suit a particular end. This is because although often large in their own right, giants ultimately turn out to be fragments of something bigger and far more difficult to grasp. They express deep desires and awaken intense fears even while they conceal, and deflect attention from, their own complex realities and the true source of their creators' needs and concerns. Giants are therefore the targets of "false fear"—a term I use to mean the anxiety generated by an entity that is ultimately not the real source of concern.[34] (We say we are worried about particular tropical rain forests when we are really worried about our own ability to breathe and our grandchildren's survival.)

While these "gigantic" fragments, or containers, succeed in obscuring important aspects of the whole, they inevitably reveal contradictions that underscore their partial character. A tree whose irregular outlines suggest a hulking human form, for instance, may provide a convenient container for a whole dark forest full of fearsome creatures that remain invisible and, therefore, formless. Reports of immigrants who sneak across our borders, introducing social problems and diseases, may become a giant container for far more diffuse fears about globalization and the blurring of national borders. The California cougar, whose growing population has become the focus of acrimonious debates about the boundaries and the rights of "wild" nature, is a giant that encapsulates larger concerns about the loss of wildness in the modern world.

Although the concept of a giant extends beyond the Amazon, it applies with particular force to a region that no one ever describes as small. The specific giants that interest me in the following pages are all images of Amazonian nature. The genuine distinctiveness and immensity of this nature have long challenged, inspired, and often horrified outsiders. As a result, the Amazon has prompted the selective highlighting of some of its aspects and the consequent concealment of others. The golden city of El Dorado, for instance, singles out the region's supreme, if inevitably elusive, wealth. Early accounts of barbaric female warriors (and the frightening jungles or Green Hells that are their descendants) stress tropical nature's more grotesque and dangerous—if perversely attractive—side. Both as a Lost World full of primeval beings and as a bio-diverse Rain Forest, the Amazon encapsulates tremendous unrealized potential.[35]

The identity of the Amazonian giants who will appear here changes over time. Nonetheless, giant-making as a process that involves a series of specific stories passed down from one person to another persists over the centuries. For the early European explorers, the giants might have been the warrior women with whom they expected to do battle, or the golden king whose purported riches led them to endure a hunger so great as to force them to eat their own shoes.[36] For us today, the giant may be the bio-diverse Rain Forest whose myriad species demand computer cataloguing before they go up in smoke. It may be the gold miners who, by polluting lakes and streams with mercury, endanger a whole web of life. It may be a particular group of indigenous people about whose survival international rock stars passionately sing.[37] Or it may be all of the above, since different giants can easily coexist, and one giant often turns out to have multiple identities and uses.

Gigantifications are more often exaggerations than outright fabrications. When I argue that the great majority of outsiders' most influential portrayals of Amazonia (golden treasure trove, primeval wilderness, threatened Eden) are different sorts of giants, I am not denying the physical reality or the importance of the biological diversity of the rain forest, or the vast material wealth that finds expression in El Dorado. Nor am I casting doubt on the simultaneous hostility and allure of tropical nature embodied in the warrior women. Rather, I am suggesting that the ability of these particular images to move viewers owes in part to their success in concealing other facets of a much larger reality. Unlike the crown, which immediately conjures up the king, the giant is a piece of something that people either cannot, or would prefer not to, see. Were a particular crown to deflect attention from the king and ideas of royal power, it too would be gigantic.

The Amazons of Greek mythology block out the genuine strangeness of the landscape for early Europeans by rendering it, in some sense, familiar.[38] So, I argue, the Stone Age Indians who live in perpetual harmony with a fragile, bio-diverse Rain Forest effectively cloak for us the long-standing complexities of the human interface with nature in the Amazon, such as the gathering and selling of Brazil nuts by fugitive or former slaves, the harvesting of rubber, and even the search for gold. This complicated interface tends to reassert its presence in what I call "seepage"—visible contradictions in the giants who serve as objects of false fear.[39] In the case of the Stone Age Indians, for instance, a photo-graph that reveals a satellite antenna behind a native village may under-cut the "timeless" character of the people in the picture and raise ques-tions about who and what the idea of their immutability may serve.

If giants change over time as groups' and individuals' shifting aims lead them to reformulate old stories, they nevertheless remain selective magnifications that continue to conceal or exclude larger entities. While it is true, for instance, that the "strange, beautiful, imperiled world" on nature posters and ice-cream cartons allots a growing space to Indians and other "traditional forest peoples," the cast of characters remains limited.[40] The concept of "virgin" (or, at best, selectively peopled) for-est similarly obscures recent archaeological data that suggest that the pre-Conquest Amazon may have supported not just a dense population, but a civilization that may have been every bit as rich and complex as that of the Incas or the Maya.[41]

The present-day exclusion fostered by our Rain Forest giant perpet-uates injustices to Amazonians. Although Amazonians have demon-strated skill in turning outside images to their own ends, our long-stand-ing focus on nature and a select cast of natural people has shut the bulk of the population out of relevant dialogues and political processes that directly affect their lives. This exclusion stymies the quest to protect the forest by blinding us to the real dimensions of—and our own involve-ment in—the problems we hope to overcome.

The Amazon as "Shape-Shifter"

Amazonian "insiders" have regularly adopted and transformed the gi-ants of outsiders, which give a fixed form to the Amazon's frightening immensity. At the same time, they have often favored images of shape-shifters in their own accounts of the Amazon. By "shape-shifter" I mean a creature or a natural entity (a lake, river, mineral, type of vegetation) that is able to change its outward form at will and that eschews any fixed identity.[42] As Tô Pereira indicated, Encantados (most often snakes or dolphins) can adopt human form as easily as we might put on a coat or hat. Similarly, many contemporary miners tell of a living gold that may appear as a lovely woman or a fearsome caiman. And Amazonian de-scendants of runaway slaves speak of a lake within a lake that shows up in one location only to disappear and resurface, moments later, in an-other. The tendency of different Amazonians to employ these figures as a way of talking about human beings' relationship to nonhuman nature provides a striking contrast to the legacy of environmental giganticism that has characterized many outside (and some inside) accounts of the Amazon. These more sinuous stories emphasize the mercurial character of both the natural world and relations among people. In emphasizing the futility of fixed definitions that would permit them to be known and controlled by outsiders, shape-shifters call attention to, rather than conceal, a larger whole. The contrasts between shape-shifters and giants in a long string of shifting narratives thus highlight important similarities and differences among images of the Amazon and spur us to think about these images' practical effects.

I have chosen to focus on stories of Encantados, or Enchanted Beings, as one example of a larger theme of mutability within Amazonian expressive culture in part because of my familiarity with a tradition that spans parts of all the Amazonian countries.[43] Tales like those that I first heard in Tô Pereira's shop, although not universal among people of mixed origin, remain part of the daily lives of many of them. Their presence in children's textbooks and in regional folklore festivals has brought them to the attention of a variety of Amazonian publics. What's more, the marked parallels between the Encantado stories and contemporary Amazonian Indian myths suggest these stories' roots in indigenous cultures (with frequent African and European borrowings) even though their tellers are generally of mixed blood.

Although persons of mixed heritage presently account for 98 percent of the Amazonian population, they remain largely unknown to the outside world. The Brazilian rubber tappers represent an important exception—but an exception all the same. Today, the great majority of *ribereños* or *caboclos,* as well as the newer immigrants often called *colonos,* still find little place in either popular or academic representations of the region, except as colonists who destroy the forest.[44] The stories told by a diverse Amazonian public therefore offer a way in to a larger Amazon that anyone who claims to care about rain forests needs to know.

"I see on TV that foreigners think that the Amazon is full of parrots and Indians in feathers," says one young woman in a "See Hawaii" T-shirt who is deftly scrubbing the scales off a large crimson fish in her backyard in what was once Henry Ford's model rubber plantation.[45] "But today we buy synthetic feathers for our festivals because to use the real ones would be to destroy the birds. Besides, there have never been a lot of parrots in this portion of the river. However, when the tourists come, we let them think that there are many. Because, in caring about the parrots, who knows if they won't come to care about a nature that includes us too?"

At the same time that these tales offer trenchant commentaries on larger social, economic, and environmental issues facing the region, they also reveal variations and different levels of meaning that illustrate the Amazon's multiplicity. To bring out these distinctions, I contrast the tales of Amazonian gold miners, or *garimpeiros,* with those of the *remanescentes,* descendants of the black slaves who fled Amazonian cacao and sugar plantations for the forest in the eighteenth and nineteenth centuries. The capricious Gold who dominates miners' stories is clearly different from the Mother Waterfall of the slave descendants. (I use capitals in both cases to indicate Enchanted Beings.) The miners want to shut out other outsiders, whereas the slave descendants want to find new allies in the battle for rights to their ancestors' land. Nonetheless, both sets of storytellers draw upon a large narrative repertoire that permits a wealth of comparisons and contrasts not only between them, but across a vast and varied Amazon.

I single out gold miners and runaway-slave descendants from a multitude of other important groups, such as the Amerindian groups and rubber tappers, for two major reasons. First, I find particularly moving both the miners' accounts of a living Gold that cries out from beneath the earth and the slave descendants' tales of a Mother Waterfall who protects fugitives. "These aren't stories at all," an older woman says with a trace of impatience. We are devouring juicy slices of a coral-colored papaya in the tin-roofed shanty she shares with her children on the outskirts of Manaus. "These are just the sorts of things that happen. Why, if you lived here, you would surely have a lot of 'stories' of your own."

Second, both the miners and the slave descendants present a conscious challenge to deeply ingrained stereotypes of the Amazon. Likewise, the stories of the slave descendants undercut the idea of an Amazon inhabited exclusively by Indians and people of mixed Indian and European lineage.

The ways in which miners and slave descendants actively engage the world beyond the Amazon also give them a particular interest.[46] Miners consciously feed outsiders' images of themselves as bloodthirsty desperados in order to keep out the governmental and commercial enterprises that would be more than happy to claim the precious metal for themselves. The slave descendants similarly transform themselves from Children of the River into this same river's staunch protectors in order to win allies in the battle for control over communal lands. Their attempts to refashion environmentalist rhetoric to their own ends leave no doubt about the contemporary import of these apparently traditional stories. When, for instance, the man beside whom I sit on a warped boat railing describes the central figure in one folktale as "a true ecologist," I know that he is doing his best to draw me into a world that Tô Pereira says outsiders can never truly understand.

These reworkings of borrowed images reflect larger social processes and tensions. The disconnect between, on the one hand, miners' tales of a deeply powerful and fickle nature that demands respect and, on the other, their environmentally destructive actions suggests that policies capitalizing on their sense of gold as a living being are almost certain to get more long-lasting results than are a host of punitive restrictions. Similarly, slave descendants' descriptions of a marvelously abundant magical lake as nature's answer to the biological reserves from which they now find themselves excluded highlight their deep resentment of reserves established by outsiders. ("Half of those 'wild' trees that they are so worried about us harming were planted by our great-grandfathers," says one older man with a rueful laugh.) These same descriptions bring home the need to weigh competing definitions of *preservation* in practical decisions about land. "Maybe we don't have legal title to the land," a young black woman says on a boat ride up the Trombetas River. "But we have a right to it because our great-grandparents buried their children's birth cords beneath these very trees."

At the same time, the stories reveal attitudes that find expression in a number of popular political movements whose members explicitly reject stories of enchanted places and beings. "I don't believe in enchanted snakes who waltz around the river bottom," says one wiry rubber tapper who is scribbling notes for the next day's union meeting. "I believe in the rich sharks who have robbed our people right here on this earth from the beginning of human history."

The Meeting of the Waters

In no way rigid, the divisions between inside and outside, giant and shape-shifter reveal numerous crossovers and contradictions. Assurances by early European explorers that the land would soon be conquered alternated with their astonished descriptions of its unfamiliar immensity. The Amazonian storytellers who recount the exploits of shape-shifting dolphins may turn out to be every bit as interested in controlling nature as were the early explorers, although often in different ways. And the same people who acknowledge nature's resistance to domination may openly express their longing to transform it. "The man who says that he can make Gold obey him is inviting her to slip between his fingers," declares a tall, dark-skinned miner whose grandfather came to the Amazon as a "rubber soldier" during World War II.[47] "But, if Gold came my way, you can be sure I'd do my best to make her do my will."

In the IMAX movie, the American scientist and the native healer nod at one another when their paths cross in an open-air market. This encounter is momentary, however, and the two men quickly go their separate ways. In contrast, the intertwining images of which I speak are more like the sustained contact between different-colored rivers in the "meeting of the waters," one of the Amazon's most famous tourist attractions.

Geographers regularly divide Amazonian rivers into "black," "white," and "clear" waters.[48] The white waters are rich in sediments that give them a pale appearance; the clear waters are largely devoid of organic matter; the black waters are warmer than both and carry less soil and more tannin than either. A "meeting of the waters" occurs when one black and one white river (or one clear and another darker or more murky river) pour into each other. The two rivers may then flow side by side for miles before the boundary between them fades. The most famous meeting of the waters takes place at Manaus, where the inky waters of the Rio Negro spill into the paler, muddy waters of the Solimões to form the enormous river known from this point as the Amazon.[49] From there, the two-toned boundary extends for well over fifty miles. Similar junctures of different-colored tributaries take place at several points within the river basin. Sometimes, as at Santarém, there are actually three rivers that come together in a swirling braid.[50]

Seen from a small boat, the single river formed by different-colored tributaries looks like a pair of intertwining ribbons. One can easily trail a hand along their sinuous seam. From the air, however, the encounter appears more spectacular and convoluted. The strands explode into a mass of shining tendrils—living bands of color that twist about each other before briefly looping back upon themselves. The "aquatic alchemy" of which Jacques Cousteau speaks thus functions on various levels. Although he is referring to a chemical reaction involving different

types of water, the larger processes of metamorphosis that his characterization underscores are immediately apparent to the naked eye.[51]

On my first trip to the Amazon, I flew over the area of northern Brazil
called the Bico de Papagaio, or Parrot's Beak, where the Araguaia and
the Tocantins Rivers come together in particularly dramatic fashion.
Best known for violent land conflicts and for a small group of guerrillas
that the military savagely suppressed there in the early 1970s, the region
was, at that moment, suffering an intense wave of human-made fires.[52]
The smoke was so heavy that we often could not see around or below
our tiny plane, causing the veteran pilot to mutter ominously. When the
thick cloud briefly parted to reveal the luminous waters, the pilot exclaimed, "What a contrast! Look at those amazing colors in the water!
How could something that beautiful not make you think of all that nature has created—and all that man destroys?"

Peering down on the huge, calm river, I found it easy to agree. However, I was soon to discover that for at least some Amazonians, the
marbled waters suggest less nature's majesty than the uneasy interface
between human and nonhuman forces. A few days later, a young, sunburned fisherman on the Araguaia told me, "My grandfather used to say
that the two rivers are two snakes who remain locked in a constant
struggle. One is a good snake, of whom we humans are the children, but
the other is a bad snake who enjoys destruction. Those people who today destroy the forest and pollute the waters so that others can no longer
hunt or fish are helping the bad snake. But the children of the good
snake remain heirs to riches far beyond those of the richest man in all of
this rich Brazil."

While the pilot, who was Dutch-born and thus an outsider, had emphasized the division between human and nonhuman nature, the young
local fisherman had chosen to evoke a world in which these boundaries
regularly blur. While it is all too easy for an outsider to see the pilot's
words as fact and the fisherman's as myth, both describe the same dazzling phenomenon, and the same material destruction. In this sense, the
two reactions to the meeting of the waters are themselves like a pair of
unevenly sedimented rivers that retain their own identities even as they
merge. Because the pilot and the fisherman remain so different in both
outlook and social status, this merger is necessarily partial. Unlike the
braided river, which eventually shades into a single color, the intertwin-
ings between insiders and outsiders remain perpetually distinct.

Nonetheless, in their overlapping visions of a nature about which both have deep feelings, the pilot and the fisherman point out the immense problems and the equally immense possibilities of today's Amazon. "Entanglements" often have distinctly negative connotations. (One "tangles with" a drunk, the IRS, a skunk.) And yet the enormous power of the world's largest river is a result of a series of confluences—of entanglements that find expression in one of the Amazon's original names, Maranhão (or Marañón), meaning "jumble" or "confusion." If a seeming infinity of smaller rivers, creeks, and seasonal "meanders" did not pour into a single, mazelike network, there would be no meeting of the waters—and, indeed, no Amazon.

These curving rivers bring me back to my friend Suzanna. "I hope I get to see the Amazon one of these days," she said later that wet March night.

"I hope so too," I answered.

What would Suzanna think about the Amazon? She'd see it differently than I do. And yet, her reactions, like my own, would be part of a much bigger story that includes the IMAX movie, the living Gold, the mysterious lake within a lake, and the tales of underwater cities that I first heard in a shoe repair shop in the river city of Parintins. These intertwining images help determine attitudes and ensuing policies that affect our lives and those of Raimundo, Tô Pereira, the young fisherman on the Araguaia River, and the woman slicing the coral-colored papaya. For this reason, even if one cares above all about protecting trees and birds and forests, understanding these images could not be more essential.

"I still think that the Amazon must be more than just a bunch of stories," Suzanna said after I had finished laying out my objections to the movie. "After all, those are real plants, real animals, real people we saw there on the screen."

"You're right as usual," I told her. "But the stories are real as well. They remind us that there are many other sorts of people in the Amazon besides the ones in the movie. And if we truly want to save the forest, then we have to learn to see and hear them, too."

A Tale of Two Cities

And as I have beene assured by such of the Spanyardes
as have seen Manoa the emperiall Citie of Guiana,
which the Spanyardes cal el Dorado, that for the
greatnes, for the riches, and for the excellent seate, it
farre exceedeth any of the world.

Sir Walter Ralegh, *The Discoverie of the Large, Rich,*
and Bewtiful Empyre of Guiana, 1596

The Encante? It's a city at the bottom of the water
that looks just like Manaus or Rio de Janeiro, only
richer, a lot richer. Humans can go there only by
invitation. And such invitations, ah, they're rare.

Tô Pereira, age sixty-eight, shoemaker
and fisherman, Parintins, Brazil, 1996

The Amazon as golden kingdom reflected in a shining lagoon; the Amazon as underwater city inhabited by dolphins and anacondas with an eerie knack for showing up in the form of one's next-door neighbor. The following pair of chapters describes two marvelous cities that diverge, but also intertwine. My focus in the first of the two is the glittering realm of El Dorado, which I see as one of the first and most important giants to represent the Amazon. My focus in the second is the shape-shifting underwater city known as the Encante, to which Tô Pereira and his friend Raimundo introduced me.

"El Dorado" is the name that the Spaniards gave to the resplendent monarch whom natives in Quito began describing to them in the 1530s. The king was said to be so rich that his servants coated him each morning with a sort of golden talc, which he then washed off in his nightly bath. El Dorado soon came to designate not just the king, but also his fabulously wealthy city, known in some accounts as Manoa. This city often was said to stand beside a golden lake (the king's natural bathtub), which also bore the name El Dorado. Sometimes king and city were supplanted by the glittering lake.[1]

More than just a tale of fabulous riches, El Dorado became the concrete, if elusive, destination of a multitude of expeditions into a forbidding interior. Rumors of a realm so rich that even the roots of weeds appear caked with gold led explorers from Spain, Germany, Holland, Ireland, Portugal, France, and England to push their way into the vast, off-putting northern center of South America.[2] Many of the earliest forays focused on the lands of the Muisca, or Chibcha, Indians surrounding Lake Guatavita, not far from present-day Bogotá. In the 1540s and 1550s, an increasing number of expeditions made their way into the Solimões River region in search of the home of the gold-rich Omagua Indians. Later, toward the end of the sixteenth century, searches for the golden kingdom often centered on the area between the Orinoco and the Amazon Rivers, and on the fabled great salt lake of Parima, said to be in the hilly region between what is now Venezuela and the Brazilian state of Roraima. The legendary golden lake of Paititi (Patiti), in northern Peru, was another frequent destination.[3]

The Encante (a colloquial form of *Encanto,* which means "charm" or "enchantment" in both Spanish and Portuguese) provides a kind of mirror image of El Dorado. Situated not on land, but at the bottom of a lake or river (there are also Encantes in the woods, but they are less common), this is the Enchanted City that appears in Tô Pereira's stories of aquatic beings who can assume human form. The Encante resembles El Dorado in its spectacular riches, its alluring mystery, and its persistent elusiveness. It is "just like" earthly cities, except for its fabulous wealth. Although it lies beneath the waters of a river, lake, or *igarapé* (a seasonal creek) with which storytellers are deeply familiar, it, like El Dorado, remains just out of reach.

And yet, its underwater location, its tantalizing proximity, and its intense mutability (it can pop up in one place, then appear in another, then return to the first) make the Encante very different from El Dorado. Despite its frequent association with a shining lake, El Dorado remains firmly anchored on dry land. Although descriptions of it are specific, its location is imprecisely defined. And the golden king El Dorado is human, not a snake or dolphin who has only assumed human form. Furthermore, while El Dorado represents a selective magnification of earthly wealth, the Encante is marvelously alien. It does not invite conquest, but instead affirms the limits of human definition and control.

In various visions of the Amazon, El Dorado, the golden dream, finds expression as an impulse toward fragmentation and containment of the natural world: the Amazon as Second Eden, as Hostile Wilderness, as Vanishing World. In the case of the Encante, the overriding sense of mutability that surrounds it takes form in present-day gold miners' accounts of a living Gold and in tales of a disappearing lake recounted by descendants of African slaves.

Despite their often dramatic differences, stories of El Dorado and the Encante reveal undercurrents that cause them to periodically intertwine. The temporary elusiveness of El Dorado, for instance, becomes outright resistance as the city appears to jump from place to place upon a shifting map, much like the Encante can disappear and reappear moments later in another spot. The elusive riches of the Encante may end up in the pockets of the plucky visitor who manages to reach it, just as El Dorado promises wealth to those who discover it. Differing accounts of each marvelous city reveal apparent contradictions that blur the boundaries between giant and shape-shifter, hinting at a legacy in which the two stories both clash and periodically converge.

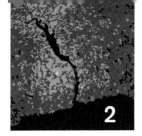

El Dorado and
the Golden Legacy

One of many early tales about New World marvels, El Dorado was not exclusively set in the Amazon. Reports of the elusive golden city also centered on the Andes and the Orinoco, as well as California, the Antilles, and Mexico. These varied locations for El Dorado continue into the present. While, for instance, journalist Patrick Tierney titled his account of how U.S. scientists allegedly triggered a 1968 measles epidemic among Amazonian Indians *Darkness in El Dorado,* the Dreamworks film *The Road to El Dorado* situates this marvelous treasure trove somewhere in Mesoamerica.[1] And yet, even while El Dorado retains its fluid geography, there is a special relationship between the Amazon and the dazzling city-kingdom (often conflated with a golden lake and a gilded monarch) that gives the tale an enduring place in succeeding visions of the region. As a result, even accounts of El Dorado that are not about the Amazon help to define what will become a recognizably Amazonian legacy.

Accounts of El Dorado

The specific textual accounts that have come down to us of a chimeric golden city vary. It would be hard to confuse Pedro Cieza de León's sober prose report of how Gonzalo Pizarro set out in search of El Dorado and the Land of Cinnamon with Juan de Castellanos' florid verse description of Sebastián de Benalcázar's march upon a marvelous mountain kingdom.[2] Both stand apart from Sir Walter Ralegh's glowing evocation of "the imperial and golden city of Manoa" in his *Discoverie of the Large, Rich, and Bewtiful Empyre of Guiana*—by far the best-known account in English of the search for El Dorado.[3] Moreover, while some of the authors were would-be conquistadores eager to celebrate past achievements in order to obtain support for new expeditions, others were skeptics who pieced together conflicting reports about the golden city. A number of the latter were Catholic priests eager to replace with Christianity the native beliefs and customs that they described.

These writers chronicled a series of expeditions that took place at different times in widely separate locations. Unsurprisingly, not just diverse topographies, but also reports of varied native customs and beliefs found their way into the narratives. Often, direct ethnographic observation mingled with snippets of myths and legends, which themselves drew on native practices such as gold mining.[4] And yet, while descriptions of El Dorado varied in content, style, and purpose, the failure of each expedition to reach its destination encouraged authors, when it did not oblige them, to conflate, rework, and augment one another's accounts. (The single golden king, for instance, may be transformed into a whole slew of gleaming warriors as time goes on.) The result was a composite sketch of a wondrously alien collection of natural riches that remained —at least in theory—*temporarily* inaccessible. This collection of spectacular wealth that became synonymous with El Dorado would come to function regularly as a giant. The presentation of the golden city as the epitome of natural wealth, and its carefully bounded (if regularly shifting) geographic location, would become giganticizing devices that functioned through idealization. The emphasis on the city's artifice, the selective use of native narratives to produce an air of mystery, and the insistence on the city's temporary elusiveness would be other such devices.

More grotesque features, such as the golden ruler's obscene wealth and the seemingly bizarre native legends that often swirled about him, would help make El Dorado a convenient focus of false fear. The fear was false because the peculiar challenges surrounding the conquest of El Dorado were readily surmountable, at least in theory. As such, they contained, and gave recognizable form to, more diffuse anxieties.

Stories of a golden kingdom arose at an important juncture in Europeans' thinking about mineral riches. For a number of the first explorers, gold was not just a precious object, but often a living thing. Convinced that the sun-colored metal must "grow" better near the equator, Diego de Ordás, an early participant in the search for what would later become known as El Dorado, applied for a royal patent to explore the region between the Amazon and the Orinoco.[5] Although the sixteenth-century Jesuit writer Father José de Acosta took care to deny gold's animate nature, he nonetheless reiterated its lifelike appearance. "And in a sense," Acosta wrote, "minerals seem to grow like plants—not because they have a true vegetative force and inner life, which belongs only to real plants, but because they emerge from the bowels of the earth as a result of the virtue and efficiency of the sun and other plants, so that over a long time they continue to grow and almost propagate."[6]

Gold evoked echoes of both medieval alchemy and a classical Golden Race or Golden Age in which humans lived in perfect harmony with each other and with nature. It was also a highly saleable commodity that conjured up cautionary stories of Mammon (the Syrian god of avarice, whose name was a synonym for earthly riches) and King Midas. "This yellow slave," wrote Shakespeare, "Will knit and break religions, bless th'accurs'd / Make the hoar leprosy ador'd, place thieves, / And give them title, knee and approbation with senators on the bench."[7]

Anxieties in Spain and Portugal about the place of these countries in an emerging European cash economy (gold became the international monetary standard in 1445) heightened a long-standing ambiguity surrounding the precious metal. In its systematic magnification of gold's more ideal qualities, El Dorado "tamed" or encapsulated the more disturbing, less Edenic side. As the epitome of mineral wealth, El Dorado stood apart from that far less ambiguous Garden of Delights, or *hortus amoenus,* that served as a primary symbol for much of the Americas (including a number of the more accessible portions of the Amazon) during the sixteenth century.[8]

The presentation of the golden city as a carefully delimited space was a necessary first step in the process of containment intrinsic to giant-making. Regardless of whether its pursuers envisioned a king, a city, or a lake ringed by mountains, El Dorado appeared as a concrete, mappable reality. Both its singularity and its elusive nature, however, separated it from a more readily accessible Edenlike garden, which existed in a series of latter-day approximations of the original paradise.

Gardens, even Edenic ones, could have practical, commercial uses. "There are also trees of a thousand kinds, all with different fruits and all so fragrant that it is a marvel, and I am greatly distressed not to know them, *for I am well assured they are all of great value,*" declared Christopher Columbus upon arriving in the Caribbean islands.[9] As, however, Columbus' use of the word *marvel (maravilla)* suggests, gardens also often inspired aesthetic and even spiritual responses (delectation, reverence). The evocation of these more intangible qualities distinguished New World Edens from an El Dorado whose worth lay overwhelmingly in its identity as the epitome of New World wealth.

Between 1503 and 1520, an astounding thirty thousand pounds of New World gold—not counting those shipments lost to shipwrecks or contraband—entered Spanish ports.[10] In that context, El Dorado appeared as a golden jackpot, the fitting climax to an ever more wondrous tale. Why, its pursuers demanded, if the New World had already yielded such astounding treasures, should the best not have remained for last?

From one perspective, the New World's golden artifacts were just another source of bullion. Thus, in 1534, when Hernando Pizarro's ship reached Seville with almost a hundred highly detailed works of art in gold and silver from vanquished Inca chieftain Atahualpa, Charles V immediately ordered them to be melted down and recast as coins. Only after royal officials pleaded to see these glittering reflections of a distant civilization did he agree to put them on public display for a few weeks.[11]

From another vantage point, these golden objects were very special transformations of an alien nature. Like Atahualpa, the golden king El Dorado boasted a "pleasure garden" full of gleaming reproductions of each and every plant and animal that existed within his realm. The high degree of artifice evident in these simulacra made the European conquest over the natives a double triumph: as the natives had already managed to convert the world around them into a series of objects with human meaning, their defeat implied a second victory over nature for the Europeans.

This artificial quality further distinguished El Dorado from the Garden of Delights, for in the latter, nature regularly surpassed art. "The hills appear as beautiful gardens and orchards, and I certainly never saw a Flemish tapestry so beautiful, with many animals of many diverse species of which Pliny neither wrote nor knew," the sixteenth-century Jesuit father Manuel da Nóbrega exclaimed about the Brazilian coast. "It has many herbs of diverse fragrance and very different from those of Spain, and certainly the majesty, the beauty, and the wisdom of the Creator shines out well in so many, so diverse and beautiful creatures."[12]

The Garden of Delights was rich in the produce that could be carted off to market and the seeds that could be made to sprout in faraway locations. But while Nóbrega's enchanting garden-forests permitted pruning and grafting, they could not survive an attack upon their roots. Once razed, these originally lush groves could quickly became water-hungry plantations that forced the Europeans to construct extensive irrigation systems, above all in the Caribbean.[13] El Dorado, in contrast, could always be refashioned. If the king got tired of the coins that he had minted from America's golden treasures, he could melt them down into an enormous lump of precious metal. Theoretically, the coins could even be recast into the very artifacts that he had initially scorned. Thus gold (and, by extension, the golden city) actually transcended both time and materiality by holding out an enduring second chance.

The wonder that the Garden of Delights inspired was a thoroughly Christian mystery. Looking at the gardenlike hills, Father Nóbrega invoked a divinity whose wisdom "shines out well in so many, so diverse and beautiful creatures." The awe that El Dorado triggered was a reflection not just of its riches, but also of a tenacious otherness that owed much to the story's partial roots in native narratives.

The indigenous rites and beliefs surrounding the golden kingdom clearly fascinated a number of European writers. The sixteenth-century explorer Gonzalo Jiménez de Quesada, for instance, described how the natives placed their dead in golden coffins, which they then allowed to sink to the bottom of the deepest lakes.[14] Almost a hundred years later, Juan Rodríguez Freyle described his frustrated attempts to fish up one of a pair of golden caimans said to lie at the bottom of Teusacá Lake. "And I confess my sin, that I entered into this long list [of greedy adventurers] with the desire to fish up one of the lake's caimans," he said. "And it so happened that, having well catechized my *jeque* ["old man" or "chief"], who had been a part of this sanctuary, I took him with me, and so when we came upon the lake and then the water, he fell face forward upon the ground, and I couldn't raise him, or get him to speak so much as a word to me." [15]

The systematic fragmentation and distortion of native beliefs within the larger process of giant-making is evident in Freyle's bemused description of the Indian's reaction.[16] This same sort of "folklorization" is particularly clear in the early-seventeenth-century Franciscan friar Pedro Simón's account of the native custom of hurling gold and emeralds into Lake Guatavita.[17] According to Father Simón's oral sources, these offerings began in earnest after the wife of an Indian chieftain threw herself and her infant daughter into the lake. Her desperate act had ample motive, since the chief had responded to reports of an affair between his wife and a member of his entourage by chopping off the man's penis and slipping it, cooked, into her food.

When the chief later sent his head shaman to retrieve his wife and child from the lake bottom, the shaman found the pair happily ensconced "in some houses and an enclosed garden of better quality than those which she had left in Guatavita." Cradling on her lap the *dragoncillo,* or little dragon, who resided there, the wife informed the envoy that she had no interest in a return to earth.

After hearing the bad news, the chief asked the shaman to retrieve, at least, his infant daughter from the lake bottom. The shaman returned with a tiny corpse whose eyes had been removed. Finally bowing to the will of "the dragoncillo whom he so revered," the chief sorrowfully returned the sightless, soulless child to the water. Shortly afterward, he began to make periodic offerings of precious objects in the center of the lake.

Scoffing at the notion that any human being could take up residence beneath the water, Father Simón in his account reduced the swirling universe of native belief to an *embuste,* or diabolic joke. He described the shaman as a sorcerer *(hechicero),* and his reference to the devil "who was accustomed to appear in those same waters in the figure of a little dragon or a great snake" invited the reader to dismiss the story as the invention of savages who had not yet seen the light of the Christian God.

The work of other colonial writers who insisted on El Dorado's elusive character reveals a similar strategy of circumscription fundamental to giant-making. In contrast to the Garden of Delights, which lay open to the newcomers as a combination living room and pantry, the golden kingdom revealed an inaccessibility that only magnified its promise. Certain that fate had reserved the best for last, the explorers swam up flooded rivers, made their beds in tree branches, and dined on snails, bats, vipers, shoe leather, and even a child or two rather than abandon the search.[18]

The inaccessibility of El Dorado was by no means total. Insistences on its *temporary* elusiveness held out new hope for the future even as they underscored its tantalizing, as yet pristine quality. ("Guiana," Sir Walter Ralegh declared with ill-concealed enthusiasm, "is a Countrey that hath yet her Maydenhead, never sackt, turned, nor wrought, the face of the earth hath not beene torne, nor the vertue and salt of the soyle spent by manurance, the graves have not beene opened for gold, the mines not broken with sledges, nor their Images puld down out of their temples.")[19] Accounts in which the golden king sends an envoy to request aid of the Spaniards likewise suggested that even though the road always ended before they got there, his glittering realm could not remain forever out of reach.

El Dorado's pursuers remained certain that the resistance they encountered stemmed from forces beyond, and not within, the golden city.

The external nature of the obstacles that barred its gates tempered the frustration that accompanied each new failure. If raging rapids, clattering cataracts, and snake-infested forests routinely got the best of the explorers, their retreat was always provisory. If only the natives had been just a touch less dastardly, if only the men had had access to another five or five hundred horses, if only the rains had—or had not—started, the expedition, this very moment, would be before the city's gleaming walls.

Even confirmed skeptics described El Dorado in ideal terms. "I would rather have the sweepings of the chamber of this Prince than the great meltings of gold there have been in Peru," asserted an unbelieving, but still fascinated, Gonzalo Fernández de Oviedo.[20] Nonetheless, many writers' focus on the almost monstrous wealth of the golden monarch injected an element of the grotesque into their tales, which helped make El Dorado an effective focus of false fear.

Rapidly converted into a synonym for a fabulously rich location, the term *El Dorado* initially applied to a chief or king so rich that his servants routinely anointed the full length of his body with a kind of resin, to which they then applied a fine overlay of golden talc. In some versions of the story, "the Gilded One" assumed this shell as part of a ritual in which he set out on a raft to deposit offerings of gold, pearls, emeralds, and other precious ornaments into the middle of a lake. In other accounts, he donned this gleaming second skin each morning, only to slough it off during a nightly bath.

To the extent that he served as a metaphor for prodigious riches, this king was clearly an idealization. However, as a literal embodiment of these riches, the gold-plated sovereign was a strangely alien, *living* object. Accounts in which the king's allies joined him in a ritual of collective gilding underscore the theme of excess. Ralegh, for instance, described how a good number of the king's allies routinely anointed their bodies with a kind of balsam, after which servants used hollow canes to blow a fine golden powder upon their naked bodies "until they al be shining from the foote to the head." They then went on to drink, continuing "in drunkeness sometimes six or seven days together."[21]

The natives' overindulgence reinforced El Dorado's more grotesque, disturbing side. Even though Ralegh refrained from disinterring a recently deceased chief who had gone to his grave along with a fabulously crafted golden chair, he clearly could imagine better uses for such an enormous chunk of precious metal. In establishing a narrative tradition in which the natives appeared alternately as direct extensions of and obstacles to the exploitation of a fabulously rich land, these instances of apparent misuse provided a rationale for European intervention. Although Ralegh did not employ terms such as "ineffective resource management," he established a pattern that has endured into the present.

Other grotesque elements simultaneously reinforce and challenge El Dorado's gigantic status. The seeming fiction of the *dragoncillo* projected onto a mythic past present-day anxieties about a nature that remained profoundly "other" by European standards. However, in its implicit challenge to Christian cosmology, tales such as that of the chief's wife who took up residence beneath the lake reveal the sort of seepage, or visible contradictions, common to all giants.

Although European writers treated them as affronts to reason, stories of the underwater city hint at a different vision of the world. The native myth's effective blurring of the boundaries between the earth and water subverted other, normally fixed divisions between human and non-human nature, and even life and death. The chief's wife found an end to her earthly sufferings and a happier, immortal home, not in some celestial paradise, but at the muddy bottom of a lake. While Padre Simón followed a time-honored Christian tradition in equating the dragon with chaos, evil, and Satan, the word *dragoncillo* remains, despite his contemptuous gloss, an affectionate diminutive. Instead of expressing fury at the monster cradled in his wife's lap, the chief proceeded to make gifts of gold and jewels to it.

If the legend's rejection of conventional boundaries between the waters and the earth challenges El Dorado's ability to serve as a giant container, so do hints that the city's elusiveness may have sprung from internal, rather than external, causes. Sir Walter Ralegh's retelling of the story of Juan Martínez in *Discoverie* provides another good example of this sort of undercutting.

Munitions master for that same Diego de Ordás who argued that a sun-colored gold must grow near the equator, Martínez incurred the captain's wrath when the expedition's entire supply of gunpowder exploded. Cast adrift in an open canoe, he was rescued by a group of natives who supposedly took him, blindfolded, on a long journey to "the great Citie of Manoa, the seat and residence of Inga the Emperor." There, Martínez met the king, who lodged him in his own palace.[22]

At the end of seven months, his royal host asked Martínez if he wanted to stay on as his guest. When the Spaniard chose instead to return home, the king ordered various servants "al loden with as much gold as they could carrie" to accompany the departing visitor as far as the shores of the Orinoco. Predictably, as soon as the servants left, thieves pounced upon him, leaving nothing but two gourds or bottles of gold beads.

Ralegh's version of the Martínez story emphasized not just the kingdom's wealth, but also the courtly demeanor that set apart its ruler from those other, more barbaric natives who routinely fell upon the Europeans. Martinez' uncommon success in penetrating the confines of the golden city suggested its accessibility to other Europeans. A closer look at this particular story, however, raises nagging doubts about just how far outsiders can penetrate the city's secrets.

For instance, at the same time that the king directed Martínez to be "well entertained" in Manoa, the Spaniard remained forbidden "to wander into the country anywhere." As a result, the munitions master never got an inkling of what lay beyond the city's gleaming gates. Even though the king was lavish in his hospitality, he did not confide in his guest. Martínez was at liberty to stay, but only on his host's terms. The king did not seek out other Europeans, nor did he appear interested in forging ties with that larger world that Martínez represented. Yet more important, when Martínez decided to leave, the king did not invite him to return. Once beyond the borders of the golden kingdom, the previously honored guest was as much an outsider as he had been seven months before.

The Martínez incident, to be sure, is just one part of a larger story. Ralegh used his account—which a number of the Spaniards' peers were quick to dismiss as sun-dazed ravings—to bolster the existence of the golden kingdom. Martínez, after all, was a mere munitions master; why should a king have had more than a passing interest in him? In the end, the failure of Ralegh's own second expedition to Manoa, and his ensuing execution, makes the contradictions in his retelling of Martínez' story, and the seepage from that giant container that is El Dorado, yet more poignant.[23]

The Amazon as El Dorado

From early on, the doubts that glimmered beneath the surface of texts such as Ralegh's *Discoverie* found direct expression in the work of other writers.[24] And yet, although the ranks of skeptics swelled with new additions, such as Voltaire's description of the ingenuous Candide's arrival in El Dorado, it took almost three centuries to extinguish lingering dreams of an actual golden realm.[25]

In his study of the emergence of a utopian discourse in the Americas, Fernando Ainsa suggests that El Dorado provided an ideal foil for a weary and conflict-ridden Europe.[26] The golden kingdom represented a melding of the Golden Age of the Greeks and Romans with the Land without Evil of the Tupi natives, a group spread throughout much of Brazil, including the Amazon. Like the Land without Evil, which continues to inspire native messianic movements, El Dorado emerged as a this-world paradise during an era of intense and often dramatic change.[27]

Nonetheless, if this metallic Eden had a positive, utopian component, it also had another, darker side. Like any giant, the El Dorado of colonial narratives overshadowed and erased other aspects of that larger whole even as it emphasized the New World's positive attributes. By foregrounding the golden kingdom's riches, its mystery, its elusiveness, and its transformative potential, its pursuers effectively erased or converted its inhabitants into incarnations of a land they saw as "pure nature." The tale of El Dorado thus laid the groundwork for one quite particular sort of gigantic vision of tropical nature in which natural entities regularly overshadow people, who themselves often emerge as commodities. The alternating idealization of the natives as rich beyond measure and denunciation of them as bad stewards continued even after outsiders discarded the notion of a gilded king, and remains with us today.

Ainsa presents the golden kingdom as a metaphor for all of the Americas. However, El Dorado evokes some corners of the New World far more vividly than it does others. The Amazon, one of its most common locations in the sixteenth century, has retained especially close links to the golden kingdom over time. As late as the 1770s, for instance, the chief magistrate of Rio Branco complained that stories of Parima lake or river, which "geographers in the fantastic disposition of their maps locate near the sources of our Rio Branco," had inspired some sixty Spanish, Dutch, and English expeditions.[28] Maps that placed the golden lake somewhere between the Amazon and the Orinoco continued to appear well into the nineteenth century.

This golden legacy is readily visible in the explicit links among a number of the texts that have exerted a profound influence on outsiders' conceptions of the region. Although, for instance, Ralegh located his golden city somewhere in the Guianas, his *Discoverie* relied heavily on Spanish sources that described expeditions in various parts of South America, including the Amazon.[29] The appearance of the German naturalist Robert H. Schomburgk's edition of Ralegh's text in 1848, the year of their own departure to the Amazon, may or may not have influenced the great British naturalists Henry Walter Bates, Alfred Russel Wallace, and Richard Spruce.[30] However, these men unquestionably absorbed other, more popular accounts of dubious scientific value, whose authors revealed an El Doradian vision every bit as glowing as that of Ralegh.

Wallace, for instance, began the preface to his *Narrative of Travels on the Amazon and Rio Negro* (1853) with a reference to an account by the American writer William H. Edwards, whose florid prose bore out his self-description as "a lover and devout worshipper of Nature." ("My attention was directed to Pará and the Amazon by Mr. Edwards' little book, 'A Voyage up the Amazon,'" wrote Wallace, "and I decided upon going there, both on account of its easiness of access and the little that was known of it compared with most other parts of South America.")[31]

In turn, the British naturalists' descriptions would later have a direct effect on early-nineteenth-century writers such as Theodore Roosevelt and the great Brazilian essayist Euclides da Cunha, who will reappear in chapter 8. Even the salty narrator of H. M. Tomlinson's *The Sea and the Jungle* is quick to cite Bates, Spruce, and Wallace as inspirations for the "noble journey" that turns out to be a nightmare.[32] Still later writers, such as the structural anthropologist Claude Lévi-Strauss, would incorporate or consciously reject these illustrious forebears. Thus, even though today's readers and writers may be unfamiliar with actual sixteenth-century accounts of El Dorado, the golden city, with its intermingling of native and European sources, remains part of the ongoing story of the Amazon.

This ensuing legacy of giganticism would continue to reinforce a selective vision of Amazonian geography. Although the Amazon reveals a variety of land formations, the genuine immensity of its rivers and its forests, and the dramatic strangeness of its flora and fauna, would encourage the sort of magnification and distortion so evident in accounts of the golden city. The region's vast distances would intensify a sense of insularity. So would the tangled quality of an interior whose rapids and seasonal streams precluded easy passage. While some parts of the Amazon would continue to recall the earthly paradise (the late-nineteenth-century baron Frederico José de Santa-Anna Nery would compare the region to "an immense hot-house"), other writers would conjure up a series of maddeningly elusive treasure troves.[33] At the same time, the drastic effects of European settlement on the Amazonian natives would fuel El Doradian notions of native peoples as either extensions of a rich land or obstacles blocking its proper use.

The narrative legacy of selective exaggeration has changed over time. However, the ideas of spectacular natural riches, mystery, elusiveness, and vast transformative potential that swirl about the golden city have resurfaced in a plethora of changing forms. Only a few of the countless possibilities, the following examples suggest giant-making's continuing force.

The Amazon as Second Eden

The German naturalist Alexander von Humboldt's relegation of Ralegh's "imperial and golden city of Manoa" to "the poetic imagination of mankind" at the dawn of the nineteenth century signaled the definitive waning of belief in a golden king. However, Humboldt's vision of tropical nature as "an inexhaustible treasure trove" and his definition of El Dorado as a hydrographic—and therefore, scientific—problem was, in many ways, less of a rupture than a metamorphosis.[34]

The emergence of the Amazon as a Second Eden that redefined, even while it ostentatiously rejected, earlier tales of fourteen-karat monarchs is nowhere more evident than in the writing of Henry Walter Bates. Originally published by John Murray in 1863, four years after the author's return from an eleven-year sojourn in the Amazon, his *Naturalist on the River Amazons* was reissued by the Penguin Nature Library in 1989, almost a hundred years after his death.[35]

At first glance, Bates' narrative could not be more different from sixteenth-century tales of El Dorado.[36] His focus on a wealth of species and subspecies, rather than on precious objects such as gold or cinnamon or sarsaparilla, sets him apart from the colonial conquistadores.[37] So does his interest in science for science's sake. And yet, although Bates appears far more interested in the bats and the beetles that are his real passion than he does in social ascent, his investigations propelled him out of his tradesman status (Bates' father was a hosier) into the lower reaches of the British upper middle class.[38] Moreover, the results of his intensive investigations unquestionably furthered European economic exploitation of the Amazon. Though Bates himself remains largely impervious to the connection, the research in which he engaged helped to fuel the Rubber Boom, whose negative effects upon the landscape he decried in the conclusion to his book.

Unlike the would-be conquistadores who approached Amazonian nature as a set of obstacles to be overcome, Bates and his fellows viewed it as both inspiration and object of respectful study. Bates' text, like that of so many others of the period, oscillates between expressions of awe and the sort of meticulous description suggested by his rambling subtitle (*A Record of Adventures, Habits of Animals, Sketches of Brazilian and Indian Life, and Aspects of Nature Under the Equator, during Eleven Years of Travel*). Although part of the stock vocabulary of Romanticism, terms such as *exuberant, luxuriant, colossal, prodigious, profuse, magnificent, primeval, virgin,* and *perennial* aptly convey Bates' astonishment before a green world from which the mist rose like "the gauze veil before the transformation scene at a pantomime."

At first glance, the single biggest difference between early accounts of El Dorado and Bates' descriptions of a forest distinguished by its "endless variety" lies in his apparent success in confronting the object of his quest. Where his predecessors had perceived a host of obstacles in nature, Bates saw the bee that stung him and the bat that drew blood from his toes as precious sources of information. Unlike the pursuers of the golden kingdom, who expressed frustration with their surroundings, Bates delighted in finding himself in the midst of a "most bewildering diversity of grand and beautiful trees."

And yet, while the British naturalist celebrated Amazonian nature, on one level it remained as inaccessible to him as El Dorado did to the sixteenth-century explorers. A fragment of a larger whole, the marvelous forest regularly overpowered all else, including the teeming river and the region's big and little cities. To the extent that he dreamed of a yet bigger prize even while he catalogued a myriad of new species, Bates the scientist resembles a long parade of earlier explorers.

The prize Bates sought was nothing less than a future union between European civilization and tropical nature, destined to produce a "glorious new human race under the Equator." The elusiveness of this goal, however, forced him to stress the Amazon's transformative potential. Even while he continued to celebrate the forest's beauty, he saw it as raw material that human beings would have to mold into a yet more perfect form.

The barriers that kept this glorious dream elusive were not primarily physical. Unlike an Ordás or a Benalcázar, Bates rarely railed about the raging torrents or thick forests in his path. In his view, it was not nature that threw up barriers to his vision, but rather his fellow humans when they stubbornly refused to exercise the faculty of reason.

Embracing the hierarchies that were part and parcel of their particular brand of determinist science, the nineteenth-century naturalists took as fact the superiority of white, European civilization. Bates' more socially prominent colleague Charles Darwin, for example, had absolutely nothing good to say about the population of Tierra del Fuego. ("Their attitudes were abject, and the expression of their countenances distrustful, surprised, and startled," Darwin observed by way of introduction.) [39]

Bates' attitude toward the people he encountered in the Amazon was more complex. He expressed admiration for his native oarsman and outright tenderness for the young Indian girl Oria, whom he nursed during a grave illness and then insisted on burying in a Christian cemetery. However, his passionate longing for a Second Eden regularly overshadowed his feelings for particular human beings. Time and again, he judged people in terms of how he thought they related to nature. The contrast between the stately forest and the unkempt humans in weed-ringed huts with which he chose to begin his book is telling in this regard. "It was mere fancy," he remarked, "but I thought the mingled squalor, luxuriance, and beauty of these women were pointedly in harmony with the rest of the scene, so striking, in the view, was the mixture of natural riches and human poverty." [40] The Indians' supposed inability to conceptualize a divine creator posed a similar impediment to human union with an all-abundant nature that Bates and his fellows perceived as demanding reverence. [41] His certainty that only the exercise of reason could bring his dream to fruition made him yet more outraged at "the revolting superstitions of the lower Portuguese." "I have often travelled in the company of these shining examples of the European enlightenment," he sourly declared. "They generally carry with them, wherever they go, a small image of some favourite saint in their trunks; and when a squall or any other danger arises, their first impulse is to rush to the cabin, take out the image and clasp it to their lips, whilst uttering a prayer for protection." [42]

The naturalist's unwavering attachment to the idea of a new and splendid alliance between nature and civilization all but guaranteed a seepage that recalls colonial accounts of El Dorado. He insisted, for instance, that the disappearance of the Passé Indians could be no cause for lament, given their absorption into a supposedly more evolved Brazilian society. Nonetheless, the old Passé chief's tearful lament that his grandchildren would no longer see themselves as a distinctive people clearly distressed Bates. Although he rationalized his dismay as a reaction to the

Indians' premature death from a disease "which seems to arise on their simply breathing the same air as the whites," this explanation would strike most readers as hollow and unconvincing.

Bates experienced a yet greater discomfiture upon returning to his original starting point outside what is today the teeming metropolis of Belém do Pará. Forced to hire a boy to show him the path that led to what was only a decade earlier the outskirts of the city, he observed with consternation that "the noble forest trees" had been cut down, creating a grim scene of naked, half-burnt trunks amid a welter of "ashes, muddy puddles, and heaps of broken branches."

The shaken naturalist denied the permanence of this destruction. "In the course of a few years," he wrote confidently, "a new growth of creepers will cover the naked tree-trunks on the borders of this new road . . . and luxuriant shrubs form a green fringe to the path: it will then become as beautiful a woodland road as the old one was." [43] Not just his sorrowful hindsight, but also his too-hearty protestations of nature's capacities for self-rejuvenation hint at an unbridgeable gulf between the reality of European civilization's impact on nature and Bates' own golden dream. At the same time, his periodic expressions of exasperation with a theoretically magnanimous nature suggest that this nature was considerably more complex than he cared to admit. "Rain, rain, rain, rain," the sodden traveler remarked at one point in his pocket diary with a monosyllabic despair every bit as eloquent as the most self-consciously lyric passages in *Naturalist*.[44]

These contradictions highlight the perceived elusiveness of Amazonian nature. In so doing, they link the naturalists' Second Eden to a much earlier El Dorado. The suggestion that impediments to the dream of glorious union may lie not in exterior obstacles, but rather within the very civilization that spawned his vision makes Bates' *Naturalist* far more than a catalogue of living objects. Moreover, although these doubts and tensions find particularly clear expression in his travelogue, they are in no way exclusive to him. Expressions of desire for a nature that evades the naturalist even as he labors to define and thereby contain it, these nineteenth-century accounts of the Amazon as a future terrestrial paradise attest to the selective magnification common to many varieties of giant-making. Thus, even while the social and political circumstances within which these authors wrote were very different from those of the early conquistadores, they continue to draw on a far older symbolic legacy.

The Amazon as Hostile Wilderness

The early twentieth century saw the resurgence of the chaotic nature that blocked the path to El Dorado in colonial narratives. While accounts of the Amazon as a Green Hell are as different in their own way from narratives of El Dorado as are accounts of the region as a Second Eden, they too reveal a tendency toward fragmentation and distortion.

Moreover, there are direct, textual links between Bates and early-twentieth-century writers such as U.S. president Theodore Roosevelt, who took *The Naturalist on the River Amazons* with him on his own two-month journey in the Amazon in 1914. ("No book since written has in any way supplanted it," he declared.)[45] Initially published as a series of articles in *Scribner's* magazine, Roosevelt's *Through the Brazilian Wilderness* departs from the accounts of the nineteenth-century naturalists in its emphasis on a beautiful and bountiful nature's thorny underside.[46] However, he, like a number of his contemporaries—W. H. Hudson in *Green Mansions,* Sir Arthur Conan Doyle in *The Lost World,* H. M. Tomlinson in *The Sea and the Jungle*—continued to envision Amazonia as a giant.

Roosevelt set out for South America in 1913 after losing a bid for a second elected term as U.S. president.[47] The expedition was thus a sort of consolation prize, which he wistfully described as "my last chance to be a boy."[48] While he referred briefly to the initial, more state-oriented portions of the tour at the book's beginning, he quickly moved on to his journeys through the Amazon.[49] The book is above all an account of Roosevelt and Brazilian colonel Cândido Mariano de Rondon's joint expedition in search of the mouth of the Rio Dúvida, or River of Doubt.[50] (The name reflects the reigning uncertainty regarding the river's course.)

Although Roosevelt described it as a "wilderness," his depictions of the interior through which he moved will strike most modern readers as more of a hostile jungle.[51] This Amazon had little in common with the lands he had so vigorously lobbied to transform into U.S. national parks.[52] While the rugged, seemingly limitless terrain through which he hacked his way was "a tract or region uncultivated and uninhabited by human beings" (Indians remained, for Roosevelt, a separate, not-quite-human category), it did not invite the repose and recreation of a present-day Yellowstone or Yosemite.[53]

Roosevelt's "wilderness" (a word that has no direct equivalent in either Spanish or Portuguese) was also no nineteenth-century terrestrial paradise. In striking contrast to Bates, who began his book with a description of the luxuriant forest, Roosevelt devoted the first seventeen pages of his narrative to a discussion of the poisonous snakes whose dangers the British naturalist made a point of downplaying. The similarly sensational descriptions of "blood-crazy" fish, "biting" and "venomous" ants, "blood-sucking" bats, and "vicious" piranha that pop up throughout the text testify to the more grotesque side of Roosevelt's gigantic nature and provide an obvious focus for false fear. It is hard to recognize Bates' intricately festooned creepers in the tangled mass of parasitic fig vines that Roosevelt compared to the tentacles of an immense cuttlefish digging its hooklike claws into the "dead carcass" of a palm tree. "Water stood in black pools at the foot of the murdered trees, and of the trees that had murdered them," the author noted with an almost gleeful grimace. "There was something sinister and evil in the dark stillness of the grove." [54]

And yet, despite this taste for the macabre, which regularly turned his would-be report of a "scientific expedition" into a harrowing adventure tale, Roosevelt joined Bates in celebrating the grand variety of Amazonian nature.[55] Some of the passages in *Through the Brazilian Wilderness* rival the British naturalist in lyricism, as when Roosevelt described a grove of buriti palms as "gorgeous with the brilliant hues of a flock of party-colored macaws." However, it is not simply Roosevelt's more poetic evocations of Amazonian nature that recall the nineteenth-century naturalists and, beyond them, the sixteenth-century chroniclers of El Dorado. Like the British naturalist's bounteous nature, but also like the golden kingdom before it, Roosevelt's tangled interior was the epitome of something he held precious. "The last great wilderness on earth," the Amazon condensed and contained within it not just a staggering array of flora and fauna, but also a particular idea of untrammeled nature.[56]

The overpowering immensity of Roosevelt's Amazon found expression in superlatives. The River of Doubt emerged as "an absolutely unknown river" in "an absolutely unknown wilderness remote in time as well as space." "Every now and then," Roosevelt asserted, "someone says that the 'last frontier' is now to be found in Canada or Africa, and that it has almost vanished. On a far larger scale this frontier is to be found in Brazil—a country as big as Europe or the U.S.—and decades will pass before it vanishes." [57]

Like a Columbus quick to cite the monetary worth of the New

World's "marvels," Roosevelt had a healthy appreciation for the practical uses of the Amazon's flora and fauna. "This fruit is delicious and would make a valuable addition to our orchards," he wrote of the *cajazeira,* or hog-plum. At the same time, however, and unlike his various predecessors, the former president was deeply taken with the primordial quality of Amazonian nature. "The exceedingly rich bird fauna of South America," he declared, "contains many species which seem to be survivals from a very remote geologic past, whose kinsfolk have perished under the changed condition of recent ages; and in the case of many, like the hoatzin and screamer [both birds], their like is not known elsewhere." [58]

Roosevelt's enthusiasm for a primordial past did not keep him from celebrating the region's immense transformative potential. "Such a rich and fertile land cannot be permitted to remain idle, to lie as a tenantless wilderness, while there are such teeming swarms of human beings in the overcrowded, overpeopled countries of the Old World," he remarked, as if stating a self-evident truth. [59] Expressing an enthusiasm for gold mining apt to make many of today's environmentally sensitive readers shudder, he went on to envision "big manufacturing communities, knit by railroads to one another and to the Atlantic coast." What at the time was a vast forest could become an equally vast industrial park in which "the very rapids and waterfalls which now make the navigation of the river so difficult and dangerous would drive electric trolleys up and down its whole length and far out on either side."

This giganticizing vision once more overshadowed people. Like Bates before him, Roosevelt often saw the Amazon's inhabitants as obstacles to "the spirit of the new Brazil." Unlike Bates, however, he openly expressed an attraction to the primitive. [60] "Nowhere in Africa," he remarked with obvious enthusiasm, "did we come across wilder or more absolutely primitive savages." [61] Lacking blankets or hammocks, the Nambikwara Indians, who did no more than lie down in the sand to sleep, exerted a particular fascination on him. "They are not even in the Stone Age," he observed with wonder and a trace of grudging admiration.

If the Brazilian cowhands' throbbing tom-toms evoked "a savage ancestry near by in point of time and otherwise immeasurably remote," the Nambikwaras' wholly unaccompanied melodies conjured up a space yet further back from civilization. "It was a strange and interesting sight to see these utterly wild, friendly savages, circling in their slow dance, and chanting their immemorial melodies, in the brilliant tropical moonlight, with the river rushing by in the background, through the lonely heart of the wilderness."

The aura of mystery that the "naked Nhambiquaras" evoked in the ex-president recalls a number of early writers' reactions to native legends of El Dorado.[62] While Roosevelt's focus on his hosts' lack of clothing cannot help but suggest a touch of prurient curiosity, nakedness, to him, was the ultimate link to past generations and the original human pair. Following a long line of writers over the centuries, the former president explicitly compared the Indians to Adam and Eve before the fall.[63] However, if the Nambikwara recalled the denizens of Eden, they were also like unruly children in their attempt to steal the expedition's silverware by naively sitting on the forks. Roosevelt's fascination with the monkey seated atop a woman's head further removed the Nambikwara from the august company of the biblical first pair by blurring the boundaries between the animal and the human. So did his descriptions of particular animals as "merry" or "meditative" and his characterization of the Nambikwara as "at ease and unconscious as so many friendly animals."

The pull that the Nambikwara exerted on Roosevelt lay in the same precariousness that led him to value the hoatzin and the screamer. Strikingly unlike Bates, who a mere half-century earlier had confidently declared that the razed forest would reclaim its past luxuriance, Roosevelt had no illusions about the irreversibility of such destruction. "There is every reason," he declared, "why the good people of South America should waken, as we of North America, very late in the day, are beginning to waken, and as the peoples of northern Europe—not southern Europe—have already partially wakened, to the duty of preserving from impoverishment and extinction the wild life which is an asset of such interest and value in our several lands."[64]

Yet the same author who hailed the value of preservation was engaged in a fact-finding mission that could not help but hasten the eventual disappearance of the wilderness that he so needed and loved. While he himself saw no contradiction in his position, today's readers may find his book a prime example of "imperialist nostalgia" for or regret about something one has helped to destroy.[65]

The competing impulses in Roosevelt and the resulting seepage in his wilderness container are nowhere clearer than in his own anticlimactic treatment of the discovery of the mouth of the River of Doubt. Though he was quick to pronounce the expedition's identification of the river's final outlet a "great feat," what most excited the big game hunter was the chase, and the chase was over. A source of deep pride, the rebaptism of this nine-hundred-mile-long river as the "Roosevelt" or "Teodoro" nonetheless signaled an end to his great escapade.

Roosevelt's ambivalent reaction to his own success calls to mind Frederick Jackson Turner's celebrated thesis that the frontier transforms the would-be transformer.[66] For Roosevelt, this transformation had a high price. The real challenge to the apparent triumph of progress and civilization lay less in anything that the "true wilderness explorer" said than in what he could not bring himself to admit. The expedition took a terrible toll on an overweight and out-of-shape man who had already battled malaria during his Rough Rider days in Cuba. At one point in the journey, having lost faith in his own endurance, a gravely ill and emotionally exhausted Roosevelt urged his companions to go on without him. The ex-president duly noted this terrible moment, as he did the near death of his son Kermit in a rash attempt to ford perilous rapids. However, he minimized the effects of both by inserting them into an account of various other trials and tribulations that incited false fear. Only a shadow of what must have been a soul-shaking anguish made its way into his travelogue and the buoyant accounts of his voyage that appeared in U.S. newspapers when he finally emerged from the wilds. (Roosevelt was "in excellent spirits," reported the *New York Times* upon the expedition's jubilant arrival in Manaus.)[67]

The stakes were too high for Roosevelt to acknowledge the price of conquest to others, let alone to himself. Not just a personal adventure, *Through the Brazilian Wilderness* is the tale of a United States intent upon asserting its control over both nature and other nations within the Americas.[68] Many of Roosevelt's readers were thoroughly caught up in this "can-do" tale, in which doubt was literally banished, and progress rewrote the landscape abroad and at home. No wonder they were shocked when, five years later, Roosevelt, his health broken by the seemingly victorious journey, died before he could make one more run at the U.S. presidency.[69]

Unlike El Dorado, Roosevelt's hostile wilderness yielded to the march of progress. And yet, like Bates' Second Eden, it still proved elusive. Perched on a log overlooking "an unknown river in the Amazonian forest," bundled in sturdy gauntlets, heavy boots, and a helmet with a veil of mosquito netting, Roosevelt savored "the delightful La Fontaine, the delightful but appalling Villon." The Amazon, however, continued to envelop the self-styled "wilderness explorer" even as he sat immersed in his books.

A Disappearing World

Roosevelt's jungle of a wilderness lives on today in any number of adventure movies, glossy brochures advertising "thrilling, good-for-the-earth, sensibly-priced eco-expeditions," and newspaper accounts of enormous snakes and dread diseases. Over time, however, it has come to coexist with a series of new giants, for example the fragile Rain Forest that replaced the clawing, biting wilds as the predominant image of the Amazon in the latter part of the twentieth century. The Rain Forest had another important predecessor, however: the primeval refuge that emerged with particular force after World War II.

This wondrous but increasingly imperiled world, of which early hints appeared in the writings of Roosevelt and various of his contemporaries, found one of its first and most eloquent expressions in Claude Lévi-Strauss' *Tristes tropiques,* first published in 1955.[70] In this famous meditation upon travel and the postwar world, which includes an extensive account of his fieldwork among five groups of Brazilian natives in 1938–39, the French anthropologist described a doomed quest for the keys to an increasingly remote, elemental past.[71]

Lévi-Strauss began his book (itself a sort of travelogue) by openly rejecting the travel genre of which both Bates' *Naturalist* and Roosevelt's *Through the Brazilian Wilderness* are prime examples.[72] "Adventure," he declared with an almost audible harrumph in the first paragraph, "has no place in the anthropologist's profession; it is merely one of those unavoidable drawbacks which detract from his effective work through the incidental loss of weeks or months." His preoccupation with the previously isolated native groups who found themselves forced into contact with a larger world signaled a more generalized rejection of the faith in a glowing future that Bates and Roosevelt so passionately embraced. The tropics of his title were "sad" precisely because progress had become a problem rather than a panacea, not just for him, but for many of his generation. And yet, despite its striking differences from Bates and Roosevelt, *Tristes tropiques* reveals its own brand of giant-making and its own resemblances to El Dorado.

Lévi-Strauss devoted a good portion of his book to a description of Amazonian Indian cultures, including the Nambikwara who had so fascinated Roosevelt almost exactly a half-century earlier. Once again, these natives were presented as the epitome of something. In this case, they were the living embodiments of "proportionality," or that equilibrium between land and people in which Lévi-Strauss saw a gleam of redemptive hope for humanity—and, thus, himself. Convinced that true liberty resided not in legal rights but in the access to sufficient space, he proclaimed the Indians to be freer than the great majority of modern Europeans, with all of their proud juridical traditions.

Unlike most of the earlier authors who described the Amazon, Lévi-Strauss did not conceal, but rather called attention to the particular giant-making impulse that lay behind his forays into the interior.[73] He was the first to scoff at his own hope of finding a human society reduced to its simplest expression ("that state which—as Rousseau also says— no longer exists, has perhaps never existed, and probably will never exist, and of which it is nevertheless essential to form a correct notion in order rightly to judge our present state"). Nonetheless, despite his acknowledgment of the probable futility of his endeavor, he persisted in the quest for primordial secrets, a quest that would become increasingly common in the 1950s and 1960s.

This search had a dramatic urgency. The Amazonian Indians, Lévi-Strauss suggested, contained within them a sorely needed antidote to a civilization that he described in terms of its "blight," "corruption," "destruction," "tarnish," "mortification," "contamination," "noxiousness," and simple "dirt." "Our great Western civilization, which has created the marvels we now enjoy, has only succeeded in producing them at the cost of corresponding ills," he said in a lament foreshadowing the neo-Romantic back-to-nature movement of a counterculture that would emerge in the 1960s.[74] As a result of the "prodigious mass of noxious by-products which now contaminate the globe," the first thing the traveler encountered was "our own filth, thrown into the face of mankind."

This sense of impending doom distinguished Lévi-Strauss' Disappearing World from the first explorers' El Dorado, the nineteenth-century Second Eden, and the Rooseveltian Hostile Wilderness. However, it too revealed an enormous transformative potential. The most minute details of indigenous culture acquired a magnified importance as clues with which he hoped to solve a far more universal puzzle. "Nothing is settled; everything can still be altered," the author declared in one of the most pivotal passages in the book. "What was done, but turned out wrong, can be done again. The Golden Age, which blind superstition had placed behind us, is in us. The brotherhood of man acquires a concrete experience, the lessons of which we can assimilate, along with so many others."[75]

Immense in its possibilities, Lévi-Strauss' Amazon subsumed within it the larger mystery of creation. Despite his seemingly anti-Romantic stance, the landscape that he described was a thoroughly marvelous "Genesis-like" world. Living fruits that seemed to dance on the tree branches brought him and his readers back to the very beginning of the world. "The birds did not flee at our approach," the bedazzled traveler declared with undisguised enthusiasm. "Like live jewels wandering among the dripping creepers and overgrown torrents, they were part of the living reconstitution, before my astonished eyes, of those pictures by the Brueghels in which Paradise is marked by a tender intimacy between plants, beasts and men, and takes us back to the time when there was as yet no division among God's creatures."[76]

Although this paradise remained elusive, the external quality of the obstacles that surrounded it provided a familiar glimmer of hope. Eventually, Lévi-Strauss did encounter a group of never-before-contacted Indians, who appeared quite capable of guiding him back toward Rousseau's "unshakable basis of human society." However, he explained, because the Tupi-Kawahib became known to him only at the last moment, he had no time to undertake a serious study. Not only were the material resources at his disposal severely limited, but he and his companions were physically exhausted. Worst of all, the rainy season, with its threat of malarial fevers, loomed, giving him no choice but to turn back in the face of triumph. "There they were, all ready to teach me their customs and beliefs, and I did not know their language," he ruefully observed. "They were as close to me as a reflection in a mirror; I could touch them, but I could not understand them. I had been given, at one and the same time, my reward and my punishment."[77]

The wealth of ethnographic detail in *Tristes tropiques* makes it impossible to confuse the Bororo with the Caduveo, the Nambikwara with the Tupi-Kawahib. Lévi-Strauss' clear-eyed, generally positive descriptions of individual humans—the chief who tried to bolster his own standing with the members of his tribe by pretending to write, for instance—contrast with the often sweeping generalizations about Indians ("they do not believe in a Supreme Being") that appear in the work of many earlier writers.[78] Nonetheless, at the same time that Lévi-Strauss' study underscores the cultural diversity of Amazonia, his obsession with a common denominator that would allow an ailing civilization to rethink its own past and future undercut his insistence on each group's distinctive traits. Like all giants, his carefully delimited, still-primeval refuge crowded out other features of a larger, at once more complex and amorphous entity.

If, for instance, Lévi-Strauss' overriding concern for a cure to the ills of his own epoch led him to search out the most isolated natives, it also prompted him to ignore other human groups in the Amazon. The non-Indian residents of the region made only a brief and thoroughly unflattering appearance in his book. Unlike the "naturally robust" Indians, the mixed-blood women of the rubber camps had to apply a thick layer of rouge to create the illusion of well-being. Fresh from their baths in filthy streams, these sickly specimens suggested the "staggering contrast between the flimsy appearances of civilization and the monstrous reality which lay just outside the door."

Furthermore, the author's preoccupation with the Rousseauian secret periodically nudged him toward caricature. Itself a reformulation of ideas that go back to the sixteenth century, his celebration of the Indians' direct relationship to their surroundings would reappear in any number of other, less self-conscious representations of Amazonian natives as extensions of the land. Thus, even while *Tristes tropiques* rejected Roosevelt's vision of the Nambikwara as a childlike and uncomplicated people, Lévi-Strauss indulged in his own version of giant-making when he invoked a harmonious and still-virgin world.

The postwar portraits of the Amazon as a primordial island in an increasingly dirty sea of civilization reveal a seepage characteristic of earlier portrayals of the region as an El Dorado, a Hostile Wilderness, and a Second Eden. In the case of *Tristes tropiques,* this seepage is immediately evident in Lévi-Strauss' excuses about his failure to pursue the Tupi-Kawahib. In the end, the Indians were elusive less because the anthropologist lacked the time to ferret out their secrets than because he did not want to discover that they did not possess the key he sought. Convinced of the necessity of retaining "the illusion of something which no longer exists but still could exist, if we were to have any hope of avoiding the overwhelming conclusion that the history of the past twenty thousand years is irrevocable," Lévi-Strauss walked away from the so-near-and-yet-so-far natives.

In turning his back on the solution to Rousseau's mystery, the man of science recalls those much earlier explorers who abruptly halted their march on a golden city whose spires rose before them.[79] By blaming the failure of his quest on such externalities as rain, lack of supplies, and the threat of fevers, Lévi-Strauss held out the possibility of victory for another day. Perhaps some other explorer, perhaps he himself on some more felicitous occasion, would succeed in plumbing the psychic depths of these "charming Indians whom no other white man had ever seen before and who might never be seen again." Perhaps too, the earth that continued to enchant him with its fabulous abundance would yet answer his prayer and let him in on "the secret of its virginity."

The writer's focus on himself and his own civilization constituted another sort of seepage. Despite his meticulous and often brilliant analysis of indigenous beliefs and customs, Lévi-Strauss' ultimate interest was less the Amazon or Amazonian peoples than it was Western society and its discontents. He regularly turned the magnifying glass back upon himself. When, for instance, he finally encountered the previously uncontacted Indians, he wrote of his emotions, not theirs. Thrilled to relive the experience of the first European explorers in which "a human community which believed itself to be complete and in its final form suddenly learned, as if through the effect of a counter-revelation, that it was not alone, that it was part of a greater whole," he gazed at a people who contemplated their own, unfamiliar image in the mirror of which "a fragment, forgotten by the centuries, was now about to cast, *for me alone,* its first and last reflection." [80]

Approaching the Rain Forest

Although they are only a few of the many giants that have come to represent the Amazon, the examples that appear here confirm the enduring ties between the past and present. The process of selective magnification and ensuing containment in which these writers engaged had different motives and took different forms at different historical moments. Nonetheless, the legacy of El Dorado remains clear in an ongoing string of portrayals of Amazonia. A peculiarly postwar heir to the sixteenth-century golden city, Lévi-Strauss' Disappearing World set the stage for that splendidly rich and yet elusive Rain Forest that would emerge in the early 1970s.

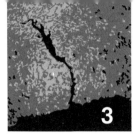

The Encante as a
World in Motion

When I retell Father Simón's story of the Indian chief whose wife takes up residence at the bottom of a lake to Tô Pereira one hot October morning some seven years after our first encounter, he listens intently.[1] "Well now, I hadn't heard of this chief before," he says as he glues a heel fashioned from a piece of used tire onto a well-worn shoe. "Still and all, the story sounds a lot like others that my Uncle Mané used to tell about the Encante. Yes, the story definitely sounds familiar. Except that I'm almost sure this priest of yours got a few things wrong."

"So, what did he get wrong?" I ask as Tô Pereira starts tapping nails into the heel.

"To begin with, the wife's lover was almost certainly not one of the chief's employees," he replies. "No, the lover had to have been an Encantado, almost certainly that dragon about whom he talks. Now then, I think that by a 'dragon,' that priest must have meant an anaconda. Because there are definitely no dragons at the bottom of the water—aren't now and never were. But there are, for sure, a lot of anacondas, and so, her lover was most probably one of the enchanted kind who was taking on the husband's form in order to sleep with the wife. And the baby, that was almost surely the Encantado's child.

"Well then, the husband was angry because he thought that the wife was cheating on him. And so, she called to the snake to come and take her and the child to the lake bottom. So then, the husband sent his best *sacaca* [a particularly powerful shamanic curer] to bring them back to earth, but getting someone back from the Encante is really very hard."

"Why is it so hard?" I ask.

"Because enchanted people almost never return," he answers matter-of-factly. "I don't think the Encantado really gouged out the baby's eyes; that's just a way of saying that the enchanted person no longer has eyes for this earth. But the storyteller was a priest, and priests don't like these stories. They say that the Encantados are just superstition, or else creations of the devil. But this isn't true. The Encantados are a thing of nature. God made them, but it is the mother of the water who tells them what to do. And the Encante, it is always with us, but it remains beneath the water, and so, far beyond the reach of me and you."

Stories and Storytellers

Tô Pereira's nonchalant analysis of a native legend contained within a European chronicle written almost five hundred years before underscores the ties between stories of enchanted places told throughout much of the Amazon today and early tales of El Dorado that have come down to us through writers such as Father Simón.[2] His remarks also invite a comparison of the two cities, which, though both prodigiously rich, deeply mysterious, and maddeningly elusive, are by no means identical. In contrast to El Dorado, which remains the terrestrial home of the golden king (described as an Indian chief in some accounts), the Encante is almost certainly a present-day descendant of that city beneath the water whose existence Father Simón derided.[3]

The dangerous and alluring subaquatic world that appears in many contemporary Amazonian Indian myths links them to a number of the Encantado tales, which are told by Amazonians of mixed blood, and to the bits and pieces of indigenous stories that show up in the work of colonial writers such as Father Simón.[4] The emphasis on aquatic seducers who appear sometimes as anacondas or freshwater dolphins, sometimes as human beings, also unites the two groups of narratives. So does the presence in the Encantado tales of personages from contemporary indigenous myths. Thus, the anaconda who is also the first shaman Unurato in Indian stories becomes the enchanted Norato or "Noratinho" (an affectionate diminutive) of *caboclo,* or mixed-blood, storytellers. The dolphin that, in animal form, seduces women in indigenous myths reappears in the Encantado stories as a handsome man in a straw hat who chases pretty girls around the dance floor.[5]

If the Encantado stories display obvious roots in the myths of indigenous Amazonians, they also reveal traces of European mermaid narratives, accounts of enchanted Moorish maidens (the *mouras encantadas*), and old Norse and Celtic legends about shape-changing walruses and seals. African influences are particularly obvious and important in the Encantado tales as well.[6] Rich in regional variations, the tales may incorporate additional borrowings from the many other groups—Syrians and Lebanese, Sephardic Jews, and Japanese—that have found their way into the Amazon over the past five centuries.[7]

Although by no means everybody in the Amazon tells these stories, they crop up throughout much of the region.[8] Linked most closely to the countryside, the Encantado tales appear as well in the big cities, where steady streams of rural migrants come and go.[9] Particularly in the poorer sections of the sprawling city of Manaus, where many of the female factory workers have husbands who remain in the countryside, from which they periodically return with a fresh supply of fish, manioc, and stories, accounts of the Encantados abound.

The ongoing influx of migrants into areas bordering new roads makes it more difficult than ever to say who is an "insider" and who is an "outsider" in today's Amazon.[10] Newcomers often learn of the underwater city and its enchanted residents through conversations with new neighbors and through children's schoolbooks that present the Encantados as *folclore*—a word that, like the much used umbrella term *cultura*, often means quite different things to different people. The Encantados also make their presence known through "folklore" floats in the nationally televised Boi-Bumbá festival, which has become one of the Brazilian Amazon's biggest tourist attractions.[11] They likewise are a recurring theme in the accompanying music that finds its way onto the radio, as well as countless tapes and CDs. "The Encante?" asks one young recent arrival from São Paulo. "Yeah, sure, it's a magic city beneath the water. You haven't heard the song?"

Cover illustrations for glossy tourist brochures and municipal telephone directories, the Enchanted Beings provide inspiration for poets, novelists, graphic artists, and composers.[12] They have served as the source of movies such as *The Dolphin* and *Where the River Runs Black,* both shot in the mid-1980s and readily available in many U.S. video stores.[13] The Encantados even play a part in political campaigns, with at least one candidate, former Amazonas governor Gilberto Mestrinho, pointedly identifying himself with the powerful, if wily, Dolphin in a catchy, made-for-television jingle. (I use capitals to indicate enchanted, as opposed to nonenchanted, beings.)

Generally told second- or thirdhand ("my cousin says . . .," "my sister's neighbor told her . . .," "everybody there in Terra Preta knows . . ."), accounts of the Encante may arise as part of ordinary conversation. "Dona Belita, wasn't she the one whose daughter was carried off to the Encante?" one person may ask another as both wait outside an itinerant dental clinic. "When was that? How did it happen?" a third person may ask, prompting a story that often proves to be the first of many. Not infrequently, tales of the Encante alternate with other accounts of extraordinary and not-so-extraordinary events that people exchange as they sit wedged into a stuffy bus that lurches through the city, or as they hunt for turtle eggs at midnight on a moonlit beach.

The stories' close association with things and places that play a fundamental role in daily life within the Amazon sets them apart from other, more universally familiar stories of ghosts, forest monsters, or UFOs. Even people quick to dismiss the underwater city as a fiction are apt to have seen the stretched skins of one or another great snake harpooned by fishermen or to have heard the telltale snorts of river dolphins coming up for air in the sultry stillness of the night. Likewise, almost everyone knows at least one person who claims to have seen the lights of a great city shining beneath a stretch of water over which big and little boats routinely pass. "I don't say that I believe in the enchanted city, but almost everybody here in Água Fria has seen lights beneath the river," one older man in a frayed straw hat says between puffs on a hand-rolled cigarette.

The fact that many different sorts of people tell—or at least recognize—these stories ("Yeah, my granddad always used to talk about these enchanted dolphins") ensures a wide diversity of attitude and opinion. A handful of the tales about enchanted cities and enchanted beings are firsthand testimony. "You know, I once talked with an Encantado on the beach there in Campo Grande," an old woman may half-whisper, smoothing back a wisp of silver hair. "Me, yes, I can say that I have been to the river bottom," a young man may confess with a mixture of embarrassment and defiant pride.

Even those storytellers who recount events to which they claim no personal relation may have firm opinions about the stories' truth. While some people treat the underwater city as an obvious reality, many others profess genuine doubts about its existence or describe the stories as "just something I have heard." Still others dismiss the tales as outright fabrications, and some speak of the Encante as something that could or should exist. For instance, Tô Pereira's eighteen-year-old granddaughter Lucinha, a first-year university student in Manaus who speaks casually of ozone layers and habitats, rolls her dark eyes at his stories of enchanted snakes and dolphins. She nonetheless grows serious when I later ask if the Encante is just make-believe. "No, no," she says. "I think that there must be something there beneath the water. These scientists who come here with all of their fancy equipment leave empty-handed, and yet, before we know it, they are back once more. So, there has to be something at the river bottom that they really want. But these old stories that my granddad tells, I think that they are saying that the river is home to mysteries that have been ours forever and that no one can ever carry off."

The Encante and El Dorado

The supreme wealth and the stunning artifice of the Encante cannot help but recall El Dorado. Not only are the streets paved with silver, gold, or diamonds and the roofs made of gold or crystal, but the Encantados eat off plates of precious metal arranged on gleaming trays. The Encante's aura of mystery, its near-at-hand yet elusive nature, and its enormous transformative potential are likewise reminiscent of the golden city.

A close cousin to the Tupi Indian "Terra sem Mal," or "Land without Evil"—an ideal place that still inspires periodic peregrinations among some indigenous peoples—the Encante is the epitome of earthly wealth. "It is just like this world, only richer," Tô Pereira explains as he works at his old black sewing machine. Storytellers often compare the enchanted city to Manaus or Iquitos, Rio de Janeiro or Lima, but on a grander scale. "Each of the Encantados has a house as big as the president's palace in Brasília that you see on the TV," adds Tô's friend Raimundo, who has come to borrow the battered saxophone with which Tô still occasionally performs at country dances.

A young woman who is pounding laundry soap into a mound of shirts at the river's edge in Zé Açu, a hamlet near Parintins that was a thriving Japanese jute colony in the 1930s, confirms the theme of the Encante's similarities to—yet wondrous improvements on—earthly cities. "Everything that we have here, they have there," she asserts. "Streets and houses, saints' days, dances that go on till sunrise, even policemen to keep everyone in order." The residents of the Encante eat the same foods as people do on earth, but they eat more, and more often. Although the Encantados, like the storytellers, sleep in hammocks, they trade the usual rough cotton for smooth, cool silk "all embroidered with little flowers in gold thread." As within Amazonian homes, which nor-

mally shun interior doors in favor of cheaper, cooler curtains, the pala-
tial homes of the Encante employ gold and silver sheets as room dividers. "So then," continues the young woman, waving a soapy hand to
emphasize her words,

> there is no difference between the Encante and this world. It's just that every-
> thing is easier. There, there are no insects to destroy crops, no ants to carry
> off the seed that has just germinated. There, nobody comes to burn down the
> forest where people hunt in order to make room for his cattle, no one appears
> with a big boat to haul away the poor man's little fish. And the houses, look,
> the houses have all sorts of pretty things. The hammock is of shiny cloth, the
> curtain [room divider] of fine gold. And so, while it's very lovely, nobody
> finds it strange.[14]

The embroidered hammocks and the gleaming room dividers confirm
that the Encante, like El Dorado, is distinguished as much by its artifice
as by its riches. Although forged entirely from naturally occurring sub-
stances (no plastic plumbing or steel drains in its silver-shingled houses),
the underwater city reveals a high level of craftsmanship. Even its peach
palms, guavas, and towering Brazil-nut trees, which bear real fruit,
stand in perfect rows, in contrast to the tangled forest that surrounds
many storytellers' homes.

The aura of mystery that pervades the Encante also recalls the golden
kingdom. Much like the man from Água Fria who claims to have seen
the play of lights beneath the water, people may describe hearing the
cries of children, the slap of washboards, or the raucous barking of a
dog. "This is what they say," Tô's young assistant Gerineldo tells me. "I
myself have heard strange noises, but I can't say what they were."

Situated beneath a river that often laps at people's doors when it does
not wash away their houses, the enchanted city is nonetheless customarily off-limits to humans. According to Tô Pereira, entrance to the Encante is strictly by invitation. Although shamans regularly make their
way to the river bottom, the underwater city and its inhabitants remain
close, yet out of reach.

The following speaker, however, a laundress in the outskirts of Porto
Velho in Rondônia, is one who does not find the Encante to be inaccessible. Rather, like the pursuers of El Dorado, she blames a series of exterior obstacles (the wind, the darkness of the night) for her failure to
apprehend the strange and marvelous couple she and her brother once
saw walking on a far-off stretch of sand.

We had gone to hunt turtle eggs that night, me and my brother. I was ten, I think; he was, perhaps, twelve. The night was very dark. I still remember how dark it was. But the stars shone out like tiny campfires and even the water seemed to glow. We kept on hunting [for the eggs]. We had been hunting for at least two hours when we saw a pair in the distance, at the island's point. A young man and a young woman, both very blond; their hair shone like gold in the moonlight. So then, my brother said to me, "Ah, these aren't people from these parts." We ran after them, shouting and shouting, but the wind was strong and they gave no sign of having heard. And, little by little, the night closed in around them until we could no longer see a thing.[15]

Finally, the vast and elusive riches of the Encante, like those of El Dorado, initially seem to invite transformation. A single crystal pebble from the river bottom is enough to make a person comfortable for life. "I know a man there in Nhamundá who once found a stone from the Encante in the belly of a fish," reports Tô Pereira's burly cousin Paulo, who has come to town from the interior to collect the two sacks of fertilizer and bottle of cow vaccine that a local politician had promised him in exchange for his vote. "Ah, who doesn't dream of that! Today that fellow has a stucco house with three rooms, a backyard full of chickens, and a fishing boat with a new motor that my cousin says is a real beauty."

Even while the similarities between the Encante and the golden kingdom are multiple and obvious, however, they often prove superficial. Despite regular references to "*the* Encante," there are myriad enchanted places. "There's an Encante in the river close by São José dos Lagos," a person may say, "and another not too far from Japuri-Mirim." As much a state of being as an actual entity, the Encante is as diffuse and changing as El Dorado is emphatically singular and concrete. Supremely mobile, the Encante can disappear in a twinkling before popping up anew in the same or a totally different place. Tô Pereira's friend Raimundo, dressed one morning in a bright plaid shirt given to him by an Italian missionary ("It was free, but it's quite ugly"), describes how he once strung up his hammock on a beautiful white island, only to narrowly escape a midnight drowning when the island began to sink. "It happened this way," he remembers:

I was dead tired; I only wanted to sleep. And so then, I came across that island in the middle of the Amazon. An island of coarse white sand, with many trees and lots of animals to hunt, everything very pretty. I thought it strange that I had never noticed it before, but I was too tired to think twice. I hung my hammock between two mango trees full of fruit and went to sleep. So then, there around midnight, I was awakened by a great noise. And I saw the island sinking, it was heading toward the river bottom. Heck, how I jumped up! I grabbed my knapsack, I leapt into my boat, and rowed and rowed. And when I looked back, I saw only the tops of those trees to which I had tied my hammock. The hammock remained behind, also an almost brand-new cooking pot. Because that island was enchanted; it wasn't of this earth, you see?[16]

Even though El Dorado always turned out to be more than just temporarily elusive, its pursuers continued to hope that they would one day reach its gates. Such hopes are harder to pin on a fundamentally elusive Encante. Not only does the enchanted city keep floating off to new locations, but its very substance keeps dissolving into the thick river mist.

The Encante's profoundly counterfeit nature is particularly clear in stories about enchanted Dolphins of both sexes who seduce human beings with riches that soon turn into something else. One woman with a shiny gold tooth—a present from a miner boyfriend now far away in Suriname ("That's where there are fortunes to be made, and I hope that he can give me a whole mouth full of gold before his luck runs out there")—recalls a story she once heard from her grandmother in a small community not far from Santarém. "In the past," she says,

> the Encantados used to come to all the country dances. Today, no, people go to the clubs to hear disco, and so these sorts of things are far less common. But back in the old days, cases like this used to happen all the time.
> So then, my grandmother always used to tell about the Dolphin who made a habit of chasing the prettiest girl in a place. You've heard this story, haven't you? Well, this Dolphin was a real scoundrel, he would always appear in the country dances, he would dance all night. Then, he would give lots of presents to the girl and later, when he saw that the others were no longer watching, he would show up in her hammock. It's just that the next day, the diamond which he had given her would become an ordinary stone. And the pockets full of dollars that he'd left her would turn into seaweed. The golden necklace would turn into a water snake. Now then, the real remembrance with which he would leave her would only show up nine months later![17]

In contrast to accounts of El Dorado, which render an alien nature familiar through the process of fragmentation and containment, stories of the Encante emphasize its fundamental strangeness even while asserting its proximity, when not its outright permeability. Despite their access to prodigious riches and their own immense powers of transformation, the denizens of the river bottom kingdom are not giants, but rather, integral parts of a world in constant motion. More protean than the

Greek god Proteus, who eventually tires of metamorphosis and surrenders to his pursuers, the enchanted beings never seem to weary of their shape-shifting ways.

Coated from head to foot in gold dust, the golden king looks "as resplendent as a gold object worked by the hand of a great artist."[18] And yet, while his gleaming epidermis sets him apart from other monarchs, it does not challenge any physical law. Likewise, despite El Dorado's extraordinary treasures, it remains very much a kingdom of this world. To arrive there may be difficult, but it is not—at least in theory—physically impossible. The Encante, in contrast, presents a series of direct challenges to natural laws, though these challenges fail to impress many of the storytellers. ("How do people breathe beneath the surface of the water? Oh, the Encantados give them a device to put in their noses," one young man says matter-of-factly.) Nonetheless, these same storytellers may insist on the Encante's fundamental mystery. "But that's the whole point of these stories," a heavily perfumed Lucinha explains as she waits for her boyfriend, Davi. "Because the world beneath the river is very different from our world, so that even though they look like us, they can never be the same."

Unlike El Dorado, which prompts fears that prove illusory, the Encante asserts human limits in the face of an often overpowering nature. Although individual human beings regularly enter into temporary alliances with the Encantados, there is no hope of totally knowing nature, let alone producing a Batesian "glorious new race under the Equator." Raimundo's tale of the Encantado who assumes the form of a child's mother to rob the woman of her baby and Tô's story of the Dolphin who assumes the form of a man's best friend in order to seduce his wife emphasize the enduring alienness of a natural world that regularly insinuates itself into the lives of individual humans.

Whereas accounts of El Dorado stress the riches that lie just out of reach, the real point of Encante tales is the only partially penetrable nature at the heart of everyday existence. Thus, while Lucinha initially does no more than laugh when I ask what her grandfather means when he says the Encante is "another world, another planet," she abruptly returns to my question later. "I think he means that we live among things that we cannot understand no matter how hard we try to do so," she says. "Because the Encante is right here, beneath the surface of the river, but in some ways, we know no more about it than we do about the moon or Mars."

At first glance, the Encante, like El Dorado, reveals an immense transformative potential. However, it is almost always the Encantados who
do the transforming, they who carry off individual men, women, and
children to the river bottom, where the abductees quickly proceed to
grow gills that will impede their return to land. Although the man in the
following story succeeds in reaching the underwater city, he finds that he
cannot return to earth once he has seen his fill. The storyteller, one of
Tô Pereira's neighbors, tells the tale to her grandson, who listens, wide-
eyed. The "Sea Horse" to which the woman refers is no miniature marine animal, but a large white stallion that thunders off with his elated
rider into the river's depths.

> So then, that man wanted to see the enchanted city—so beautiful, so myste-
> rious, so rich, ah, so very rich! He did everything he could to get there, but
> without success. Until he finally succeeded in mounting one of these Sea
> Horses. And off they went to the Encante. There, the man was astonished.
> Because the houses of the river bottom are of real silver. And the roofs are
> made of lightning stones [aerolite, stony meteorite], and those shaman's crys-
> tals that they call *urutacu*. So then, every day, he would mount the Sea Horse
> and they would go for a ride. And things went on like this, every day another
> ride. Until one day, the man suddenly felt homesick for his wife and mother
> and his newborn son. So, he said, "Let's go, Sea Horse! It's time for me to re-
> turn." But the horse had disappeared. He called and called to it, but it was
> nowhere to be found. So then, the man had no choice but to remain there in
> that city—so rich, so lovely, but so far away, my heart, my pretty little bird,
> so very far away from here.[19]

The transformations that the Enchanted Beings effect may enrich particular humans. A tone-deaf man whom they whisk off to the river bottom may return a consummate musician. The shy and awkward teen-
ager at whom pretty girls laugh may come back an accomplished healer
over whom the same girls quarrel. Nonetheless, it is clearly the Encantados who select the human objects of these metamorphoses, not the human beings themselves. Those men and women who attempt to effect
their own sorts of transformations almost always fail. Although people
may succeed temporarily in spiriting off a pocketful of crystals from the
river bottom, these usually turn into stones or worthless glass before the
adventurer can exchange them for something of lasting value. Should
the fisherman accustomed to bringing home whole boatloads of giant,
bony-tongued *pirarucu* from a particular lake or river suddenly incur its
enchanted owners' displeasure, he is almost sure to find himself with an
empty boat.

Blurred Boundaries

Consummate impersonators, the Encantados are definitely not human. Nonetheless, particular Enchanted Beings often seem far more like people than does El Dorado's golden king. The fact that the Europeans' interest in the king seldom went deeper than his gleaming skin under- scores his identity as a mere embodiment of gold. In contrast, at least some of the Enchanted Beings are individuals who display a range of emotions, including envy, greed, remorse, and compassion. While some Encantados are remote and largely faceless, others possess distinctive personalities and even proper names. "That Dona Julita!" exclaims one older woman seated behind a plastic tub of shrimp in the marketplace. "She always shows up on the beach near the Mocambo, she says things to the young men that encourage them to sweet-talk the young women, ah, she's a real matchmaker!"

Sometimes, the normally untrustworthy Encantados appear as role models, thereby converting the Encante into a foil for human societies and underscoring a recurring theme of justice and injustice in these sto- ries. "Down there in that city of theirs, no one ever goes hungry," one thin young woman says as she presses a piece of bread into the hand of a whining child. "The Encantados always help each other. They don't fight, they don't steal, they are more human, more Christian than we here on earth."

Unlike those of their number who regularly cart off the objects of their desire to the river bottom, a handful of Enchanted Beings actually seek to abandon their enchanted status in favor of becoming human. Usually, these renegades turn out to be the offspring of one enchanted and one human parent.

"But why would the Encantados give up a life of luxury at the river bottom? Why would they want to lose their immortality?" I ask Rai- mundo, who has stopped by to give Tô Pereira a slab of silver fish. Rai- mundo considers my question as he carefully wraps the fish in a banana leaf and lays it in the shade.

"You've got me there," he says with a laugh. "Life is so much easier at the river bottom than it is here on earth. No one has to work, every- body eats well, and every night there are big parties with dancing until dawn. Me, I wouldn't leave that life to sit out on the river in the cold of night, surrounded by mosquitoes, waiting for a fish to bite!"

Tô joins in the laughter, but then looks solemn. "The Encantados are very rich," he says, "but they are prisoners of nature. Their servants bring them fruit on silver trays from dawn to dusk, but they have no control over their own lives. We humans, now, even the poorest person has more liberty than they do, down there in that city all of gold. Because we are owners of our own lives, free to choose at every moment between good and evil, while the Encantados have no choice but to do as nature wills."

The handful of Encantados who make the decision to abandon their life of luxury beneath the river cannot perform this act of reverse alchemy single-handedly. In order to effect their own disenchantment, they must seek out a human ally willing to follow instructions. These instructions may require feats such as firing a shot into the forehead of a monstrous snake that suddenly looms up from the water, or breaking an egg or squeezing a lemon over this same monster's ugly head. Should the human partner waver, the Encantado will be forced to disappear beneath the waves. ("They say that his enchantment will be tripled!" exclaims Gerineldo, who had been listening quietly.)

The single most familiar story of disenchantment throughout much of the Amazon is almost certainly that of the great snake known as Cobra Norato.[20] Storytellers often begin with an account of the conflict between Norato and his twin sister, who has a nasty habit of capsizing boats and gulping down their passengers. After one particularly fierce fight in which the sister blinds Norato in one eye, he decides that he has had enough of the enchanted life. He seeks out a soldier whom he asks to help him in his quest for disenchantment. "And so when the third wave broke, Noratinho [in this case, an ironic diminutive] arrived in the body of that monstrous snake," explains Gerineldo's pretty young cousin Rosane, whose husband is off working in Manaus as a taxi driver while she tends to their newborn son.

> The soldier was very frightened, he broke out in a cold sweat, he wanted above all to run away. But he screwed up his courage [literally, "he made a heart of his intestines"] and *pahhh!*—he shot that monstrous snake right in the middle of the forehead. With that, the snake's shell split wide open and that man, who was Noratinho, came walking out. Afterward, he gave the soldier an enormous diamond. And he went off to live in the interior near Alenquer. He still lives there with his wife and a whole raft of grandkids. He's old now, but he still shows up at all the country dances. My aunt heard him play the fiddle once and she says that she never heard anything like it. The dance to which he had been invited never ended before dawn.[21]

Although Rosane begins and ends with Norato, the intrepid soldier is an essential figure in the tale. His role is yet more pivotal in other versions of the story, which exhibit an El Dorado–like emphasis upon material riches. Not only does the soldier dominate the action in these cases, but he succeeds in permanently transforming to his own advantage the normally elusive—and illusive—treasures of the river bottom. The following storyteller, a man nicknamed Charuto (Cigar, a reference to his stocky build and dark complexion), often works with Gerineldo's father, a modest *regatão,* or river merchant.[22] Initially reluctant to tell the story ("I've forgotten half of what I knew—get Gerineldo's dad to tell you"), he quickly becomes engrossed in its telling, pausing in the midst of unloading bulging sacks of yellow flour to act out the events that he describes.

> Heck now, I'm telling you, this fellow became stinking rich! Because he took the stone from the river bottom which Norato had given him and he sold it for a fortune. What a lot of money it was worth! [Here, he waves his hands enthusiastically.] So then, he went on to buy a whole herd of oxen, land, an apartment in Santarém and another in São Paulo, all furnished, with a uniformed doorman. He even bought himself a little airplane to go on joy rides. [More hand waving.] Now, they say that the shell is what is most valuable of all. Because it can cure any illness—cancer, hepatitis, evil eye, you see? They say that a shell like this is very dangerous. But, I swear to you that if I found myself nearby, I'd grab it. [Here, Gerineldo rolls his eyes, causing Charuto to repeat the assertion.] You can make fun if you want, boy, but it wouldn't scare me. And even if I were scared, I would grab it anyway.[23]

In yet other versions of the Norato story, the former Encantado becomes one of that special class of shamanic healers called *sacacas.* Unlike the less powerful healers called *pajés* and *curandeiros,* these *sacacas*—like the "sorcerer" in Father Simón's story of the little dragon—can travel at will to the river bottom.[24] Their ability to do so undercuts the elusiveness of the Encante and challenges the absolute power of the Encantados, whom they may urge (or even order) to cure a sick man or to return a kidnapped child. "Look," says Raimundo, "I knew one of the most powerful *sacacas,* his name was Raimundo Buritama—Raimundo just like me, see? Now then, this man would go to the river bottom like you or I would go to Palmares or the Francesa [both neighborhoods of Parintins]. He'd light his cigarette and jump into the water. Minutes later, he would resurface, his clothes still dry, puffing on that cigarette!"

Because a healer on the order of Raimundo Buritama is so clearly extraordinary, his ability to penetrate the borders of the underwater city is scant proof of its accessibility. However, other stories in which ordinary people manage to barge, bluff, or wheedle their way into the Encante present a more direct challenge to the idea of the underwater city as off-limits to human beings. In contrast to the fisherman who merely stumbles across a pebble from the Encante that he trades for a three-room house with a backyard full of chickens, the man in the following story, who unexpectedly finds himself at the river bottom, succeeds in raiding the Encante. Precisely because the happy ending is an exception to the rule in which such disrespectful actions are severely punished, his account underscores not only the permeability of the boundaries between the earth and the Encante, but also a similarity between stories of El Dorado and the Encante.

> Well, when this fellow opened his eyes, he was in the Encante. He didn't know how he'd arrived there, he just saw that everything was different and very rich, you see? So, he quickly filled his pockets with those little stones. Then, he ran as hard as he could, he ran and ran and ran until he couldn't any longer. He closed his eyes and when he looked around him, he was again on the beach. And look, his pockets were full of sand, of pebbles, but there was one, just one of these pebbles that turned out to be an enormous pearl. And this pearl alone was enough to buy a boat that is the equal of a luxury hotel. Its name is *Enchanted City* and it makes the trip from Manaus to Belém every second Friday of the month. If you book passage on it, the crew will tell you the same story. That I guarantee![25]

In theory a source of danger to be avoided, the Encante in practice may be so attractive that people throw caution to the wind. ("They were so beautiful that I forgot to be afraid," confesses one man who describes his encounter on a shadowy beach with a trio of Encantados dressed in clothes the color of sea foam.) Moreover, the same Encante that exerts an ominous power in many stories may become the butt of jokes in others. Gerineldo loves to recount the tale of the man dragged off to the river bottom by a group of Dolphin policemen furious that he has wounded their chief with his harpoon.[26] Usually, this tale ends with a description of how the man returns to earth laden with gifts after he succeeds in healing the injured chief. Gerineldo, however, laughs delightedly at his own conclusion, in which the turtle-guide who extends his paw in a farewell handshake ends up in the soup pot. "You really think you're funny, don't you, Gerineldo?" scolds Lucinha, trying hard to frown while Tô Pereira shakes his head.

Ongoing Interchanges

The tenuous nature of the division between El Dorado and the Encante becomes obvious if one compares the Encantado stories with a number of contemporary Amazonian Indian accounts of shape-changers. The greater fluidity of boundaries in the native narratives indicates the Encantado tales' intermediary status between European and native Amazonian accounts. The presence of this third strand of stories also makes clear that even when the Encante provides a vivid contrast to El Dorado, the relationship between giant and shape-shifter is no simple, binary opposition. The boundaries between the Encantado stories and native narratives, and between these stories and accounts of El Dorado, are blurred enough to leave no doubt about the continuing interplay between various groups within and outside the Amazon.

Unlike giants, such as the golden king, who are content to strain the imagination, the Enchanted Beings actively transgress physical laws. Thus, while the native legend Father Simón incorporated into his own chronicle only hinted at an ongoing commerce between the world of human beings and another world beneath the water, these ties are far more explicit in Encantado stories in which Dolphins and Anacondas make love to men and women.

In the countless stories about amorous male Dolphins and insatiable females ("She was one hot dame!" one man who claims to have been pursued by a blond and blue-eyed Dolphin exclaims to a group of friends and neighbors), however, the Encantados inevitably take on human form before embarking on their escapades. In that way, they stand apart from indigenous Aquatic Seducers, who often retain their animal form during intercourse.[27] Frequently casual or even humorous descriptions of lovemaking between humans and Encantados undercut the seriousness of the fundamental unity that is the point of native myths. Different from the Encantado stories in their generally more self-consciously solemn tone, indigenous myths often reveal a somewhat different vision of the human relationship to the nonhuman world.[28] A contemporary Shipibo myth from the Peruvian Amazon, a piece of which appears here, offers an excellent example. The nephews of a woman hide on the riverbank and watch a dolphin emerge from the water, approach their sleeping aunt, and have intercourse with her.[29]

> When he was very, very close, the woman began to sleep—*hëën* [a Shipibo word for the heavy breathing indicating that someone has fallen asleep]. When the dolphin reached her, he entered her. The two nephews then began

to approach the copulating couple. The dolphin carried an *iscobina* [a ceremonial costume that involves a cotton poncho from which dangles a bunch of four bird feathers] around his dorsal fin. He wore it thus on his back as he entered the woman's mosquito netting. When he was leaving it afterward, one of the two nephews began to shoot arrows at him with his bow. The dolphin fell to the ground impaled. He struggled to raise himself on his ventral fins and crawled with great difficulty toward the lake. The other nephew then shot him with an arrow when he was very near to the port. Then he gave the dolphin a blow with his *macana* [presumably, a club]. The wounded dolphin managed nonetheless to crawl into the water and escape.

Mixed-blood storytellers often describe the Enchanted Beings as *mães*—an ambiguous term in that these "mothers" of the woods and waters can be either masculine or feminine in form.[30] However, despite the term's implication of sexual duality, gender distinctions in the Encantado stories are very clear. My question as to whether a male Dolphin could be attracted to an adult man elicits gales of laughter. "The males are very macho" (*Os machos são bem machos*), Tô Pereira assures me as Lucinha coughs discreetly and Gerineldo snickers. The fixed quality of gender distinctions in the Encantado stories contrasts with the greater ambiguity of contemporary Indian myths, in which the Fish Woman may be at once the daughter of the Anaconda and one of the Anaconda's many alter egos, which include the World Tree and the Cosmic Dragon. The presence of a serpent within her own vagina is just the most obvious proof of Fish Woman's dual sexual identity.[31]

And yet, if the boundaries within the Encantado stories are generally more fixed than they are in native myths, there is at least one significant exception. Whites or gringos are almost always strongly negative personages in contemporary Indian narratives. In them, figures such as Cobra Norato exist in opposition to the whites.[32] In the Encantado tales, the Enchanted Beings themselves may actually be whites.[33] The ensuing ambivalence that storytellers display toward these personages underscores the blurring of ethnic boundaries in much of present-day Amazonian culture.

In one Arapaço retelling of the Cobra Norato story from the Vaupés River basin, in the northwest Amazon, a shape-changing snake who lives in a house beneath the water seduces a woman whom he sees bathing in the river. The suspicious husband then posts a companion woodpecker in a nearby tree. When the snake arrives, the husband shoots the snake with a poison dart, fishes it out of the river, and cuts off its penis. Next, like the chief in Padre Simón's story, he cooks the penis, which he then slips into the wife's food.

Though the wife vomits upon learning what she has just eaten, she nonetheless gives birth to Unurato. While she goes on to take up residence within the river in the form of a huge *pirarara* (a bright red catfish), her son grows into an enormous snake who regularly attends parties on earth in human form. One day, he asks a white man to meet him at midnight on a beach and to hurl an egg at his head. The man, however, becomes afraid when he sees Unurato in the form of an enormous snake. Instead of following Unurato's directions, he shoots him. The snake skin falls into the water, and Unurato, suddenly bereft of his supernatural powers, has no choice but to remain in human form upon the beach.

Forced to labor for the whites who have been the cause of his misfortune, Unurato heads off for Brasília, where he gets a job as an ill-paid construction worker. After saving up enough money, he returns to Amazonia in the form of an enormous, brightly illumined submarine crammed full of goods. The machines he has purchased allow the "snake-beings" called *wai-masa* to build an enormous city beneath the river, whose purpose is to bring renewed prosperity to the Arapaço.[34]

This version of the Unurato story shares many features with *caboclo* accounts of Cobra Norato. Indeed, the majority of Encantado stories of the great snake are far closer to indigenous myths than they are to certain contemporary retellings of the Norato tale, such as one available in a glossy comic book.[35] The initial seduction of a human woman by a snake, the snake-child's penchant for attending parties in human form, and Unurato's instructions to a human regarding his fearsome appearance are key elements in both. While the sojourn in Brasília is almost certainly a recent Arapaço addition, the time-honored theme of a great Anaconda boat appears in many of the Encantado tales.[36] The single most important difference between the two concerns the gringo character, who appears in most Encantado tales as "a soldier" of indeterminate race, and as a faithful ally. This same figure betrays Unurato in the Arapaço story. Then too, although Unurato turns out to be the original ancestor of the Arapaço, the Enchanted Beings remain suspect and often treacherous figures in the Encantado tales.

The term *gringo* refers not just to white skin, but above all, to power over others. (A *casa de branco,* or "white's house," can just as well belong to a rich man with darker skin.) Some storytellers expressly compare the Dolphin to the old-style rubber barons who cruelly exploited rubber tappers, or to new-style production bosses who work their employees to the bone. "Look," says one young woman who has lived all her life in one rubber colony on the Juruá River. "The Dolphin is just like the owner of the rubber camp in my grandfather's time. If one of his workers didn't bring in enough rubber, he would have his hired thugs beat up the whole family. Today, the Dolphin is more like the factory owner, who doesn't want to hear that a worker has a headache, who won't let a mother leave her shift five minutes early to pick up a sick child."

At the same time, however, that the Dolphin—unlike Unurato—is not to be trusted, he possesses tremendous healing powers. Not only are his cures powerful and certain, but, unlike expensive "drugstore medicines," they are, as Tô Pereira says, "a thing of nature, and so, freely given." In addition, the Enchanted Beings oversee an abundance of natural riches. While they may share these with human beings, they inevitably take their treasures with them when they pull up stakes. "The Encantados can be scoundrels, but they can also be good friends to us," observes Gerineldo's mother as she mashes a banana for the baby whose tiny toes he gently tweaks.

The Enchanted Beings also make life considerably more interesting. Frightening in their caprice, they nonetheless inject a note of the unexpected into an often grueling routine. "My mother knew a woman there in the interior who claimed to go to the river bottom every evening to dance with the Encantados," Lucinha says.

> By day, she was a laundress, she washed and ironed from dawn to dusk, but each night she would go to the Encante and dance away the night. My mother told her that she must be dreaming, that no one could go like that to the river bottom. But the woman talked in such detail of what she saw and did in that underwater city that one would almost think it was all true. And my mother says that once she saw that woman at dawn emerging from the river, fully clothed, completely dry, with a big bouquet of white, very fragrant flowers. And so, people still argue about what really happened. That's why my granddad says that the Encante is the mystery of this earth.

At the same time that the Encantados are often cruel and deceitful, they evoke a fascination that few storytellers find themselves able to resist. The fact that the former governor of Amazonas was able to turn to his own advantage his critics' negative identification of him with the lustful and deceitful Dolphin is a prime illustration. A barrage of ads that portrayed him as a strong leader capable of marvels offer vivid proof of this enduring ambiguity.[37] In this sense, the Encantado stories, with their grudging celebration of the gringo, offer a reverse image of early chronicles of El Dorado in which the native *dragoncillo* exercises a perverse allure. In short, while there is no confusing the giant with the shape-shifter, the two are part of specific narratives that regularly intersect, and mirror each other, in many ways even as they rework similar elements for different ends.

Entangled Worlds

Tô Pereira's reinterpretation of my account of Father Simón's written version of an oral legend calls attention to the multiple overlappings between accounts of El Dorado and the Encante. The fact that Tô later goes on to repeat my version of Father Simón's account to Lucinha suggests that the native legend will continue to go through new permutations in the future. ("My granddad told me all about that chief who gave the snake to his wife for dinner!" she says to me a few days later with a twinkle in her eye.)

The contemporary quality of the Encantado stories, like that of native myths in which the snake-man Unurato goes on to become yet another faceless migrant to Brasília, resides partially in storytellers' insistence on the continuing presence of the Enchanted Beings in their own lives. It also owes to the storytellers' awareness of that larger world that presses in upon themselves and the Encantados. "Of course you won't find any sign of the Encante in the city!" exclaims Gerineldo's brother Pedro Paulo when I ask if has heard reports of enchanted beings in Manaus. "Do you think that the Cobra Norato is going to rent an apartment and install a telephone? No, no, the Encantados aren't going to live in dirty rivers into which people throw old Coke bottles and all sorts of other garbage. They won't put up with a place all full of factory fumes where your eyes itch and burn any time of night or day. No, they like peace and quiet, they like to bathe in clear rivers and to stroll through the woods at dawn. You can still find a few here in the Aréia Grossa [a sandy stretch that was once the lonely outskirts of a rapidly expanding Parintins], but they're getting to be fewer and fewer as more houses crop up where once there was nothing except trees and sand."

For most people in today's Amazon, "El Dorado" is not some shining treasure trove, but rather, that tiny rural community in the Brazilian state of Pará where police gunned down a group of landless peasants in April 1996.[38] Talk of the tensions between El Dorado and the Encante therefore would have little meaning for them.

At the same time, however, that the storytellers would frown at terms such as *giant* and *shape-shifter*, they are quick to note that their own conception of the Amazon and Amazonian nature is very different from that of most outsiders. Some are equally quick to see the Encantado stories as an expression of this difference. "Where you live, there are no Encantados," says Gerineldo as we sit on a grassy knoll above the river, waiting for Charuto and his father to anchor the small wooden boat crammed with plantains and bulging burlap sacks. "But then again, there are hardly any anacondas. You don't even have *pirarucu* fish. So, everything is very different, it is not like here at all." The interest that such tales continue to excite in the people who hear and tell them ("Do you think these things are true?" storytellers often ask each other) is in part a tribute to the intriguing events that they describe. However, curiosity about the Encantados also attests to differing levels of awareness that these accounts express a vision of nature presently under assault from without.

Those Amazonians who reject the Encantado stories as mere superstition are usually well aware that the Encante represents another vision of the world. Their negative assessments of these stories often reflect their own desire to appear as rational and modern in outsiders' eyes.[39] "In the old days, people were very ignorant," one of Tô Pereira's regular customers declares as he wraps her resoled sandals in newspaper. "We here in Amazonia lived at the end of the world. Today, no, we are more up-to-date, we know all about the greenhouse effect, biodiversity, and sustainable development. So, nobody talks anymore about the Encante, or the Encantados. Except, perhaps, my next-door neighbor, who likes to talk about how he once went to the Encante. But this is just a story; no one can breathe at the bottom of the river. We all know this very well."

Some people do not reject the Encante so much as relegate it to a past fundamentally different from the present. In the stories I recorded, the differences in the actual narratives were often far less striking than were divergences in the commentaries surrounding them.[40] "The Encante comes from the beginning of the world," explains one man who is waiting for Tô Pereira to repair the heel on his small daughter's sandal. "It is the chaos on which Christ was able to impose order and only this little remnant remained there beneath the water as a reminder of the past." "I don't know if there is an Encante," muses a lottery-ticket vendor who has stopped to drop off Tô's weekly ticket. "But I am sure that there used to be one in those times before what they called 'progress' came knocking at our door."

In many cases, the Encante becomes part of an era preceding large-scale deforestation and urbanization, a recent and yet mythic time when, supposedly, no one ever had the slightest trouble finding enough to eat.[41] "There was still an Encante when my father arrived here in Tefé. But today it no longer exists, because it has disappeared with all the movement," says one young man in the once-sleepy city now overrun by petroleum workers bound for a platform in the forest.

"These things of the Encante are from a distant past when the birds still used to speak with people," Gerineldo asserts, mopping the sweat off his face as he prepares to close the shop for lunch. "Because long ago, in the past, the birds knew our language and we could speak their language too."[42]

"So when did the birds stop talking to people?" I ask him.

"Oh, at least twenty, maybe even thirty years ago," he says. "In that time before people started burning down the forest and the Encantados had to leave."

While some storytellers see the Encante as a Disappearing World on the order of Lévi-Strauss' *Tristes tropiques,* others attempt to understand it in terms of the new language of environmentalism that reaches even the most remote villages through TV or radio programs, as well as via children's schoolbooks. (Today, even tiny rural communities often have a single television that runs on a generator that provides energy to the central square for a few hours every day.)[43] Often, the Encantados emerge in the new guise of environmental guardians and a sort of supernatural rain forest police who regulate resource consumption.[44] "The Encantados are the owners of everything in nature and they don't let anybody mess with it," explains one young woman who has slung her hammock beside mine on a crowded boat bound for the gold camps of the Madeira River. "They protect the forest, they don't let people pollute the river or fish too much. And if somebody doesn't respect nature, they give him a really hard time so that he learns not to do these things again."[45]

Other storytellers, including a number of Lucinha's fellow university students, often make the same point in a more abstract way. "I don't believe that there are anacondas that turn into boats," says her boyfriend, Davi, an agronomy major whose high, straight nose has earned him the nickname "Índio." "And I don't think that dolphins go around getting women pregnant. But I do believe that people here have their own way of saying that humans have to respect nature, that if we continue to destroy the environment, everyone is going to suffer, that we Amazonians will go hungry in a land of great abundance. And so, you could say that I almost believe in the Encante, because I am convinced that what these stories say about caring for this world of ours is true."

In contrast to Tô Pereira, who shrugs diplomatically when I ask him what he thinks of Davi's comment, Tô's friend Raimundo bristles at Davi's rejection of a more literal interpretation of the Encantado tales. "Your father, Davi, was born in the interior," he says to the young man. "He fished and hunted in the woods and so, he knew a thing or two about the Encantados. You were born there too, and you'd still be there, fishing and hunting deer and tapirs, if your mother hadn't moved you to the city after he got sick. Well then, what you know of the Encantados, you have learned from others. You aren't your father, who once saw one face-to-face."

Although Raimundo takes issue with Davi and rolls his eyes at non-colloquial terms such as *the environment,* he reserves his scorn for the outsiders who scoff at the Encantados as superstition while they mine the waters for fish in enormous trawlers. Davi joins Raimundo in expressing anger at their contemptuous attitude. "Perhaps I don't believe in the same way that you and my father believe in the Cobra Norato," he says to the older man. "But I never say that the Encante is a lie. It makes me angry to turn on the TV and to see only Indians and parrots on the programs about Amazonia. It makes me even angrier to hear outsiders say that we don't know how to take care of nature when it is they who come here to steal our fish and cut down our trees." The recurrent protest in these stories against humans' injustices to one another, and against humans' mistreatment of nature, also unites Raimundo and Davi.

"Master, I will show you where it lies," one native said to the owner of a gold mine almost three hundred years ago when the owner asked the man to show him the location of El Dorado. "You will see it from afar, but you won't be able to reach there because it has been enchanted by the ancestors."[46] Only one of countless forms of popular expression in a vast and varied Amazon, the Encantado stories prompt multiple reactions. Nonetheless, the interchange between Davi and Raimundo underscores a larger vision of nature with deep roots in a centuries-old narrative tradition upon which both "insiders" and "outsiders" continue to draw.

Amazon Women

These women are very white and tall, and have hair
very long and braided and wound about the head,
and they are very robust and go about naked, [but]
with their privy parts covered, with their bows and
arrows in their hands, doing as much fighting as ten
Indian men, and indeed there was one woman among
these who shot an arrow a span deep into one of the
brigantines, and others less deep, so that our
brigantines looked like porcupines.

Gaspar de Carvajal, *Discovery of the Amazon,* 1542

And so, I tell you that gold has no owner. There are
people who think that gold is just a rock, that it is
lifeless, but it is every bit as alive as you or me. And
gold appears to us one minute in the form of a lovely
woman, all in white, but in the other like a repulsive
snake or ugly caiman. And while gold makes some
men rich, no one, and I mean no one, tells gold what
to do.

Gold miner, age seventeen, Tapajós River gold camp, Brazil, 1994

Although he was one of the most enduring figures in the swirl of early narratives surrounding the Amazon, the golden king was by no means the only giant. Transposed to the New World, the warlike Amazons of Greek myth figured among his principal rivals in terms of fascination and staying power.[1] It is they, not he, who gave the region originally known as "the Freshwater Sea" (Mar Dulce) or Marañón (Maranhão) the name by which we still know it.[2]

In reality, the Amazons were not so much competitors of as they were complements to the gilded monarch. With their domain often situated close beside El Dorado on old maps of South America, these warrior women, like the golden king, represent an uneasy confluence of European and native stories. Also like him, they regularly functioned as exaggerated fragments of a rich, alien, and seemingly limitless nature that threatened to swallow up the astonished Europeans. Only slightly less elusive than the golden king, they too withheld their riches from the eager Europeans.

However, unlike accounts of El Dorado, which generally played down the more unsettling elements of tropical nature, tales of the warrior women actively highlighted the tension between the New World's stupendous wealth and its grotesque and frightening aspects. They also initiated a long and ongoing tradition of female personifications of the Amazon region by outsiders and insiders.

The first chapter in this section begins with a consideration of the warrior women's roots in both Greek myth and Amazonian tradition. It then goes on to discuss the New World Amazons and some of their equally "gigantic" descendants. The second chapter contrasts female figures from the Encantado stories with the warrior women. Here, the Gold of gold miners' stories serves as my prime example. (As before, I use capital letters to distinguish an Enchanted Being.) Many different women all in one, this capricious femme fatale also may appear as a chaste and beneficent Woman in White, or as a snake or caiman who protects the ravines where men dig for precious ore.

And yet, if the warrior women are giants while Gold turns out to be a consummate shape-shifter, the miners who describe "her" often redeploy others' images of themselves as rapists of a virgin land, thus purposefully drawing attention as the subjects of false fear. While I do not wish to minimize the genuine environmental destruction the miners cause, or to play down the often calamitous effects of their assaults on native peoples, I stress the ways in which these men serve as convenient villains in an international drama. As a result, even as my examples newly illustrate the division between competing visions of the Amazon, they also reaffirm the fluid boundary between them.

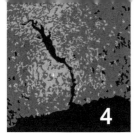

4

Warrior Women, Virgin Forests, and Green Hells

Genuinely striking, the milky green stone that dangles from a leather cord around the neck of the older man on the splintered wharf keeps drawing my eye. "Is it a frog?" I finally ask, no longer able to contain my curiosity.

The man nods. "This stone is very old. It is called '*muiraquitã*,'" he says, shading the pendant with his hand so that I can get a better look.

"You mean one of those talismans that the Amazons are said to have given to their lovers as a token of their encounters?" I ask, suddenly connecting a word I had carefully sounded out in books (moo-ee-rah-kah-TAH) to the smooth, cool, and curiously luminous object that he now slips off and places in the cup of my hand.

"Yes," he says. "Perhaps it is true, and perhaps it isn't, but I like to think that one of those women warriors could have given this frog as a gift to one of my great-great-grandfathers long before the Europeans ever dreamt of setting foot here."

Present in accounts by various European writers, jade amulets such as this one still turn up from time to time in today's Amazon.[1] Called *muiraquitã, murayataka,* or *takua,* these frog-shaped stones give a tactile presence to a multitude of stories about the warrior women who have long claimed a privileged place in images of Amazonia.[2] In bestowing the name of these women upon the world's biggest river and the vast lands that surround it, sixteenth-century Europeans underscored the simultaneously alluring and hostile aspects of New World nature. Unlike the coquettish female figures who appeared alongside them in a number of early representations of the Americas, the warrior women embodied a world at once enormously dangerous and immensely rich.

The Amazons as Classical and Old World Myth

Enigmatic from the start, the Amazons—a name that does not appear to be Greek in origin—made their first known appearance in early versions of the *Iliad*. The epic formula "Amazones antianeirai," or "Amazons like unto men," marked them as a race of females who were the equal of males in battle. Indeed, it was said they cut off their right breasts in order to better wield their bows and arrows.[3] Some classical authors located the Amazons near Greece; others consigned them to Libya and even Atlantis, and still others, including the fourth-century B.C. historian Herodotus, placed them in Scythia or Asia Minor.[4] Contemporary archaeological evidence argues for the myth's partial basis in a historical people of the southern Russian steppes called the Sauromatians, among whom the women (who rode horseback) appear to have enjoyed a privileged status.[5] While there is no proof that these horsewomen were the origin for the Greek stories, which probably were in circulation long before the Greeks became aware of the Sauromatians' existence, they most likely played a part in the progressive "barbarization" of the Amazons.[6]

With time, the Amazons grew not just more bellicose, but more complex and mysterious. Transformed from women seen as men's equals into women openly hostile to men, they began acquiring individual personalities in later epics. One of the first and most memorable of these figures was Penthesilea, queen of the Amazons, whom Achilles slew in battle when she took the part of Troy against Athens.[7] The coupling of belligerence and sexual allure in the figure of Penthesilea—whose name means "she brings sorrow to the people"—constituted a thorny problem in terms of the Greek honor code.[8] In the course of fighting, the Amazon queen had exhibited a healthy dose of the martial valor called *thumos,* which the early Greeks saw as a property exclusive to males. Achilles therefore had done battle with a suitable opponent. Because *thumos* was said to leave the body upon death, however, the corpse at Achilles' feet was that of a beautiful woman, whose slaying was cause for shame and not rejoicing.

The balance between the Amazons' allure and their off-putting fondness for combat shifted over time to reflect new social and political realities. In early Athens, stories of Amazons summarily crushed in battle played a key role in bolstering a marriage system that had little place for independent women. With the passage of the centuries, different stories emerged. The tale of the Amazon invasion of Athens in revenge for the rape of the princess Antiope followed the Persian invasion of the city in the fifth century. Achilles and Penthesilea, the original warring couple, later reemerged as lovers, while another Amazon queen, Thalestris, jumped into bed with Alexandros instead of confronting him on the battlefield.

And yet, although ideas about the Amazons changed dramatically in accord with historical circumstances, representations of them in Greek epics and in vase and mural painting, sculpture, mythography, and funeral oratory continued to encapsulate a series of contradictions. Depicted alternately as passionate and hostile, as women who must be won by strong men and female warriors who would rather die than submit to male authority, the Amazons in art and myth almost certainly mirrored shifting roles among, and attitudes toward, Greek women.[9] Likewise, the warrior women's fluid identity allowed their passage over time into other cultures.

A number of medieval European authors based their accounts of Amazons on classical sources such as Herodotus.[10] However, the Amazons were unquestionably best known to the general public through the accounts of medieval travel writers. One of them was Sir John Mandeville, who referred to the inhabitants of the all-female island of "Amazonia" or "Feminye" as "noble and wise warriors." Another was Marco Polo, who extolled the great riches of the women on the Female Island of the Arabian Sea. These travel accounts in turn fed into those sorts of chivalric romances of the sixteenth century that Miguel de Cervantes would later lampoon in *Don Quixote*.[11]

The increasingly close association between the Amazons and prodigious wealth in the late Middle Ages may have stemmed from classical authors' descriptions of their gold and silver armaments. The fifth-century B.C. historian Hellanicus, for instance, identified the Amazons as a "golden-shielded, silver-axed, female, man-loving, male-infant-slaying" army.[12] Heavily metaphoric (gold and silver were too soft to be used as weapons), these classical descriptions illustrated the warrior women's suprahuman prowess in battle by placing them in the company of mythic figures such as Calypso with her gold belt, Cupid with his golden arrow, and Apollo with his gold cloak, bow, and lyre. Medieval travel writers, eager to impress their readers with the exotic riches of foreign lands, made far more literal connections between the Amazons and precious metals. In fact, the impetus for later descriptions of warrior women who traipsed about in golden crowns, oversaw great subterranean mines, and wept tears of purest silver lay in the very concrete quest for New World treasures.[13]

New World Amazons

References to the "women without men" of Matinino (variously identified as Martinique, Montserrat, and Guadalupe) appear in the writing
of Columbus, who thought he had reached the Indies and was therefore
looking for Marco Polo's wealthy Amazons.[14] He thus did not register
surprise when, in January 1493, a native informant told him about an
island inhabited solely by women and very rich in *tuob*—an indigenous
term for gold or copper. In a letter summarizing his first voyage, written
some two months later, Columbus reported that these women were said
to use bows and spears to attack others and to protect themselves with
plates of armor made of bronze. Recasting earlier accounts of a "masculine" and "feminine" island, he situated the Amazons beside a neighboring island to the west of Matinino inhabited exclusively by men.[15]
His claim that the Amazons periodically mated with these men—whom
he identified as "*canibales*"—established a direct and early parallel between the New World Amazons and a group of men who feasted on human flesh.

And yet, despite their partial roots in Old World sources, the warrior
women were more than a collection of preexisting stories that the Europeans imposed wholesale on the New World. The Amazons had closer
ties to a long-established narrative tradition than did the golden king,
but they too were hybrid creatures. At the same time that the writers
who described them looked to medieval travel writers for embellish-
ment, they drew on a variety of native stories and beliefs as well.

Native reports of Amazonlike women were not limited to the Caribbean islands where Columbus had reconnoitered. Strikingly similar
traditions cropped up among Cariban, Arawakan, Salivan, and Tupian
linguistic affiliations throughout Amazonia, the Orinoco basin, the Guianas, and the West Indies, from as far south as the Araguaia, Tocantins,
and Paraguá Rivers in eastern Brazil and northern Bolivia to as far north
as the greater Antilles.[16] North of the Amazon River, these women were
often called Aikeam-Benano, or "women-who-live-alone." South of the
river, they were likely to be known as Cougnantaisecouima, or "women-
without-men."[17] There were also reports of a queen or leader of the
Amazons called "Cuna Ateare" or "Conori." Usually placed at the
headwaters of the Trombetas River, this Amazon queen is said to have
ruled over seven settlements in the Guiana highlands.

These early references to all-female societies find present-day echoes
in native Amazonian myths about women in an early time who pos-

sessed a series of sacred pipes or ceremonial flutes that guaranteed their dominance over men.[18] At the time, these reports all but ensured the emergence of a series of composite narratives by the Europeans. The Amerindian elements that crept into the explorers' first- and second-hand reports in turn prompted the authors of chivalric texts to emphasize particular elements in their accounts of warrior women.[19] For example, Columbus' reports of an "island without women," themselves a meshing of medieval and native sources, reverberated in the description of the Amazons in the extremely popular chivalric romance *Las sergas de Esplandián,* by Garci Rodríguez de Montalvo, first published in 1510.[20] Quite likely following Columbus' lead, Rodríguez de Montalvo placed his island of women on the right-hand side of the Indies close to the Terrestrial Paradise. Big, bold, and black (rather than very white, as they were in most medieval accounts), his Amazons shared the predilection of Columbus' natives for the martial arts. His explanation that the warrior women's weapons were made of gold "because it was the only metal on the island" echoed Columbus' borrowed descriptions of an island rich in *tuob.* Even Rodríguez de Montalvo's claim that the Amazons fed captive men and their own male babies to griffins trained to eat any man who landed on the island echoed Columbus' reference to the cannibals with whom the women supposedly mated from time to time.

Thus, the "women-without-men" who emerged in early explorers' reports were strikingly different from their classical cousins. Their seclusion, for instance, did not necessarily translate into martial activity directed at men. Only some sixteenth-century European writers followed classical sources in describing them as one-breasted.[21] These and other differences have led some scholars to argue that the designation "Amazon" merely may have been a way of making observations about some New World females intelligible to readers back home.[22] However, the fact that medieval Europeans had no trouble identifying Marco Polo's island full of equally unwarriorlike women as "Amazons" argues for a more literal understanding of the term.

Hernán Cortés, for instance, appeared convinced of the Amazons' flesh-and-blood existence. In 1518, the explorer—an avid fan of chivalric novels—received a contract from the Spanish governor of Cuba, Diego Velázquez, to explore westward from the islands. "It is said," the governor affirmed, "that there are people with large, broad ears and others with faces like dogs, and also where and in what directions are the Amazons, who are nearby according to the Indians whom you are taking with you."[23] In a letter written in 1524 to Charles V of Spain, Cortés referred to reports of "numerous, well-populated provinces along the coast adjacent to the towns of Colima" where the natives claim there is "much treasure" as well as "a district inhabited by women without men." Although his ensuing search for the Amazons failed, it was Cortés who, in 1535, named the supposed "island" of California after the Amazon queen Califia, who appeared in the fifth book of Rodríguez de Montalvo's romance.[24]

The Amazons' physical presence was yet more palpable in the Dominican friar Gaspar de Carvajal's description of a group of female warriors whose arrows quickly made the Spanish brigantines of Francisco de Orellana bristle like porcupines.[25] Nothing in this narrative— one of the earliest descriptions of New World Amazons by a European, and almost certainly the most influential—suggests that the friar found these fearsome, long-haired warriors to be anything less than flesh-and-blood descendants of the female warriors of Greek myth.[26] It is precisely this ability of the Amazons to transcend boundaries of time and space that rendered them suitably gigantic fragments of a New World nature whose hugeness and unfamiliarity inspired, even as they terrified, the Europeans.

The Amazons as Giants

To the extent that they encapsulated irresolvable tensions about the place of women in society even as they deflected attention from "the unknown, the limitlessness that terrified the Greeks," the Amazons of classical antiquity were themselves giants.[27] However, their larger-than-life qualities underwent important changes in the hands of sixteenth-century explorers. While the New World Amazons continued to incorporate anxieties related to an untrammeled female sexuality, the primary object of concern in Carvajal's famous account of the warrior women was not their threat to particular social institutions, but their embodiment of a simultaneously rich and forbidding New World nature. This nature appeared to the friar not just as *a* female, but as at least two very different sorts of women, hostile and alluring.[28] As human containers of immense, forbidding alien surroundings, Carvajal's "Great Mistresses" did not trigger the same sort of physical desire as a Penthesilea, whose likeness men prayed they might find in their bed on returning home from war.[29] They did, however, inspire an all too obvious lust for New World riches.

Like virtually all of his fellow chroniclers, Carvajal set out to describe in detail the people and places that he and the expedition encountered during their passage down the Amazon in 1541–42.[30] The friar had more pressing aims, however, than the usual desire to secure recognition for past discoveries while drumming up the funds for new ones. Above all, he sought to justify and celebrate the actions taken by the leader of the expedition, Captain Francisco de Orellana, and his men in the face of charges of treason. Orellana's principal accuser was Gonzalo Pizarro, under whom he had set out to look for El Dorado and the Land of Cinnamon. After the expedition quickly ran out of supplies, Pizarro sent ahead the captain and some sixty men, including Carvajal, to look for food. Unable or unwilling to return to the main party, Orellana and his crew continued down the entire length of the river on a momentous nine-month journey that Pizarro, shamed and angry at his own resounding failure, saw as a betrayal.[31]

The presence of the Amazons in the midst of a hotly contested mission that brought back little or nothing of material value set Carvajal's chronicle apart from any number of other accounts of New World expeditions that had failed to produce significant riches. His firsthand report of the encounter between the men and the warrior women would serve as a basis for paraphrasing and endless embroidery for a large number of subsequent reports by other writers.[32] Primarily second- and thirdhand accounts, only a handful of these narratives would describe allegedly face-to-face meetings between the Amazons and particular Europeans, and none would be nearly as dramatic. For example, although Columbus' son Ferdinand asserted in retrospect that a group of aggressive female prisoners had led the admiral to give credence to reports of Amazons on the island of Matinino, Columbus himself never claimed to actually have seen the warrior women.[33] Likewise, almost a century after Carvajal penned his famous chronicle, Bernard O'Brien described how his father, Cornelius, and four other Irishmen made their way up the Amazon and encountered "masculine women" called Cuna Ateare, who had "very small right breasts like men, [treated] by arts so that they do not grow, in order to shoot arrows."[34]

The proximity of the author to the alleged eyewitness distinguishes O'Brien's account from most descriptions of the warrior women. Nonetheless, his narrative lacked both the novelty and the epic dimension of Carvajal's original firsthand description of a full-fledged battle involving significant numbers of natives and Europeans. Carvajal's account is also distinguished by its forceful conflation of the at once hostile and alluring Amazons with a rich and yet off-putting land. His chronicle provided a different, ultimately complementary vision of the region and of the New World from the one embodied by the golden king.

Although the friar devoted only a few paragraphs to others' reports of the Amazons' rich kingdom and a scant page to his own description of the men's furious battle with these "Great Mistresses," their presence permeated an account marked by its intense ambivalence. While the golden king had been an effective and alluring icon for great wealth that remained maddeningly elusive, the Amazons embodied a land that inspired both desire and fear. Although the sorts of contradictory sentiments they instilled in Carvajal were not unusual in colonial chronicles, his oscillation between positive and negative descriptions pushed these tensions to an extreme.

Like El Dorado, the land of which the Amazons were the supreme rulers was distinguished by its enormous wealth. The white-as-alabaster villages that followed one upon the other boasted a surfeit of turtles, meat, and fish, as well as biscuit (manioc) in such abundance as to feed "an expeditionary force of one thousand men for one year." Crammed with game animals, fruit-bearing trees of all sorts, and vast stores of what looked to Carvajal like acorns, wheat, and olives, the lush riverbanks seemed to him to be "as good, as fertile, and as normal in appearance as our Spain." [35]

Extensions, like the golden king, of a prodigious nature, the Indians of this new country initially appeared every bit as rich and wondrous as the land. While their tortoiseshell armor and brilliant headdresses struck the Europeans as thoroughly exotic, their "jewels and gold medallions" suggested the presence of a series of reassuringly familiar treasures. Decked out in "gold and [splendid] attire," the natives were as welcoming as the lush riverbanks full of fruit trees and animals. Exhibiting a wealth of "manners and good breeding" that again recalls the gilded monarch, they showered the Europeans with food and drink "and all with as much orderliness as if all their lives they had been servants."

If the lands through which the men passed were rich, those that they did not get to see were said to be even richer. Secondhand reports of these marvelously wealthy territories emphasized the "very great wealth of gold and silver" in the Amazons' direct possession. These treasures, like those of El Dorado, were distinguished by their artifice. No dense lair of primeval vegetation, the Amazons' "excellent land and dominion" included a glittering city with not just one, but five very large buildings that served as places of worship. The gold and silver with which the city brimmed had been crafted into wondrous objects including "many gold and silver idols in the form of women, and many vessels of gold and of silver for the service of the Sun."

The use of jewel-toned feathers to decorate the ceilings of their temples underscored not just the Great Mistresses' astounding wealth, but also their cultured, more courtly side. Like the golden king, they displayed a regal bearing—at least when at home. Carefully attired in cloaks of fine wool, they wore their flowing hair loose to the ankles. Atop their heads perched golden crowns "as wide as two fingers." At a time when many Europeans still ate with their hands or with rustic table implements, those Amazons "of rank and distinction" employed gold and silver eating utensils as casually as we today would make use of plastic picnic forks.[36]

And yet, if the Amazons were every bit as rich as the golden king and their city every bit as much a display of artifice, their kingdom was unlike El Dorado in its vast dimensions. El Dorado compressed the riches of the Americas into a carefully contained space (a walled city, a kingdom, or a lake ringed by mountains), but the realm of the Amazons appeared to sprawl without limits. Thus, while Ralegh's Juan Martínez reached the golden city of Manoa after a relatively short journey, a man who sought to traverse the Amazons' domain was "destined to go a boy and return an old man."

Moreover, whereas the golden king was the very model of civility, the Amazons displayed a number of frankly barbaric traits. Alluring in their supreme wealth, they could also be extremely hostile. "Very white," "very robust," and "of very great stature," the Amazons demanded description in superlatives and were giants in the most literal sense. However, as the moniker "Great Mistresses" suggests, they were also giants in terms of the power they wielded over others. Both their prodigious wealth and their exceptional fierceness set them apart from the other Indians. ("They are rich and feared," Nuño de Guzmán wrote succinctly in a 1530 letter to the Spanish king.)[37]

The other Indians' fear of the Great Mistresses did not mean that they themselves were pacific, however. The same supposedly docile and courteous natives who welcomed the Spaniards with shows of the land's bounty regularly turned on them with "murderous" and "evil" intentions as soon as the men turned their backs. Tormented at night by great clouds of mosquitoes, the Spaniards found themselves by day obsessed with the lack of food when the natives began withholding their bounty. The beauty of the scenery that rose up before them could not sustain the

men, who, fearful of native ambushes, found themselves reduced to eating the boiled leather of their own belts and shoes rather than venture
into a dangerous forest that may have been full of game, but also was
full of Indians. ("Hunger was our only sauce," Carvajal noted grimly in
one version of his narrative.) [38]

Even at their most cruel and murderous, these other Indians were no
match for the Amazons, whose ferociousness they tauntingly described
to the Spaniards. Unlike the golden king, the Great Mistresses possessed
a taste for riches surpassed only by their fondness for war. The discomfiting boundlessness of their kingdom found echoes in their unbridled
savagery upon the battlefield. As frightening to their own troops as they
were to the Spaniards, the Amazons would summarily execute any man
who showed the slightest sign of hesitation in the heat of battle. Carvajal described how in a fierce battle that erupted on 24 June, ten or twelve
of these female captains fought so courageously that "the Indian men
did not dare to turn their backs, and anyone who did turn his back they
killed with clubs right there before us, and this is the reason why the Indians kept up their defense for so long." [39]

Quick to exhibit their mastery over men on the field of battle, the
Amazons also flaunted their dominance when it came to lovemaking.
Thus, while accounts of El Dorado only hinted at the more grotesque
aspects of a king who literally became a golden object, accounts of the
Amazons pointed to their openly unnatural use of men for their own
pleasure. When, as Carvajal noted delicately, "that desire came to
them," they made war on a neighboring overlord, taking captives whom
they kept as lovers for "the time that suited their caprice." [40] Once pregnant, they sent their erstwhile partners packing. (The friar's account
made no reference to the Amazons' alleged custom of bestowing jade
keepsakes upon their lovers in a manner that Sir Walter Ralegh would
later compare to the exchange of valentines.) Following the birth of the
ensuing children, they destroyed or sent away the male offspring to their
fathers, raising the females "with great solemnity" and instructing them
"in the arts of war."

Their fierceness in battle situated the Amazons somewhere between
the golden king and a whole assortment of New World monsters. To the
degree that sex and eating were often linked semantically (the English
"he devoured her with kisses" still finds multiple analogues in colloquial
Spanish and Portuguese), the sexually dominant Amazons constituted a
special class of cannibal. Although they did not actually eat people, their
unnatural appetites made them apt containers for an all-consuming na-

ture.[41] In this sense they resembled less the gold-plated king than they did other, far more fearsome aberrations such as the Ewaiponoma, whom Ralegh later described as men with eyes in their shoulders and mouths in the middle of their breasts.[42]

Their refusal to submit to any man, including the far better armed intruders convinced of the superiority of their civilization, distinguished the Amazons from a number of other female personifications of the Americas. Their essential wildness prompted artists to depict them as surrounded by fierce animals (usually lions or stags, meant to evoke the hunt) and often naked and armed with a bow and arrow. These illustrations provided a dramatic contrast to myriad portraits of voluptuous, even coquettish Indian princesses wearing grass or parrot-plume skirts and carrying lacy-looking feather fans. Laden with fruit and wreathed in flowers, those more pacific and welcoming Americas were the obvious extensions of Father Manuel da Nóbrega's Garden of Delights. Sometimes overtly flirtatious, often suggestively recumbent, their tousled hair and naked shoulders implying a luxuriant seductiveness and accompanying spirit of accommodation, they were entirely foreign to their warlike sisters.

The Amazons' martial impulses and their willful use of men in procreation flouted European gender expectations.[43] Like the golden king's apparent squandering of natural riches, their belligerence seemed to cry out for intervention from without. Not surprisingly, sixteenth-century European literary treatments of the Amazons often ended with the warrior women abjuring their martial ways. Converted to Christianity, they cheerfully surrendered not only their religion but also their matriarchal culture to become model wives and mothers.[44]

However, as I already have suggested, the warrior women were far more than a particularly graphic expression of sixteenth-century anxieties about gender. Although the mingled fascination and terror that they inspired in the Europeans had much to do with actual male-female relations, it sprang first and foremost from encounters with a New World nature that regularly placed men, as Carvajal said, "in great danger of death." For the friar, the meeting of the waters (in this case the Solimões and the Rio Negro) was no shimmering testament to nature's grandeur. Rather, it was all too vivid proof of nature's violence and terrifying force.[45]

An embodiment of this tremendous power, the Amazons inspired false fear because they, like Penthesilea—or a Dolphin on land—were mortal. They succeeded in peppering the Spanish ships with arrows, but

the better-armed Europeans were able to pick off a number of their assailants. "Our Lord was pleased to give strength and courage to our
companions, who killed seven or eight—for these we actually saw—of
the Amazons, whereupon the Indians lost heart, and they were defeated
and routed with considerable damage to their persons," Carvajal reported. The Amazons did, however, force the Spaniards into a hasty retreat, undercutting their triumph: "The Captain ordered the men to get
into the boats with very great haste, for he did not wish to jeopardize the
lives of all, and so they got into the boats, not without some trouble, because already the Indians were beginning to fight again."[46] Nonetheless,
the encounter with the warrior women promised an eventual victory
over a land that the friar identified as the personal property of the Great
Mistresses.

By making the Amazons the object of concern in his account, rather
than a far more immense and amorphous nature, Carvajal played into
false fears and assured the Amazons' identity as giants. Further illustration of this is found in Carvajal's insistence that the Spaniards readily understood the natives, and that the natives comprehended them.
Unwittingly confirming that the real object of the men's fear was not the
Amazons per se, Carvajal time and again described how the natives
listened in deferential silence or with "keen interest" to Orellana as
he "speaks," "urges," "commands," "explains," "reports," and "proclaims." Some of these passages would be downright funny if their future import for the natives were not so ominous. When, for instance, the
captain explained that the Spaniards were Christians and "not like them
[the natives] who walked in the paths of error" by worshipping stones
and man-made images, the "very attentive" audience appeared to nod
its assent.[47]

By no means the only chronicler to minimize or to deny obvious difficulties in communication between the Europeans and the natives, Carvajal still outpaced many of his peers.[48] Words actually took the place of
food as Orellana regularly "sustain[ed]" the starving men with assurances that they would prevail.[49] The captain's ability to create "a haven
of clear understanding" carved out a comforting alternate space for men
besieged on every side by a terrifying nature that found expression in
a people who eschewed language for "senseless" yells, bewildering
dances, and a cacophony of trumpets, pipes, and drums.

The tremendous fear of the unknown that lay behind the friar's insistence that the natives clearly understood the Spaniards further solidifies the Amazons' importance as a particular sort of giant. Alien on the one hand, the warrior women, with their deep roots in Western literature, were, on the other, almost familiar and thus oddly reassuring. Moreover, as the stuff of myth, they conveniently transcended boundaries not only of gender, but also of time and place. In so doing, they conferred a larger-than-life status upon the beleaguered Spaniards.

The New World Amazons' ability to bestow such a mythic aura helps explain an otherwise puzzling facet of Carvajal's text. Although the friar repeatedly condemned the other natives as "warlike," "arrogant," and "devilish" and deplored their "wicked sacrifices," he had almost nothing bad to say about the Great Mistresses. Since it is they who commanded the other natives, the Amazons bore direct responsibility for the crew's travails. Nonetheless, even when their troops wounded him in the side ("If it had not been for [the thickness of] my clothes, that would have been the end of me") Carvajal did not denounce the warrior women, but rather called attention to their valor. ("More than an hour was taken up by this fight [between the Spaniards and the natives], for the Indians did not lose spirit, rather, it seemed as if it was being doubled in them, although they saw men of their own number killed, and they passed over them, and they merely kept retreating and coming back again.")[50] This lack of criticism is doubly strange, since these women's sexual license, lust for battle, and fondness for graven images would all appear cause for the strictest censure on the part of a Roman Catholic priest.

The friar's admiration for the manlike Amazons served in part to feminize the other Indians, who surely would have run away from the better-armed Europeans were they not so afraid of their women captains. So although the Amazons were indeed courageous, their valor highlighted the cowardice of the men whom Carvajal described on other occasions as fighting "like wounded dogs."[51] At the same time, the friar's genuine wonder at the Amazons again confirms their identity as giants who magnified the Spaniards' own achievement in confronting a nature so immense it ensured its own mythic status.

A number of Carvajal's contemporaries were quick to dismiss his claims as fabulation—or, at best, confusion on the part of a crew whose members mistook a group of long-haired men for women. However, the king's swift acceptance of his and Orellana's version of the story confirmed the Amazons' hold upon the imagination of many of these men's peers.

It is possible that Carvajal and Orellana cynically invented a battle
with the Amazons in order to divert attention from Pizarro's accusations. Loath to face a disgruntled king—and a charge of treason—
empty-handed, the friar constructed a fantastic interlude that transformed what would have been a grim list of battles and privations into
a grand and heroic achievement. However, his urgent tone and the concrete details he offered argue for an actual encounter between the fright-
ened and exhausted Spaniards and what they believed to be a New
World incarnation of Greek myth. Moreover, the alacrity with which
the great river down which they had sailed became known back home
as "the Amazon" (and not, for example, "the Orellana") suggests the
enduring fascination of this particular set of at once native and European giants.

The Amazons and Their Legacy

On the surface, stories of the Amazon had less of a direct impact on European colonization than did accounts of the golden kingdom, which
played a major role in opening the interior of South America to settlement and exploitation.[52] In addition, while both the king and the warrior women were distinctly peripatetic (reports of Amazons continued to
surface in various locations, from Chile to Paraguay to California), there
is an obvious semantic bond between the Amazons and Amazonia.[53]
Then again, while some contemporary writers see El Dorado as outshin-
ing all other colonial accounts of the Americas, others pronounce stories
of these women to be "the most authentic and luminous of all New
World myths." [54] In reality, the two figures, and the larger stories about
nature that they embody, are profoundly intertwined. Not only did the
Amazons signal the proximity of El Dorado, but they served as the more
wild and dangerous flip side of an ostensibly pacific golden king.

The active resistance to intruders so obvious in accounts of the sixteenth-century Amazons contrasts with the subversive quality of an El
Dorado that always remained just out of reach. The warrior women's
willingness to fight to the death foreshadowed later struggles in which a
theoretically female (but often, actually sexually ambiguous) Amazonian nature would fight back with all its might against intruders. Much
like the lowland Indian, or *auca,* onto whom early-twentieth-century
European rubber magnates would project their own propensity for violence, the Amazons possessed something that the Europeans needed and

wanted. The mystery of the Amazons, which went beyond purely material riches, lived on in the native shamanic powers that would awaken both fear and wonder in later Europeans, whose own cures would prove no match for tropical ills.[55]

Their ability to encapsulate the immensity of Amazonian nature helps explain the Amazons' enduring appeal among European writers. After noting that these "manlike women have their abodes in great forests, and on lofty hills," the seventeenth-century Jesuit father Cristóbal de Acuña expressed his conviction about the reality of the Amazons' existence. "A lie of this magnitude," he declared, as if stating the self-evident, could not have taken hold "in so many tongues and so many nations, with so many hues of truth."[56]

A full century later, in the 1740s, Charles de la Condamine, one of the first and best known of a long line of European "scientific travelers," again referred to the reputed presence of warlike women in the interior of Guiana.[57] Eighteenth-century maps continued to show islands inhabited by the warrior women, and as late as 1818, Drouin de Bercy, author of a comparative study of Europe and the Americas, argued for their existence.[58] Likewise, even while he lent scant credence to the Amazons of Greek myth, the nineteenth-century German naturalist Robert H. Schomburgk reported hearing accounts from the Macusi and the Carib Indians of "separate hordes" of warlike females toward the head of the Corentyn River.[59]

While the Amazons, like the golden king, gradually ceased to be an object of pursuit, the portrayal of Amazonian nature as a warrior woman continues into the present.[60] Even though the region does not hold a monopoly on belligerent landscapes, the Amazon has regularly inspired such images at different points in time. One of the single most obvious descendants of the early Amazons is the Green Hell of early-twentieth-century Latin American novels, essays, and short stories. Much like Roosevelt's hostile Brazilian wilderness, this verdant inferno flaunted its riches even as it resisted conquest from without.

Rooseveltian Wildernesses and Green Hells

Full of feathery bamboo, tall trees with foliage "as delicate as lace," and swarms of "gorgeous butterflies," Roosevelt's distinctly female wilderness could be both beautiful and fragile. This same wilderness, however, had a more violent side. "The very pathetic myth of 'beneficent nature' could not deceive even the least wise being if he once saw for himself the iron cruelty of life in the tropics," the ex–U.S. president declared. "Entirely indifferent to good or evil," this nature "works out *her* ends or no ends with utter disregard of pain and woe."[61]

Roosevelt juxtaposed this female nature with a virile Anglo-Saxon civilization destined to wrap both the wilderness and a series of less developed and less vigorous cultures in its transformative embrace. Nonetheless, even while he clearly thought of Amazonia as a female presence to be subjugated in this Darwinist drama, he did not develop the idea of the region as an actual woman. In this sense, he was very different from a number of Latin American writers of the epoch. Not just theme and setting, the hostile wilderness became an actual personage in works such as Alberto Rangel's *Inferno verde,* or Green Hell, a collection of short stories that opened the door to a series of early-twentieth-century *novelas de la selva,* or "jungle novels."[62]

Supremely rich and actually beneficent on some occasions, Rangel's Green Hell on others was a lethal entity. Much like Carvajal almost four centuries before him, Rangel described alternately a forbidding tangle and a luxuriant expanse. On the one hand, his Green Hell was a "MOST FERTILE VALLEY-kingdom of running Waters, orchard of Orchids and Palm Trees, empire of the rubber trees." On the other it was an "undifferentiated, dense, disordered mass of leaves and branches, twisted fronds caught up in knots of vines that claw each other by the legs."[63] Not only did this fighting, biting jungle lash out against itself in an unbridled fury, but it attacked any intruder foolhardy enough to throw himself into the fray.

Perversely attractive in its chaotic energy, Green Hell displayed an erotic side that recalled the Amazons of classical antiquity. At the same time, Rangel's description of an invisible pollen that would alight upon the necks of unsuspecting passersby in a caustic caress foreshadowed any number of later evocations, including the Colombian novelist José Eustacio Rivera's allusions to "the aphrodisiac parasite that covers the ground with dead insects" and "the disgusting blooms that throb with sensual palpitations, their sticky smell as intoxicating as a drug" in *La vorágine,* or The Vortex. "No cooing nightingales here, no Versaillian gardens or sentimental vistas!" exclaims the book's narrator, lest the reader of this most famous of all early "jungle novels" somehow fail to get the point.[64]

Despite the heavy air of sexuality that, many decades later, would lead German filmmaker Werner Herzog to equate Amazonian nature with "overwhelming misery and overwhelming fornication, overwhelming growth and overwhelming lack of order," Green Hell also had a primeval, even virginal side.[65] Rangel anticipated Roosevelt, as well as a number of later Latin American writers, in his focus on the Edenic aspects of this verdant inferno. In the first story in his collection, for example, a "tender tapestry of grasses" curiously reminiscent of Father Nóbrega's *hortus amoenus* leads to a lake ringed by every imaginable species of animal—a scene that the narrator compares to a rustic illustration for the Book of Genesis.

Very unlike the *hortus amoenus,* however, this marvelous tapestry quickly becomes a tangle of fetid grasses when the sun appears. Only when the rains return does the pestilential swamp and "veritable catalogue of insect life" revert to a luxuriant lagoon. Like the jungle in the Portuguese writer Ferreira de Castro's later novel *A selva,* which remains "a fantastic and spectacular play of shadows and light," it inspires admiration at the same time that it prompts a visceral horror.[66]

Even when they focused on the landscape's primeval, paradisal aspects, Rangel and his fellow authors continued to insist upon the need to transform this "ogre who devours worlds."[67] In his stories, as in a number of novels by other writers of the period, the apparent protagonist is almost always an urban transplant whose dreams of personal profit are part of a larger vision of national integration of which Roosevelt undoubtedly would have approved. In the end, however, it is inevitably a defiantly enormous nature that dominates these often pedestrian works.

Although these dreamers failed where the U.S. president appears to have emerged triumphant, their defeat was meant to be provisory. Rangel, for his part, actually had his jungle prophesy its own eventual capitulation to a worthy suitor who had yet to make his presence known. "I am," asserts the vocal (indeed, quadrilingual) jungle, "the land promised to superior, vital, vigorous races, blessed with strength and intelligence and fortified with money: and one day, they will come to plant in my bosom the definitive work of civilization, which the first immigrants, the poor and humble *pionniere* of the present, trace confusedly between curses and the gnashing of teeth."[68]

Green Hell's assurances that later generations would come "to the tamed and cultivated land, to lay the deep foundation of the *urbs,* where once stood the provisory shelter of the *settler*" would seem to second

Roosevelt's view of the inevitability of progress. In so doing, Rangel appears to have drawn back from the image of a perennially defiant warrior woman. However, much like Bates' dream of a "glorious new civilization under the equator," Green Hell's vision of her own impending transformation from the "Gehenna of tortures" into "the mansion of hope" was set in an indefinite future. Despite these assurances of her ultimate domestication, Green Hell continued to rout all would-be invaders with a violent energy far more convincing than her florid words.

The single biggest difference between the early-twentieth-century Green Hell and Carvajal's warrior women lies in the reasons for their hostile actions. While the Amazons fought because it was their nature, Green Hell expressly responded to provocations from without. Rangel, who wrote during the dizzying apogee of a Rubber Boom that extended from the mid–nineteenth century into the beginning of the second decade of the twentieth century, was very clear about the motives for Green Hell's often lethal actions. In one story, "Maiby" (the name of an Indian woman), he described the frenzied search for rubber in terms of rape and crucifixion.

Impaled on a rubber tree like some "extravagant brunette orchid," the at once Christlike and bizarrely sensual victim is an all-too-obvious double for the land itself. ("The martyrdom of Maiby, with her life trickling into the little basins used by rubber collectors, would still be less than that of an Amazon offering itself up as nourishment for a commerce that exhausts it," the narrator asserts.)[69] It thus represents a larger crime "committed not out of Love, by an insanely impassioned heart, but out of the collective Ambition of thousands of souls crazed by a universal greed."

The specific historical context and political message of the early jungle novels underscores the varying possibilities and purposes of the Amazons as a broadly defined narrative legacy. Although clearly a descendant of the sixteenth-century warrior women, Green Hell was no mere re-creation of a timeless myth. Written for a Latin American public, rather than a European one, these novels reworked the old theme of a threatening, elusive nature to new, nation-building ends. If Carvajal's warrior women served as convenient containers for a landscape that threatened to devour the explorers, the Green Hell of writers caught between their own admiration and distrust of Europe embodied, even as it concealed, the contradictions in official modernizing schemes.[70] Fearsome in its resistance, the jungle of the jungle novels was also marvelously original. The often involuntary admiration that a defiantly virginal Green Hell inspired in the Latin American reader distinguished these accounts from the superficially similar Rooseveltian celebrations of a kind of progress in which an early-twentieth-century U.S. public was coming more and more to place its faith.

Second Eden as "the Second Sex"

Particularly obvious in descriptions of a walking, talking jungle, the legacy of the Amazons goes far beyond personifications of a resistant female nature. Time and again, the warrior woman reappears beneath the surface of seemingly El Doradian portrayals, such as the majestic forest that Bates pronounced "grand in its perfect equilibrium and perfect simplicity." The margins of Amazonian streams were "paradises of leafiness and verdure," the sparkling brooks were full of "perennial and crystal waters," and even the parasites were part of a parade of wonders in an Amazonia that abounded in "little Edens." [71]

An infinitely desirable woman, tropical nature regularly appeared as an ideal spouse for an implicitly male, European-style civilization. [72] However, in order to produce a glorious new human race under the equator, she first would have to be wooed and won. This courtship process—which took the form of scientific investigation—was unflaggingly reverential. Thus, even while some of Bates' descriptions are mildly erotic (the solitary scarlet passionflower "set like a star within the green mantle of creeping plants," the juxtaposition of the "massive, dark crowns of shady mangoes" with Amazonian women's glossy and luxuriant hair), nature remained a "solemn temple" that demanded the utmost respect.

And yet, while this contained eroticism only enhanced the nineteenth-century naturalists' enthusiasm for an ideal nature, hints of a less than templelike Amazon often crept between the lines of their accounts. For instance, although Bates described the voracious leaf-cutter ants with his usual enthusiasm, he went on to blow up these pests with gunpowder. His portrayal of an earth "encumbered with rotting fruits, gigantic bean-pods, leaves, limbs, and trunks of trees," that was at once the birthplace of "the great world of vegetation" and a grotesque cemetery revealed an ambiguity similarly reminiscent of the warrior women's fearsome allure.

Bates' contradictions also confirmed that the "sovereign nature" that he would woo with science could be a royal pain. "I enjoyed the voyage on the whole," he wrote in one of various sections of the book guaranteed to please armchair travelers. Yet he also complained of the scanty fare, the confinement of the canoe, the trying weather—frequent and drenching rains, with gleams of fiery sunshine—and the woeful desolation of the river scenery.[73]

Likewise, although he followed his account of a seemingly interminable march through tepid shallow water with a celebration of the "lusty health" that one enjoyed while living "this free and wild life on the rivers," his description of a "brain-scorching vertical sun" is all too believable. While similar accounts of obstacles are routine in Roosevelt's *Through the Brazilian Wilderness,* Bates' attempts to play down his discomfort give these episodes a particular vividness. "A drizzling rain fell all the time, and the ground around the fires swarmed with stinging ants, attracted by the entrails and slime which were scattered about," he wrote before going on to assure the startled reader that the journey was, "by and large, quite pleasurable."[74]

The resistant underside of Bates' elsewhere "perfect," "bounteous," and invitingly beautiful (female) nature is nowhere more visible than in his account of his return to England: "The want of intellectual society and of the varied excitement of European life, was also felt most acutely, and this, instead of becoming deadened by time, increased until it became almost insupportable. I was obliged, at last, to come to the conclusion that *the contemplation of Nature alone is not sufficient to fill the human heart and mind.*"[75] So, although he continued to call for the union of civilization and nature, he himself abandoned his long courtship by returning home.

Virgin Forests

Similar acknowledgments of the concealed willfulness of an outwardly beneficent, distinctly female nature mark portrayals of the Amazon as a Disappearing World. Although his focus on tropical nature's primordial qualities set Lévi-Strauss apart from Bates, he and a number of subsequent writers revealed a similar frustration with this nature's resistance to their own grand schemes.

The near obsession with surfaces in Lévi-Strauss' descriptions of the clouds whose feeble, hollow shadows recalled the flats of a stage set and of the forest that first struck the visitor as "a mass of congealed bubbles, a vertical accumulation of green swellings" attests to this frustration.[76]

Although its jewel-like landscape was breathtaking in its beauty, the Amazon of *Tristes tropiques* was also often full of dust, of bleak, treeless expanses, and of mud. It therefore comes as no surprise that this resolutely elusive nature flatly refused to answer his prayer by letting him in on "the secret of its virginity." The Amazon's more obdurate qualities came to the fore once more when the threat of torrential rains and malarial fevers forced him to retreat precisely in the moment when he finally encountered a previously uncontacted tribe. Although he continued to invoke the splendors of wild nature, with its accompanying freedom, the constraints that this same nature placed on the expedition could not be more clear.

The fierce and sometimes brutal nature that glimmers beneath the surface of some of the most apparently ideal depictions of Amazonia lives on in images of a harsh and untamed jungle that coexists with today's fragile Rain Forest. The ads presently used to attract eco-tourists to the Amazon highlight the same dual nature that found expression in both Green Hell and the sixteenth-century warrior women. It is true that one can trace an evolution from calls to experience the "great adventure" of "the lush, dark, exciting jungle" in the 1980s to shimmering invitations to explore an intricate web of flora and fauna in the "Virgin Forest" of the 1990s. Nonetheless, both virgin and virago remain not just present, but inextricably intertwined, in current images and accounts of the Amazon. Although they have different meanings than they had fifty or five hundred years ago, they are both part of larger chains of narratives that periodically converge.

"Rich beyond measure" in terms of its biological diversity, the "endangered" forest is also a "thrilling habitat" full of "Stone Age Indians," "untamed wildlife," and "astonishing surprises that will set your hair on end." [77] Thoroughly gigantic in its natural wealth and plethora of yet-to-be-discovered species, this Rain Forest recalls a scene from one of the later "jungle novels" in which a newcomer to the Amazon stares into a night illuminated by "colossal fireflies." "Behind these forests," he warns his companions with equal measures of dread and anticipation, "lies the great beyond!" [78]

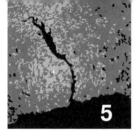

Gold as a Woman

From the outside, Angela Maria's modest stucco home looks like twenty others on the sun-drenched side street just a few minutes' walk from Tô Pereira's shoe repair shop. The inside, however, is different from any other in the neighborhood. Two bright-blue brocade sofas with protective plastic covers on the cushions vie for space in the living room with a massive, modern grandfather clock. The tile kitchen boasts a slightly rusted cherry-red refrigerator atop of which sits a set of cookie jars shaped like an eggplant, a glossy pepper, and a plump tomato. The money for these uncommon luxuries, Angela Maria is quick to inform anyone who shows the slightest interest, reflects the year, seven months, and eight days she spent working as a nurse in a gold camp called Lucky River. The Tapajós River, on which the camp is situated, was a major mining center in the 1980s, when high gold prices and a relative abundance of surface gold kept its tiny airport humming. Although the region has since been eclipsed by the state of Roraima (in northern Brazil near Venezuela) and by Suriname and French Guiana, it is still an important source of gold in the Brazilian Amazon.

More than ten years have passed since a then thirty-three-year-old Angela Maria cashed in the last of the handful of pea-size nuggets that she had managed to smuggle past federal police in the frenetically busy Itaituba airport by packing them into the hollowed-out heels of a pair of high-heeled shoes. Although the shoes now gather dust on the floor of her bedroom closet ("I can't bring myself to throw them out!" she confesses with a sheepish chuckle), her store of tales about gold camps and gold miners appears as fresh as ever. Detailed accounts of the people and places that were part of her daily life in Lucky River mesmerize me and Lucinha as we slump comfortably in the well-worn plastic deck chairs that Angela Maria has set out for the three of us on the narrow strip of sidewalk before her front door.

"Gold," she informs us as she tugs a comb through her short auburn-tinted hair in the sudden cool of this June evening, "is always a woman for the miner. Now then, 'she' can take very different forms. Sometimes, Gold appears as an old lady. But more often, she is a beautiful woman in white who tells men where to dig. Sometimes, too, she can take the form of an ugly snake or caiman, which a miner dare not kill or all the gold within the ground will disappear. But even as a snake, Gold remains a woman. Because she is the *mãe* [mother, tutelary spirit] of what looks to us like shiny metal, but which the miners believe is a living thing."

When we look incredulous, Angela Maria lowers her voice and proceeds to tell us how she too once found herself face-to-face with a mysterious woman all in white. "It doesn't seem possible," she admits, "but I swear that this really happened. Late one night when the moon was full, just days after I first arrived in Lucky River, I was returning from giving one of the men an injection when suddenly I saw a tall, blond woman in a long white dress at the edge of the woods. She raised her hand and beckoned to me, but when I started to go toward her, she disappeared into the shadows of the trees. 'That's odd,' I thought. 'Who could she be?'

"Early the next morning, I asked Seu Luiz [the owner of the mine] about the beautiful woman who had disappeared into the woods. 'Ah, my dear,' he said, 'you have seen the woman all miners long to see. Had you not spoken to me of her, she would have reappeared to you this very night and shown you where to dig for gold. But the Woman in White does not allow anyone to speak about her to another human being.' And so, if I had known this, I could have been very rich today."

Lucinha frowns. "And so you're sure it was a woman you saw there in the shadows?" she asks skeptically.

"I'm absolutely sure," Angela Maria says. "If someone had told me all this beforehand, I wouldn't have believed him. But the gold camps are full of strange and marvelous things."

In its unmistakably female identity, the Gold that meanders through Angela Maria's accounts of her own eventful, often trying life in Lucky River recall the warrior women and their various descendants. Irresistibly rich, this often grotesque Gold can be as headstrong and independent as any sixteenth-century Amazon. Unwilling, like the Amazons, to submit to any man, she fills her pursuers with both an intense desire for conquest and sense of deep unease. "Every man wants to meet the Woman in White, because she will show him where to find gold," Angela Maria tells us. "But the miner who meets her is no longer the

owner of his life, because for her to help him, he must do exactly as
she says."

To the extent that the Gold she describes is every bit as dangerous and
alluring as a warrior woman, it is a giant who contains and deflects attention from a larger, all-devouring nature. However, despite its more
gigantic aspects, this Gold is a consummate shape-shifter who reaffirms
a protean nature's power. The object of a quest for personal fortune in
which each miner competes against his fellows, she unites men well
aware of her capriciousness.[1] ("Ah, brother, don't take it so hard, she
dumped me too," one miner may declare by way of consolation to another who has been drilling for weeks in an apparently promising location, only to come up empty-handed.) The enduring mutability that
finds expression in Gold's multiple identities underscores at least some
miners' sense of nature as a living being that permits and even invites
momentary intervention but defies full conquest and control. Ostensibly
about a willful Nature, these stories about Gold also permit the men to
express their anger and frustration at powerful outsiders. In their tales,
the government, commercial gold companies, and foreign environmentalists with good intentions but little knowledge of regional realities all
emerge as usurpers bent on destroying a poor man's only chance at a better life.

Present-Day Gold Miners

Mining has long been one of the very few avenues to riches open—at
least in theory—to even the very poor. Thus it resembles a sort of hands-
on lottery in which people accept slim odds for the chance at a bonanza.
As in the lottery, part of mining's appeal lies in the aura of possibility
that comes to surround even the least favored participants. Whereas
one's investment in a lottery may be minimal, however (a dollar here, a
dollar there, on trips to the corner market), the miners routinely risk
their lives. Gold mining is hard work, and the men often labor from
dawn to dusk seven days a week. Mining is also dangerous, since acci-
dents, diseases, and acts of violence are rife. Most of all, gold mining is
psychologically taxing, since a man must cooperate with others without
ever letting down his guard.

Reports of gold and gold mining in the Amazon (Amapá, Rio Branco,
and the neighboring Andes and Guianas) date back to the sixteenth cen-

tury and the early tales of El Dorado.[2] In colonial Brazil, gold was primarily associated with the center-west (often pictured as an extension of
a fabulously rich Peru on sixteenth-century Spanish maps).[3] Amazonian
gold became a focus of international attention only in the twentieth century, with the discovery of gold in the Tapajós area in 1958.[4]

A dramatic spike in the price of the precious metal in 1979, and the
discovery of the giant lode at Serra Pelada later that year, converted the
search for gold into a veritable fever.[5] It was during this time, in which
Brazil emerged as the world's fifth-largest gold producer, that Angela
Maria signed on as a nurse in Lucky River. Young and single at the time,
she had never dreamed of working in a gold camp until a chance conversation in a Belém dentist's office with a seemingly unexceptional older
man changed her life. The man, Seu Luiz, turned out to be the owner of
Lucky River. "Two days later," Angela Maria recalls, "I was on a plane
for Itaituba. He even offered to pay for a gold tooth to replace the one
that I was having treated, and though I find gold teeth ugly, I was impressed—he was so rich!"

Despite the later drop in gold's value and the increasing need for expensive machinery to extract ore from deposits ever more difficult to
reach, mining continues to attract sizable numbers of men to the Brazilian states of Pará, Rondônia, and Roraima.[6] There are also mines and
miners in portions of the Spanish-speaking Amazon (above all, in Peru,
Bolivia, and Colombia), as well as in Suriname and the Guianas.[7] Although current population estimates are more often in the tens of thousands than the hundreds of thousands, mining, with its sense of adventure and lack of need for formal qualifications, remains an important
occupation in the Amazon.

The gold camps are known in Brazil as *garimpos* after the verb *garimpar,* which means "to scratch or dig," "to prospect," and also, collo-
quially, "to pick one's nose." [8] Their single most outstanding characteristic is their variety.[9] Some, known as *fofocas* (rumors), are mere flashes
in the pan. Others are small cities complete with a fleet of single-engine
airplanes, a police force, and one or more computers. Mining may take
place directly in rivers, but the majority of sites are placer mines situated near or beside rivers. Although most mines presently employ rudimentary hydraulic drills much like those used in the California gold rush
of 1849, the level of technology may range from highly sophisticated
machines (rare) to a simple metal basin (even more rare today in many
areas, given the increasing lack of readily accessible alluvial gold).[10]

The system of ownership in the mines also varies, with some *garimpos* in the hands of a single owner and others offering a complex patchwork of competing claims. During the 1960s, for instance, the Tapajós gold fields were almost all "closed," or "wild" *garimpos,* which meant that the mine owner (most often a gold buyer, merchant, supplier, or pilot) controlled access to the area. With time, however, and with the advent of more expensive technologies, differences in ownership and administration began to appear.

Because *garimpos* rarely take up large areas of land, they are not a major, direct cause of deforestation. However, the runoff of silt and overburden may choke roots and undergrowth in the forests where men have carved out a *garimpo,* thereby indirectly causing considerable destruction. Those *garimpos* that employ machinery may tear huge piles of earth from mountainsides, clogging rivers and severely eroding the land. However, the greatest destruction caused by mining is a direct result of the massive and almost completely unregulated use of mercury in the mines.

Common as well in nineteenth-century California, mercury is used as an amalgam to which the gold clings. In the last stages of the collection process—be it manual or mechanized—the amalgam is usually tipped into a piece of finely woven cloth (which can be something as simple as the miner's T-shirt), and then twisted hard enough to expel any excess mercury, which usually runs into the river, killing fish and contaminating a food chain that includes humans as well as birds and other animals. The miners then heat the amalgam with a butane torch, causing the remaining mercury to evaporate in a toxic white gas, which they inhale nonchalantly, unaware of the nerve disease, impotence, and eventual death that sustained exposure causes. ("They say it's bad for you," one miner says fatalistically, "but here I am, here is the gold, and what would you have me do?") The same negative effects may be visited in somewhat attenuated form upon nonminers, since the pollution of streams and rivers can affect hundreds and even thousands of miles of waterways.

Generally poor, and often illiterate or semiliterate, the miners vary in terms of their geographic origins. Some are Indians or blacks, but most are of mixed blood. Although many are from within the Amazon, some are from neighboring states. In the case of Brazil, a large percentage of the miners come from the northeastern states of Maranhão and Ceará, or the south-central states of Goiás and Paraná. During the height of the rush on Serra Pelada in the early 1980s, and the ensuing frenzy in the mass media, the Amazon became a magnet for fortune seekers from a host of the most diverse locations.[11]

Most outsiders' image of the Amazonian gold rush *is* Serra Pelada, which became a symbol for an entire region thanks in good part to Brazilian photographer Sebastião Salgado's striking portraits of antlike men winding their way up and down an abyss that was once a mountain.[12] A media spectacle from its very start, the mine was anomalous in various other ways as well.[13] Far bigger than most *garimpos* (at its peak in 1983, Serra Pelada, situated in southeastern Pará, produced more than a metric ton of gold a month and contained a population of close to a hundred thousand miners and related merchants and tradespeople), it was also distinguished by its hillside, as opposed to riverine, location. The Brazilian military government's decision to place control of Serra Pelada under Major Curió in 1980 was another differentiating factor, and the ensuing prohibition of mercury and the almost complete exclusion of women from the mine were two important direct results of this control. The politicization of the miners in the *garimpo* was another. Curió, for example, was elected to the Brazilian Congress when he ran in 1982, and his allies took eight out of nine seats on the city council in neighboring Marabá.

What was depressingly similar about Serra Pelada to other *garimpos* was the small number of people whom it benefited. About a quarter of the gold production there was controlled by just over a hundred persons. Likewise, fewer than a thousand people—about 2 percent of the total registered *garimpeiro* population of 48,000—pocketed more than 70 percent of the income from the gold during Serra Pelada's boom period.[14]

The punishing routine associated with gold mining has led the *garimpeiros* to describe themselves as "penitents" forced to atone for the "sin" of nonconformity with the poverty into which most of them were born. ("The priest says that the poor are blessed," says one young miner, "but what would he know about the man cheated out of his land by a pack of lawyers or the young girl who becomes a prostitute in order to feed her little brothers?") When the hot sun does not beat down upon their heads, heavy rains convert their camps into a sea of slime. Moreover, even the rare man who manages to escape malaria and hepatitis—no easy feat in settings where logs jam rivers that look more like curdled milk than water—often finds himself succumbing to a contagious solitude. Because meals are often staggered so that the digging, hauling, and sifting of earth can continue without interruption, and the racket of machinery makes conversation all but impossible in any case, most men have little direct contact with their coworkers by day. When night finally comes, many head for makeshift bars *(cantinas)* where they drink, dance with prostitutes, and talk for hours. These conversations may continue in the tents and lean-tos located just above the gullies, called *barrancos,* where the men drill for ore.

Barring the so-called *peões rodados,* or men who move from mine to mine in an eternal pilgrimage, prospecting tends to be an on-again, off-again occupation. Likewise, many of the women who work as cooks, laundresses, and shopkeepers in the *garimpos* and surrounding settlements, called *corrutelas,* spend only a certain amount of time there before returning home.[15] As a result, it is just as easy to hear the sorts of stories miners tell in places where there are no mines, and it is certainly easier to tape-record outside the *garimpos,* where the racket of machines, dynamite, and tractors drowns out voices and the men are usually too busy or too exhausted to converse by day.

After Angela Maria first got me interested in gold miners, I went on to record large numbers of tales on the boats that serve the cities of Santarém, Itaituba, and, later, Maués. I also spent day after day in the crowded malaria wards of public hospitals and clinics in these cities, where virtually all of the patients are from *garimpos.*[16] Although it was unnerving to record a person who might suddenly start shaking with a fever I had no way of assuaging, a thick ring of miners regularly formed about me in the outdoor courtyards where many patients milled about, waiting for a doctor. "It makes the time pass," one man with almost yellow skin said when I nervously asked if he ought not to be lying down instead of talking. He had just flown in to Itaituba from a gold camp on the Tapajós River and looked very ill. "Besides, where would I lie down if there aren't any beds here?" he asked, causing the other men to laugh sardonically.

I recorded other stories in the gold camps themselves, which I visited with the pilots of tiny planes who regularly supply the camps, above all in the Tapajós. Usually friends or acquaintances of friends, these men allowed me to perch atop sacks of potatoes on runs that usually began at dawn and ended just before nightfall. ("There's no way you'll find me there when the mosquitoes and the men start drinking," declared one grizzled pilot with whom I often traveled.)

In Rondônia, where most mining sites are situated on or directly beside rivers, I spent almost a month accompanying an engineer friend who regularly serviced machinery in the camps. Although he laughed at the flowered cotton dresses I wore on these outings ("You look as if you're going to a garden party!"), the long skirts gave me the freedom to clamber over hills and into muddy gullies while warding off the insects. They and the small silver cross I wore around my neck also served to immediately establish a respectable identity for me in locations where women who are not mistresses or wives tend to be "secretaries" (a word that may refer to domestic help, but is also a common euphemism for prostitutes).[17]

"You sure don't look like a missionary, miss," said one young man, after surveying me from the top of a rusted tractor. "But then again, you don't look much like those girls in the *cantina*, either."

Some miners were understandably suspicious of an outsider with no immediately apparent motivation for being there. ("You expect me to believe that you came all this way just to hear a bunch of men tell stories?" one sunburned miner growled. "Lady, everybody here is peddling something—don't you think that I don't know!") A few men worried that I might be a spy sent to find out who was hiding gold from government tax collectors. Many, however, proved poignantly eager to talk about their lives. Despite my protests that it was I who remained indebted to them, many storytellers would offer me a gift of an orange or banana, a shot of rum, or a wildly expensive Coca-Cola, sold in *cantinas* with an added charge for every ice cube. Occasionally, one or another miner would present me with a pinch of grainy powder that looked less like gold than ground ginger. ("No, no, take it," one man said when I protested. "You remind me that there is a world beyond these miles of mud.")

It was Angela Maria who led me to spend several weeks in Lucky River. Her stories of the Woman in White, who promised men great fortunes; of a black man whose bleeding body vanished into thin air when her husband, Paulo, left him to get help; and of Maria Gasolina, a prostitute who swallowed gasoline in order to abort an unwanted baby, made me want to see firsthand the people and the places she described. Now estranged from Paulo, whom she left behind in the *garimpo* ("He loved me, but he couldn't leave that life even when I had my baby"), Angela Maria was initially hesitant to contact the owner when I said I'd like to visit Lucky River. However, her own curiosity about the changes that had taken place in the years since she had left the camp eventually led her to telephone one of Seu Luiz' sons. When the son reported that he would be heading for the mine in a few days, should the *"professora gringa"* care to tag along, I saw my opportunity.[18] Armed with a suitcase full of the woolen socks and heavy work shirts that Angela Maria had pressed upon me as protection against the cold nights that she shivered to remember, I set out for Lucky River.

First founded in the late 1950s, the camp was, at the time of my visit, one of the oldest still-producing gold mines on the Tapajós.[19] I found myself tape-recording a long string of stories there from men who had spent ten-hour days knee-deep in tepid, insect-infested mud. An antidote to the grim routine they followed day after day, which was conspicuously absent from the catalogues of horrors with which my nonminer friends had regaled me, these stories portrayed a world distinguished by its resistance to fixed definitions.

The wool socks, by the way, turned out to be totally useless. The freezing nights that Angela Maria remembered turned out to be an unrelenting steam bath. Likewise, her stories often turned out to be very different from the tales of enchanted snakes and disappearing corpses that people regularly recounted at Lucky River. Even veteran miners looked quizzically at me when I inquired about the hapless Maria Gasolina and her unborn child. "Never heard of her, ma'am," said one old man, pausing in the midst of pouring a mixture of cashew juice and rum into clouded plastic glasses for the patrons of the *cantina* he had set up in his tiny living room. Stirring the thick yellow mixture, he shrugged his shoulders. "But then again, there are so many ghosts around here that it's easy for a person to lose track."

Stories about Gold

Not surprisingly, a large number of the stories that miners tell focus on the precious metal that accounts for their own presence in the *garimpo*. In part oral histories, many of these frequently first-person narratives include lengthy descriptions of different gold camps, as well as of particular people and events. They also are often rich in detail. "It was Mané Pé Grande [Manny Big Foot] who found three and a half pounds of pure gold there, two feet from that clump of trees just down the road from Boa Aventura exactly a week before Ash Wednesday," a man may declare.

And yet, while the particulars vary, the general outlines of these stories—many of which deal with lucky strikes, or *bamburros*—tend not to. It is a rare storyteller, for instance, who does not deal in superlatives.

The nuggets that the happy miner encounters are inevitably as big as oranges, if not watermelons. The strike does not simply make him rich, but transforms him overnight into a millionaire. "They say that this Mané now flies in his own airplane to an apartment in São Paulo every weekend," the storyteller may declare with something between envy and jubilation.[20]

In everyday life, the owners of the mines or the machines (not always one and the same) are by far the most likely to be the beneficiaries of a major find. However, the protagonist in the vast majority of miners' stories is a "Joe Nobody." Although the storyteller may acknowledge the extraordinary character of the occurrence ("Today, these things almost never happen"), the tale nonetheless centers on Joe's ability to overcome all odds.

The following story is a clear-eyed description of the growing dominance of technology and hierarchy in gold mining, in which poor men may end up as day laborers or as *porcentistas* who reap scant advantage from a major strike.[21] It is also an expression of the narrator's hope that he may yet find himself among the lucky few. A young man with an easy smile and stiff black hair that stands straight up on his head, he begins by declaring how unlikely it is to strike it rich, then unleashes a flood of the marvelous details so common in these tales.[22] While his comparison of gold to an underground river is as old as El Dorado, the conditions he describes are thoroughly contemporary.

> Look, finding gold today is really hard. Because gold comes from a river that runs beneath the earth, and that is always changing course. In the past, miners were able to find places where the river ran very near the surface of the earth where they could seize the gold. Today, one needs machines, one needs a whole team of men in order to extract it—and so, the person who gets rich is the one who already has a lot of money. Really, the ones who make big fortunes are the ones who sell the food and medicines, the ones who own the hydraulic drills, the computers, the airplanes and who can charge outrageous sums. Still, sometimes, Gold takes a liking to some poor man, but it's not every day; you have to be really lucky. [Here the young man flashes a winning smile.]
>
> In the past, yes, everything was easier, a man might find gold on the ground, people filled whole tins of Leite Ninho [a brand of powdered milk] with enormous nuggets. Back then, in those old days [the 1950s and '60s], there was a man named Inácio who struck it fabulously rich. Look, the gold he found filled two whole airplanes. One plane almost fell out of the sky because it was so heavy. And with this gold, he bought apartments in Rio de Janeiro, in Brasília, in New York, and Paris. Even his dog got a house of his

own. This man would have lunch in the *garimpo* and dinner in Belém. He'd
sleep in a bed of real wood with gold decorations and then, early the next
morning, he'd be back here again.[23]

In part a catalogue of gold's rewards, the young man's story is also a
description of a personal relationship. The Gold in his story is every bit
as alive as the sun-colored, plantlike metal that inspired Diego de Ordás
to roam the steamy equatorial zone in search of El Dorado. Moreover,
as Angela Maria notes, this Gold is distinctly female. The language of
these stories is often one of courtship and seduction. Although *gold* is a
masculine noun in Portuguese *(o ouro)* as well as in Spanish *(el oro)*, a
man occasionally may employ the feminine pronoun (*ela*, as opposed to
ele) before making a quick correction. The existence of a feminine variant, *bamburra*, on the masculine *bamburro*, further underscores the
gendered identity of Gold.

"Gold, yes, it is a woman," says Carlinhos, a short, friendly man who
has worked almost five years as a machinist for Angela Maria's estranged husband, Paulo. "It would have to be, ma'am. Because it is always growing, always giving birth to more gold. It's true that it can appear as a big, black snake too. But," he adds, with a mischievous wink,
"it is more apt to appear to us as a pretty woman—tall, white, blond,
and blue-eyed."[24]

Gold's ability to command respect sets her apart from the women in
most miners' daily lives. ("Men like to order women around, but it is
Gold who tells them what to do," explains a moon-faced woman who
has been working as a cook in Lucky River for "two months now, but
this is my fourth time here and I swear by all the saints that it will be the
last if I come down with malaria again.") The same man who brags that
he would never take "no" from any woman may find himself meekly
submitting to a deceptively fragile-looking Gold. While miners laugh
and roll their eyes at tales of how a once fearless *garimpeiro* meekly
obeys the Woman in White's instructions, they grudgingly agree that
they would do the same in his place. "We swallow the toad [a colloqui-
alism that refers to putting up with something] because we all want
something better," says the youngest man in the camp, who is counting
the days until his sixteenth birthday.

Look, this fellow was the bravest of all the miners for miles around. No one
dared to cross him, see? Because if he were to get angry, there would be some
mother weeping [for her dead son] before the day was through. But when this
Woman in White began to appear to him, he'd become tame as a little child.

[Here, the men snicker a bit uncomfortably.] He'd go down there by the river around midnight and only return at dawn. Now then, everybody talked behind his back, but no one was ever fool enough to ask him where he'd been.[25]

The welter of taboos surrounding men's behavior in the mine underscores Gold's power. A man, for instance, should never spit or urinate in a gully that miners are excavating. He should refrain from cursing or from speaking in a loud voice and should not clean the mud from his rubber sandals until after climbing out of the excavation pit.[26] Menstruating women are expressly forbidden from so much as looking at a gold site, and even "healthy" women should be careful not to touch any of the miners' tools. Thus, although my status as a foreign guest gave me access to excavation sites, a number of the miners looked uncomfortable when the owner's son invited me to examine a hydraulic drill. They went on to offer a series of excuses as to why I should not do so. "It's too heavy for her," objected one older man with a red bandanna around his forehead and a tarnished medal of Saint Barbara on his sunburned chest. "It's very dirty," chimed in his slightly younger, copper-skinned companion. "You don't want her to get her hands all full of mud."

Above all, a man must take care not to attack Gold directly. The present-day belief that the precious metal may assume reptilian form recalls colonial chronicles such as Juan Rodríguez Freyle's account of his search for a pair of golden caimans rumored to lie at the bottom of a lake. The man who kills a snake or caiman that turns out to be one of this Enchanted Being's various manifestations brings catastrophe not only upon himself, but on the community at large.[27] Even if the miner and his fellows quickly move on to another site, they may remain *panema*—an indigenous term that most commonly refers to a lack of success in hunting or fishing brought on by disrespect for carefully defined taboos.[28] The drills and sluices in use in the particular locale where a miner kills one of Gold's reptilian manifestations may remain similarly jinxed. In a few cases, these machines may even require purification by a healer.

"Yes, miss, I can say that I have seen this," pipes up one normally shy young miner with a thickly bandaged index finger caught earlier that morning in a wayward gear. The good-size gold camp on the Tapajós in which we find ourselves has been in existence for only a month.

In the last *garimpo* where I worked, a fellow killed a very big snake in the excavation pit and all of us became *panema*. No one could find so much as a fleck of gold for weeks. Even the machine became *panema*. No, no, don't laugh [he says this to several friends of his who are listening to the story].

There wasn't a mechanic who could fix it. One of them would come and repair it and immediately afterward, it would break again. Finally, we had to
pay one of these *pajés* [shamanic healers] who really knows what he is doing
to come and blow smoke over the machine so that it would begin working.
[Here one of the other men laughs, but the others don't join in.][29]

Not simply strong-willed, Gold is often frankly capricious. There is
little a man can do to secure her continuing favor. Once Gold tires of a
particular individual, she discards him, Angela Maria says, "like a banana peel." As a result, while miners tell countless stories of lucky
strikes, they are even more likely to recount instances of *blefes,* or busts.
A word with strong connotations of deception and betrayal, the verb
blefar awakens a sense of rueful amusement, at least when it applies to
others. Beyond losing all of his money, the man who is *blefado* has been
"swindled," "duped," or "screwed." In contrast to the noun for lucky
strike, which, as already noted, may be feminine in colloquial usage, a
blefe (or, less frequently, a *blefo*) is always masculine.

Willful and capricious, Gold is also profoundly strange. Indeed, she
has an attraction to human blood that makes her as grotesque as any
warrior woman, if not more so. The man whom she favors has to have
"*sangue bom para o ouro,*" or good blood for gold.[30] Although in some
stories Gold favors those with particular skill or virtue, the great majority of tales eschew any sort of moral. Failure or success is ultimately
a question of destiny. A man may labor for months in one spot without
finding so much as a single nugget, while a newcomer may hit pay dirt
in the very same location on his first or second try. Reputed to have a
murderous temper, the seventy-year-old man who tells this story looks
like someone's sweet-faced grandfather as he squints up into the early-
morning sun and speaks reverently of Gold and the men on whom she
smiles.

Everybody wants to get rich. No two ways about it. But Gold is mysterious,
she does exactly as she wills. Look here, there was a miner who spent more
than three months working in a gully. Genisvaldo was his name. A very good
person, very hard working, but he had bad blood for Gold. So then, he
couldn't take it any longer, he went away. And another came, a very young
man who didn't know a thing about mining. So then, he began to work
Genisvaldo's gully. Look, on the second day, this other fellow hit pay dirt. In
other words, he had good blood for Gold. There are people who said, "What
a shame that Genisvaldo left too soon!" But I say that Genisvaldo could have
stayed there another three months or another three years, and nothing would
have happened, he would not have found a thing.[31]

Gold's customary failure to reward hard work or personal virtue does not discourage most miners. The belief that it is blood more than actions that determines if one will be lucky provides a degree of consolation in the face of disappointment. At the same time, because blood's true character is not always immediately evident, the miner who has not hit pay dirt need not surrender hope. Unlike the economic system about which the men are unhappy but can do little to change, Gold remains supremely unpredictable. The men complain bitterly about this unpredictability, but it is actually a prime source of Gold's appeal.

"Do I believe that men have good blood or bad blood for Gold?" asks Seu Luiz, who began his life as "a *caboclo* just like any other." A short, sinewy man, now almost seventy, he has been regaling me with tales of his last trip to Paris as we drink a fine merlot with a lunch of freshly caught fish. "No, I don't believe in this business of good blood versus bad blood. But I do think that some men have a better head upon their shoulders and that Gold respects both courage and intelligence." He says this as he refills my glass with the wine whose crimson color is not lost on either of us.

"Tell me," he says, "how is Angela Maria?"

"Oh come on, I bet you have good blood for Gold," I say.

Gold as Enchanted Being

Gold's identity as an at once hostile and alluring female recalls the Amazons and their various descendants. Unlike them, however, she is not a person. Nor is she, at least technically, a personification, since she takes on various forms, not always human. Even the Woman in White, who does assume the shape of a particularly beautiful female, comes and goes in ways that defy physical laws.

Gold is also different from certain familiar embodiments of Amazonian nature; though she might still boast her maidenhead, Ralegh's Guiana did not appear impervious to conquest. Bates' bountiful nature turned out to reveal many different facets, but "she" exhibited an underlying logic that the patient naturalist, at least in theory, would eventually grasp. Likewise, even though Lévi-Strauss' bejeweled Eden stubbornly refused to divulge her secrets, he made no suggestion that the secrets were themselves incomprehensible. Gold is not so easily grasped.

Because of Gold's deeply mysterious nature, her relationship with the miners is neither a simple contest on the order of the Spaniards' armed confrontation with the Amazons, nor an enduring union such as that which Bates envisioned between tropical nature and European civilization. As in the case of other Enchanted Beings, Gold holds out the possibility of an alliance that brings overwhelming benefits to humans. The fact that this partnership inevitably crumbles confirms the precious metal's identity as an Encantado and sets it apart from its more gigantic counterparts even in those moments when it seems to act most like a giant.

Less openly hostile than giants such as Carvajal's Amazons or Theodore Roosevelt's clawing, biting wilderness, Gold is far stranger and more frightening. Her strangeness is nowhere more evident than in her attraction to human blood. Although Gold actively shuns murderers in a number of stories, she inspires a greed that triggers acts of violence which may result in death. Moreover, even though Gold never directs one man to kill another, she displays a disturbing propensity to show up in places where blood has been shed. This means that although the man who kills another does not profit by his actions, others unassociated with the crime may benefit from the unhappy event.

Born in the interior of Amapá, the following man, a heavyset card player in a purple tank top, had recently arrived in Lucky River following a stint in Suriname.[32] He recalls how a gully that had never yielded anything before the brutal assassination of a young miner begins producing large quantities of gold immediately following the man's bloody death.

> People call me "Tião" [a common nickname for Sebastião but also the word for *top* in Portuguese] because I spin from one place to another like a children's toy. An itinerant miner such as myself has seen a lot in this world, and he has a lot to tell. And look, it's true that Gold likes human blood. Because once when I was working near Maués, there was a *garimpeiro* of a very bad sort who picked a fight with a young man. So then, the young man went to defend himself and the first man fell upon him with a knife. He stabbed him so many times that the body looked like the sides of meat that you see hanging there in the market. The dust beneath our feet turned into a crimson mud. And the very next day, an enormously rich vein of gold appeared in that very spot. Yes, yes, I swear that what I'm telling you is the solemn truth. Now then, the murderer himself never touched a bit of it. He too met a bad end.[33]

The profound and abiding strangeness of Gold means that a man can hope for little more than a passing alliance with her. Unlike early tales of an El Dorado whose treasures eventually would be seized once and for all, accounts of Gold are charged with a sense of bemusement and resignation. "Gold comes and goes like smoke," says a young prostitute with bleached blond hair and eyes the shade of cinnamon who has worked in a dozen camps along the Tapajós for the last two years. "It can remain with a man for an hour or a year, but one day it disappears." Born in Belém, she regularly returns home with bundles of purchases for her mother, who believes that she is working in a bank in Santarém.

Even when Gold is with a man in her form as the Woman in White, her presence is provisory. As Angela Maria suggests in her account of her own encounter with this woman, the person whom the Woman in White favors is expressly forbidden to breathe a word about her to anyone. "Procópio, poor thing, wasn't used to keeping to himself like Gold demanded," says one older man with large, freckled hands, who enjoys recounting how he was born on a boat on the Amazon in the middle of a storm. "He got rich, for sure, but he was never again quite right in the head. By day, he was like you or me, but when night came, he would suddenly start talking out loud to people whom no one could see." By the same token, even the man who strikes an enormous vein of gold must take care to act in a way that will ensure Gold's favoring him again.

"Oh, yes, a man can do things to make Gold return to him," a young man in a World Cup shirt assures me when I ask. Dissipating the proceeds of a lucky strike in a thoroughly flamboyant manner, for instance, signals the lucky *garimpeiro's* confidence that Gold will one day reappear. Thus, while outsiders dismiss miners' penchant for conspicuous consumption as proof of their ignorance or profligacy, the men in question often see these actions as an investment in the future. "Why would a man spend all his money if he weren't sure that this were the best way for him to get more?" Angela Maria asks ruefully. She is almost certainly thinking about the breakup of her marriage following Paulo's refusal to quit mining after making the biggest *bamburro* of his life.

And yet, if the Gold of miners' stories often hints at the dark side of nature, her defiance of fixed forms and limits is part of her allure. Moreover, even at her most capricious, Gold is usually more even-handed and more generous to miners than are the representatives of a system in which they see themselves imprisoned. "I personally prefer life in the *garimpo* to life on the streets of Manaus," says one man who has wrapped a lime-colored towel around his head as protection from the sun. "Because Gold comes and goes, but she is not like the rich man who will never help the poor man no matter what. Besides, she does not ever pledge her word, and then go on to break it."[34]

Like one of Carvajal's warrior women, Gold's allure lies partly in her spirited refusal to submit to any man, no matter how convinced he is of his own superiority. Unlike the Amazons, however, who prove vulnerable to the Spaniards' harquebuses, Gold inevitably turns out to be stronger than human will. Indeed, she is even stronger than the economic hierarchies that weigh down miners. Because of this, the stories about her are not simply expressions of a fluid nature that interacts with humans, but protests against a social and economic system that pushes people toward the gold camps.

"The man who says he understands Gold is a liar," one older miner from the interior of Itaituba says with a deep sigh, waving his straw hat at the sand flies that buzz about our heads at the end of a stifling afternoon in Lucky River. "Of course," he adds, "if anyone did understand her, he would be a very rich man, and there would be no hope for the rest of us." [35]

Violence as a Link between Competing Worlds

The central role that violence plays in many miners' stories suggests, at first glance, that the tellers are blithely unaware of a larger world that is quick to regard them as both ignorant and savage. Certainly, for those men and women who find themselves stranded in the midst of the forest, the *garimpo* can seem a world apart. The frequent lack of the most rudimentary comforts intensifies the sense of isolation. So do debts to the mine owner that may make men virtual prisoners in camps far from any road. Furthermore, the use of the word *perna* (a leg of a flight) as a standard unit of calculation for goods and services in many gold camps on the Tapajós and in Roraima emphasizes the *garimpos'* dependence on the sporadic presence of tiny—and expensive—planes.

Nonetheless, despite the isolated quality of many camps, residents of even the most remote *fofoca* keep an eye trained on the larger world. Only dire necessity would cause most miners to miss the TV or radio newscast that gives that day's gold-price fixing. Their well-founded fears of being cheated may lead men with no more than a year or two of grade school to master complex currency conversions. At least some *garimpeiros* speak as casually and knowledgeably of international financial markets and gold futures as they would of last night's soccer game.

The Brazilian government's decision to seize direct control over Serra Pelada during the gold fever of the 1980s did much to politicize miners, who have since begun to elect local legislators and to participate in political parties. *Garimpeiros'* success in forcing government authorities to modify, when not rescind, a number of their directives in Serra Pelada brought home to them their power as a group.[36] One obvious result of this growing political consciousness and participation is the election of a number of miners to state and local offices. Nilson Pinheiro, who discovered the Tapajós gold fields, was later elected a state deputy in Pará. Angela Maria's estranged husband, Paulo, has served as a local representative and has dreams of entering politics, should he ever succeed in tearing himself away from the *garimpo*.

A second look at the actors and the actions in many tales involving violence reveals the ways in which miners regularly rework others' negative images of them to their own purposes. While, for instance, *garimpeiros* inevitably figure as the villains in newspaper accounts of gold mining ("In the Gold Rush, Nature Is Viciously Trampled," exclaims one set of headlines), they are apt to emerge as victims in their own narratives.[37] Stories about an unquiet soul who roams the gully where a too-trusting miner fell into an ambush are often warnings as much to oneself as to others that a man, even when he feels most lonely, should not confide in anyone. "That young fellow was a hard worker, everybody liked him, but he was much too trusting," the narrator—himself a very young man, with a frayed blue ribbon around his wrist reading "Souvenir of Our Lady of Sorrows"—concludes with a shake of his head.[38]

> It happened like this, it's a sad thing, I don't like to talk about it: There was a young man from Maranhão, very hardworking, a friend to everyone, who hit pay dirt one day. A great big block of gold, I saw it with my own eyes. But he didn't know how to keep the good news to himself. So then, they killed him. Because he didn't know how to be suspicious. He was walking up there on that ridge where you see that tree early one evening when they fell upon him. They stabbed him so many times that his own mother would not have known him. Even today, we see ghosts, hear cries, and I become sad. Because he had no guile, poor thing, but the others did.[39]

This focus on the solitary individual who must confront violence all alone would appear highly alienating. Nonetheless, these accounts of brutal actions may exert a paradoxically humanizing effect by attributing to flesh-and-blood actors fears and anxieties far harder to fix on invisible microbes and abstract social hierarchies. In recounting these stories, the miners make more comprehensible and even perversely glamorous what otherwise might appear a stultifying, if genuinely perilous, routine. They also create a peculiar sense of community. Certainly, the storytellers remain well aware on some level of the odds against them. "The problem is not the *garimpo,* the real problem is the world that makes Brazil, Brazil," says one young man whose faded orange visor shades his large, dark eyes. Nonetheless, the common caricature of the violent *garimpeiro* gives men the courage to go on. To the extent that this caricature serves as a focus for false fear (since one can confront another miner in a way that one cannot an unjust social system or a malarial mosquito), these villains serve as giants within a larger narrative of ongoing metamorphosis.

The villains are not always fellow miners. They are often unscrupulous mine owners in the mold of old-style rubber barons, or investors in faraway São Paulo, or a government that tries to prohibit *garimpeiros* from exercising what they feel is their legitimate livelihood. A confirmation of the violent character of *garimpos,* the following story is also, first and foremost, a stinging condemnation of the system in which gold miners find themselves enmeshed. The narrator is a middle-age shopkeeper with two gold front teeth, whom Angela Maria once nursed through a bad case of food poisoning. Born in Itacoatiara, he moved to Santarém while still a baby. "All my family is there," he says, "but somehow, I keep finding my way back to Lucky River. Tell Angela Maria she was right—mining is like a disease!"

> It happened this way: The man came from Maranhão to do battle in the *garimpo.* He went on for some seven months without finding anything until one day he struck pay dirt. But when he went to sell the gold, the owner of the *garimpo* only wanted to give him a pittance. So then, he got angry and said, "Fine, I'm going to do my selling in Itaituba." Well then, the owner said, "That's OK with me, but no one leaves here except in one of my planes, and the price of the flight will be half of all the gold you've found." So, the man left in a huff. "The hell with that guy's airplane, I'll make my way by water," he said to his friends. He waited for night to come, he set out upon the river, but the owner sent two hired assassins after him, and they killed him in the hour. Because he should have pretended to agree with the owner and then fled. The rich man always wins in contests of force, so the poor man has to be smarter. Now, his soul still wanders about here. The other day, a new arrival asked, "Who is that tall, thin man with the sad face whom I see wandering down around the river?" Well, everybody knew, of course, but no one had the heart to say.[40]

The strained laughter that follows the tale's conclusion confirms that this story strikes a raw nerve in the listeners. "Oh yeah, they're are all in cahoots with one another," asserts one young man who flips through a

comic book and flirts with a woman in a very short green dress. "The
mine owner pays off the government malaria prevention workers so that
they do not come here. Then, when a man gets sick he has to pay three,
four, five *pernas* for a remedy that costs pennies in the city. The same
thing with food, with machine parts, you name it. The owners have a
monopoly on all these things so that even when the poor man makes a
lucky strike, most of it goes right away to paying off his debts. Then too,
today half of the *garimpo* owes money to the crack and marijuana deal-
ers. You probably owe them too, eh, sweetheart?" he says to the young
woman, who frowns and studies a peeling crimson fingernail.

Aimed in part at outsiders, images of the miners as trigger-happy outlaws are intended in part to deter corporate interlopers who otherwise
might be quick to horn in on what remains a largely unregulated and
technically clandestine and illegal operation.[41] The prospect of having to
deal with a horde of wild-eyed miners has effectively slowed the entry of
extraregional commercial ventures into gold extraction. Unfortunately,
it also has often led government agencies and nongovernmental environmental organizations to dismiss miners as beyond the pale of education, thereby further marginalizing them. To the extent that the miners
actively encourage a vision of themselves as hopelessly unruly, the nonminer friends who had cautioned me about the dangers of the *garimpo*
were playing admirably the role scripted for them. And they were by no
means alone in this respect. Over time, I came to recognize my own
place in the supporting cast.

On an initial stroll down the dirt street of one of the first gold mines
that I visited in the Tapajós, for instance, I noticed a dark stain in the
dust. Even before I asked, my hosts volunteered the information that I
was witnessing the last traces of blood from the knife wounds inflicted
on a young miner who had gotten into a fight with another man almost
a week ago. Primed by innumerable stories about the ferocity of *garimpeiros,* I was spellbound by the horrific details of how the first man had
stabbed the other "seventeen times right in the heart, the blood gushed
out all over" in an altercation over a woman said to have eyes only for
a third man. ("The woman over whom that man stabbed the other
didn't like either of the two!" a young machinist said with a click of the
tongue.)

When I thought about the incident months later, I still had a visceral
reaction to the half-moon of sunbaked blood. Nevertheless, with each
new trip to the *garimpos* I became more aware of the near pleasure that

the storytellers took in my dismay. Although they might express sadness about the death of a particular individual, or revulsion at the senseless-ness of a particular brutal action, it was important to them that their stories have a visible effect upon me. In those cases in which I did not re-act strongly enough to satisfy them, they would produce new, even more horrific details until I finally did.

My point is not that the heinous events to which storytellers refer are a mere figment of their imagination, or that miners are a peace-lov-ing lot whom others have wrongly maligned. Although some gold camps are more dangerous than others, few are entirely free of a violence that periodically spills over into attacks on Indians and other local groups.[42] The miners may see these groups as obstacles to their extractive activi-ties, particularly when the groups hold legal title to the land, as native peoples sometimes do. They also may find these groups to be convenient scapegoats for their own frustrations, since Indians in particular tend to be even lower than themselves on the social scale. That a significant number of miners have some portion of Indian blood makes their hos-tility toward native people a bitter irony.

If miners' stories confirm the harshness of life in the gold camps while seeking to deter outside intervention, they also seek to make their tellers feel better by presenting violence not just as a fact of life, but as a pecu-liar source of pride. The following storyteller—a tall man known iron-ically as "Zé Pequeno" (Joe Little)—does not dismiss the doctor as a coward. Rather, his point is that miners possess a fortitude, even a hero-ism, that outsiders lack. Like Angela Maria, from whom I first heard this story, he insists that "living in the *garimpo* is not something that just anyone can do."

> Then, this doctor who arrived in the *garimpo* didn't sleep a wink because of the spirits. At six in the morning he asked for an airplane to leave that place. "I saw a lot of unquiet souls, a lot of things," he said. "Look, Seu Joaquim [the owner of the *garimpo* and his host], there are three spirits who are wan-dering about the *garimpo*. All three died a terrible death. In addition, they died with gold in their mouths, they had gold teeth but no one removed them. [Gold left anywhere in or on the body is believed to tie the soul of the dead person to earth.] One was a young man whom they killed down there in the gully. They killed him out of spite, a very young man. Another was an older man, poor thing, he died an ugly death. The third was a woman—tall, with dark brown hair, and slender. Her jealous lover plunged a knife straight through her heart." So then, that doctor explained absolutely everything. And so, *mana* [a colloquial form of address that literally means "sister"], you can see why living here is not for everyone.[43]

Stories that initially appear to celebrate bloodshed often turn out to be affirmations of a mystery that many *garimpeiros* see as surrounding Gold. By setting apart the *garimpo* from the humdrum world beyond it, violence gives its occupants new status. Though a source of deep anxiety ("Who will take care of my wife and eight children back there in Imperatriz if I die here tomorrow?"), it transforms a grueling routine into a high-stakes adventure that defies the social odds. This aura of deep enigma is particularly obvious in two differing accounts of a bleeding black man whom Angela Maria's estranged husband, Paulo, encountered one day around dusk. In the first version, Angela Maria stresses the grisly nature of the event; in the second, Paulo emphasizes its mystery.

> A horrible thing, Cândida, the *garimpo* is a hell, it's full of death, of things that would make anyone afraid. Because, look here, Paulo had gone in search of a wrench to change a part in the motor. And when he entered the machine shop, he saw that black man sprawled out on the floor. Full of blood, that man was bleeding from the chest, the neck, the head. A stranger, someone he had never seen before—heavyset and very dark. The man was still alive but he was bleeding so much that he was on the point of death. There was blood everywhere. "Gosh, that's one more gone, they've knocked off yet another," he [Paulo] said. And he went to find the others. But when they returned, the black man wasn't there. And what's more, there wasn't even so much as a drop of blood!

When I later got to meet Paulo in Lucky River, he took me to see the now-abandoned shed in which the event had occurred.[44] However, although he too described the bleeding body, he was far less interested in stressing its gruesome appearance than he was in impressing on me the enigmatic quality of the event. "I still don't understand it," he declares at the conclusion, outlining with a finger that once-bloody spot on the chipped concrete.

> Because look, that man was full of blood, the blood was gushing from his head. He was a strong man, but there is no one who could survive a wound like that. So I went to get help. And when I returned with the others—it was Dr. Joaquim and Joe Little, I no longer remember who else—there was absolutely nothing. No black man, no blood. The whole thing seems like a lie, a joke. [Here, he laughs a bit sheepishly.] But that's the way it was. Look, you can see that this shop has just one door. If someone had gone in or out, everybody would have seen. I have no explanation, I only know that the *garimpo* has its mystery, that here things happen that don't happen in any other place.

A number of possible motives for the differences in these versions are readily apparent. Angela Maria's estrangement from Paulo, her distance from the *garimpo* in both time and space, and her identity as a woman and a nurse almost certainly influence her rendition of the story. Paulo's desire to impress a foreign female visitor with his courage and his consciousness that anything he says is likely to get back to Angela Maria are obvious factors in his account. Nonetheless, the intermingling of the mysterious with the macabre that marks his version of the story is part of a pattern visible in other miners' tales.

At the same time that miners routinely rework others' caricatures of themselves to their own purposes, stories about a Gold that defies even the rich men who normally lord it over them bring home miners' deep ambivalence about a nature that they themselves would like nothing better than to exploit. "Ah, if a man could make Nature do exactly as he wanted!" one man with four gold front teeth exclaims in a small gold camp near Maués called "Now-You-See-It, Now-You-Don't" *(Vê, não vê)*. The striking contrast between miners' vision of an all-powerful Enchanted Being that demands respect and the effects of their daily activities (direct or indirect deforestation, wholesale pollution of lakes and rivers, often devastating attacks on local populations) underscores the competing forces that play upon these men.[45]

Outsiders' accounts of *garimpeiros* as assailants of a virgin land are no less contradictory. For all their vocal concern about the rain forest and so-called forest peoples, nonminers in Brazil and elsewhere are more apt to see nature as an object to be manipulated through either protection or development than as a living being that demands respect. Moreover, they have their own motives for presenting the gold miners as bloodthirsty giants. A convenient embodiment of the more savage aspects of tropical nature, the wild-eyed outlaw provides a focus for larger fears about environmental destruction: "Gold miners extract tons of gold from Yanomami lands and transform Roraima into a caldron of conflicts," declares an article titled "The New Gold Fever."[46] Articles by foreign journalists with titles such as "Gold's Lure versus Indians' Rights: A Brazilian Conflict Sets the Amazon Aflame" (the *New York Times*), "Gold Lures Hordes of Miners into Yanomami Domains, Despoiling Rain Forest" (a subsection of one piece in a larger report in the *Wall Street Journal* titled "Amazon Tragedy"), and "Motley Miners Pursue Amazon Gold" (part of the series "The Last Frontier" in the *Washington Post*) are equally critical of *garimpeiros*.[47]

The caricatures of gold miners in these articles provide a ready scapegoat for an assault on tropical nature whose causes go far beyond the miners themselves.[48] Multinational logging and mining ventures, government development policies dictated in large part by international monetary pressures (Brazil's need to pay off the interest on a staggering international loan while attempting to control inflation), and the burning of forestland for large-scale cattle ranches are only the most obvious of the other causes. Hydroelectric plants, roads that necessitate and foster ongoing deforestation, and waste-producing industries are ultimately far more destructive than limited-scale mining. Although miners have killed many native people through direct attacks and the indirect spread of disease, these larger enterprises have had a much more significant effect on a regional population that includes the sorts of ordinary men and women who turn to mining when deprived of their traditional livelihood. Nonetheless, the "scruffy," "ragtag," and "desperate" *garimpeiros* make particularly effective targets, because they divert attention from destruction in which newspaper readers might find themselves complicit.[49]

The miner as environmental villain permits readers in Washington and Tokyo, Lima and São Paulo to bemoan the destruction of the Amazon while continuing to consume hearts of palm salads at mahogany dining tables or to package handfuls of "Rainforest Trail Snax" in gleaming sheets of foil made from Amazonian bauxite. Moreover, while it would again be wrong to minimize the consequences of miners' destructive actions, the wholesale condemnation of them conceals the extent to which the Rain Forest they are routinely pictured as despoiling is itself a giant. Like the teenage women who find themselves working as prostitutes in some gold camps—an occurrence that also has received heavy media coverage—Amazonian nature in these articles is depicted as profoundly vulnerable.[50] Just as the young women are "imperiled," "imprisoned," and even "mined" in "hellholes" where "just about everybody packs a .38" and violence is "a simple fact of life," nature itself is routinely degraded.[51] Newspaper reporters regularly describe *garimpeiros'* use of toxic mercury and their attacks on Indians as a "violation" and a "rape of the land." ("Police Raid Amazon Saloons Said to Enslave 22 Girls," reads the subtitle of one article that goes on to decry the desecration of "untamed tropical forest.")[52]

Thoroughly virginal, this land full of great trees and Indians clad only in beads and feathers has no defenses against the gold-hungry "barbarians" who turn what ought to be paradise into hell. The ironic contrast between the noble-looking jaguars on "Save the Rain Forest" posters and the "wildcat" miners in the press coverage attests to the idealization of a nature whose less appealing aspects are routinely projected onto a particular group of human beings.

Quick to accept the vision of themselves as tough men inured to violence, miners nonetheless deny that they are enemies of nature. Their reasons are practical in part. While the image of themselves as swashbuckling outlaws keeps out intruders, portrayals in which they appear as enemies of nature and of native peoples lead to demands from environmentalists and human rights groups for official intervention. Responding to international pressure, the Brazilian government has sought to keep out miners where it cannot control them, periodically bombing rudimentary airstrips that serve a host of *garimpos* in Roraima, where miners have engaged in egregious attacks upon the Yanomami.[53]

The notion of the *garimpeiro* as an environmental outlaw reinforces ideas of gold mining as a disease and of miners as dangerous carriers of a moral virus that, in the words of the *Washington Post,* threatens to "contaminate society as much as mercury pollutes the rivers."[54] "If Latin American governments do not work together to curb the rape of the tropical rain forests [by the miners and similarly destructive individuals], the entire planet may be endangered," reads the subtitle of an article in *USA Today.*[55]

If, however, *garimpeiros* have good practical motives for contesting the image of themselves as destroyers of nature, they also have more emotional reasons. "These people who call us enemies of the forest don't live side by side with us in the mud; they only see those pictures of birds and butterflies on television," scoffs an older man in a malaria ward in Itaituba, who tells me how his one lucky strike at Serra Pelada paid for the "big cloud of silk with shiny beads all over" that came all the way from Paris to serve as his granddaughter's wedding gown. "Half an hour here would be enough to stop them from talking nonsense. But which of these *doutores* [an umbrella term for anyone with money] is going to leave his soft bed to do penance in the sun?"

Miners' startling assertions that they are the ones who understand and truly respect nature underscore the gaps between word and action. Their apparent disregard for nature in their search for gold makes it easy to dismiss those claims and the accounts of a living Gold. Yet what looks to outsiders like a series of contradictions may not strike the miners as such. Most of the men, for instance, find it hard to believe that mercury does any sort of lasting damage.[56] "They don't understand all this talk about how *garimpeiros* are poisoning the waters," says Angela Maria.

"They see the wind carry off that little trail of smoke into the air and ask how it could end up in the river. 'These people who claim that we are making ourselves sick just want to scare us into leaving so that they can take our place!' they say." [57]

Many miners argue that the environmental destruction they wreak pales beside that of the powerful developers who are often quick to paint themselves as friends of nature and who may sponsor preservationist efforts that improve their own public image. "Do you think that these people have a shred of real interest in the monkeys or the jaguars?" demands one man in Lucky River, tapping the end of a hand-rolled cigarette against a table strewn with playing cards. "They say that they want to protect the forest for our grandchildren, but just look at what they do. If you want to see dead fish, ma'am, go there by the refinery. If you want to see dead trees, go look at the drowned forests there in Samuel and Balbina [both enormous dams that flooded vast areas of forest]."

The environmental organizations that decry the miners' genuinely destructive actions may come in for similar criticism based on their seeming lack of interest in people of mixed blood. "These know-it-all environmentalists cry when the turtles die or when some Indian gets measles, but they couldn't care less when our children go to bed with an empty stomach," adds one of the man's regular blackjack partners, prompting three or four other miners to nod energetically. "As far as I'm concerned, the pack of them can go to hell." [58]

Although few of the storytellers acknowledge the discrepancies between their words and actions, it is often these very contradictions that make their tales compelling. Thus, while Gold is clearly a woman in these stories (or, rather, a series of women), she remains a projection of the severely constrained miners' own fierce desire for a richer, freer life. "Why do you stay here?" I impulsively ask a thoughtful, funny eighteen-year-old in a fly-infested gold camp near Porto Velho; he is still recovering from his third bout with malaria. "You're smart and mining's going to get you nothing but more malaria—why don't you catch the next plane out of here and do something else?"

"What else is there for me?" he answers. "Are you offering me a job?" We both laugh too hard and I feel embarrassed by my question. "Besides," he continues, now entirely serious, "in the *garimpo,* almost anything can happen, almost anything, you see?"

It is this at once escapist and defiant sense of a shape-shifting Gold's enduring mystery and potential that first drew me to the stories told by Angela Maria. While the terms *victim* and *villain* are ultimately too simple to describe a large and varied group of people united only by their desire for something better than what would normally be their lot in life, the miners are unquestionably both.

As for Angela Maria, when I returned from my sojourn in Lucky River, she was waiting for me on the dock. "It was terrible, wasn't it?" she said as we trudged up the hill with my suitcase full of scratchy shirts and unused woolly socks. Newly conscious of the stock role that out-siders play in miners' portrayals of the *garimpo,* I found myself wanting to tell her that Paulo's version of the story of the mysterious black man was very different from the one she'd told me, that no one in the camp had ever heard of Maria Gasolina, and that Lucky River in July is as hot as hell. But the words stuck in my throat. On the one hand, I didn't have the heart to disappoint a friend who had gone out of her way to help me. On the other, I found myself thinking, "The real problem is not the *garimpo,* the real problem is the world that makes Brazil, Brazil."

The Amazon as Water, the Amazon as Woods

Save the Rain Forest!

A hundred different posters

Nature doesn't permit humans to destroy it. Mother Waterfall enchants the fish, the turtles, so that they become invisible to human beings. We look around and think that the abundance of which our grandfathers spoke has vanished when it really has gone off to that lake within a lake which is the true biological reserve. And there it remains, beyond the reach of intruders who cut down the trees and kill the fish with poisons from their refineries. But one day, when the world finally comes to its senses, that enchanted lake will become disenchanted. And those riches which outsiders say are just a story will be the joy of all humanity.

Woman, age thirty-six, Trombetas River, Brazil, 1995

Both rich realms of nature, the bio-diverse rain forest that appears in the headlines of countless newspaper articles and the mysterious lake within a lake of contemporary Amazonian folk stories are very different. The first is a distinctly terrestrial universe; the second is the aquatic equivalent of a Russian doll or Chinese box. A series of readily mappable habitats, the rain forest stands apart from the overtly fabulous waters that some storytellers describe as dwarfing the Amazon itself. "How can these lakes be still larger than the river? Well, of course, they are enchanted," one older woman with a stiff cloud of silver hair patiently explains.

Once more, however, the division between these seemingly different portrayals turns out to be far less fixed than would first appear. Despite its concrete biological foundations, the Rain Forest encapsulates far larger fears and longings about the human place in nature. At the same time, it conceals considerably more immediate desires to possess and control distant resources for the profit of outsiders. As a result, the overwhelmingly "natural" Rain Forest becomes as much a giant as El Dorado or the Land of the Warrior Women.

Conversely, tales of a shape-shifting lake within a lake often turn out to be more rooted in concrete economic and political objectives than one might expect. These tales, which in this book stand in for a much wider array of Amazonian stories that give a prime—though not exclusive—place to water, are as contemporary in their own way as are news reports on an endangered biosphere. The storytellers' insistence that the lake within a lake is a more genuine "biological reserve" than its official equivalents underscores the role of these folk accounts in urgent debates over land ownership and use. ("It is we who are the true environmentalists, not those people who are paid to throw us out of our own homes," declares one woman with an emphatic thump of a wooden cooking spoon.)

The first chapter in this section begins with a brief description of the emergence of the Rain Forest as a near-synonym for Amazonia. I then look at the gigantic features of three depictions of the Amazon Rain Forest. These examples highlight the scientific (or pseudoscientific) aura, the openness to use, and the sense of a fragile equilibrium that characterize a much larger group of Rain Forest representations. Finally, I consider various changes in portrayals of rain forests over time.

The second chapter looks at stories of a lake within a lake as a contrast to accounts of "our" Rain Forest. Tales of this enchanted lake teeming with fish and plant life are particularly popular among descendants of runaway black slaves on the Trombetas and Erepecuru Rivers, a region rich in bauxite and other minerals. Here, I am concerned both with the shifting meanings that storytellers give this particular outpost of the Encante and with the ways in which traditional and new environmentalist vocabularies collide and intertwine. Intriguing in their own right, the differences between gold miners' stories and tales by the slave descendants bring home the multiplicity of an outwardly homogeneous narrative tradition.

Illustrations

"How the Nobility of Guiana would cover themselves in Gold when feasting," from an engraving in the Frankfurt edition of Theodor de Bry's *America*, 1599. One man (presumably a servant) blows gold dust from a pipe onto the naked body of a nobleman covered in oil. The image is based on text in Sir Walter Ralegh's *Discoverie of the Large, Rich and Bewtiful Empyre of Guiana*.

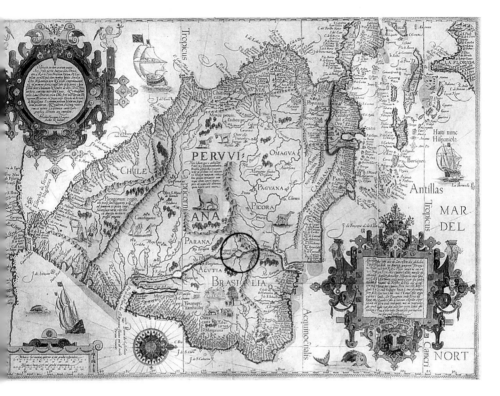

Map of America from a colored copperplate engraving by
Arnold Florentin van Langren in 1596. The map shows
El Dorado in the form of a lake connecting the Amazon and
La Plata river systems, just south of the mountains. (Courtesy
of the Staats und Stadtbibliothek, Augsburg)

"How the Indians mine Gold from the Mountain," from an
engraving in Theodor de Bry's *America*, 1599, which served
as an illustration to some editions of Ralegh's *Discoverie*.

Indians mining for gold. This de Bry engraving from the 1590s bears a striking resemblance to photographs of contemporary alluvial mining in the Amazon. It also appears as an illustration in some editions of the *Discoverie*.

Depiction of a ritual performed by a golden figure in a feather crown with ten attendants (also wearing crowns) on a golden raft, created by Muisca Indian craftsmen. The discovery of the golden object at the bottom of Lake Siecha, not far from present-day Bogotá, suggests a historical basis for the legend of El Dorado. Because the Muisca did not produce gold, but traded for it with other tribes, their gold objects tended to be small. (Courtesy of the Museo del Oro, Banco de la República, Bogotá, Colombia)

Panoramic wallpaper with a scene of El Dorado produced in 1848 from a design by E. Ehrmann, Fr. Zipelius, and A. Fuchs in Rixheim im Elsaß, Germany. (Courtesy of the Deutsches Tapetenmuseum, Kassel)

Mobbed by Curl-crested Toucans, an illustration from an
early edition of Henry Walter Bates' *Naturalist on the River
Amazons*, first published in 1863.

Claude Lévi-Strauss and his companion, the monkey Lucinda,
seated at his feet, in the Amazon during his journey there in
1937. (Photograph from *Saudades do Brasil,* reprinted by
permission of Claude Lévi-Strauss)

Colonel Roosevelt and Colonel Rondon
At Navaïté, on the River of Doubt
From a photograph by Cherrie

Theodore Roosevelt (left) and Colonel Rondon on an out-
cropping at the falls of Navaïté on the River of Doubt in 1913.
The photographer was George K. Cherrie, a naturalist at
the American Museum of Natural History, which partially
financed the expedition. (Frontispiece to Roosevelt, *Through
the Brazilian Wilderness*)

Candace Slater, in a similar pose and helmet, surveying a gold-producing gully in the Lucky River gold camp, on the Tapajós River, some eighty years later.

Father and son eating manioc, Parintins. The father is a
taxicab driver who tells various stories of Cobra Norato.
(Photo by Candace Slater)

Boy fishing with bow and arrow, Paraná de Abuí, Trombetas River. His straight black hair suggests Indian blood and underscores the ethnic mixture in some *remanescente* communities. (Photo by Candace Slater)

Girl on a hammock that serves as both chair and bed, country-side near Maués. Her mother has just told us a story of how the girl was almost carried off to the Encante. Her father has been working in the gold mines a day's journey from their home ever since she was born. (Photo by Candace Slater)

Boys outside an automobile repair shop in Parintins. Both participate in the Boi-Bumbá festival and have learned numerous stories of the Encantados from their grandmother, as well as from schoolbooks. (Photo by Candace Slater)

A teller of Encantado stories, Parintins. The woman claims
to have once visited the Encante herself. (Photo by Candace
Slater, previously printed in Slater, *Dance of the Dolphin*)

Old man in a doorway, rubber camp, Juruá River. The man
was born in the northeast and intersperses stories about
northeastern outlaws with others about Enchanted Beings.
(Photo by Candace Slater)

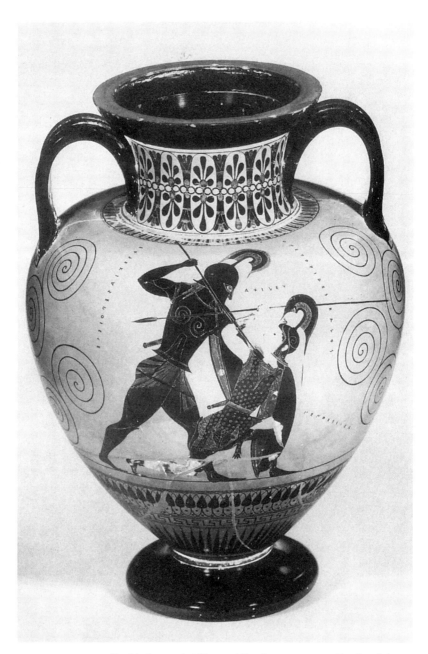

Duel between Achilles and the Amazon queen Penthesileia.
Attic black-figure neck-amphora, by Exekias, ca. 530 B.C.
(Courtesy of the Trustees of the British Museum)

Detail from a world map by Sebastian Cabot, 1544,
showing the fighting Amazons. From *El Patiti, El Dorado,
y las Amazonas,* by Roberto Levillier. (Courtesy of Emecé
Editores, S.A.)

AMERICA.

Eſtrix dira hominum ſcatet auro America: pollet
Arcu: pſittacum alit: plumea ſerta gerit.

43.

L'amérique cruelle a devoré beaucoup d'hommes, elle
produit de l'or, est adroite à tirer l'arc; nourrit
des perroquets et porte des ornemens en plumes.

America, by Theodor Galle, from the series *Proposgraphia*, published by Philipp Galle around 1600. The personification is of an Amazon "devourer of men," who carries a feathered spear in her left hand and the head of a vanquished rival in her right. (Courtesy of the Kunstsammlungen der Veste Coburg, Coburg)

Cover illustration, AMAZON GAZONGA, BAD GIRLS OF THE
JUNGLE, proves that the Amazons as a concept remain alive
and well. (© JASON WALTRIP)

Alluvial mining in the Tapajós region. Miners may spend hours or even whole days up to their knees or waists in mercury-contaminated water that resembles curdled milk. (Photo by Candace Slater)

Blasting with a water jet. The water dislodges sediment that
is then scrutinized for gold. It also erodes large chunks of
previously forested land. (Photo by Candace Slater)

An older miner with a rosary around his neck. "White Rat" has worked in a succession of gold mines in different parts of the Brazilian Amazon and French Guiana for more than twenty years. "If things don't pan out here, my next stop is Suriname," he says. (Photo by Candace Slater)

Miners parked in front of the *remanescente* community of Pancada, on the Erepecuru River, attempt to load a horse into their small boat. (Photo by Candace Slater)

Young miners in Rondônia. During the 1980s and 1990s, raft mining, which employs divers who descend from platforms directly on (as opposed to on the banks of) a body of water, was common on the Madeira River. The man in the bandanna, a diver, died less than a week after this photo was taken when his air hose was cut by a jealous fellow miner. (Photo by Candace Slater, previously printed in Slater, *Dance of the Dolphin*)

Miner from the interior of Maranhão, Tapajós River. Note the rain forest images on his shirt. Although the man's mouth is closed here, his four front teeth are gold. (Photo by Candace Slater)

Our rainforest policy.

5

The two versions of the McDonald's
Rain Forest flyer. The text on the flip
side begins with the assertion

Our rainforest policy.

"Tropical rainforests play an important role in the Earth's ecology." (Used by permission of the McDonald's Corporation)

A photograph of the rain forest taken in the late 1930s
by Claude Lévi-Strauss and printed a half-century later
in *Saudades do Brasil*. (Reprinted by permission of Claude
Lévi-Strauss)

A Stream in the Forest, an illustration from *A Narrative of Travels of the Amazon and Rio Negro*, first published in 1853 by Alfred Russel Wallace, with whom Henry Walter Bates journeyed to the Amazon. Although the subject is ostensibly the water, it is the trees that dominate the scene.

(Top left and right) Simoniz car wax ad, featuring Chief Tunabi. The fine type at the bottom of the ad reads, "The harvest of carnauba wax does not damage the Brazilian carnauba palm." (Simoniz Corporation)

(Bottom right) Young Cashinaua Indians in the Peruvian Amazon looking through the photographs of Brazilian native peoples in Claude Lévi-Strauss' *Tristes tropiques*. (Photo by David Allison, used by permission)

"I bring carnauba wax from the Amazon to new Simoniz. May it make your car's finish the envy of your village."

–Chief Tunabi

Easy-to-use wax and polish mysteriously unified in one. Transcendent total finish for all cars. No dust or streak demons. Magically beads rain.

The harvest of carnauba wax does not damage the Brazilian carnauba palm.

Remanescente paddling through the flooded forest on an *igarapé,* or seasonal stream, on the Trombetas River in an area that has seen violent land disputes. (Photo by Candace Slater)

Remanescente in the city of Oriximiná, waiting to embark on the boat that will take her back to her community on the Trombetas River. (Photo by Candace Slater)

The waterfalls called Chuvisco (Drizzle) and the accompanying rapids, Erepecuru River. (Photo by Candace Slater)

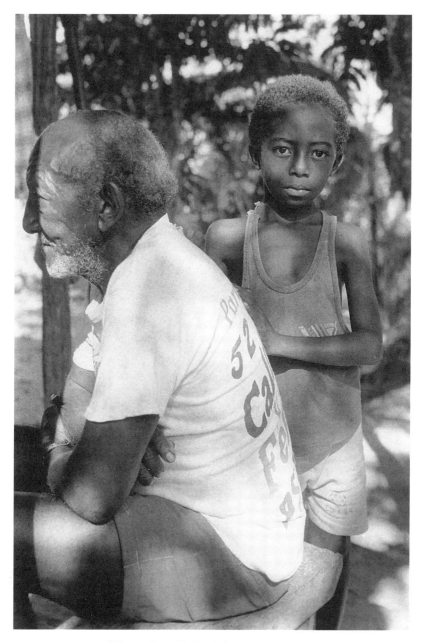

Old man from Abuí with his grandson in Boa Vista. It is he who tells the story of how he once entered the golden church. He also recounts how his father used to go to visit the old man named Higino, who had privileged access to the lake within a lake. (Photo by Candace Slater)

Family on Abuí Lake. The woman, who is smoking a hand-rolled tobacco cigarette, is a gifted storyteller who recalls her grandfather's accounts of how the *remanescentes* fled the pursuing soldiers with the help of Mother Waterfall. (Photo by Candace Slater)

Man in the community of Silêncio, on the Matá River not far from Óbidos. The basket on his back holds tobacco leaves, which he will hang up on the fence to dry in the sun. (Photo by Candace Slater)

Two sisters outside a home overlooking Abuí Lake. The women's mother is a healer whom people from miles around seek out, and the docking place before the house is always full of small boats. (Photo by Candace Slater)

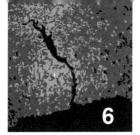

Roots of the Rain Forest

"Would you happen to have change for a dollar?" the young mother asks me as I pass in front of the Nature Company store. Eyes glued on the brightly colored Rainforest Meter just outside the front door, her son, a six- or seven-year-old boy with red hair and a baggy San Francisco Giants sweatshirt, is popping coins into the slot at a rapid clip. "Mommy, quick, another quarter!" he exclaims excitedly, running a small hand over the pictures of smiling snakes, emerald-colored trees, and butterfly-encircled jaguars spread across the meter's top.

"Listen, Danny," says the mother. "You've already saved two jaguars. Don't you want to save some parrots? Or some nice, big jungle vines? Put in these nickels and this dime now. The dime will buy ten parrots. And look, each nickel gets you half a spider monkey, a million raindrops, or five hundred vines."

As I rummage through my purse for coins, we both smile at the boy's enthusiasm. "It looks as if he's not going to let you leave until you're down to your last penny," I say to Danny's mother, who nods and laughs.

"It's a good thing for children to learn that the rain forest belongs to all of us and that we all have to work to preserve it," she says as she hands over several dimes and one more quarter. "Hopefully, when he grows up, there will still be an Amazon to save."

The Emergence of the Amazon as a Symbol

Today, as the young mother's parting comments suggest, the Amazon and "the Rain Forest" are virtual synonyms. Although other humid woodlands fan out across five continents, the Amazon is not just the biggest of these, but the most familiar to an international public. Asked to name the location of a rain forest, people in different corners of the globe may well mention the Pacific Northwest, Indonesia, or equatorial Africa.[1] Nonetheless, the word *Amazon* evokes the term *rain forest* as much as *Pacific* does *ocean* or *Yosemite* evokes *national park.*

The present closeness of this association makes it hard to imagine a time when the world did not conceive of the Amazon as a rain forest. However, the ties between the two are relatively recent. For much of the past five hundred years, the Amazon has been known as a "jungle," a "wilderness," or simply a "forest."

Two principal occurrences help explain how and why "the Rain Forest" became synonymous with Amazonia in the 1970s. The first is the opening of the Amazon Basin in the 1960s to large-scale development such as oil and gas extraction, highway construction, and massive colonization. The second is the emergence of an international environmental movement in the early 1970s, which saw the destruction taking place in rain forests in the Amazon and other areas, such as Southeast Asia, as a threat not just to the region, but to the planet as a whole.[2]

Human transformation of the land and waterways is nothing new in Amazonia.[3] Long before the first Europeans arrived, indigenous people practiced raised-bed agriculture in the Beni wetlands in what is now Bolivia. They also managed forests throughout much of the Amazon Basin.[4] The introduction of metal tools into the Amazon in the sixteenth century, as well as the forcible reorientation of existing internal trade networks into an export economy based on resource extraction, could not help but introduce important changes into a long-inhabited land whose contours native populations had helped to define. The seventeenth century also had seen forests begin to give way to cattle ranches on Marajó Island in the Amazon estuary, in Rio Branco and on the savannas extending from modern-day Roraima to the interior of Guiana, and on parts of the Mojos and the Venezuelan llanos (plains).[5] Thus, although one might expect an account of environmental disaster in the Brazilian Amazon to chronicle events of the last few decades, documentation such as David Sweet's "A Rich Realm of Nature Destroyed" reaches back to the seventeenth and eighteenth centuries, when missionaries, traders, and slavers pushed their way into the interior.[6]

Not just the colonial economy, but colonial demography occasioned transformations throughout much of the Amazon. In various corners of the interior, the Jesuit missions served as early population centers, drawing in the natives from outlying regions and converting them not just into Christians but into a viable labor force. Slaving expeditions and diseases quickly made inroads on a densely populated landscape. Later, in the nineteenth century, the wealth that flowed from the Rubber Boom transformed once-sleepy provincial outposts into cities of some note. Although Manaus would become the largest and most famous of these newly cosmopolitan locations, many smaller trading centers emerged throughout the upper Amazon.[7] Cachuela Esperanza, on the banks of the Madre de Dios River in Bolivia, for instance, became the capital of the Suárez brothers' personal empire. The town included not just office buildings, villas, a radio telegraph station, school, and chapel, but also a hotel, restaurant, cinema, theater, billiards salon, lighted tennis courts, a state-of the-art hospital under Swiss direction, and a library with books and periodicals in four languages.[8]

Unfortunately, these emblems of progress were undergirded by the debt bondage, serfdom, and slavery that further decimated Indian populations and created suffering among immigrants in many corners of the Amazon.[9] Moreover, although rubber tapping was generally not environmentally destructive, Bates' account of the transformation of a previously "noble" forest around Belém into a welter of "ashes, muddy puddles, and heaps of broken branches" as the city became increasingly important to international commerce foreshadowed the great wave of deforestation that would swell the region's cities more than a century later.[10]

And yet, if human action on the land goes back not just centuries but millennia, the scale and intensity of changes in the past cannot compare to those that mark the second half of the twentieth century. Overseen directly by national governments, rather than by the individual entrepreneurs and companies that usually had been the prime movers in preceding centuries, this new brand of development had multiple motives and effects.[11]

The desire to tame and modernize an Amazon long seen as a vast backwater was a principal factor behind the development programs of the 1960s. Especially in Brazil, this desire took on heightened significance with the rise in the 1950s of a civilian government. The creation of Brasília as the country's new capital would go hand in hand with construction of the Belém-Brasília highway, designed to open up the Amazon interior. In some ways a revamping of former president Getúlio Vargas' earlier "Westward March," which in the 1930s had sought to integrate the Amazon into a modernizing nation. The renewed push to fulfill Brazil's manifest destiny through the incorporation of a previously marginal region found echoes in other Amazonian nations, such as Ecuador.[12]

This concerted drive to open up the Amazon also reflected pressure from the United States. Shaken by the success of the Communists in Cuba, the Kennedy administration instituted the Alliance for Progress in 1961, which offered sweeping economic aid to Latin American countries that could show themselves to be energetically embarked on a course of modernization.[13] Investments in the Amazonian portions of Colombia, Ecuador, Peru, and Bolivia by U.S. companies, including petroleum giants such as Texaco, were one result. In a number of the Amazonian countries, tax incentives to foreign companies willing to invest in agribusiness, manufacturing, logging, and mining ventures became part of a larger Amazonian development drive that would move hundreds of thousands of colonists into the region.

Intended in part to relieve mounting social pressures in other parts of the country, the push to colonize and develop the Amazon, previously seen as a remote realm of nature, was also designed to generate new sources of revenue. Another purpose was to secure the national borders against possible insurgents—a recurring obsession on the part of the military in Brazil.[14] Often, however, the newcomers found themselves largely stranded in their new homes. Along the Caquetá River in San Vicente del Caguán and Aracuara in Colombia, for instance, huge resettlement projects failed when crops unsuited for the terrain withered or when newly arrived peasant farmers could not get their produce to market, forcing them to feed the fruits of their labors to their pigs. Faced with a lack of money and intense land speculation fueled by large-scale developers' growing interest in the region, settlers throughout many of the Amazonian nations sold their small farms and moved to cities, where new factories were sprouting up.

Accompanying this urban expansion was the growth of hydroelectric dams, commercial fisheries, and yet more highways, which occasioned deforestation and environmental destruction on an unprecedented scale.[15] Intended in part to link growing settlements in the interior to markets in other parts of the region, as well as to open up parts of the Amazon still inaccessible by land, some of these highways also made possible the influx of more colonists and new commercial enterprises.[16] They also facilitated the construction of oil and gas pipelines, which cut through lands long inhabited by indigenous peoples. Even in Ecuador and Peru, whose military governments were relatively progressive, these new "corridors" were initially hailed as a source of added revenues that would benefit the same native populations on whose lands they encroached.

The ever greater assault on the Amazon's forests and forest peoples coincided with, and helped prompt, the emergence of a broad-based global environmental movement in the early 1970s. This movement was marked by events such as the first Earth Day (April 1970), the convocation of the first United Nations Conference on the Human Environment (1972), and the publication of influential books and reports such as the Club of Rome's *Limits to Growth* (1972) and *Mankind at the Turning Point* (1974).[17] Shaken by growing evidence of pollution and species extinction in the United States and Europe, the leaders of this movement cast the Amazon as a prime focus for new, international campaigns against the destruction of nature.

The parameters of this concern would change over time (biodiversity and sustainable development, for instance, emerged as major issues in the late 1980s). As different environmental interest groups developed distinct agendas, the Amazon Rain Forest itself would become less of a unifying umbrella. Nonetheless, it has remained one of the most powerful icons of a new millennium. The Amazon's ongoing ability to elicit large-scale concern owes much to the striking, rapid transformations taking place there. However, it also reflects a long tradition of environmental gigantification that allows outsiders to continue to focus on the region's identity as quintessential Nature, despite the ample evidence of alteration of both land and water by many different human groups over the centuries. "If the Amazon is in danger, what is *not* in jeopardy?" the leaders of the movement demanded of a primarily U.S. and Western European public worried about the effects of far-off fires on the roses and tomatoes in its own backyard.

The Rain Forest as Giant

"Rain forests" are sometimes equated with jungles and wildernesses. People may use these terms interchangeably, or even in tandem, as when newspaper reporters speak of the "Amazon rainforest wilderness" or invoke the rain forest's "jungle allure." In general, however, the term *rain forest* has quite different connotations from either *wilderness* or *jungle*.[18] These connotations are critical to differing assessments of what activities are, or are not, appropriate for rain forest areas.

Much like the term *environment,* which the new movement's leaders carefully appropriated as a substitute for what they found to be an overly Romantic-sounding *nature, rain forest* is of relatively recent vintage. (The first entry in the *Oxford English Dictionary* dates from 1898, some eight hundred years after the initial entries for *wilderness* and well over a century after the first notations in English of the term *jungle*.)[19] A direct translation of the German *Regenwald,* it lacks not just the multiple and shifting meanings of these far older terms, but also their apparent imprecision and often frankly lyric cast. "The Rain-Forest is evergreen, hygrophilous in character, at least thirty meters high, but usually much taller, rich in thick-stemmed lianes, and in woody as well as herbaceous epiphytes," Andreas Franz Wilhelm Schimper explained crisply in his early botanical treatise *Plant-geography.*[20]

A descendant of the *Regenwald,* the Rain Forest that emerged in the 1960s and 1970s had acquired an aura of science. A rain forest, according to the latest edition of *Merriam-Webster's Collegiate Dictionary,* is "a tropical wooded area with an annual rainfall of 100 inches (254 centimeters) and marked by lofty, broad-leaved evergreen trees forming a continuous canopy."[21] By this definition, if a wooded space receives 99.9 inches of rain, it cannot be a rain forest, and while different people may have different criteria for "lofty," there is no way that the trees in a rain forest can be small.[22] Likewise, if the sky appears where there should be a thick green ceiling, the place in question is no rain forest.

This scientific overlay led to portrayals of the rain forest as both a storehouse of valuable commodities and a key to global environmental health, which in turn invited the sorts of symbolic transformations by outsiders evident in mass market movies such as *Medicine Man.* Starring Sean Connery in the role of a reclusive research scientist, this 1992 movie revolved around the race to find a cure for cancer before bulldozers razed the area where Connery harvested special flowers for the serum.

Unlike today's wilderness, which the U.S. Wilderness Act of 1964 defines as "a place where man remains a visitor," the Rain Forest does not necessarily resist development.[23] On the contrary, while active transformation, or even organized human habitation, threatens the identity of the wilderness, the Rain Forest remains a Rain Forest until the trees disappear. Moreover, in contrast to the jungle, whose chaotic vegetation resists rational use by humans, the forest often described as a "marvelous cornucopia" does not repel, and may even invite, exploitation on the part of humans.

Rain forests' uneasy equilibrium also sets them apart from jungles, with their tough and thorny "hearts of darkness." [24] And although wildernesses may exhibit a fragility similar to rain forests, their image is less exuberant, more austere. The Rain Forest, with its intricate balance of flora and fauna, is portrayed as profoundly vulnerable to disturbance from without. As a result, this Forest giant is hardly a Warrior Woman, but a damsel in distress. (At least one "Rescue the Rain Forest" button pictures a virginal figure with pale green skin and tangled hair adorned with butterflies.) [25]

The idea of rain forest areas as delicately poised natural laboratories that invite use even as they help regulate and ensure the planet's environmental balance is not necessarily false. The problem is that particular elements of this Green Cathedral (for example, the flora and the fauna, the indigenous peoples) are gigantic enough to displace or conceal others that are just as important (cities, plains or swamps, nonindigenous Amazonians).

The gigantic qualities of the Amazon Rain Forest are particularly obvious in three examples from the 1990s. I have singled out this trio of portrayals from myriad possibilities because of the clarity with which they illustrate the process of selective magnification. Easy targets in their own right, they call attention to the more subtle ironies and contradictions in the overall variety of rain forest portrayals.

Amazonia without Myths

The 1992 U.N. report *Amazonia without Myths* invites attention because of the overtly antimythic stance summed up in its title.[26] The report is also interesting as a preliminary position paper for the important U.N. Conference on the Environment and Development, better known as the "Rio Earth Summit" or "Eco 92," which took place in June 1992 in Rio de Janeiro.[27] Prepared at the behest of the Amazon Cooperation Treaty and underwritten by the Inter-American Development Bank and the United Nations Development Programme, the report outlines policies aimed at conciliating the demands of environmental preservation and economic development.

The official compilers of this publication are the members of the Commission on Development for Amazonia, an ad hoc group comprising a half dozen former presidents of Amazonian nations, the president of Brazil's Center for Indigenous Rights, the head of the Brazilian National Council of Rubber Tappers, the Brazilian minister of education, former U.N. secretary general Javier Pérez Cuellar, and Nobel Prize–winning novelist Gabriel García Márquez. The names of the technical specialists who actually prepared, edited, and translated this document appear somewhat later, in the preface. Printed in soy-based ink on recycled paper, *Amazonia without Myths* sets out to "explain, interpret and, where necessary, destroy myths" so that "development and well-being can be firmly joined in forging a better future."

The authors' initial step in this future-building mission is to denounce a long line of fallacies. First among them is El Dorado, which they describe as "now almost totally discredited" and therefore undeserving of further examination. Other myths at which the report's writers take aim are the homogeneity of the Amazon, the empty or virginal Amazon, and the region as a panacea for national problems. They also denounce "the internationalization of the Amazon," or the developed world's proprietary vision of tropical nature as a universal human heritage. In place of this pernicious "world of fantasy," they offer a vision of a region genuinely rich in the "biodiversity of its ecosystems, its flora, its fauna and the native germ plasm." It is this Amazon that transcends myth to offer "true possibilities for sustainable development."[28]

The barrage of facts and figures that accompany the report (minerals in the Brazilian Amazon alone are worth approximately $1.6 trillion; two thousand species of Amazonian plants produce "a wide array of useful oils, greases, waxes, varnishes, aromatic essences, [and] condiments") makes this ostensibly myth-free Amazon very different from the descriptions of Carvajal, Bates, Roosevelt, or Lévi-Strauss. So does the initially sober-sounding program that the report outlines with the help of numerous graphs and charts. Unlike Bates, who sought a "glorious new human race under the Equator," or Lévi-Strauss, who pursued the Rousseauian secrets that would unleash "the Golden Age that is within us," the authors set their sights on "strategies and alternatives for sustainable development." Their goal is not the transformation of the world's last wilderness into a splendid stage for civilization or the conquest of a thorny jungle, but rather "an adequate balance between the environmentally sustainable exploitation of goods with existing markets, and an effective assessment of, and compensation for the functions and services Amazonia performs for mankind." This emphasis on the economic uses of nature's bounty underscores the Amazon's modern-day Rain Forest identity.

And yet, despite this apparently rational, technical-sounding agenda, *Amazonia without Myths* is a veritable compendium of myths. Chief among them is the vision of the Amazon's rain forests as a stage for a planetary drama with unmistakably utopian overtones. An "ultimate paradise" in the world's imagination, the Amazon's "slow and silent agony poses one of the most dramatic threats to human survival." Its "salvation" thus becomes "not merely a heroic feat of its natural trustees [by which the authors mean native peoples] but a crusade that all humankind no longer can defer."

The religious language that creeps into the report with terms such as *paradise, salvation,* and *crusade* suggests a self-consciously "scientific" Amazon with deep roots in the very myths that the report's authors would dismiss. As a model for a world "on the dawn of the Third Millennium," the Amazon of *Amazonia without Myths* holds out "a new pact of lasting solidarity for all peoples" united around "a cause that represents today, as it has for many centuries, the adventure of man on earth." To the extent that sustainable development becomes an answer not just to pressing economic needs, but to the age-old ills of injustice, hypocrisy, and exploitation, it is one more mythical panacea. Thus the Amazon as a whole becomes a specifically late-twentieth-century incarnation of the colonial El Dorado that the authors so unequivocally dismiss. What's more, although quick to identify native peoples as the legitimate stewards of the region, the report once again discounts, when it does not actually efface, the persons of mixed blood who constitute the great bulk of the Amazonian population.

Transcendent Total Finish

The theme of the Rain Forest as teeming with unrealized potential is yet more obvious in an advertisement for Simoniz car wax that features an Amazonian Indian identified as "Chief Tunabi." Even while its playful tone stands in sharp contrast to the sober language of the U.N. report, the ad is an even more emphatic statement of the utility that sets the Rain Forest apart from the wilderness or jungle. It is also a vivid testament to the symbolic weight of both the Rain Forest and Amazonian native peoples at the end of the twentieth century.[29] Designed as a two-page spread but also distributed in several more compact versions (one occupying a page, another a single column), the ad appeared in a variety of niche-market magazines during the spring of 1995, including *Sports Illustrated, Rolling Stone, Car and Driver, Home Mechanix,* and several in-flight airline publications.[30]

The ad's purpose was to sell a car finish whose primary ingredients include a wax from the Brazilian carnauba palm. In the two-page version, the entire left half of the ad pictures the brightly ornamented Indian chief, who stares out at the reader as he stands before a backdrop of frondlike leaves. The right half of the ad depicts a sleek black bottle of Simoniz Advanced Total Car Finish, its bright yellow half-sun set in a red band that echoes the band of red paint that accents Tunabi's dark eyes. Grainy in a way that recalls bark or raw silk, with its much-touted "natural imperfections," the pale background provides a contrast for the streamlined, high-tech bottle, above which a quote from the chief appears: "I bring carnauba wax from the Amazon to new Simoniz. May it make your car's finish the envy of your village."

A double line of type beneath the bottle identifies the contents as "easy-to-use wax and polish mysteriously unified in one" and goes on to promise a "transcendent total finish" on each and every car. "No dust or streak demons," it announces. "Magically beads rain." An irregular turquoise border with an artisanal-looking geometric design runs down and across the outer margin of each of the two pages, drawing chief and bottle into a common graphic universe. The red-brown earth-tone highlights of the border create further links between the two. The fine print in the right-hand corner below and outside the border offers the assurance that "the harvest of carnauba wax does not damage the Brazilian carnauba palm."

At first glance, the ad appears to be no more than a good-humored spoof aimed at drawing attention to the exotic extra in this "advanced total car finish." While few Amazonian native peoples would find Tunabi's folkloric sentiments or pidgin English funny, the designers clearly did not expect magazine readers to take seriously the dust and streak demons or the tongue-in-cheek reference to the magic beading of the rain.

The ad does more, however, than simply tout the virtues of a particular car wax in a novel way. Simoniz' claim that the harvest of carnauba wax does not damage the palm tree asserts a vital balance between development and preservation that links the ad to *Amazonia without Myths.* At the same time that it is meant to be lighthearted, it plays on serious hopes and fears about the planet's future. And much like the golden king almost five centuries earlier, the chief is the extension of a rich land. The red and black face paint, the bead earrings, the luxuriant tangle of seed necklaces, and the brilliant blue feather aureole around his head suggest natural riches. The thick ornamental bands around each of his upper arms and the heavy pectoral of silver-coated feathers emphasize the wealth of his leafy El Dorado.

Far beyond any talk of dust and streak demons, the true magic that the ad invokes is the promise of development free of any cost.[31] The visual links between Tunabi and the sleek black bottle suggest the possibility of commerce between two very different worlds. Just as the half-sun on the bottle reappears in the forest's dappled leaves, so the gold medal on the bottle finds echoes in the wreath of silver around the chief's neck. The earth-toned frame that unites the two halves of the ad emphasizes the theme of shared riches, as well as of a shared authenticity that stems from a closeness to tropical nature. ("*Genuine* quality" the label on the bottle reads.)

Above all, the Simoniz chief invites car owners to feel good about a wax that does not hurt an environment into which their automobiles regularly pour carbon monoxide. Just as "his" trees yield their bounty without suffering the slightest damage, Tunabi can afford to be generous with the magic of a self-renewing Forest. However, his lack of interest in any return on nature's largesse makes him unlike flesh-and-blood Indians such as the Kayapó or the Yanomami, with their increasingly vocal objections to trespassers upon their land.

The contrast between Tunabi and the real peoples who inhabit today's Amazon creates an underlying tension. So does the gap between the carnauba palm that the chief hastens to share with the global village and the tree that actually grows on Brazilian soil. Native to the very driest areas of the country's arid northeastern interior, the carnauba is not adapted to rain forests and does not figure among the approximately 150 species of palms common within the Amazon.[32] Since the glossy coating on its leaves is the tree's way of conserving moisture in a climate subject to catastrophic droughts, it would take a true magician to fulfill Tunabi's claim to bring Amazonian carnauba wax to new Simoniz without damaging the trees themselves.

The droughts that even today periodically force poorer northeasterners to seek their fortunes elsewhere drove some three hundred thousand of them to the Amazon during the heyday of rubber in the latter part of the nineteenth and early twentieth centuries.[33] Those few carnauba palms that do grow in the Amazon today are almost all found in the home gardens that these northeastern transplants established.[34] Vivid proof of the human urge to reshape nature to fit particular needs and longings, these transplanted palms undergo a second transformation in the ad into pillars of cost-free development. In masking the toll that this development necessarily takes on both plants and people, both Chief Tunabi and "his" palm trees become yet another giant.

Rain Forest Arches

If *Amazonia without Myths* underscores the Rain Forest's scientific overlay and the Simoniz ad points toward its symbolic and material uses, a McDonald's Corporation flyer titled "Our rainforest policy" illustrates this same Forest's uneasy equilibrium. Widely distributed in the fast-food chain's restaurants throughout the United States in the first part of the 1990s, the flyer was a response to the threat of boycotts of the chain by environmental organizations concerned about allegations that McDonald's was getting its beef from pasture created by deforestation in the Amazon.[35]

Still available as late as 1998 in scattered locations, the double-sided, single-sheet statement bears one of two photographs.[36] The first shows a stand of tall trees to the left and a series of delicate ferns in the right-hand corner, their brilliant green enhanced by a long funnel of light reaching down through the trees. A second, somewhat later version of the flyer pictures a darker, denser woodland with no sunbeams to provide a focus. Moss covers the trunks of mighty trees whose crowns remain far out of sight. A fan-shaped tree fern in the background brings to mind an exotic feather headdress, while the smaller ferns that crowd the foreground suggest a kind of living filigree.

The greens and browns that dominate both photos bring into relief the primary colors of the McDonald's logo—a red square with golden arches—which appear below them. The heading on both is followed by the numeral 5 in the top right-hand corner, indicating that this is the fifth of approximately a dozen handouts that promote the corporation's policies on nutritional and environmental themes ("We're lowering our cholesterol," "We're keeping our waste out of landfills," "McRecycle," and so on).

The statement on the flyer's flip side begins with an affirmation of the fragility of the feathery forest. "Tropical rainforests play an important role in the Earth's ecology. And their destruction threatens the delicate environmental balance of our planet," reads the first paragraph. An assurance that McDonald's uses only local beef in the United States, Canada, and Europe leads in to the concluding affirmation that the corporation will continue to monitor its beef suppliers and adopt "policies and practices aimed at protecting the global environment on which we all depend."

Invoking the Forest's key place in a "delicate equation" that includes not just the Amazon, but the world as a whole, the flyer focuses on a convenient false fear: global ecological breakdown. The vulnerability of the Rain Forest reflects a level of destruction all too real, but, the flyer reassures, responsible, environmentally conscious policies of the sort that McDonald's is adopting can maintain the balance that allows hamburger patrons to slather ketchup on their Big Macs without having to worry about their role in destroying some distant endangered environment.[37] Their attention is thus diverted from problems every bit as big and much closer to home.

The two McDonald's woodlands provide an excellent example of the Rain Forest's ability to contain, and to impose order on, an increasingly chaotic world. Blissfully devoid of people, both the radiant bower of the first photo and the mysterious glade of the second provide refuge from a world of highway billboards and meals seized on the run. Oases in a sea of neon signs, they promise respite from the specter of burning forests that metaphorically, if not literally, cloudy skies from Seattle to New York City.

Like the Simoniz ad, however, the flyers are constructed around a fiction. Despite the opening allusion to the importance of tropical rain forests, the woodland in the first photo is no tropical rain forest.[38] To begin with, the dense canopy of a rain forest normally blocks out the type of golden light that bathes the leafy floor in the photo, thus permitting very little surface vegetation of the type the photo shows. The lack of epiphytes ("air plants" that grow on other plants or objects, on which they depend for support), standard in most rain forests, also confirms this impression. Indeed, the trees in question are actually temperate conifers completely alien to the tropics. Compounding the irony, the abundance of new growth in the photo reveals some sort of relatively recent disturbance. Although this disturbance may have had natural causes, nonnatural causes—above all, logging—remain a distinct possibility. The image chosen to illustrate the call to preserve the planet's fragile equilibrium is therefore, more accurately, a portrait of destruction.[39]

While the forest in the second photo probably does lie somewhere between Cancer and Capricorn, it is a montane mesophyllous forest, also known as a cloud or a fog forest—a type found on upland slopes. Devoid of the thick trees with buttresses and heavy canopies that characterize wetter woodlands, it does not fit the image of a classic lowland rain forest. What's more, the veneer of moss that coats the slender trunks confirms the presence of light. Likewise, the absence of orchids, bromeliads, or other epiphytes suggests that the forest is subtropical at best. The scene might be in Chile—or even in New Zealand. It is not, however, typical of forests like the Amazon.[40]

In short, the Rain Forest that both versions of the flyer portray in word and image is, in every sense, a gigantic landscape that consciously reinforces a skewed vision of the Amazon for the profit of a corporate entity. ("The forest doesn't look a bit like either of these pictures!" Angela Maria exclaimed in exasperation when I showed her the flyers. "How can these big companies have so much money and still not get things right?") While there are practical reasons for the choice of a non-classic rain forest (for example, the corporation's desire for a dramatic lighting effect difficult to obtain beneath a dense canopy), these concerns are not the whole story. The flyer makes an appeal to a society that regularly looks to nature for the raw materials to sustain its commodity-intensive way of life even while it expresses longing for an escape from this life back into a simpler existence.[41] The redemptive gleam at the end of a menacingly dark tunnel of destruction, these idyllic groves hold out the hope not just of global balance, but of some sort of equilibrium within the mundane details of daily life.[42]

The Amazon Rain Forest at the Beginning of the Twenty-first Century

Never just one thing, the Amazon Rain Forest at the beginning of the twenty-first century is more resoundingly multiple than it appeared in the early 1970s. And yet, even though present-day representations vary, it is possible to identify some general transformations over time.[43]

A number of portrayals of the present-day Amazon Rain Forest are considerably more accurate than various earlier representations. Greater knowledge about rain forests among a general public, the new importance of local people in rain forest representations, and an increasingly hardheaded admission of the need for difficult environmental choices can be seen as positive developments. However, it is also possible to see these same portrayals as giants of another stripe.

The Amazon Rain Forest of the beginning of the twenty-first century is more a part of daily life than it was in the 1970s. Its familiarity owes in good part to a growing commodification that has helped change the spelling of *rain forest* (a two-word noun) to *rainforest* (a single-word adjective) and has placed Rain Forests on a wide array of shampoo bottles and cereal boxes. If this same familiarity has somewhat deflated the initial sense of crisis that led quite diverse environmental groups to join the call to save the Amazon Rain Forest, it has also made rain forests a more generalized concern.

Although, for instance, McDonald's no longer distributes Rain Forest flyers in its fast-food restaurants, its new promotional pamphlet called "The Planet We Share" continues to stress rain forests' importance. The preservation of rain forests has assumed an established place alongside recycling and "source reduction"—a fancy term for downsized trash—as one of the corporation's and the public's primary environmental concerns. "The Amazon?" demands my neighbor's nine-year-old daughter. "Yeah, it's the world's biggest rain forest. You can find giant snakes and a thousand different kinds of insects in a single tree. This is the second time this year we've studied it in school and I'm doing my report on monkeys. The last time I did frogs."

This new familiarity is obvious too in changes in the marketing of rain forest products. While the 1980s saw a proliferation of products (shampoos, juices, ice creams) that contained actual rain forest ingredients, such as Brazil nuts and guaraná berries, the 1990s witnessed an increase in other products that treat rain forests and the Amazon Rain Forest as a more diffuse, if equally saleable, idea.

"It's like meeting in the Rain Forest!" proclaims an ad for Coty's Raw Vanilla men's cologne.[44] Intended to capture the appeal of a purer and less harried realm of nature for consumers trapped in an urban jungle, the Rainforest men's outerwear collection has little or nothing to do with actual forest areas. Waterman's Amazon Green Ballpoint Pen, with its "long-lasting refills," has no direct connection to the region whose name it invokes. Likewise, the choice of "Amazon" as a name for the huge on-line bookseller undercuts its abstract, high-tech character. "Amazon suggests great size, of course, and a compendious database, but it's also overflowing with so much third-world, underdog, eco-conscious goodwill that every click on Amazon.com feels like a vote for the rain forest," asserts Peter de Jonge in an article about the company in the *New York Times Magazine*.[45]

The tenaciously escapist elements of these examples suggest that what has become familiar about today's Amazon Rain Forest is that which is most predictably exotic. This blend of familiarity and exoticism at the beginning of a new millennium is nowhere more obvious than in portrayals of Amazonian peoples. Almost certainly, the single most important difference between the Rain Forest of the 1970s and that of succeeding decades is the expanded, newly vital role of its human inhabitants.[46] Although unpopulated green expanses still appear on a host of calendars and fruit juice bottles, they now coexist with other representations in which people appear. Even the openly fictitious Chief Tunabi is proof of this larger and more serious change. Were the Simoniz ad to have appeared in the 1970s or 1980s, the chief's place would almost certainly have been occupied by a leafy palm tree.

The reasons for the new presence of Amazonian peoples in popular representations are easy to pinpoint. The increasingly vocal presence of various indigenous peoples' movements on the international stage during the 1980s makes it hard to portray an Amazon that is home exclusively to jaguars, vines, and parrots. At the same time, the presence of a series of flesh-and-blood natives who do not look or behave like one another challenges the idea of Amazonian peoples as uniform embodiments of nature.

Back in the 1970s, few readers outside the Amazon would have been able to name a single Amazonian Indian group. Today, even if readers still cannot pronounce the names, numerous articles on groups such as the Kayapó and Machiguenga and Yanomami make it more likely for them to have a sense of rain forests as a home to diverse peoples. The appearance in 1992 of a very serious-looking Kayapó chief Paiakan on the cover of *Parade,* a Sunday magazine with wide national circulation, signaled the new role of Amazonian Indians on an international stage. ("Can this man save the world?" the caption asked millions of readers.)[47]

The bitter controversies that embroil these native peoples confirm their shifting importance within Amazonian nations, as well as outside them.[48] In the 1970s, for instance, the Brazilian newsweekly *Veja* ran a series of articles about the "gentle giants" and "Stone Age savages" whom road builders were encountering.[49] In other articles celebrating this "Decade of Conquest" in which "millions of Brazilians" were "staking bets on the riches of the enormous mineral deposits and on the

benefits of cattle ranching," one could find pictures of near-naked Indians posed beside giant orchids. The tone of most of these articles was
a slightly bemused fascination with these human embodiments of an
Amazon that the writers described over and over as "limitless," "dazzling," "fabulously wealthy," and "mysterious," as well as unfailingly
"gigantic."[50]

However, with the resounding failure of Brazil's "century of progress
in a single decade" and the ensuing conversion of the Amazon from "a
redemptive cornucopia" bound to solve the country's financial problems
into a much less immediately saleable genetic storehouse, native peoples
became less easy to romanticize. No longer gentle giants or innocents at
play in Amazonia's immense garden, the Indians increasingly emerged
as flesh-and-blood people fully capable of using international environmental organizations to press regional and local land claims. Their
growing political involvement led publications such as *Veja* to portray
them as naïfs and even "gigolos" who consorted with British rock stars
and European heads of state to bring dishonor on the good name of
Brazil.[51] *Veja*'s furious attacks on Paiakan, whom a young Brazilian
woman would accuse of rape on the eve of the Rio environmental summit, confirm native people's new international importance.[52] Represented as a front for foreign interests, once mysterious and appealing native peoples became outright traitors to the nation in later articles.[53]

The new actors in the global environmental drama are not only native peoples. While before the 1990s few, if any, non-Indians appeared
in portrayals of the Amazon, the growth of other sorts of grassroots organizations gave new prominence to people of mixed ethnic heritage.[54]
The assassination in 1989 of Chico Mendes all but guaranteed the presence of other sorts of "forest peoples" on an international stage.

Important new scholarship that debunks the idea of the Amazon as
a "counterfeit paradise" by emphasizing a long-standing and sizable human presence there has bolstered a growing insistence on people as full-
fledged actors in an ongoing environmental drama. However, this insistence only goes so far.[55] Although the Rain Forest of the 1990s and
beyond unquestionably has more room for a wider variety of local
voices than did earlier representations, it continues to favor certain
kinds of people and certain scripts. For instance, as soon as the Brazilian media attacked Paiakan as a rapist while describing the tribe's deal-
ings with loggers and miners, the Kayapó's support among many environmental groups disappeared.[56]

This support could erode so quickly because it was, and remains, largely superficial. "Local knowledge" has often been little more than a corollary to the preservation of the plants, animals, and ecosystems that are many environmentalists' real concern. Thus, although *Amazonia without Myths* begins with an insistence on people as "the Heart of the Amazon," the authors devote no more than five of the report's ninety-nine pages to the region's inhabitants. Not only do the green, leaf-textured letters of the *Amazonia* in the book's title reaffirm the region's primary identity as a forest, but the handful of references to humans inside centers on "indigenous and forest people" whose "ancestral wisdom" seems likely to translate into material benefits for all of humanity.

Even considerably more nuanced portrayals of Amazonians often equate "local peoples" with "traditional" groups who appear as protectors of the marvelously abundant forest that remains the outsiders' true concern. The descriptions of "the Stone Age Yanomami" that abound in present-day newspaper reports employ the language of endangered species when they identify the group as an "imperiled Amazon tribe" or "South America's last major untouched tribe to roam freely" over a "wilderness" the size of Missouri.[57] At the same time, reporters who describe the entrepreneurial Kayapó often question outright whether Indians who would sell their gold and timber can be "true" Indians at all. ("Indians accused of being 'jungle maharajahs'" reads the subtitle of one article.)[58]

Amazonian Indians, much like people in other rain forest areas, have proven adept at mastering "environmentalese" to express their own beliefs and political aspirations.[59] In some cases, they have managed to expand this borrowed vocabulary to include the idea of human rights. In this way they are much like the gold miners, who have a similar flair for turning outsiders' images of themselves to their own ends. Nonetheless, even those groups who have been most successful at manipulating the symbolic space at their disposal find themselves facing new challenges, such as a growing pessimism about the future of the world's rain forests in an age of globalization in which economic progress frequently translates into environmental loss.

The proponents of the new pessimism are, above all, natural scientists (conservation biologists, primatologists, ornithologists), economists, and environmentalists thoroughly disenchanted with the idea of sustainable development.[60] Although they speak with different emphases, most would agree that "the marriage of conservation and development has been a disaster for much of tropical nature" and that "a greater effort must be made to protect tropical parks and reserves from human interference—while some large, relatively untouched natural ecosystems remain." Dismissing as sentimental myth the notion that human beings "will attempt to live in harmony with nature if given the chance," these individuals are apt to proclaim the inevitability of a future driven by global markets in which ever more tightly interlocking networks of technological and economic networks obliterate remaining cultural and biological differences.[61]

What its advocates see as a new, necessarily hard-eyed vision of rain forest preservation programs has a number of positive aspects. Although a wide variety of critics labeled *sustainable development* an oxymoron from its beginnings, its present-day attackers have succeeded in drawing popular attention to the often contradictory nature of its goals. They have been equally good at underscoring the dangers of hyperbole and of a rote celebration of local knowledge that denies the fully human identity of particular groups and individuals by insisting that they function as unswerving environmental champions.[62] Likewise, these critics' emphasis on the corporate networks that increasingly transcend national boundaries raises critical questions about the relationship between development and preservation. Their insistence that economic development inevitably destroys some measure of nonrenewable resources presents an open challenge to Chief Tunabi.

If the new pessimism has succeeded in underscoring the scope and character of some of the Amazon's most pressing problems, it has its own decided drawbacks, above all for the human inhabitants of rain forests. The attack on sustainable development as an untenable ideal often becomes a blanket rejection of people's capacity to interact in a nondestructive way with their surroundings. Although the critics rarely denounce local knowledge per se, they insist that rapid worldwide change makes it impossible to use this sort of knowledge as a cornerstone for action. Attempts to understand local ways of thinking are, by extension, nostalgic and ultimately a waste of time, since there can be no real place for humans amid the remnants of a wild nature that outsiders might fight to save.

The implications for the Amazon of the new pessimism are particularly clear in "A Dying World," by conservation biologist John Terborgh, which appeared in the *New York Review of Books* in January 2000. In this essay—a review of Wade Davis' *One River* and Nigel J. H. Smith's *The Amazon River Forest*—Terborgh describes the present-day

Amazon as "a continent-sized region at the crossroads between a mysterious and often violent past and a mundane future in the modern economy." However, his Amazon-to-be will retain little, if any, hint of this still vivid past. "Already the children of nearly every tribe receive instruction in Spanish or Portuguese, and as the younger generation crosses the language divide, so will it cross the cultural divide," Terborgh asserts. "Literate, and aware of the larger world around them, the young will slip unnoticed into a sea of brown-skinned people. They will drink beer, watch television, and be fans of the national football team, just like everybody else." [63]

Terborgh claims to sympathize with Smith's affection for Amazonia's mixed-blood residents, describing him as "understandably fascinated by [the *caboclos*'] intimate ties to the rhythm of the river." He nonetheless dismisses as impossibly romantic Smith's plea that native biodiversity continue to serve as a cornerstone for agricultural intensification. "I would argue, to the contrary," Terborgh says, "that the caboclo lifestyle is foreordained to go the way of spears and stone axes. We should not forget that pioneers living on the North American frontier two hundred years ago gathered fruits and nuts from the forest, selected the proper wood to be used for dozens of specialized purposes, and treated their ills with poultices and teas made from native plants. But who among us now still lives by the lore of two hundred years ago, however rich and insightful it may have been at the time?" [64]

Many readers' first reaction to Terborgh's assertions will be a quick nod of the head. No, Americans today don't run out to the forest for a medicinal tea or poultice. And yes, the Amazon, like the rest of the world, is almost certain to be different tomorrow than it is today. The inevitability of change seems to support Terborgh's call for the more efficient policing of a threatened nature that conservationists' visions of development cum social justice have failed to protect. But the apparently commonsense quality of these assertions is less self-evident than it initially appears. It is true that the species extinction, deforestation, and industrial pollution to which Terborgh points are dramatically visible in the present.[65] And yet, although they are genuine problems, we have seen that loss itself is a narrative theme with a long history. The intervention and control that Terborgh and his fellows advocate as a response to what they see as today's unprecedented crisis is as old as El Dorado. If the golden king is dumping precious gold into a lake, then someone who has better uses for such treasures has the right, if not the obligation, to remove it from his possession. If present-day Amazonians cannot put a stop to deforestation and species extinction, then they should cede the land to others who can more effectively protect it.

However, even while the pessimists' combative language calls attention to authentic failures, it obscures other aspects of a larger whole. The sharp insistence on irreparable loss that is a hallmark of the new pessimism (itself a retooled version of the calls to save "pure nature" common in the 1970s) creates a great divide between the past and future, tribal Indian and cultureless beer guzzler, predatory human and threatened nature, the precious "wild" and the unexciting "tamed." In so doing, it conceals a less totalizing, far less clear-cut world in which partial change and surface transformation are at least as common as is outright disappearance. To the degree that it conceals this more complicated present in which some humans, in some circumstances, destroy nature while others seek to preserve it, the fragmented forest becomes its own giant.

Even though few North Americans today run out to the forest for headache cures, packages of herbal tea increasingly cram supermarket shelves, websites that dispense advice about homeopathic remedies abound, and alternative health products are a multimillion-dollar industry. Moreover, the Pilgrims' attitudes toward New World nature as a paradise to be recovered by the (suitably enterprising) righteous live on in our own attitudes toward the potted plant in our kitchen window as well as toward rain forests halfway around the world. Certainly, we do not think in exactly the same way as our great-grandparents. But if our tenuous and yet enduring connections to the past surface in a hundred minor details, why then should Amazonians be all that different? Do we really wish them to refrain from becoming "literate, and aware of the larger world around them"?

Saudades do Brasil

The dual identity of loss as a response to particular present-day events and as a potentially giant-making device with a long narrative history is nowhere clearer than in Claude Lévi-Strauss' *Saudades do Brasil* (literally, Nostalgia for Brazil). Published in French in 1994 and in English translation a year later, the book is a collection of photographs of Indians from central Brazil and the Amazon, which the French anthropologist took in the late 1930s. These remarkable portraits gathered dust in a São Paulo archive before coming to light again a half-century later.

Saudades' graphic suggestion of cultural demise provides a distinctly personal-sounding correlate to lists of facts and figures documenting the extinction of various plant and animal species. Although, in many ways, a sequel to Lévi-Strauss' earlier *Tristes tropiques,* this gallery of vanished individuals and whole native societies does not offer the slightest glimmer of hope that Rousseau's keys to the beginnings of human civilization may yet reveal themselves to us. The Indians seated in circles with their backs to the viewer, the natives laughing at an unseen camera or engaged in conversations no one can remember, are the black-and-white remains of a once brightly colored world.

In his prologue to the photos (which also appears as the lead article in the 1995 Christmas issue of the *Saturday Review of Books* under the title "Photographs and Memories from the Lost World of Brazil"), Lévi-Strauss dispels any lingering doubt that the past can be retrieved. Even though the photos confirm the former existence of particular people and landscape, they "do not evoke them" for the photographer, let alone "bring them materially back to life." Should the reader set out to find the world captured in these pictures, it "would be unrecognizable and would in many respects have simply vanished."[66]

The present-day Indians whom the French anthropologist describes are little more than walking specters. The same Nambikwara who once lay down to sleep in the still-warm ashes of their remote campfires now live on the margins of burgeoning cities or make their temporary homes by the side of heavily traveled roads. Once all but oblivious to a larger world, the members of the tribe have come to depend increasingly on handouts from missionaries and government officials. Reduced by previous smallpox epidemics to a mere seven or eight hundred people, these descendants of Theodore Roosevelt's "Adam and Eve before the Fall" reserve their new passion for consumer goods. When a film project flies them to Mexico so that they can appear in a documentary about vanishing cultures, they make use of the opportunity to scoop up cheap transistor radios as well as to pass out pamphlets in English, Spanish, and Portuguese denouncing abuses by gold miners.

As in *Tristes tropiques,* the Amazonian Indians of *Saudades* call attention to processes and concerns that go far beyond them. The true subject of both books is not the Brazilian Indians or the Amazon, but rather a Western civilization that is as precious to Lévi-Strauss as "wild nature" is to today's conservation biologists. The enemy, in Lévi-Strauss' view, is much the same process of globalization that Terborgh and his fellows describe. "The victim of circumstances of its own making [over-

population, commodification in the name of economic progress], Western civilization now feels threatened in its turn. It has, in the past,
destroyed innumerable cultures in whose diversity lay the wealth of humankind. Guardian of its own fraction of this collective wealth, weak-
ened by dangers from without and within, it is allowing itself to forget
or destroy its own heritage, which—as much as any other—deserves to
be cherished and respected." [67]

Time and again, Lévi-Strauss' concern for Western civilization pushes
him toward metaphor. As the group that impressed the young anthropologist as the most genuinely Rousseauian in their simplicity, the Nambikwara retain a particular meaning for him. They also account for an
unsurprisingly large space in his gallery of images. However, more than
a particular group of people he once knew, the Nambikwara are a symbol of what has happened or is happening to other native peoples
throughout much of the world. In their newfound enthusiasm for transistor radios, they are one with those Pacific Coast Indians of Canada
who stick a likeness of Mickey Mouse amid the tribal masks that Lévi-
Strauss saw in 1974, and which he describes in *Saudades* as "among the
highest creations of world sculpture."

The forces of globalization have done more than destroy once vital,
marvelously resilient native cultures. If, in the 1950s, the Amazon could
strike Lévi-Strauss as a great green island in a rising sea of consumerism,
those waters have now engulfed it too. As a result, the world that he describes in *Saudades* is no longer *"tristes tropiques"* but rather, *"triste
planète."* "Dispossessed of our culture, stripped of values that we cherished—the purity of water and air, the charms of nature, the diversity of
animals and plants—we are all Indians henceforth, making of ourselves
what we made of them," he declares in what is, without a doubt, the key
sentence of the book.[68]

Lévi-Strauss' lament underscores the larger political stakes behind
images of today's Rain Forest. If his portrait of a bygone Brazil is un-
abashedly nostalgic, the lyric language of his "Lost World" finds fewer
open echoes in Terborgh's "Dying World" and in his *Requiem for Nature*—a book that attests to the "relentless onslaught of civilization" in
even "the most remote corners of the planet." [69] To be sure, Terborgh
and his fellows are far more interested in formulating policies than is the
eighty-six-year-old anthropologist who looks back over his long life in
the pages of *Saudades*. Nonetheless, chapter headings such as "Paradise
Fading" and "The Last Bastions of Nature" use a similarly Edenic language to underscore the theme of loss. The presence of one of Henri

Rousseau's jungle paintings on the cover of *Requiem for Nature* further links this plea for a hard-edged science to Lévi-Strauss' quest to find Jean-Jacques Rousseau's building blocks of civilization.[70]

The destruction of the last four decades is, again, no fiction. However, in *Saudades*, as in Terborgh's "Dying World," the insistence on the totalizing quality of this loss obscures the diversity of peoples and cultures that continue to exist. There is almost no room in Lévi-Strauss' preface for those Amazonian Indians who have managed to survive what he describes as "a new cataclysm." There is even less space for those indigenous political organizations that have succeeded in calling international attention to injustices visited upon their members so as to reestablish native hold over a series of communal lands. The Nambikwara's distribution of pamphlets denouncing the gold miners appears in *Saudades* as more proof of loss and attenuation. So does their trip to Mexico in order to appear in a movie that protests injustices against native peoples. However, it is just as easy to see these actions as an eloquent expression of their adaptability and their ongoing will to live. Likewise, while Lévi-Strauss views the Nambikwara's interest in transistor radios as evidence of an unseemly consumerism, the fact that they buy radios instead of toasters or designer sneakers suggests a desire to tune in to that larger world to which, for better or for worse, their destiny is linked.

Moreover, even as Lévi-Strauss' vivid prose and haunting images bring to life an ever fainter past, he appears to ignore or even disdain those people of mixed blood who are, in many cases, the Indians' descendants. Much as the diseased, rachitic rubber tappers in *Tristes tropiques* served as a foil for the healthy natives, so detribalized Indians and members of hybrid culture are, by implication, pale imitations of something more precious and authentic. Like Terborgh's "Dying World," Lévi-Strauss' "Lost World" conveniently ignores complicated but essential questions of transformation and the continuing resilience of half-buried stories and beliefs. Although he never goes so far as to describe present-day Amazonians as "brown-skinned beer guzzlers," he clearly finds little of interest in their attempts to live within a shifting present. In offering the presence of Mickey Mouse amid the tribal masks as confirmation of the death of native culture, the anthropologist stifles any impulse to ask what exactly Mickey might mean to the natives in question or what the Nambikwara think they are hearing on their cut-rate radios.

"We are all Indians," says Lévi-Strauss by way of conclusion, but this assertion, albeit startling and poignant, is half true at best. Even if one accepts the premise that the homogenizing forces of globalization have led all of the planet's residents to share in a sense of loss that Lévi-Strauss associates with the Amazonian Indians, different social groups participate in these processes in quite separate ways. All of humanity is surely, in some sense, the poorer as one more stretch of trees goes up in flames. However, the Tukano and the Machiguenga, the Kayapó and the Yanomami, experience the destruction of their homes and prized possessions in a far more immediate and catastrophic fashion than do a group of Japanese computer programmers, an Australian rancher, or an eminent French professor of structural anthropology.

"But why would he say we are all Indians?" demands a genuinely curious Tô Pereira when I ask what he thinks about Lévi-Strauss' assertion. "My grandfather spent almost six months with the Indians once, he lived among the Sateré-Maué tribe. They were kind to him, he was well treated, but there were many things they wouldn't teach him, even though he asked. Because the whole thing about Indians is that they don't want to be the same as others. They are proud of their way of life, they don't want to share their secrets or to leave their houses in the forest for a house like yours or mine. Your professor friend is right that the whole world suffers when the trees burn. But those who truly suffer are those who live closest to the trees."

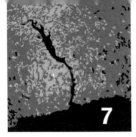

Lakes within Lakes

"In the time of the candles, the masters forced our ancestors to serve as human lamps," says the graceful young black woman named Benedita, one of my traveling companions on this, my second of two trips up the Trombetas River. Although the smell of just-brewed coffee has begun to waft from the galley kitchen, we remain huddled in our hammocks, talking, as the slow-moving boat pushes its way through a thick and chilly morning fog. "They would have to stand there with an outstretched palm full of oil that held a burning wick, which often seared their skin," Benedita says, blowing on her own slim hands to warm them. "And so, whenever they could, they fled into the *mata* [bush]—that is, they fled into the *floresta* [rain forest]. And that is how we, their descendants, ended up here, far above the cataracts that held back the soldiers that came after them, you see."

"What's the difference between a '*mata*' and a '*floresta*'?" I ask.

"Oh, there is no difference," she says, stretching out her arms to a newly present sun. "It's just that the rain forest is something about which outsiders care. If I say 'the bush,' you might not listen. But if I say 'the rain forest,' then everybody wants to hear."

The sun is a great deal hotter as I later sit at a rustic table, listening to the tall and normally quiet Manuel Pedro, the shorter and far more loquacious Mundico, and the stout, steely haired Dona Amélia, who wishes out loud that she could be God for just half an hour. ("I'd give the world a good, hard shaking!" she exclaims.) The three are exchanging jokes and stories mixed with gossip after lunching on fried piranha and the tasty little *pacu* fish that Manuel Pedro caught before dawn. "Now, these are all lies!" Mundico assures me with a pat on the shoulder and a conspiratorial wink. When I ask to hear more about the "time of the candles," however, they describe in solemn detail how their enslaved ancestors came to seek protection of the *Mãe Cachoeira,* or

Mother Waterfall, when they fled their masters and were pursued by the soldiers, who were stopped only by a thundering wall of water behind which the escaped slaves came to reside.

Listening to them talk, I remember Benedita's distinction between a *mata* and a *floresta* and suddenly realize that it is neither of these terms, but instead the river and its interactions with the land, that dominates their accounts. Why, beyond the obvious material reasons, I wonder, is water so essential in a large number of the stories told by contemporary Amazonians? Why, conversely, is there not a single fish or turtle on Danny's Rainforest Meter? Why does Roosevelt, in hot pursuit of the River of Doubt, follow Carvajal and Bates in describing a largely terrestrial flora and fauna? How and when did Benedita's *mata* get to be a *floresta,* and in what ways does the enchanted lake within a lake become a kind of shorthand for a much larger group of stories in which concerns about human justice and injustice regularly intermingle with a conviction about nature's power and enduring mystery?

The Children of the River

Just as miners' accounts of an animate and ever-changing Gold offer particularly eloquent testimony to the partial overlapping of competing visions of the Amazon, so do the accounts of present-day Amazonian *remanescentes de quilombo.* These *remanescentes* are literally "remnants," descendants of the runaway African slaves who founded independent fugitive, or Maroon, communities (known in Brazil by the initially pejorative terms *quilombos* or *mocambos*) in many different parts of Latin America.[1]

Fugitive slave communities existed in various corners of the Amazon. The Maroons of Suriname comprise a particularly large, important, and well-studied group.[2] The descendants of runaway black slaves in Colombia, Venezuela, and Ecuador are also commanding increasing attention.[3] Here, my focus is the communities on the Trombetas and Erepecuru (also known as the Cuminá and the Paru do Oeste) Rivers, as well as around the cities of Santarém and Óbidos, in the western part of the Brazilian state of Pará.[4] These communities account for approximately a fifth of the ex-*quilombos* in the state. Although their numbers are small in absolute terms (about sixty-five hundred persons in total), they offer a particularly effective illustration of the cultural, political, and economic networks that extend far beyond them.[5]

Unlike their counterparts in a number of other countries, the Brazilian *remanescentes* are only now beginning to develop a strong sense of themselves as an ethnic group with a long history and a specific political agenda.[6] Although Article 68 of the Brazilian Constitution of 1988 guarantees ownership of ancestral lands to the descendants of former slaves, *remanescentes* throughout Brazil are presently engaged in legal battles to assume in practice what is theirs in theory.[7] As a result, the communities of the greater Trombetas find themselves continuing to battle both multinational mining companies and government agencies for legal as well as practical control over these properties.[8]

The history of the *remanescentes* in the Amazon extends back to the mid–eighteenth century. Eager to create a lucrative export crop for Portugal within the Amazon, the powerful Portuguese prime minister Pombal began encouraging the growth of a plantation economy through the monopoly company known as the Companhia Geral do Grão-Pará e Maranhão.[9] These new plantations produced sugarcane, rice, cotton, and—above all—cacao. A royal edict encouraged the planting of cacao on the higher banks of the Amazon floodplain from around what is now Parintins downstream to the estuary, resulting in groves containing as many as forty thousand trees.[10] Amazonian growers sent raw cacao to Spain and Portugal. From there, it was reexported to Genoa, Venice, and Naples for processing and then shipped back to the Iberian Peninsula, as well as to other countries where the demand for chocolate—a luxury beverage whose popularity predated coffee—was high.

When wild, the sun-colored cacao fruit yields a single harvest, but under cultivation, it produces twice a year.[11] This increased harvest required a new source of labor that the existing Indians and caboclos could or would not provide. To meet the demand, Pombal began importing significant numbers of African slaves into the Amazon.[12] Their presence helped make cacao the Brazilian Amazon's principal export for close to a hundred years.[13]

Cacao's dominance subsided only with the Rubber Boom, which effectively siphoned off for extractive activities the labor that formerly had been devoted to floodplain crops. By the end of the 1850s, the international trade in latex had skyrocketed.[14] Although rubber quickly undercut what had been an expanding plantation system, substituting short-term extractive ventures for long-term investments in the region, it did not obliterate it entirely. Plantation crops, and with them slave labor, remained the mainstay of the economies of the cities of Santarém, Óbidos,

Alenquer, Faro, and Monte Alegre—none of which were rubber centers.[15] The plantations themselves entered into a definitive decline only in the late nineteenth century, when growing cacao production in the state of Bahia destroyed the Amazon's primacy within Brazil as a producer of the fruit.

As Benedita's account of the time of the candles makes clear, some of the slaves tried to flee oppressive masters.[16] While attempts at escape would escalate during the massive popular rebellion of 1835–39, known as the Cabanagem, they began in the eighteenth century and continued long after the uprising had failed.[17] Possibly inspired by the example of Maroon communities in the neighboring Guianas, to which the Trombetas River system eventually connects, groups of fugitives began settling in the Curuá River region in the latter part of the eighteenth and the early nineteenth centuries.[18] However, government troops, who destroyed the communities of Inferno and Cipotema in 1812, pushed the slaves into successively more inaccessible locations. These included the lands above a series of forbidding cataracts on the Trombetas and Erepecuru Rivers.

In 1821, the slave Atanásio, who had fled in the raids on the Curuá, headed a force of some forty slaves who founded a new *quilombo* on the Trombetas, which eventually attracted more than two thousand inhabitants.[19] Although government troops seized Atanásio when they destroyed this second *quilombo* some two years later, he staged a new escape. The slaves went on to found a community called Maravilha (Marvel), to which some of the oldest *remanescentes* still refer.[20]

Relatively self-sufficient, these fugitive communities did a surreptitious trade with white merchants, regularly exchanging a highly prized variety of tobacco and various forest and river products (sarsaparilla, Brazil nuts, turtles) for coffee, sugar, tools, and cloth.[21] Punitive missions against the *quilombo* dwellers—whom one writer of the period described as "absolute rulers of the region"—nonetheless continued right up till abolition.[22] After the freeing of the slaves in 1888, the *remanescentes* began to descend the rivers, often establishing communities near large stands of the Brazil nut trees (some planted by their ancestors, some naturally occurring) that had achieved a new economic importance as cacao production waned. Too poor to afford boats large enough to transport the harvest, the slave descendants continued to rely on middlemen, who pocketed a good percentage of the profit. Later, in the twentieth century, members of the regional elite began buying legal title to the lands that these same slave descendants had worked for generations. The new owners would then parcel out the land to individual families, periodically sending representatives to collect the bulging sacks of nuts, for which they paid a pittance.[23]

Today, the old elite has lost much of its power. However, new pressures on the slave descendants have replaced the old. The huge multinational bauxite processing plant at Porto Trombetas—a response to the discovery of a 4-billion-ton deposit that suddenly made Brazil the world's third-largest supplier of the raw material for aluminum—is the most obvious source of tension. Heralded at its founding in 1979 as "a new nucleus of civilization in the very midst of the Amazon jungle," the plant, only minutes by motor boat from the *remanescente* community of Boa Vista, has generated tremendous profits for the multinational conglomerate, whose partners include Alcoa and Reynolds Aluminum.[24] However, its industrial wastes have poisoned the woods and waters where Boa Vista residents used to hunt and fish. While new cleanup procedures have contained a portion of the pollution and somewhat repaired past damage, the *remanescentes* continue to reap only limited benefits in terms of jobs, and few of the health and educational services that the multinational enterprise originally had promised have materialized.[25]

As the ongoing growth of the city-refinery of Porto Trombetas, with its approximately eight thousand inhabitants, has had a direct effect on Boa Vista, so have virtually all of the nearby black communities felt the results of the establishment of two huge land reserves intended to offset the impact of new mines and refineries on a species-rich and previously sparsely settled region. The Brazilian government's environmental protection agency, IBAMA, in 1979 declared one huge tract of land along the right side of the Trombetas River a biological reserve off-limits to its former occupants.[26] A year later, an entire community of twenty-five *remanescente* families was summarily expelled from the lake of Jacaré. The official demarcation of a second reserve along the opposing bank as a national forest ten years later closed huge tracts of land to the hunting, fishing, and extractive activities essential to the *remanescentes'* way of life.[27]

Suddenly trespassers upon their own lands, the residents of the twenty-one communities in the greater Trombetas area responded in 1989 by founding a political association known as ARQMO (Association of Descendants of Former Quilombos of the Municipality of Oriximiná).[28] Through membership in larger regional associations with outside backing, such as the coalition that organized in opposition to a wave of dam building for hydroelectricity throughout much of Amazonia in the 1980s, and involvement with foundations such as the São Paulo–based Indian Support Commission, this group has managed to find a national and international forum for its grievances.[29] Beyond Amazonia, the rise within Brazil and other Latin American countries of various black-rights movements provides this movement a second avenue of support.[30]

Well organized and politically agile, ARQMO has responded with legal action to the multinationals' drive to buy up individual properties in the former *quilombos*. Boa Vista gained formal title to its lands in 1995, followed by sixteen other communities on the Erepecuru and the Trombetas Rivers between 1996 and 1998.[31] And yet, while these actions represent an important moral as well as pragmatic victory, the *remanescentes* remain engaged in new court battles over land, ongoing skirmishes with IBAMA officials, and campaigns against new multinational mining projects. They also must find the means of continuing economic and cultural survival even as they seek a satisfactory definition of what constitutes a "*remanescente*" and who, by extension, has a legal right to work and live in the former *quilombos*.[32] In addition, they must struggle to get their story out while the far more visible and amply funded bauxite companies portray themselves as environmental champions in the international media. ("Hope for the Amazon Jungle," read the approving headline of one recent Associated Press report on Porto Trombetas.)[33]

Recording the *Remanescentes*

My first contact with the *remanescentes* occurred when I discovered that a good number of the people whose stories I was tape-recording in the cities of Óbidos, Santarém, and Oriximiná, and on boats that linked these locations, were the descendants of runaway slaves. Many of them had been born in ex-*quilombos* where members of their families still lived. Intrigued by the sometimes striking differences between the *remanescentes'* stories and those told by other Amazonians, I jumped at the opportunity to spend several days in the community of Silêncio do Matá (literally, Silence on the Matá River). My host was a young man whom I had met through a grassroots pastoral organization in the colonial city of Óbidos, some of whose ornate pastel mansions still have leg chains rusting in the basement. I then had the opportunity to make several visits to the former *quilombo* of Arapemã, just across the river from the burgeoning urban center of Santarém, where the remains of a whipping post and pillory stand in one public square in which children now whoop and play.[34]

A journey of several weeks up the Trombetas River followed. Because virtually no public transportation exists beyond the giant refinery at Porto Trombetas, I rented a small boat in Boa Vista. By great luck, the boat's owner, Zé Cândido—who agreed to ferry me from one community to another as part of the rental—turned out to be a member of the ARQMO leadership. During the day, we visited Zé's friends and relatives. At night, he would ask one or another family if I might sleep in their home while he and a young nephew strung their hammocks in the ramshackle boat he jokingly referred to as his "stray dog." Surprised by the unexpected presence of a curious and dependent stranger, who had arrived with no food and little knowledge of things they deemed essential, my hosts would talk with me for hours. They would then often leave a candle burning so that I would not wake up in the dark. Thanks to their generosity, I returned home with dozens of hours of taped stories and warm memories, including that moment when a boat, with only blacks aboard, made a wide arc across the river at Porto Trombetas to collect me, astonishing a group of white engineers assembled on the pier. ("I can't believe you're getting on a boat with people who would lie about the time of day to their own mother," one said disapprovingly. "What I can't believe is that these mistrustful so-and-sos would go to all that trouble to help someone who wasn't black," declared his friend.)

These experiences, which led me to largely dismiss others' past and present descriptions of the slave descendants as closed and suspicious, when not downright hostile and deceitful, left me wholly unprepared for my second trip up the Trombetas and Erepecuru Rivers almost exactly a year later.[35] Presented with the unexpected opportunity to tag along with three young filmmakers who had obtained ARQMO's permission to make a documentary about the communities, I rushed to buy several weeks' worth of spaghetti, soap, and coffee—staples we would need on board the boat that would serve as our hotel and floating restaurant. An hour later, I found myself on the boat with the team and representatives of the various communities that had been slated to receive the visitors.

Because the video that the team was planning would be aimed at a public beyond the Amazon, the *remanescentes* were understandably concerned about its content. Moreover, the four of us—all white—

seemed to them to be a de facto group, which triggered obvious, often uneasy questions. ("What do these people want?" "Who has sent them and where did they get the money to show up here?" "How do we know that they won't tell lies about us that will hurt our efforts to get title to our land?") Our presence also brought to the surface long-existing rivalries and disagreements within and among the various communities. ("Why are they interviewing him and not her?" "Who said that they should spend two days in Place X when they are not even stopping in Place Y?" "Why are they asking questions about such-and-such rather than this or that?") Self-conscious about speaking before an often temperamental video camera, people were apt to recount stories very different in emphasis, and sometimes in content, from those I had previously heard.

At the time, I found it unsettling and sometimes painful when people who had taken me into their homes on my last trip barely acknowledged my presence this time. It was equally discomfiting when Benedita, Mundico, and other community members whom I liked and respected would exchange knowing winks or whisper, or would overtly attempt to manipulate the video team to their own ends. The very different quality of these experiences—in retrospect, unsurprising—affords a privileged glimpse at a people with a long history of betrayal by outsiders suddenly forced to navigate their way among them. The stories themselves point to the tensions prompted by the *remanescentes'* increasing need to translate a history of injustice and the vision of a powerful and always-changing nature into terms comprehensible to an outside public whose images of the Amazon rain forest do not include enchanted beings—or, for that matter, blacks.[36]

Varieties of Transformation

The mineral-rich soils of the Trombetas regularly attract gold miners. There is a *garimpo,* for instance, just outside the *remanescente* community of Pancada on the Erepecuru River, and supply boats—full of crates of beer bottles, machine parts, and sometimes even skittish horses who appear to dance to the music of a blaring boom-box—regularly dock beside the residents' canoes. Even though the slave descendants as a whole are apt to have harsh words for the *garimpeiros,* whom they see as inflicting malaria, venereal disease, and drunken brawls upon them, individual *remanescentes* often turn out to have spent various intervals in the gold camps. As a result, despite striking differences there also is a clear overlap in the stories told by the two groups.[37]

Remanescentes and gold miners are apt to mingle bits and pieces of oral history with folk narrative. Rooted in personal experience but drawing on a rich legacy of symbols, *remanescentes'* stories, like those of the gold miners, often describe both acts of violence and enchanted places and beings.[38] Unlike the miners, however, who often surround brutal events with an aura of glamour, the *remanescentes* decry the violence that they see as directed at them by outsiders. For example, they condemn the recent actions by IBAMA and by various multinational companies, which they see as endangering their own survival.

"Reserves, reserves, reserves, that's all whites talk about today," grumbles one of Mundico's sisters-in-law. "They go around destroying nature, but when they talk, it's always 'reserve' this, and 'reserve' that. And what about us? Where should we live? In the middle of the river? Shall we build our houses on the water? Or turn ourselves into fish? In the old days, the river was our supermarket and the woods our drugstore. Today, we have no money, and yet, we are not supposed to hunt or fish or even gather the fruits and nuts that just rot there on the branches."

The violence in the slave descendants' narratives has far deeper roots in Amazonian history than that which permeates the tales of miners. Not surprisingly, "the past" for the miners, a heterogeneous and constantly shifting group, seldom extends back beyond the 1950s. Indeed, the term often refers to the 1980s and a time before the widespread use of machines. In contrast, the *remanescentes'* collective memory reaches back over the centuries. Time and again, they refer to today's forced evictions from their homes, the pollution of lakes and streams with refinery wastes, and the closing of large tracts of forest as "a new slavery."

The relationship between the individual and the community in *remanescentes'* tales also distinguishes them from the gold miners' stories. For example, an angry *mãe,* or guardian, is almost certain to pack up her riches and move on if a *garimpeiro* kills a snake or caiman in the gully he happens to be excavating. His actions thus directly affect the fate of every man in the camp. Yet the tales miners tell about such incidents reveal little sense of collectivity. The *remanescentes'* tales, in contrast, display a strong group awareness. For example, in the following story, João Gringote (literally, "John Whitey") pointedly ignores his

mother's warnings about the consequences of his actions toward a giant
turtle, an animal that has long played a key role in the *remanescentes'*
diet and symbolic life.[39] His unhappy fate is thus strictly his own fault
and has no negative repercussions for the group. The speaker is a young
woman recently engaged to one of Zé Cândido's nephews.

> And then, this John Whitey caught sight of that enormous turtle, very differ-
> ent from all of the other turtles, because of its white head. "What luck, this
> turtle is going to make me rich!" he said. And so, in that moment, the *mu-*
> *tum* bird began to sing. For the person who doesn't understand the language
> of the birds, that *mutum* was just singing like birds do. But the woman, who
> had knowledge of the speech of animals, understood that the *mutum* was say-
> ing, "John Whitey, the turtle is going to carry you off." So then, she said to
> him, "Oh, my son, don't go down to the beach because the turtle is going
> to carry you off." But he said, "Ah, grandmother, don't talk nonsense, I'm
> going, yes I am!" And so, he grabbed the turtle with both hands, and his
> hands remained stuck to its shell. He tried to free himself with his feet, but
> they stuck to the shell as well. So then, there was no remedy. Even today, we
> sometimes see that man seated on the turtle. He shows up in the midst of a
> multitude of dolphins and his hair is very long and greenish from having
> passed so many years within the river. We shout to him, but he seems not to
> hear us as he goes riding by.[40]

The possibility of direct communication between human beings and
animals is central to this and to a number of other *remanescente* stories.
The *mutum,* or curassow, who sings out a warning to the foolhardy protagonist recalls African birds of augury who alert listeners to what is
about to happen. Then too, the protagonist, whose whiteness (if only in
name) sets him apart from other community members, shows disrespect
for not just the unique white-headed turtle, but for his own mother,
who, as a curer, understands the language of the animals. The storyteller's seemingly unconscious transformation of Whitey's mother into
his grandmother in the middle of the tale only highlights Whitey's lack
of respect for the elders who embody a collective wisdom that appears
in opposition to individual monetary gain.

The strong communal loyalties that allowed the *remanescentes* to
survive in the face of extreme and repeated danger find equally clear expression in a handful of stories about saints who pluck people from the
clutches of the Encantados. Not only does the community as a whole set
out to find the kidnapped woman in the following story, but the black
folk-saint Anthony replaces the more customary shaman in the search.
This substitution is highly unusual in the Encantado stories as a whole,
in which the saints customarily control the heavens, leaving the waters

to the Enchanted Beings and the shamanic healers who regularly communicate with them.[41] The storyteller, who works as a laundress for the
bishop of Óbidos, explains how her father called on the saint to rescue
his mother, whom two Enchanted Beings in the guise of children had imprisoned in a hollow tree.

> Everybody looked everywhere for Dona Claudina. She heard their shouts,
> but she wasn't able to respond. So then, she spent the whole night there, a
> night of heavy rain. And look, when she finally managed to escape the fol-
> lowing morning, her clothes were dry, completely dry. So then, she showed
> everyone that big tree trunk in which she had spent the night. She had not
> gone to the river bottom, but still, it was a thing of the Encante. They were
> Encantados in the form of small boys who had shut her up inside that tree.
> Well, after that, she remained a bit touched in the head—it wasn't long be-
> fore she died. But if my father had not made that vow to our Saint Anthony,
> if he had not asked for her return in the name of everyone, no one would ever
> have laid eyes on her again.[42]

Dona Claudina's triumphant return is a tribute to the community,
which has willingly suspended its own pursuits on her behalf. Her return also underscores the power of the black saint on whom her son calls
in the name of all. More like one of the African deities called *orixás* than
a Roman Catholic holy figure, the Saint Anthony who effects her rescue
moves with consummate ease between the known world of the *mata* and
the uncharted realm of the Encante.[43] The saint's success reconfirms the
special relationship between the *remanescente* community and a larger
natural universe that gold miners inevitably confront on their own or
with the help of charms specially designed to attract gold, or prayers or
talismans designed to "close" the body against injury. It also underscores much larger differences between the *remanescentes'* and the miners' uses of their shared narrative tradition. Although miners do call on
the saints for protection, these saints never actually cross paths with an
enchanted Gold.

While the general absence of saints in the Encantado tradition gives
those tales in which saints appear a special interest, the more important
figure in *remanescentes'* stories is an Enchanted Being: Mother Waterfall. Although she is as strong-willed and as alluring as the Woman in
White, Mother Waterfall is very different in the overwhelming sense of
justice that leads her to shield the oppressed. Steadfast protector of the
waters and all of the creatures who live within them, she is a parent to
the Children of the River. Severe but loving, she—in bitter contrast to
human beings—does not betray those who earn her trust.

So then, this is a story that even children tell. Everybody knows how Mother Waterfall welcomed those slaves who were fleeing their masters. Poor things! They arrived here full of hunger, full of thirst, full of fear of the soldiers who were right behind them with their guns and chains. And the soldiers would certainly have grabbed them if Mother Waterfall had not wrapped them in a heavy veil of mist. So then, the soldiers could see nothing, they were forced to turn back in defeat. And our grandparents were saved. They had come there with nothing more than the shirts on their backs, but Mother Waterfall gave them courage, she gave them food, she gave them peace. So then, they made their little houses there above the cataracts where no soldier would ever have the nerve to follow. Because Mother Waterfall felt sorry for our grand-parents, who could not live cooped up like a songbird in a cage. [Here the storyteller goes on to relate how the slaves, with the aid of Mother Waterfall, successfully repelled various attempts to capture them through both armed confrontation and deceit.][44]

The heroine of this and countless other stories, Mother Waterfall is in no way abstract. "Here is our mother," Manuel Pedro tells me as the great waterfall called Chuvisco (Drizzle) comes into view after a long, hot hike through spiny brush. The emotion in his voice, together with the sudden sight of the droplets that spew up into the sky like an infinity of glass shards, makes me want to cry. Sensing my reaction, Manuel Pedro looks startled, then laughs loudly. "You are thinking that the slaves showed great courage in escaping," he says, almost gaily. "But we today think that they were foolish not to have simply killed their masters from the start." I nod, aware that this show of mirth is meant to convert the brilliant shards into water once again.

Although Gold eventually will deceive a man, he must do everything within his power to enjoy her favor for long as possible. This sense of nature as a potentially hostile presence also crops up in some of the accounts of slave descendants. "God gives people a second chance, but nature doesn't," Zé Cândido declares as we huddle beneath a sheet of blue plastic while a sudden storm causes our small boat to lurch from side to side. "The wild waters of the rapids, they forgive nothing, they pull down a person to the river bottom where they kill him right away. Because God created human beings in his own likeness, but nature, no, it's something different. If we do not enter into her rhythm, then we will be destroyed."

And yet, even when seemingly cruel and unbending, Mother Water-fall is not capricious. Her actions have a logic that human beings can understand and use to their own benefit. Entering into nature's rhythm allows one to protect both oneself and the riches nature provides. By listening to nature, humans can outwit those who would force their will on themselves and on her.

Many *remanescentes* tell stories about a man named Domingos Xavier, who, like John Whitey's mother, could understand the language of the animals. Unlike Whitey's mother, Xavier's special abilities centered exclusively on the turtles. "They say that this Domingos Xavier had to do no more than whistle and the turtles would begin climbing up on land," Manuel Pedro says as Mundico sprays DDT on the plump, defiant cockroaches camped out beneath a metal stew pot. "He would whistle and before long the entire beach would be black with turtles," Mundico confirms, in between a fit of coughing brought on by the DDT.

One of Manuel Pedro's best friends, a young man named Samuel who sports an orange baseball cap and Nike knockoffs, describes how the turtles summon Xavier to the river one day to advise him of the impending arrival of a group of officials. The officials, they explain, are planning to force the *remanescentes* to round up the turtles for a politicians' banquet in Santarém. Xavier hurries to relay the turtles' message to the community so that its members will not be pressed to perform a task they would consider an affront to both nature and themselves. By the time the officials arrive, the entire community has hidden in the forest. Although the officials shout threats into the brush, there is nothing they can do to make either the people or the turtles reappear.

"So then, the politicians all ate roast beef in that banquet," Samuel says, completely deadpan. "I myself was too busy to attend, but I hear that the food was very good."

Gold's penchant for metamorphosis is a drawback for the miners, who express frustration in their retellings of the widely familiar story of a golden church that suddenly crops up in the middle of the forest. Heralded by ringing bells and bright streams of firecrackers, the church displays a maddening propensity to disappear as soon as someone gets too near it. In contrast, the slave descendants regularly convert the story of the church into a fable about the high price of greed. The following storyteller, Seu Tico, an old man who still loves to fish and hunt, concludes the story by remembering the time that he too came upon the church.

> Well then, everybody knows the story of the church that shows up here in the middle of the forest from time to time, a huge church all of gold. So then, one day a priest was walking through the forest and he heard the church bells ringing. When he looked up he saw firecrackers bursting over a tower of pure

gold. So then he thought, "Look at all that gold that I can cart home for my altar!" and he pushed open the church door. But as soon as he did that, he was overcome by the stench of the *azinhavre* [verdigris], which is like sweat, because gold is a living thing.[45] But he didn't want to leave the gold, and when they found him a day later in the middle of the forest, he was dead.

So then, I too once saw this church and was dazzled, very dazzled. It appeared before me one day when I was hunting in the middle of the woods. I saw that the door was open, and without even thinking, I went in. But in the moment in which I entered, I smelled that strong smell and then I fainted. And when I opened my eyes I was beneath some trees. There I remained, unable to move, unable to speak, until my son came upon me. Now then, I didn't die, like that priest who tried to steal the gold for his own altar. No, what he did out of greed, I did out of wonder. That is, I saw that radiance and I couldn't resist.[46]

Although the priest in Seu Tico's story has no name, he is often identified as "Father Nicolino," who was a historical personage—Father José Nicolino Pereira de Souza, who founded the parish of Oriximiná and who traveled extensively in the Trombetas area between 1877 and 1888, where he recorded the first baptisms of residents of the *quilombos* before dying of a fever contracted during one of these journeys.[47] The focus in the story on the gold's offensive smell recalls the early-eighteenth-century friar Juan de Santa Gertrudis' account of a native description of El Dorado that features a mountain that weeps tears of gold and threatens all those who approach it with thunder, lightning, and "an evil-smelling green smoke."[48] Here, the smell is not so much a sign of gold's base nature as a confirmation of its identity as a living being who, like the *remanescentes,* resists domination and commodification by outsiders interested in their own gain.

For the slave descendants, many of whose communities still lie hidden behind a protective fringe of forest, the golden church's evanescence is often less a source of frustration than a welcome concealing device. Much as Mother Waterfall rescues the fugitives from certain death by wrapping them in a thick mist, so her descendants prevail upon the local shaman to convince the Mother of the Forest to enchant the El Doradian church so that it will not prompt the miners to invade their lands in search of gold. After that, though the church continues to surface from time to time, it does so noiselessly.

"So then," explains one man on a boat to Porto Trombetas,

a whole bunch of *garimpeiros* suddenly showed up here in search of the golden church. They wanted to dismantle it, to carry off the pieces. So they set up a *garimpo* in the middle of the forest and began throwing mercury in the water. It got so that no one could hunt or fish. So then, the *remanescentes* went in search of a powerful *pajé*. "Make the church disappear!" they begged him, and he did. That is, the church still appears from time to time, but the bells have stopped ringing. And the firecrackers that used to pop and crackle now explode in a silent rain of light.[49]

Nature's ability to protect and conserve through transformation is even more evident in stories of the enchanted lake within a lake, which some *remanescentes* compare to a biological reserve. Often said to be situated near Abuí, one of the more remote and particularly beautiful *remanescente* communities, this lake—which remains off-limits to everyone except an old man named Higino—is the epitome of natural abundance. In some versions of the story, its invisibility infuriates those *remanescentes* eager to share more fully in its bounty. In others, its elusiveness only confirms Nature's resolve to preserve the riches she has set aside for the exclusive use of the Children of the River. The story is a continuing source of inspiration for storytellers such as Seu Tico's wife, whose silver hair spills out of the bun atop her head as she describes Higino's marvelous catch.

> This lake within a lake about which everybody speaks is pure abundance. It is enchanted because one moment you can see it and the next, it disappears. It is a bright blue lake that changes color like a shaman's crystal. Its waters are full of fish, and in the center is an island of white sand full of animals and many trees. Now then, this Higino was an elderly *remanescente* who lived nearby here; a person could leave at nine in the morning and be arriving at his house before the end of the afternoon. The lake, no, it was far more distant, but Higino would go there and be back within the hour with a boat full of fish, of turtles, of manatees. The onlooker would be astonished to see that multitude of fish. Once, my father asked Higino if he could accompany him to that lake. So then, Higino told him, "Ah, *mano* [a colloquial form of "brother"], that lake is so big, so far away, that you would be exhausted." Because that lake was not Higino's, but a thing of the Encante that not everyone can see.[50]

The comparison of this enchanted lake within a lake to today's biological reserves allows the *remanescentes* to bring the story into the present. Often, the enchanted lake becomes a symbol of threatened abundance and a kind of prophecy. Its openness to at least some humans (the wise and generous Higino, who respects nature and distributes its bounty to all members of the community) also provides a point of contrast with the biological reserves in which there is no place for human beings. Even those *remanescentes* who express doubts about the Encante may use it as a symbol of a nature that interacts with the community.

> That enchanted lake of which my grandfather used to speak was a kind of biological reserve. He didn't use the word *reserve* when he talked about it, but it was a lake within another lake that was sheer abundance—the water teemed with fish and turtles, there were great crowds of manatees. The lake was hard to reach, but there was an old man by the name of Higino who knew the way. Every time he went there, he would bring back a whole boat-load of delicious fish that he would give away. Because that enchanted lake was meant for us Children of the River. Its abundance was a gift in which all were meant to share. So then, that lake was a reserve, but not like these reserves today in which the guards let no one enter, and even burn the boats of the hungry men who try.
>
> This story is very old. But it still reminds us that whoever speaks of preservation always needs to speak a little word of justice [*uma palavrinha de justiça*]. Because what is fragile is not really the forest. What is fragile is rich people's interest in poor people's rights.[51]

The Children of the River as Protectors of the Woods

The slave descendants' use of traditional folk stories to position themselves in relation to a larger world provides an important link between them and other Amazonian storytellers. Like various Amazonian native groups and rubber tappers, the *remanescentes* seek to garner allies in the fight to retain control over their lands.[52] In this sense, they are very unlike the miners, who redeploy others' negative images of themselves in ways intended to scare off potential competition.

The changes the *remanescentes* introduce into their accounts in an effort to influence outsiders may show up in the stories they tell each other. Although they are relatively skilled at switching from one vocabulary to another (which leads their enemies to call them "two tongued"), the two parts of their lives are impossible to separate completely. As a result, even as they attempt to turn outsiders' language toward their own purposes, they cannot help but become partially caught up in borrowed words.[53]

Accounts of the time of the candles offer an excellent example of ongoing changes in the accounts of slave descendants. Because the parents and grandparents of today's *remanescentes* often found the history of slavery too painful to discuss directly, their children's impressions of the past are often largely visceral.[54] Now almost a hundred years old,

Manuel Pedro's great-grandfather still thinks back upon the elderly Dona Julita, whose shriveled right hand served as a flesh-and-blood reminder of a legacy of pain. ("To see her was to smell scorched flesh," he says with a sigh.) Another old man recalls the elderly neighbor with a pierced ankle through which the then-teenager's owner had passed a heavy chain. ("I was only six or seven, but I still remember how it never healed right—I didn't want to look and yet I couldn't take my eyes off it," he says.)

The memories of their parents' terror of outsiders confirm the past's hold upon a community that today actively confronts its enemies with this past as both justification and ammunition.[55] Dona Amélia recalls how her father began to sweat and tremble when the news arrived that a group of soldiers was on its way to recruit the *remanescentes* for "a great war." "He and the other adults were so afraid that they immediately killed all of the animals so that their barking and cackling would not betray us. They stuffed the babies' mouths with rags so that they could not cry and then we set out for the woods. We hid there for almost a week in a steady rain. But I still remember how my father—who was black as the bird you see on that log there—turned white as a sheet."

These powerful recollections contrast with present-day accounts of the time of the candles, which even ten-year-olds recite. More than simply evoking a past in which Mother Waterfall enveloped fugitives with mist in the face of the pursuing soldiers, these often detailed descriptions create sympathy for the *remanescentes* among outsiders by prompting revulsion at the harsh treatment of their ancestors. Not necessarily true in literal terms, accounts of how the slaves' masters forced them to take a daily "bath of lashes" nonetheless bring home the larger truth of an injustice that extends into the present. The oppressive treatment of her forebears is less important for one of Dona Amélia's grown nieces, still known to everyone as "Nené" (Baby), than is the menace of what she labels "a new slavery." Although Nené's voice remains calm throughout the story, the pace at which she jabs a needle through the torn mosquito net that she is mending quickens as she proceeds.

In those old days, the owners wore gold crowns and the slaves had nothing. They didn't have so much as a straw hat to protect them from the sun. Every day that the blacks returned from work, exhausted, they would take two baths. The first was called a bath of lashes with a stick studded with bits of broken glass. After this bath, which was a whipping, that left his body full of cuts and gashes, he'd take another bath with salt water so that their wounds would not become inflamed. Only afterward would they get to eat. And so,

of course, they fled. Mother Waterfall enchanted the slaves so that the soldiers could not follow them. And they began a new life there, above the
crashing waters of the falls, where the only sort of baths they took were river
baths. So then, that time is over, but today, there are the beginnings of a new
slavery. This IBAMA takes everything away from the poor man—his boat,
his fishnet, the fish with which he aims to feed his children, sometimes his
very life.[56]

While storytellers such as Nené stress the continuities within the *remanescentes'* history, others focus on the differences between a bitter
present and a hard but happier past.[57] Thus, Mundico's mother—a
small, spry woman who shades herself from the sun with an umbrella
emblazoned with a likeness of Marilyn Monroe—finds the dangers of
the present to be more pressing than those that her ancestors faced.

> At least in the old days, the slave descendants could take refuge in the forest.
> We lived with nature, we had peace and plenty. And when outsiders came to
> bother us, the adults could run into the forest while we children would curl
> up in one of those big outdoor ovens made of clay or in the hollow of a tree.
> Once, in fact, I fell asleep inside an oven, and my mother nearly tore the place
> apart looking for me once the coast was clear. But today, there are airplanes,
> and so, there is no place for anyone to hide. So then, we *remanescentes* still
> live with nature, but nature can no longer protect us like it did when I was
> young.[58]

The strategic sweetening of the past is particularly common in descriptions of the Brazil-nut trade. While some *remanescentes* have bitter
memories of how members of the local elite bought title to the lands
where their forebears had gathered nuts for centuries, others see this
time as happier and more healthful.

"Look, there is no harder work than having to carry fifty, sixty boxes
of Brazil nuts a good five miles in the hot sun or the pouring rain," says
one of Mundico's uncles, a bony man with very white hair who is weed-
ing the tomato seedlings in a beached canoe full of earth that now serves
as a planter. "We were slaves of the whites. Because the nuts were ours,
because it was we who gathered them, but the white man bought them
for the price of his own choosing. Not only did what we earned fail to
cover a tenth of the sweat we wasted, but sometimes, the black would
actually end up owing money to the whites!"

In contrast, one of Benedita's friends, a young woman with bright
black eyes who works as a grade-school teacher, speaks of a time in
which whole families set up camp in the forest. Her description of how
the adults sang as they gathered nuts and the children played hide-and-

seek and feasted on wild berries makes this era sound almost like a
group summer vacation. ("People liked to sleep beneath a sheet of stars
there deep within the woods," she says as she scrapes a layer of mud off
a well-worn rubber sandal.)

Asked about the problems that the older man described in bitter detail, Benedita's friend acknowledges their existence but argues that they
pale before those of today. It is meaningful to note that the man told his
story to a group of neighbors among whom I was seated, whereas the
woman addressed the video camera later that same afternoon. When I
ask Manuel Pedro whose version is correct, he shrugs. "Maybe both are
right," he says. "Well then, who do you think is righter?" I persist, but
he only laughs.

The re-creation of the past with an eye to present-day objectives is
equally apparent in assessments of the first *remanescentes'* relations
with the Indians whom they encountered in their flight into the woods.[59]
Accounts in which the natives appear as one more dangerous obstacle
confronting the fugitives alternate with others that depict the two as
natural allies united by persecution as well as by a common quest to live
in liberty.[60] The first speaker here is Dona Amélia's middle-age neighbor
Dona Lia, whose words are punctuated by the sizzle of the fish she is
frying. The second is Benedita, who sits next to me on a stump beside a
steel-colored river a few days later in the community of Bacabal as we
wait for the film crew to return from a shoot. When I ask if it is true that
the Indians treated her forebears badly, Dona Lia nods her head.

> We have always been a persecuted people; our ancestors had to confront
> many things—hunger, fear, the ache of solitude. We were sold in the mar-
> ketplace just as if we were a sack of lemons—so much for a woman, so much
> for a man. So then, our ancestors fled and they arrived here and there were
> only Indians—treacherous, cruel, and crafty as wild beasts. But our ances-
> tors confronted them too, just as we today confront the IBAMA that takes
> the land to which we have no title, and yet, every right.[61]

> They are our brothers, the Indians; they always were. Because they helped
> our ancestors a great deal, they taught them many things. Both peoples knew
> how to respect nature, both simply wanted liberty to live within the virgin
> forest. And so, the Indians helped us as, today, we seek to help them and
> everyone who struggles to save the *floresta* from its enemies.

Different *remanescente* communities almost certainly interacted differently with the various Amerindian groups with whom they came in

contact at diverse points in time. (The Kaxúyana and the Tiriyó, for instance, are particularly likely to appear in historical sources as the *remanescentes'* allies.) Dona Lia's and Benedita's accounts are ultimately less about things that happened than they are about the future that they seek to shape. That both sets of "forest peoples" face serious threats to their survival leads Benedita to take issue with Dona Lia's negative description of the natives even while she reiterates her emphasis on past sufferings.

The idea of the first slaves as charter members of an alliance based on an intimate understanding of and respect for nature goes hand in hand with a vision of them and their descendants as long-standing protectors of Mother Waterfall. Thus, Rosa Acevedo and Edna Castro, authors of the most detailed study to date of the Trombetas *remanescentes,* speak of the "continuous ties of complicity" between nature and these "Guardians of the Forest and Rivers." [62] This shift from children of a mighty river to respectful overseers of a besieged and newly needy nature does not seem in any way illogical to a number of the slave descendants. "Well, the son grows up and takes care of his old father, right?" says one man as we watch the rain clouds swell over the river above the community of Tapagem on a dark summer afternoon. "And so, the moment has come for us to take care of our mother, who is nature." All the same, this new role of protector—a response to changes in the political as much as the physical landscape—demands considerable adjustment on the part of a people accustomed to the notion of an all-powerful Mother Waterfall.

The movement from needy children to stalwart, environmentally sensitive guardians is particularly evident in stories of Domingos Xavier, the *remanescente* said to speak the turtles' language. While some storytellers reiterate the old man's role as longtime confidant of these creatures, who warn the slave descendants of impending danger, others convert him into the turtles' human leader. In the first of the next two stories, the turtles let Xavier know when danger is imminent. In the second, Xavier, no longer a mere conduit between the turtles and the humans who have long depended on them, sounds the alarm himself. Likewise, while the turtles let him know when the coast is clear in the first version of the story, it is he who bids them to reappear in the second. Although the storyteller in both cases is the same person, a heavyset man named Chicão (Big Frankie), one of Zé Cândido's relatives by marriage, the stories come from recordings made on my two separate trips. In the

first, Chicão speaks to Zé and various other community members seated
with me on a log outside his door. In the second, he speaks directly to
the video crew.

> Domingos Xavier had the trust of the Encantados. As a result, the turtles al-
> ways gave him information in his dreams, they always told him what was
> about to happen. And so, when these officials were about to arrive, they told
> the *remanescentes* that they should go hide in the woods. After the coast was
> clear, he dreamed again of the turtles. And they told him to fill a turtle shell
> with herbs. It was for him to send up that wisp of smoke there on the beach,
> and they would return.

> So, Domingos Xavier knew very well that the officials were going to arrive,
> and he told the turtles to hide. And when he saw that there was no longer any
> danger, he sent up a wisp of white smoke so that the turtles would appear
> again on the sandbank where they lay their eggs. Because he was their second
> captain, you see? He had the trust of the Encantados. He would fill a turtle
> shell with herbs. Then, he would send up that white smoke there on the beach
> and they would begin arriving. It's in this way that the *remanescente* always
> knew how to protect nature, to protect our forest, the plants and animals. Be-
> cause if it hadn't been Domingos Xavier who took care of the turtles, those
> officials wouldn't have left a single one here, of that you can be sure.[63]

Chicão's stress on the mysterious links between the human and nonhuman world in his first version of the story contrasts with his emphasis on the slave descendants' commitment to the defense of the forest in
the second. Although he uses the word *mata,* not *floresta,* in both cases,
the vulnerable nature that he evokes in the second evokes the Rain Forest that has become an international concern.

As Benedita made clear, one important difference between a *mata*
and a *floresta* lies in the speaker's intended public. Beyond that, however, a *mata* tends to be a forest full of landmarks readily familiar to the
community. Much like its English equivalent (the bush), the *mata* can be
an unknown and frightening territory. However, the word alternatively
may suggest a series of familiar, largely unsensational surroundings that
inspire a host of personal and collective memories.[64] It is in the *mata*
where one finds "that lake full of piranhas" or the three tall mango trees
behind which lie a thick stand of Brazil-nut trees. It is also the *mata*
where José's or Ana's or Inácio's mother buried her newborn child's um-
bilical cord.[65] In contrast, it is the *floresta* that one fights to save from
the destruction unleashed by multinational enterprises, the *floresta* that
the *remanescentes'* lawyers invoke when they go to court seeking to gain
them legal title to their land.

The passage from *mata* to *floresta,* and the ongoing tension between the two, implies far more than a shift in vocabulary. It may mark a new attitude not just toward an outside public that cares about the Amazon's rich flora and fauna, but also toward the natural world in whose midst the *remanescentes* live. Evident in testimony aimed at an international public, transformations in the portrayal of the human relationship to nature are equally obvious in the stories of enchanted beings and enchanted places that people continue to tell one another. In various cases, for instance, the tale of Higino's Lake—once an affirmation of nature's mystery—becomes a saga of destruction.

Higino's willingness to serve as intermediary allows all of the *remanescentes* to share in the lake's bounty, but his death places its wealth out of reach. By no coincidence, the old man's demise is often concurrent with the establishment of Porto Trombetas in these stories. Higino actually foretells the impending catastrophe in extensive detail in some accounts. Today, the environmental devastation associated with the giant mining ventures dooms new searches for the lake. And yet, despite the gravity of the events that Zé Cândido describes in the following story, his account is less a lament than a protest, which he peppers with a deep, contagious laugh.

> My cousin and I went in search of that lake, back in '82. We blazed a trail some three miles long behind the mountains, till we got to a big gorge, a kind of waterfall, and we almost reached there. Almost. We could actually see the deep blue stain of the water in the distance just beyond the hills. Today, no, no one ever gets that close. Because the mud of the refinery kills all the fish in the river, the dust of the refinery kills all the game and all the trees. There was a time in which there was so much dust that you couldn't see the green of the leaves, there was only the red of the dust, that very bright, bloodred, everywhere you looked. And the boat would drag itself through the mud as if it were a caiman. So, no one ever gets to that big gorge before the lake now. Not even Higino, if he were alive, would be able to find the path.[66]

Some *remanescentes* are not content to recast time-honored stories. Concerned that the golden church and the enchanted lake may serve as escapist fantasies, they may reject these "old tales" out of hand. "Why do you ask about these things?" Benedita demanded in a sharp tone when I once asked Dona Amélia if she had known an old man named Higino. "I think it's much better to talk about Atanásio and how he struggled against the whites. It's a story that has a lot to teach us, a story for today, and so unlike these old tales that are too often full of lies."

Although her question was directed at me, it was Dona Amélia who responded. "Oh, Benedita, all I know about this Atanásio are the things you've told us," she said with a puzzled frown. "They are very interesting, but my father used to talk about how his own father used to go to visit this Higino, and so, even though I myself never met him, I know how to tell the story. And that lake, look here, it is a thing of nature. And nature is no lie."

Benedita shrugged and dropped the subject, but Dona Amélia's words clearly had not changed her mind. For her, as for a number of other young *remanescentes,* the Encante has become not just a fantastic story, but a potential obstacle to the political awareness crucial to the community's continuing survival in a time of rapid change. "These sorts of tales may be very pretty, but, in the end, they are just dreams that keep people from fighting for their rights," she later told me coldly. "You yourself, an educated person, can't really believe that there is such a thing as a lake within a lake!"

Stung by the anger of someone whose resolve I admired and whose company had come to take the chill off foggy mornings, it was hard for me to explain that yes, I did believe. Or, more precisely, to the extent that the enchanted lake gave people a way of talking about a nature that resisted domination and filled them with a sense of their own ties to their surroundings, it struck me as a far more vivid protest against oppression than the more direct statements I had heard time and again.

I also couldn't find the words to say that I did not consider the stories of Atanásio and Higino to be mutually exclusive. Like accounts of the first slaves' heroic resistance, their descendants' continuing dreams of abundance struck me as affirmations of a fierce will to survive. Moreover, while tales of Higino were less direct than the catalogues of all-too-real injustices that Benedita regularly offered, I saw both as eloquent expressions of the *remanescentes'* anger at "false" biological reserves. It was because these "lies" made real to me the truth of a people's creativity and courage that that I had asked about Higino and could not forget the story of the lake. However, when I tried to convey this, my words sounded dry and academic. "I have no idea of what you're saying," Benedita declared before rolling over in her hammock, leaving me to stare into a starless night.

Later, when I found the courage to talk to Manuel Pedro about the two exchanges, he brushed off Benedita's words. "It's that she's worried about how we *remanescentes* are going to look in the eyes of outsiders," he said, offering me a cigarette he knew I would not smoke.[67] "If we look ignorant and superstitious, no one will take us seriously in the fight to keep our lands. Everybody knows these stories—Benedita herself could probably tell you that story of the lake. But she is worried that you and your friends will turn out to be one more group of whites who use us to make a pile of money while we just look ridiculous to people back there in your world." [68]

His explanation made me feel worse instead of better.

In the face of history, Benedita had every right to be afraid. Why, when I knew the story of the slaves, and of whites' often cruel and deceitful treatment of them, had I expected a few moments of friendly conversation to erase whole centuries of distrust? How, after well over twenty years of fieldwork among Brazilians, could I have failed to anticipate how Benedita might react?

"And what do you think about Higino's Lake?" I finally asked in a small voice. Manuel Pedro waved one hand noncommittally and laughed. "Me, I don't think anything," he declared with a long puff on the cigarette.

A heron streaked across a sky the same color as the river as I slumped a little lower in my deck chair. "I don't think anything," Manuel Pedro said again as we both watched the heron stage a second swoop. "Now then, my mother says that Higino's Lake is the true biological reserve, unlike all of the false reserves invented by these people who want to rob us of our lands. She says that all the turtles are going there now, that there you'll find more animals than exist in the whole forest, more species than there ever were in all of Noah's Ark. Higino's Lake, she says, was always intended for the Children of the River. But today, it is the legacy of all those who are against destruction and against these false reserves. She says that she holds this lake close inside her, like a hope, like a promise, like a mirror of something that, perhaps, never existed and yet, one day could be."

"That's a wonderful story," I said.

"Yes it is," said Manuel Pedro. "But the story of Atanásio is very good as well."

"Do you say 'mata' or 'floresta' when you want to talk about the place you live?" I asked abruptly. "Or does it all depend on the person with whom you're talking at the time?"

"Ah," said Manuel Pedro. "Sometimes it's 'mata.' And sometimes it's 'floresta.' But, you know, I don't think all that much about the person with whom I am talking. Mostly, I think about what it is that I want to say."

8

Beyond Eden

Truly, the Amazon is the last, as yet unfinished page
of Genesis.

Euclides da Cunha, A Lost Paradise

My mother says that Higino's Lake is something
that she holds close inside her, like a hope, like a
promise, like a mirror of something that, perhaps,
never existed, and yet, one day could be.

Manuel Pedro, age twenty-six, Lago de Abuí, 1995

In its marvelous diversity, its threatened abundance, and its significance
to all of humanity, the lake that Manuel Pedro's mother holds up as a
mirror of the future presents a striking contrast to the Rain Forest
packed with marvelous flora and fauna that dominates present-day descriptions of the Amazon by outsiders. Even while Higino's Lake blurs
fixed distinctions between the earth and water by serving as a refuge to
both land and river creatures, accounts of it underscore the centrality of
aquatic imagery in many of the stories told by contemporary Amazonians. In doing so, the lake underscores the identity of these stories as visions of the world that intertwine with our own visions, thereby allow-

ing us to see beyond a long legacy of environmental giganticism and to approach not just rain forests, but all of nature, with new eyes.

The ultimate shape-shifter, water is not just a physical presence — something that acts on people and that people, in turn, actively transform. It is also a symbol of resistance to fixed definitions and hierarchies in which Amazonians have regularly found themselves at the bottom. In this sense, the tale of the enchanted lake, which provides a shelter to the hunted and shares its bounty only with human beings of its own choosing, is less different from accounts of the rebel leader Atanásio than initially might appear.

There are obvious material reasons why water, in its ever-changing relationship to the land, should play an essential role in a number of these narratives. Rivers have long been the lifeline of this "land of waters."[1] It is they that continue to connect far-flung human settlements hemmed in by an often fear-inspiring forest, they that renew the rich soils of the riverbanks through yearly flooding, and they that partially define human movement by creating islands or summarily carting off whole chunks of land.[2] While humans have regularly modified watercourses, they cannot actually create the rivers, creeks, and lakes that provide water for drinking, washing, and cooking, and which offer up the fish that have long served as most Amazonians' primary source of protein. Though roads have opened up the Amazon interior in the last three decades, even people who depend on them to get from one place to another still need a steady source of water for their crops and cattle. City dwellers need water too. Were it not for the huge new dams such as Samuel and Tucuruí, which provide them with light and power, the big cities of the Amazon would grind to a halt.

There are equally concrete reasons why land should regularly overshadow water in the minds of many outsiders. The first explorers pushed their way into the Amazon in search of particular terrestrial commodities — gold, cinnamon, and that wealth of other regional products known collectively as *drogas do sertão*. While the eighteenth- and nineteenth-century naturalists depended upon rivers to get them from one field site to another, Alexander von Humboldt's name for the Amazon, "Hylaea," comes from the Greek root for *forest,* not for *river.*[3] His successors' passion for cataloguing found a focus in terrestrial species, as Bates' much-loved beetles in *Naturalist on the River Amazons* attest. Calculations of biodiversity also concentrate heavily on terrestrial flora and fauna (for example, "3.5 million ants in a single acre of Amazonian rain forest").[4] Finally, large-scale deforestation has refocused international attention on a place where the effects of environmental destruction are often more immediately visible on the land (burnt earth, severed tree trunks) than they are on the equally affected rivers.

Despite these ready explanations, outsiders' tendency to concentrate on the land, even while paying lip service to the water (the Amazon as source of 20 percent of the world's freshwater, etc.) has more than a purely material basis.[5] It is also the fruit of a particular Judeo-Christian narrative tradition that begins with the tale of an earthly Eden. Even though four diverging rivers flow through this terrestrial paradise, it remains a plot of solid earth.

The Amazon, I have argued, has long tended to strike outsiders as a series of shifting El Dorados—rich, if elusive, realms of nature that invite transformation. However, even while the golden city's manifold uses set it apart from a Garden of Delights, where one is content to simply tarry, it too can be seen as an heir to and variant on the biblical Eden. The idea of conquest at the heart of giant-making is as old as the injunction of God in Genesis that humans assume dominion "over the fish of the sea, and over the fowl of the air, and over the cattle, and over all the earth, and over every creeping thing that creepeth upon the earth." To the extent that El Dorado invites control over its marvels—be it in the form of exploitation or preservation—it is a special, postmedieval kind of terrestrial paradise.

Water defies domination even as human beings help shape its flow.[6] Man may claim dominion over the fish of the sea, but not over the sea itself. ("The fish that someone catches belongs to that person," says Dona Amélia. "But these newcomers who rush in here claiming that the lake is theirs—they make me cry with anger, but most of all, they make me laugh.") Every schoolchild knows that rains and rivers transform rock as much through slow erosion as through the violence of cataracts or floods. If the roots that reach deep into the earth make Amazonia's forests easy to insert into a vision of a Second Eden, the Encante, for its part, remains the original chaos, the world before it has been baptized or even definitively molded by a divine hand. The Encante is the stone that dances, the patch of moss that suddenly dissolves into a puddle, the bird that chats with the turtle, the gold that appears and disappears.[7] It is also a nature that, like both Gold and Mother Waterfall, responds to human beings' treatment of one another and of plants and animals.

Even when Amazonian storytellers express doubts about the truth of a particular occurrence, their narratives remain an affirmation of the precarious and shifting balance between earth and water in a land where, as Benedita says, "the river is our backyard and the trees our second roof." [8] Not just a place, Higino's Lake is also that time when, as Dona Amélia suggests, "nature still spoke to human beings and they spoke back to nature." [9] Though some *remanescentes* relegate it to a vanished past, others insist on the lake's continuing presence in their lives. "It's that we no longer know how to arrive there," Manuel Pedro's mother says. "Higino knew how to open the gate, but we no longer know. Now then, this gate is not a fence, a door that opens and closes with a key and padlock—it is those magic words which would transport a person to the lake. Today, we have forgotten how to get there, but one can still make out the curving lines of its white waters within the darker waters of that other lake. One can still catch a glimpse of that island ringed with white sand beaches, and in whose center rise the palm trees on which gypsy-birds and parrots perch."

Water is also, once again, a fluid arm in many Amazonians' struggle to assert their own identity. "No one knows these waters like we Children of the River," Benedita tells me as we shiver in the morning mist. "Someone who isn't from here can spend a week going round in circles looking for the entrance to the lake any twelve-year-old could find. We say 'Mother Waterfall' because the land is ours, but we ourselves belong to the waters that helped us escape from slavery and that give us the courage to fight on against those who would make us slaves once more."

Visions of the Amazon

Earth and water, giants and shape-shifters, El Dorados and Encantes— the swirl of these images and stories provides the foundation for more effective action in regard to the preservation of the peoples, plants, and animals of the Amazon. Important in part because of what remains dissimilar among them, the portrayals that collide and intertwine throughout the preceding pages draw attention to disparities in lived experience. They also underscore social and economic inequalities that can never be fully bridged. Even so, they pave the way for an understanding of the Amazon that goes beyond the glittering realm of nature at the heart of both the sixteenth-century El Dorado and the twentieth-century IMAX movie. These varied portrayals make us question the Rain Forest of a hundred TV documentaries and the tradition of giganticism to which they point. They help us to find the courage—perhaps the audacity—to look at the Amazon as if, almost five hundred years after Orellana's voyage, we were discovering it for the first time.

The portrayals we have seen have practical implications. Gold miners emphasize the violence that they hope will keep out powerful intruders. The McDonald's Corporation depicts a fragile woodland that it claims to protect. Conservation biologists speak grimly of a dying paradise in order to rally support for the botanical equivalent of gated communities. The descendants of runaway black slaves talk about the *floresta,* rather than the *mata,* in order to attract allies who can help finance the battle for legal title to their land. The designers of the Simoniz ad use an "Amazonian Indian" to suggest that the buyers of their car wax are helping the environment even as they zoom down a highway steeped in smog. The producers of the IMAX movie choose spectacular scenes that will make viewers pay to be transported to a realm of nature very different from the one just outside the theater door.

At the same time that these portrayals serve specific interests, they influence popular perceptions, individual actions, and official policies. If I think that the Amazon is a jungle full of violent people and dread diseases, I am far less likely to slip a nickel into a Rainforest Meter than I am to invest in chain saws and tractors. If you see the Amazon as a place in which people have always coexisted with plants and animals, you may give money to community conservation projects. If your good friend Sam sees humans as intruders, he is far more likely to help underwrite a "wilderness reserve." Likewise, if the members of the Brazilian congress decide that gold miners' ambivalence about nature might have positive consequences, they may use monies previously destined for bombing clandestine airstrips to fund educational campaigns. If lawmakers from Lima or São Paulo or Hoboken equate the Amazon with wild nature, they are unlikely to vote for a program focused on the cities whose fate is inseparable from that of Amazonia's forests.

Seemingly offhand narratives often turn out to be portrayals of the Amazon which convey deeply rooted ideas and beliefs. The fact that tales of enchanted cities are, for many people, "only stories" means that they may use them as springboards to address much broader questions in a largely unselfconscious way. If one were to ask Angela Maria to elaborate on her vision of the human place in nature, she would probably laugh uncomfortably. "How could I even begin to answer that?" she might demand. And yet, the stories that she tells about the mysterious Woman in White have everything to do with the interface between gold mines and a living, breathing Gold. Likewise, the obviously humorous quality of the Simoniz ad or the frankly fictive villains of an adventure movie such as *Anaconda* do not negate the serious nature of the concerns on which they play.[10] Indeed, these portrayals are effective precisely because of their success in addressing indirectly the possibility of sustainable development (Simoniz) and outsiders' fearful fascination with tropical chaos *(Anaconda).*

The differing portrayals of the Amazon also allow—indeed, force—the recognition of divergences and points of contact *within* the sprawling categories that I have labeled "outsiders" and "insiders." The differences between Raimundo's and Davi's attitudes toward the Encantado and Cobra Norato stories, for example, say much about the changes that the Amazon is presently undergoing. They also confirm that transformation does not always mean a simple rejection of the past.

The dissimilarities in Bates' vision of a "glorious new civilization under the Equator" and Lévi-Strauss' *Tristes tropiques* underscore crucial differences in historical perspective. So do the gaps between descriptions of the Amazon as a Warrior Woman and the forest as a bejeweled paradise. At the same time, unsettling similarities between El Dorado and today's Rain Forest draw attention to a continuing narrative legacy whose resilience is as important as the changes it regularly undergoes. While many people today would be quick to condemn the explorers' rapacious search for a golden kingdom, present-day injunctions to protect a "rich genetic storehouse" often mask a similar desire to wrest an ostensibly mismanaged treasure from Amazonians. Conservationists might argue that the explorers acted out of greed, whereas they seek only the good of humanity, but most Amazonians would find the distinction unconvincing. "Both want what belongs to us," Davi says with a shrug.

Comparable departures *between* "insiders" and "outsiders" are equally, if not more, important. The "pink" dolphin that has become a standard feature of TV documentaries bears scant resemblance to the *red* dolphin *(boto vermelho)* who regularly affirms nature's power over humans in the Encantado tales.[11] There are things about Angela Maria's Woman in White that her most painstaking explanations will never make entirely clear to me. She, in turn, shakes her head at the appeal of the McDonald's flyers.

However, at the same time that differences between "inside" and "outside" portrayals can jolt us out of thinking that our view of nature is either right or natural, points of contact between the two are equally illuminating. Gold miners' strategic appropriations of newspaper accounts of themselves as villains underscore their connections to a world far beyond the muddy trenches where they drill for gold. Benedita's rejection of Higino's Lake as the sort of superstition that could hurt *remanescentes'* standing with middle-class outsiders confirms this "traditional community's" ties to a larger world. As a descendant of an El Dorado that is both European import and New World story, "our" Rain Forest contains deep within it native viewpoints that have helped to shape our understandings of the Amazon even as they hint at a long history of exploitation.

The sorts of portrayals that appear in the preceding pages demand that we look beyond present-day visions of the Amazon as a pan-human biological legacy (the Rain Forest as a Global Commons), which outsiders have been quick to treat as their own property.[12] They encourage us to see the region not just as a singularly valuable collection of flora and fauna, but also as a common symbolic heritage that we share with Amazonians. In relation to this heritage, both we and they are simultaneously borrowers and lenders. Much as Tô Pereira passes on my version of Padre Simón's retelling of early native stories about El Dorado to Lucinha, who will almost certainly share what she has heard with Davi and Gerineldo, so I have passed on this story of a story to the reader, who is now also a conscious part of a living chain.

An awareness of this give-and-take can help bring into focus the real people on whose daily lives real policies impinge. To the degree that they do or don't fit stereotypes that serve particular political and economic interests, the people of the Amazon—Tô Pereira, Angela Maria, Manuel Pedro, Benedita—are regularly ignored or disdained. In providing concrete examples of the ways in which their tellers echo, challenge, and transform our own accounts of Amazonia, the stories make it harder to turn one's back on Benedita, harder not to look Tô Pereira in the eye. This, above all, is why they are important. This, above all, is why they are memorable and precious.

The living chain of which I speak is no harmonious circle that confirms the simple dictum that "variety is good." The tangled strands we have examined are part of an often bitter exchange between unequals— Padre Simón and his Indian informants, gold miners and reporters for the *Wall Street Journal,* Benedita and the bauxite companies—in which some people win and other people lose. And yet, if the consequences of these encounters have often been unhappy, the fact that our destinies have long been intermingled is also cause for hope. If we can see our own part within an Amazon that holds yet more surprises than that marvelous forest of the IMAX movie, we can see its problems, as well as its wonders, in new and unexpected ways.

Benedita is not just playing with words when she distinguishes between the *mata* and the *floresta*. She knows all too well that her small daughter's claim on the "wild" cacao trees that her own grandfather planted will depend in part upon the *remanescentes'* ability to engage a distant world. The fact that violence is a rhetorical device in gold miners' stories does not mean that there is not real violence in their lives—that which they perpetrate on local populations, and that which they themselves experience as members of the Brazilian (and Colombian and Peruvian) poor.

A critic might object that we have no time to worry about images and stories if we want to save the Amazon's rain forests from destruction. But these same images and stories are nothing less than a debate about people's place within nature and nature's place within our own and others' hearts and heads. Nothing could be more essential for the future of Amazonia. Nothing matters more in the Amazon today.

Giants, Shape-Shifters, and "the Last, as Yet Unfinished Page of Genesis"

The logical consequences of accounts of giants and shape-shifters as they translate into differing attitudes and distinct programs of action are nowhere clearer than in the writings of the early-twentieth-century essayist Euclides da Cunha. One of Brazil's greatest writers of any epoch, Euclides (Brazilians use only his first name) is the author of a series of remarkable essays about the Amazon.[13] A member of a southern elite far more apt to travel to Paris than to Pará, he was at once an "insider" and an "outsider."[14] From that position, he consciously made use of contradictions to construct two at first competing but ultimately intertwining visions that today suggest two quite different lines of policy. His description of the Amazon as "the last, as yet unfinished page of Genesis" echoes the Edens of my title. The unexpected ties between him and contemporary Amazonian storytellers underscore the sorts of entanglements that have appeared throughout these pages.

The first, giganticizing strand in Euclides' essays found expression in images of a "barbarous land" whose sheer size repelled attempts at civilization. The logical extension of this vision was the sort of forcible incorporation of a long-marginal Amazon into a modernizing nation, evident in the official colonization schemes of the 1960s and 1970s. The second, shape-shifting strand encouraged a vision of an Amazon that moved in from the margins to become the creative center of a defiantly autonomous Brazil. This vision's logical extension was a collaboration—as yet unrealized—between human beings and nature in a nation that would stop emulating foreign models in order to explore the riches that lay within. In this vision, the Amazon emerged not only as a realm of nature, but as a human creation in which social and economic forces exercised a power as formidable as that of a raging river or a blazing sun.

Born in Brazil's rapidly industrializing south, Euclides was a military engineer who soon found his temperament unsuited to a career in the army. It was therefore in the role of journalist that he accompanied the military forces that mounted four separate expeditions against a messianic community in Brazil's vast, dry northeastern backlands during 1896–97. In 1902, he published *Os sertões,* or Rebellion in the Backlands, a sweeping, justly famous book that forced educated Brazilians to confront the meaning of the terms *civilization* and *barbarism* in the republic that had replaced the monarchy in 1889.[15] Two years later, at the age of thirty-eight, he set out for the first time for Amazonia as the head of a national delegation to a joint Peruvian-Brazilian commission. Charged with delineating the boundaries of the rubber-rich Purus River region, an area claimed by Peru, Bolivia, and Brazil, the group spent some seven months in Amazonia preparing an official report.[16]

During this time, Euclides began to write a series of sketches of an Amazon whose "watery desert" provided a fitting complement to the "arid ocean" of the Brazilian northeast.[17] These essays were meant to provide the basis for a future book called *Um paraíso perdido,* or A Lost Paradise.[18] However, his death in 1909 during an armed confrontation with his wife's lover assured that the essays would remain forever incomplete.[19] Their unfinished quality gives added force and poignancy to his description of the Amazon as a work in progress.[20]

Euclides did not simply sum up different images and ways of thinking about Amazonia. Unlike the "jungle novelists" of the period, who made considerable efforts to conceal their own contradictions, he reveled in entanglements. His own repeated insistence on contrasts and paradoxes makes opposing readings of his essays not just possible, but obligatory.[21] While some authors might have said one thing when they really meant another, the Amazon appears to have inspired genuinely conflicting feelings in Euclides. These feelings found expression in descriptions of an "opulent disorder" that was at once a giant and a shape-shifter.[22]

Euclides' dazzling double vision continues to hold out hope for ourselves, as well as for Amazonians. The point is not that Euclides—who was both a member of an official mission and a "son of the land" who remained "passionately in love with her"—came to view the Amazon the "right" way, or that metamorphosis is inherently superior to giant-making. Rather, it is that one can transcend—albeit imperfectly and momentarily—one's own assumptions about nature, one's own historical circumstances, and one's own social class. If Euclides, largely despite himself, could come to recognize an alien Amazonia's shape-shifting features, then we too—you, me, Suzanna, red-haired Danny—can see beyond the gigantic images of the Rain Forest that inspire but also blind.

At first glance, Euclides' Amazon looks very much like one more El Dorado. Immensely rich, this "very vast Canaan" was a "millenarian storehouse" overflowing with valuable commodities, including the rubber that, by 1900, had become Brazil's second most important export. The land, rather than the river, dominated this first, unapologetically gigantic vision. Its sheer immensity elicited lists of numbers that anticipated the self-consciously quantitative language of *Amazonia without Myths*. ("No less than fifty million hectares worth no less than a half billion Peruvian pesos," Euclides wrote in one description of a long expanse of rubber trees.)[23]

This area was also brimming with another sort of potential. As "the newest land upon the planet," a "portentously virgin" Amazon exhibited a "surprising, very precious, disjointed" physiography that made it a fitting stage for the great human adventure that Euclides saw as then unfolding. ("It is along [the river's] boundless bed that one of the most daring lines of our historical expansion is being traced out today," he wrote.)[24] Breathtaking descriptions of a "Paleozoic" universe that instilled the "torturous sensation of a retreat to the most remote of eras" thus provided the backdrop for a tale of heroic conquest.[25] Here, it was the "Titanic caboclos" who emerged as the front guard of Western civilization. In a manner that sometimes foreshadowed the work of Brazilian photographer Sebastião Salgado, Euclides saw human beings as inextricably caught up in the drama of a land that itself exuded a strange humanity.

When Euclides called the Amazon "a land without history," he—like many others before him—was defining "history" as only that which was relevant to European civilization. Convinced that civilization itself required the transformation of *terras* (lands) into *territórios* (administrative jurisdictions), he made relatively little mention of the native pop-

ulations that had made their home within the Amazon for millennia.[26]
Instead, he celebrated the rubber tappers, who had come from other
parts of Brazil and Peru. It was these newcomers who were engaged in
the portentous task of "carving" themselves into a resistant earth. "In
the land without history, the first events inscribe themselves, few and
as yet scattered, in the names of places," he explained. Thanks to the
rubber tappers' heroic efforts, the traveler could literally read the landscape, in the form of wooden place markers suspended over rustic
houses. Names such as *God Help Us, Nostalgia, St. John of Miseries,
Hidden Away,* and *Inferno* shared an emerging map with other settlements, called *Triumph, New Enchantment, Liberty,* and—of course—
Paradise.[27]

 And yet, despite the enormous efforts of the men who had begun to
"tame" a land that resisted cultivation, the Amazon, like all El Dorados,
remained defiantly elusive. If the land's "unfettered amplitude" repelled
these newly arrived "nomads," so did the "tumultuous inconstancy" of
the river, which attacked its own creations. "Every six months," Euclides wrote, "each flood that passes is a wet sponge upon a badly made
sketch." This sponge "erases, modifies, or transforms the firmest and
most salient features" on this boundless canvas as if it were the wandering brush of a superhuman and eternally dissatisfied artist.[28]

 The stubbornly unfinished quality of this nature made it alien, even
ugly, to the gigantic eye. "Naturally, the land is sad and awkward, because it is new. It is still in the process of becoming," Euclides asserted.[29]
Immense beyond conception, Amazonia's expanses ran together in a
way that robbed space of its normal meaning and blotted out time itself.
As travelers moved up the great river, they found themselves confronting
"the strange immobility of landscapes of a single color, of a single
height, and of a single form" that instilled in them the "anguished sensation of a sudden hiatus" within the ebb and flow of daily life.[30] This
disturbing uniformity prompted a fervent longing for not just "one's native land, but of Earth, of the forms of nature traditionally linked to contemplation."[31] To the extent that it defied known categories and cos-
mographies, the Amazon was not just elusive, but subversive. Euclides'
distress at an earth that seemed to melt into the sky without even a token wisp of a horizon thus recalls Padre Simón's much earlier horror at
a world where the boundaries between earth, air, and water, which defined the Christian cosmos, blurred or disappeared.

 Worst of all, from Euclides' initial viewpoint, the land that rejected
civilization was ultimately a traitor to the nation. Not simply capricious,

this river that delighted in destroying human settlements and carting off whole islands summarily dumped Brazilian soil into an ocean that then washed up this earth on the Carolina shores. The Amazon that often became a symbol of Brazil in international quarters thus turned out to be "the least Brazilian of rivers." Fully complicit in this act of telluric treason, the land "abandons its inhabitants" and "goes in search of other latitudes."[32]

This rebellious nature demanded control and transformation. If the Brazilian government did not take concrete measures to adopt this enormous "stepchild" into the framework of the nation-family, Amazonia was bound to stray.[33] ("The Amazon, sooner or later, will detach itself from Brazil, naturally and irresistibly, as a planet becomes detached from a cloud—by the centrifugal expansion of its own movement," Euclides wrote.)[34] Going on to cite Humboldt's vision of the region as a dazzling stage "where, sooner or later, the world's civilization will become concentrated," he called on the new republic to forcibly secure the Amazon's place within Brazil.

The practical measures for which Euclides called were much like those that Theodore Roosevelt would outline less than a decade later in *Through the Brazilian Wilderness*. The central government must lay railroad tracks, foster further colonization, and install telegraph lines that will link the margin to the center in a "vibrant innervation of ideas." Only through these systematic measures of incorporation could the Amazon fulfill that "extraordinary destiny" in which modest, local networks of communication would reemerge as international highways primed to play their part in an alliance "of civilization and of peace."[35]

This integrative mission would require not just new technologies, but a new language. Euclides had embarked on his journey with his head full of descriptions by nineteenth-century European naturalists, including Bates. However, once he arrived in Amazonia, he found "the most exotic adjectives, the most appealing nouns, and the most brilliant verbs" to be wholly inadequate. Not only was this borrowed vocabulary incapable of delving beneath an opaque surface, it also could not express the Amazon's raw power.

Not surprisingly, given his epoch and his technical training, Euclides almost immediately encountered an antidote to imported lyricisms in the language of positivist science. Wracked by insomnia during one of his first nights on the river, he became immersed in a scientific monograph with which a foreign naturalist had presented him earlier that day.

When day finally dawned, he found that he could suddenly see beneath the surface of the water with his "newly liberated eyes." [36]

Not just powerful, the new idiom he discovered was also, in his view, universal. As a result, in practically the same breath that Euclides decried his countrymen's tendency to think "too much in French, in German, or even in Lusitanian Portuguese," he extolled science's ability to leapfrog national borders. "In the sciences," he affirmed, "thanks to their superior philosophical reflexes, establishing the universal solidarity and harmony of the human spirit, it is understandable that we humble ourselves before all external influences." [37] By embracing "a peculiar language carved out of the harshness of technical expressions," Brazilians supposedly could remain fervently nationalistic even while asserting their membership in "a global fellowship of knowledge." [38]

The essays' magnificently outmoded language (who today would speak of rubber tapping as "a grievous task" or an "eternal prison circuit in a prison without walls"?) marks them as the expression of another era.[39] However, many of the ideas underlying Euclides' "first" vision reappeared in the geopolitics that served as blueprint for the massive colonization and development efforts in the Brazilian Amazon during the 1960s and 1970s. Seen from that standpoint, his writings have a curiously familiar ring.

The term *geopolitics* had originated earlier in the century in Europe, where it owed much to theorists such as the geographer Friedrich Ratzel, who compared national states to biological organisms.[40] However, the Brazilian version was to find its immediate source in the writings of General Golbery do Couto e Silva. One of the primary architects of policy during the military dictatorship that ruled the country between 1964 and 1984, Golbery was the author of three books outlining the domestic policies that Brazil would have to follow in order to claim its rightful place as a world power.[41] That Golbery often seemed to be paraphrasing Euclides when he talked about the Amazon does not mean that he and his fellow generals drew their ideas directly from the Amazonian essays. Indeed, these ideas were in no way exclusive or original to Euclides. Rather, for Golbery, the sorts of gigantic notions that found memorable expression in Euclides possessed tremendous practical implications.

One of Golbery's primary claims about the Amazon was that it had remained virtually unpeopled. Euclides' image of the region as a blank slate on which heroic pioneers must write the destiny of an eager nation reappeared in the general's references to the Amazon as "a vast and un-populated island," as well as in official colonization campaigns that pre-sented the Amazon as a land without men for men without a land.[42] The tens of thousands of impoverished colonists whom the Brazilian gov-ernment shipped north to Amazonia in the 1970s were expected to pick up the baton that Euclides' Titans had dropped when the Rubber Boom collapsed. Their attempts to remake the Amazon initially prompted much the same sort of heroic rhetoric ("Victory in the Jungle!") that Eu-clides had lavished upon his "pioneers."

Euclides' idea that the government must make full use of new tech-nologies to secure a planetlike Amazon's place within a national con-stellation found expression in the concrete policies of the 1960s and 1970s: the major highways meant to open up a previously resistant in-terior, the tax incentives aimed at moving in new industry, the massive deforestation aimed at increasing cattle pasture, and the construction of enormous dams to provide power. All were signs that Brazil was taking an active role in realizing a practical and emotional manifest destiny.

Euclides' corollary notion that an Amazonia left to its own devices was likely to betray the nation (as did the river that carted off Brazilian soil) would find expression in later military policies aimed at cordoning off the region from both domestic and foreign agitators.[43] The discovery in 1973 of a small enclave of southern guerrillas who had taken refuge in the Araguaia River region confirmed the government's worst fears about Amazonia's treacherous nature. These fears prompted proposals for a Calha Norte (literally, Northern Trench)—a security moat around the Amazon designed to keep out foreign insurgents while controlling potential problems from within.[44] Today, these same anxieties underlie the sorts of expressions of mistrust of Amazonian Indians visible in the vitriolic denunciations of them as unpatriotic international pawns.

Finally, Euclides' idea that the Amazon had an "international des-tiny" that demanded expression through a "universal language" would resurface in a fervent faith in science and technology. At the same time that the proponents of geopolitics expressed intense misgivings about foreigners' designs on Amazonia, its leaders extolled an ostensibly neu-tral science's ability to lay bare the region's secrets. This enthusiasm for technological solutions as a way to identify and put to use the Amazon's great treasures would only grow stronger in the 1980s and the 1990s, when a vague, if much touted, "scientific research" geared toward illu-minating the mysteries (and the commercial applications) of biodiversity replaced the massive colonization and development schemes. ("SCIENCE IN THE JUNGLE: BIOLOGISTS PENETRATE THE FORESTS IN ORDER TO KNOW FIRSTHAND WHAT THEY INTEND TO PRESERVE" exclaims the headline of a special *Veja* supplement that celebrated scientific advances in the Amazon.)[45]

Although Golbery and the other generals who oversaw the opening of the Amazon during the 1960s and 1970s referred directly to Euclides on occasion, they were more apt to invoke his name than to actually quote him. Moreover, their paraphrases were selective. Thoroughly gigantic on the one hand, the Amazon of Euclides' essays was, on the other, a consummate shape-shifter. Although the essays portrayed the region as demanding forcible integration into the nation-center, they also revealed an Amazonia whose constant metamorphoses flouted fixed definitions. Golbery and company were careful to ignore this point. Even more important, the essays departed from other nineteenth- and early-twentieth-century "scientific travelers'" accounts in their unmistakable suggestion that it was a man-made economic system, and not nature, that provided the true obstacle to progress in the Amazon.

If humans could not subdue and unilaterally bend nature to their own purposes in this "second" vision, they had far less need to do so. Whereas an incorrigible river created difficulties for would-be tamers of the land in Euclides' first vision, the particular economic system called *aviamento* was the true culprit in his second. A debt trap in which large-scale buyers furnished necessary goods on credit to individual producers, who were then forced to sell the buyers raw rubber at ludicrously low prices, the *aviamento* system obliged the rubber tappers to work under harsh conditions, often with no medical help or other assistance of any kind. Since the trees they tapped were not their property, the men could be dismissed at any moment. However, they were more likely to be held hostage by their debts to the company.

The oppressive force of this economic system was nowhere clearer than in Euclides' striking portrait of the rubber tappers and their customs in his essay "Judas-Asvero."[46] Although the title referred to the Wandering Jew—an echo of the men's own rootless existence—the essay described the men's practice, during Holy Week, of constructing a straw effigy of the disciple said to have betrayed Christ for money. Created in their own likeness and attired in their own cast-off clothing, this "graceless, tragic, and chillingly burlesque" figure became the embodiment of the men's own "monotonous, obscure, extremely sorrowful, and anonymous existence."[47] In raining bullets upon the effigy as it floated down the river in a small boat on the Saturday before Easter, the men vented their fury at their own quickness to have believed others' lies about the fortunes they would amass in a distant Amazon.

And yet, if the rubber tappers' desire for easy riches had led them to sign away their freedom to the owners of the rubber camps, to whom they had become indentured, it was the unjust extractive system that emerged as the ultimate villain in Euclides' essay. Not nature, but other humans had pushed them into an unending succession of Good Fridays. Not the land, but the particular uses to which a small number of powerful men had put it had locked them into an endless circle of misery traced out again and again in their daily rounds of the rubber trees.

In Euclides' second, shape-shifting Amazon, nature itself defied the domination at which the rubber tappers chafed by resolutely repelling all human attempts to control it, or even to know it. Yet more important, it demanded that human beings transform themselves so that they could begin to comprehend it. As a result, the practical implications for how new arrivals to the region could and should relate to the unique environmental conditions they encountered were profoundly different from those that would be associated with geopolitics. This second vision also necessitated a radical rethinking of Amazonia's place within a nation for which it had become both cornerstone and inspiration, as well as its place on a planet for which it represented nothing less than "the last, as yet unfinished page of Genesis."

As rich and immense as its giant counterpart, this shape-shifter Amazon, with its unfinished quality that made the land "sad and awkward" in some parts of the essays, emerged in others with a triumphant sense of possibility. If the Amazon's commodities were the true source of its wealth in the first vision, it was the Amazon's very newness that was the font of riches in the second. Likewise, the Amazon's "flagrant deviation from the customary processes of evolution" was terrible from one perspective, but from another its ensuing uniqueness fostered innovations impossible in other corners of the world.[48]

Just as Euclides dwelled on the land's terrestrial riches (rubber, minerals, wood) in his first vision, Amazonia's waters dominated his second. A horrific animal that thrashed its giant tail at precarious habitations in some passages, the river that regularly became "a tributary of its own tributaries" appeared, in others, far more like a human being. A master engineer, it was also a "monstrous artist" who kept shaping and re-shaping a "scandalously profligate" nature.

Further, if the Amazon's vastness and intrinsic instability deeply disturbed Euclides in his more gigantic moments, this same alien immensity became, at other times, a source of astonishment and delight. "Its space is like Milton's: it hides within itself," he wrote.[49] Whether "inscribed within the geometric fatality of the earth's curve, or eluding curious glances within the deceitful cloak of its immutable features," this world inevitably concealed as much as it revealed. However, even while it "[hid] within itself," the Amazon called attention to its vastness in a way entirely foreign to a giant. "There is something extraterrestrial in that amphibian nature, mixture of waters and earth, which cloaks itself, completely leveled, within its own grandeur," a clearly mesmerized Euclides exclaimed.[50]

Conquerors embarked on a historic mission in some sections of the essays, human beings became, in others, "impertinent intruders" and "constructors of ruins." They could not hope for more than the most fleeting glimpse of an enduringly elusive whole. "The amplitude which has to be diminished to be judged, the grandeur which only allows itself to be perceived in miniature through microscopes" is "an infinity that parcels itself out, bit by bit, slowly, very slowly, indefinitely, torturously," Euclides said.[51]

Always the agents in giant-making, human beings had limited power over the torturous process that Euclides described. They could hope for a fuller vision if, and only if, they accepted an immense (but not gigantic) nature on its own terms—that is, through comprehension rather than domination. Thus, in between injunctions to lay railroad tracks and celebrations of the vibrant crackle of telegraph lines, Euclides argued that humans camped out on "the threshold of a marvelous world" had no choice but to wait for nature to decide to reveal itself, since it could not be known through force. "To see it, one must renounce all prospect of unveiling it," he said firmly.[52]

This renunciation did not mean resignation to the impossibility of ever fully knowing nature. On the contrary, Euclides declared, humans would one day succeed in comprehending the Amazon's astonishing potential. However, like his friend and protégé Alberto Rangel in *Inferno verde* (to which Euclides wrote the preface), Euclides consigned this victory to a distant future.[53] Only many thousands of years from now, at the conclusion of "incalculable efforts," would that "marvelous landscape which today exhausts our dazzled and vacant gaze" reveal its final secrets. Then, and only then, would "the almost mythic cycle" of Orellana's Amazons and Ralegh's golden Manoa fuse with "the most audacious scientific hypotheses" to allow would-be viewers of the Amazon to overcome their age-old sense of paralysis before its grandeur. In this happy moment, the long, unfinished course of natural history finally would be complete.[54]

The idea of the Amazon as a realm of nature awaiting discovery lives on in the IMAX movie's "timeless land" in which the myth and magic of Indian shamanism promises eventual cures to diseases not yet conquered. However, the language that Euclides considered "hard-edged" is impressionistic (and frequently bombastic) by the standards of contemporary science. Time and again, his calls for a new antilyrical form of expression bumped up against his own impassioned evocations of the Amazon's exultant newness. Passages in which whole islands went sailing off upon the crest of a flooded river like "monstrous mast-like boats with long, sunken prows and high sterns" could not be farther from the "harsh technologies" that he extolled. Bent on expressing the Amazon's vastness head-on, Euclides nonetheless regularly found his sober mathematics dissolving into a dizzying "dilation of marvelous numbers."[55]

Moreover, it would be hard to miss Euclides' deep personal identification with a river that, like him, was both engineer and artist. His perverse delight in the river's refusal to respect the confines of its bed is similarly clear. At the same time that the Amazon was a realm of science, it also was a near-magic antidote to Brazil's inferiority complex vis-à-vis the Old World. Even while he attempted to balance giant and shape-shifter, he did not give them equal weight in his work. Euclides' writing remains powerful throughout the essays, but it is those passages in which he describes the Amazon's astonishing fluidity that are truly incandescent.

The practical implications of Euclides' second vision could not have been more important. First of all, his indefatigable shape-shifter cast doubt on the whole idea of the Amazon as a territory awaiting demarcation. No longer an enormous footnote to the "real" story of a would-be Europe in the tropics, this stubbornly unfinished Amazon became the potential center of a defiantly original Brazil. From this perspective, the lack of history that Euclides periodically lamented became a great attraction. Precisely because the Amazon resisted comparison to temperate nature, it demanded another set of standards and a radical redefinition of key terms. Free of imported norms and preestablished expectations, the region held out the promise of new ways of seeing that would propel all of Brazil onto the center of an international stage. Its resistance to subjugation became a metaphor for the respectful relations that ought to exist between humans and nature, and also among human beings.

The world that emerged in Euclides' second vision staunchly resisted the conquest and transformation that all giants invite. Although this Amazon, in which "images replace formulae," could be known, the search for knowledge produced an alliance that was subject to continual renegotiation. The "vigorous measures" of affiliation that composed a preexisting blueprint thus became a more open-ended process of discovery in which each new step shaped the next.

Moreover, the Amazon of this second vision was, again, a social as much as a natural creation. As such, it invited ongoing interpretation. Conspicuously absent from official geopolitics, this shape-shifting, resolutely "other" nature provided the basis for some of the greatest works of Brazilian Modernism. A multistranded artistic movement of the 1920s, *modernismo* exhibited direct ties to competing political parties and initiatives in a country caught up in intense waves of immigration and growing industrialization in the south.[56] The Modernists' desire to shape the future of the country made them part of what was almost surely the single most important sea change in Brazilian cultural history. The Amazon's ability to serve as inspiration for three of this important movement's best-known works—Mário de Andrade's novel *Macunaíma*, Raul Bopp's long poem *Cobra Norato*, and Heitor Villa-Lobos' *Bachianas Brasileiras* (almost certainly the single best-known classical music work by a Brazilian composer)—recalls Euclides' vision of the region as a font of possibility.

The fact that *Macunaíma* is a barbed "rhapsody" rather than a novel, that the *Bachianas Brasileiras* mingles Bach with birdsong, and that the enigmatic *Cobra Norato* lies somewhere between epic and lyric poetry corroborates Euclides' vision of an Amazon that rejected established genres.[57] His complaint that his contemporaries relied too much on Europe found echoes in the composer and authors' searches for a specifically Brazilian idiom with roots in everyday experience—searches that went far beyond the realm of art or literature. Precisely because their creators set out to do nothing less than to redefine Brazil, all three members of this trio have become classics. For them, as for Euclides, the Amazon's shape-shifting qualities became a source of inspiration, its exhilarating vastness an escape from past constraints.

These three artists' heavy reliance upon specific Amazonian folk traditions, including the Encantado narratives, highlights in turn the unexpected links between Euclides' still-evolving Genesis and the ever shifting world of the Encante.[58] Just as Euclides' monstrous river recalls the young Araguaia fisherman's account of the warring serpents, which appears in chapter 1, so his "immensity that hides within itself" brings to mind the lake within a lake. Euclides' vision of a world in constant movement, as well as his focus on the economic hierarchies that giants conceal, reappears time and again in contemporary stories of enchanted cities told by people who may not know the first thing about him.

"Euclides da Cunha?" one woman who worked as a cook in Lucky River repeats when I inquire. "The name sounds familiar. Wasn't he the one who cut down the trees to build the Trans-Amazon?"

That the same Euclides who championed progress in the abstract almost certainly would have had deep misgivings about a highway that slashed through a forest which was also, for him, the most powerful of symbols, makes this woman's response unintentionally ironic. Her words effectively underscore the uncanny resemblances between his Amazon and that other Amazon of the oral storytellers whose voices echo through this book. To begin with, these storytellers' accounts of an enchanted world have deep roots in the native cultures that, in Euclides, are regularly overshadowed (indeed, subsumed) by a land that demands transformation from without. A number of these storytellers are, almost certainly, descended in part from the "Titanic caboclos" who went on to intermarry with Amazonian natives. Their present lives as shoemakers, laundresses, and fishermen who double as short-order cooks or bicycle mechanics nonetheless would seem anticlimactic in comparison to early-twentieth-century rubber tappers whom he portrays as engaged in a desperate but heroic struggle with the land.

Despite the gulf between Euclides and Tô Pereira, the idea of an Amazon in constant flux links his essays, full of complicated ideas and often convoluted clauses, to a host of seemingly simple tales about enchanted beings that many contemporary Amazonians continue to recount in a distinctly colloquial language. These links reassert the Amazon's identity as a joint creation—a series of both conscious and unconscious collaborations. In reaffirming how persons of unequal social status and differing viewpoints echo and take issue with each other, they point toward a more figurative "meeting of the waters" that cuts across both time and space. "That's a funny way of putting things," says Manuel Pedro's mother when I tell her about Euclides' description of an "extraterrestrial" nature that conceals itself in its own immensity. She stops grating manioc to gaze out at a river that resembles liquid caramel this hot and cloudy afternoon. "But, of course, he's right that no one can force the Encante to reveal its secrets. That's why no one knows the real location of Higino's Lake."

Beyond Eden

More than just a handy summary of conflicting attitudes toward Amazonian nature, Euclides' passionate descriptions of the land and of the water offer blueprints for very different courses of action. Whether as a basis for the geopolitics of later decades or as a mandate for a new enviro-poetics that can recognize the long-standing, if uneasy, partnership between human beings and a nature that inevitably registers the effects of humans' interactions with one another, his essays continue to raise questions whose answers have direct consequences for ourselves as well as for Amazonians. Why, they make us ask, would a divine creator have left the Amazon, and not some other place, unfinished? Who precisely is going to write this "last, as yet unfinished page of Genesis"? What will be the basis for this authorial selection? Will nature be subject, object, or coauthor of the ensuing text? How will "science" be defined, and what will be its role in the Amazon's conclusion? And what about the readers? For whom will this page be written? How will it draw in—or once more exclude—the metaphorically illiterate? And, most of all, what exactly will this last page of creation say?

There is no escape from these essential questions. The images and stories that appear and reappear here are clues to our own thinking, and to others' conceptions of a rain forest that is both place and icon, natural creation and ongoing human invention. The often surprising connections they reveal hold out new hope for the Amazon and Amazonians. The gaps they illuminate hint at what Manuel Pedro's mother says perhaps never existed and yet one day could be.

Like the torrents of water that pour down over the rain forest of the IMAX movie, the palm-studded island at the center of Higino's Lake rebuffs fixed divisions. Land and water, human and nonhuman nature remain intertwined in both sets of representations, albeit in differing proportions and toward different ends. In the case of the Rain Forest, these ends are customarily linked to claims on land that may take the form of ardent calls for preservation or equally energetic development schemes. In the case of the lake within a lake, storytellers use the idea of a pro-

tean Encante to point to their own ties to their surroundings, and to
their own histories. In so doing, they reassert their own, often increasingly difficult existence in the midst of what the IMAX movie presents
as a green utopia, as well as the pressing need to slip "a little word of
justice" into the international discussions about the fate of a forest that
turns out to be their home.

"I think that no one in the world beyond here hears our voice,"
Benedita, no longer visibly angry, says to me one evening as a light rain
tickles the canvas roof above our heads. "They don't even know that we
exist. For the people where you live, the Amazon is just tall trees and
parrots. I saw it all the time on TV when I used to work in Porto Trombetas as a maid. But the people from the outside, even if they don't want
to listen to us, perhaps they'll still hear the voice of a nature in which
trees and parrots have always lived with people, and people have always
lived with them. Perhaps in listening to nature, they will come to hear us
also, and the future will be different, and better than the past."

It will not be easy to rethink a Rain Forest whose roots reach back
over the centuries. However, we have no other choice. Yes, it will be
hard. But it will be far harder to save something that does not exist.

Chronology of Key Dates

The following chronology situates some of the texts, authors, and events that occupy a key place in this book within a broader historical and geographical context. Although purposefully eclectic, the summary outlines the larger themes of the fluidity of borders in the Amazon region, the competition among European and then Latin American nations for control of its riches, Amazonia's legacy of boom-and-bust cycles, and the continuing conflicts between longtime residents and newcomers.

600 million B.C.	The giant intracratonic Amazon basin has its origin along an ancient zone of weakness within the Precambrian Shield.
9000 B.C.	Early human groups leave pictographs at Pedra Pintada, a series of rocks on the floodplain to the west of what is today the city of Monte Alegre in the Brazilian Amazon. Other cultural remains found at the site may be as much as five thousand years older.
Late 1400s	Prosperous chiefdoms along much of the Amazon River and the adjacent uplands and interior mark the success of native societies in adapting to the Amazonian environment. Archaeological and historical evidence suggests that a number of these societies were densely populated and culturally advanced, with intensive agriculture, well-developed trade networks, and sophisticated forms of artistic expression.
1492–93	Christopher Columbus makes his first journey to the Americas. In his diaries and letters, he notes native reports about a group of women without men on the island of Matinino, whom he describes as "Amazons."
1494	The Treaty of Tordesillas divides South America between Spain and Portugal.
1500	Vicente Yáñez Pinzón, ex-commander of the caravel *Niña* during Columbus's first New World voyage, enters the mouth of the Amazon River, which he calls "Santa María de la Mar Dulce" (Saint Mary of the Freshwater Ocean).

The river is also initially known as the "Rio Grande" or the "Marañón" ["Maranhão"]). In the same year, Pedro Alvares Cabral claims the northeastern coast of Brazil for Portugal.

1508   The first chivalric novel in the widely popular ten-volume "Amadís de Gaula" series appears. *Las sergas de Esplandián,* which features the Amazon queen Califia, follows two years later.

1531   Convinced that a sun-colored gold must lie near the equator, Diego de Ordás begins to explore the Orinoco region. In the same year, Francisco Pizarro arrives in Peru and Pedro de Heredia reaches Colombia's Atlantic coast.

1533   The first shipment of Inca gold arrives in Seville, whetting the Spaniards' hunger for new treasures.

1536   Jerónimo de Ortal hears reports of Amazons dwelling along the Orinoco River. Hernán Pérez de Quesada will hear similar reports about Amazons living along the Magdalena River not long afterward.

1537   Reports of a golden king reach the Spaniards in Quito, prompting new expeditions into the Colombian interior.

1539   Three explorers searching for El Dorado—Gonzalo Jiménez de Quesada, Nicolaus Federmann, and Sebastián de Benalcázar—converge upon Muisca (Chibcha) territories in present-day Colombia. In this same year (or, according to some records, a year earlier), Pedro de Candia sets off from Cuzco in search of a golden country called "Ambaya" in what was to become the Moxos province of Bolivia.

1541-42   In late February 1541, Gonzalo Pizarro sets out from Quito in search of El Dorado and the Land of Cinnamon. The day after Christmas of the same year, Captain Francisco de Orellana leaves Pizarro's expedition with orders to sail down the Napo River in search of provisions. On 12 February 1542 he enters the main arm of the Amazon. On 26 August he reaches the Atlantic Ocean, making his expedition the first to traverse the full length of the river. Friar Gaspar de Carvajal's account of the crew's discovery of the river— which the great sixteenth-century historian Gonzalo Fernández de Oviedo will call "one of the greatest things that ever happened to men"—and his description of the men's encounter with the Amazons, leads to the rebaptism of the river as "the Amazon."

1559   Pedro de Ursúa sets off down the Huallaga and Amazon Rivers. He later dies at the hands of the rebel Lope de Aguirre, who eventually assumes control of the expedition.

Aguirre's boats reach Margarita on 21 July 1561, making him the second European to descend the full length of the Amazon and the first to cross from the Amazon into the Orinoco via the Casiquiare canal.

1570–1630s   Dutch commerce reaches the Portuguese Amazon (Rio Branco) through native intermediaries on the Essequibo River, reinforcing long-standing native links between the Caribbean and South America.

1580–1640   The crowns of Castile and Aragon absorb the Portuguese monarchy for a sixty-year period still known as "the Captivity." The Dutch take advantage of the situation to begin their conquest of Portuguese holdings from Africa to the East Indies, as well as from the Caribbean to northeastern Brazil.

1595   Based on Spanish accounts of El Dorado, Sir Walter Ralegh mounts a search for the Golden City of Manoa, supposedly somewhere between the Orinoco and the Amazon Rivers. His *Discoverie of the Large, Rich, and Bewtiful Empyre of Guiana*, which appears a year later, remains the best-known account of El Dorado in English.

1612   The French establish holdings on the Portuguese Atlantic coast (Maranhão), but are subsequently expelled.

1617   Ralegh's second expedition in search of Manoa fails, opening the way to his execution a year later. In this same year, the city of Belém is founded on the mouth of the Amazon.

1620   Maranhão and Grão Pará become a separate administrative unit from the rest of Portuguese America, which is known as "Brazil."

Early 1620s   Cornelius O'Brien and four other Irishmen make their way up the Amazon, where they are said to have encountered a group of "masculine women" who purposefully stunt their right breasts in order better to wield bows and arrows.

1627   Father Pedro Simón's *Noticias historiales* is published in Spain. Among the native legends and beliefs he recounts in this narrative is the story of the king who makes golden offerings to a "little dragon" at the bottom of a lake.

1637–38   Pedro de Teixeira ascends the Amazon from Belém to Quito. In 1639, he returns to Belém with the Spanish Jesuit Cristóbal de Acuña. The latter's *New Discovery of the Great River of the Amazons* (1641) contains a wealth of detailed information about economically valuable flora and fauna that leads the Spaniards to attempt to keep it out of print.

1640	The ascension of the duke of Bragança to the newly independent crown of Portugal marks the beginning of serious Portuguese colonization of the Amazon. Government *tropas de resgate* ("rescue troops," whose supposed intent is to save the Amazonian Indians from one another) mount a series of slaving expeditions. These forays accompany a growing commerce in regional products (cinnamon, wild cacao, turtle oil, sarsaparilla) known collectively as "*drogas do sertão*" literally, "backlands drugs."
1650s	The Jesuits establish numerous communities called *aldeias* or *reducciones* in the Amazon in order to catechize the natives, who provide the Europeans with much needed manual labor.
1670s	First indications of the systematic cultivation that will permit not one, but two yearly harvests of cacao.
1682	The Bolivian missions begin a prosperous period that ends only in 1767, with the expulsion of the Jesuits from the territory of the Audiencia de Charcas.
1689–91	The Jesuit priest Samuel Fritz leaves Quito on a mission to the Napo-Solimões region, then goes on to Belém before returning. Happily for the Portuguese, Fritz fails to interest the Lima viceroy in the need for Spain's incorporation of that part of Amazonia extending from the Napo to the Rio Negro.
1720–1820	Cacao emerges as a primary export in Venezuela, Ecuador (Guayaquil), and the Brazilian Amazon.
1743–49	Smallpox and measles epidemics kill twenty to forty thousand people, about a third of the total European and Europeanized population of the Brazilian Amazon. The resulting labor shortage in the region will lead the Marquês de Pombal to augment significantly the importation of African slaves into Amazonia upon his rise to power in 1750.
1744	The French naturalist-traveler Charles de la Condamine describes the Casiquiare Channel for a European public some two hundred years after Lope de Aguirre navigated the same trajectory. The first of a long line of northern European "scientific travelers" to visit the Amazon, la Condamine publishes an account of his travels in which he expresses his belief in the existence of both El Dorado and the Amazons.
1750	Spain and Portugal sign the Treaty of Madrid, which abolishes the Treaty of Tordesillas in place of the principle of *uti possedetis,* or right by possession, to settle disputed boundaries in the Río de la Plata and the Amazon.

1755–78	Pombal's Companhia Geral do Grão-Pará e Maranhão becomes the prime instrument for economic recovery and development in the Brazilian Amazon. The move toward greater royal control, revenue gathering, and the development of tropical export staples, accompanied by a rise in African and Amerindian slavery during this period, is equally visible within the Spanish-speaking Amazon.
1759	Voltaire mocks the lingering belief in El Dorado in *Candide*. Pombal expels the Jesuits from all Portuguese holdings. Father João Daniel takes up residence in the Lisbon jail cell where he will spend the next twenty years at work on an encyclopedic description of the Amazon that anticipates accounts by nineteenth-century naturalists from northern Europe.
1760	The Treaty of El Pardo annuls the Treaty of Madrid.
1770s	The chief magistrate of Rio Branco, Francisco Xavier Ribeiro de Sampaio, complains that fantastical stories of a golden lake are continuing to inspire a series of foreign incursions into the Portuguese Amazon.
1777	The Treaty of San Ildefonso redraws Portuguese-Spanish frontiers in South America, confirming Spain's possession of the Río de la Plata region and Portugal's possession of the Amazon.
1778	José Pavón, Hipólito Ruiz, and M. Dombey's publication of *Flora peruviana* confirms the growing interest in botanical classification throughout both the Spanish- and Portuguese-speaking Amazon.
1783–93	Alexandre Rodrigues Ferreira, a Brazilian botanist and author of the *Viagem filosófica*, leads a Portuguese natural history commission into the Rio Negro.
1790s	The failure of Pombal's monopoly company and of the Spanish silver-contraband trade prompts the decline of the trade route along the Madeira River and the decline of the Amazonian west.
1799	Alexander von Humboldt and Aimé Bonpland explore the Orinoco region, going on to make their way to the Rio Negro by way of the Casiquiare canal, earlier used by Lope de Aguirre. Humboldt redefines El Dorado as a hydrographic phenomenon demanding scientific study.
1807–25	Napoleon's invasion of the Iberian Peninsula leads to the exile of the Portuguese court to Rio de Janeiro (1807–21) and the declaration of an independent empire of Brazil in 1822. It also prompts the French exile of the Bourbons (Charles

	IV and Fernando VII) in 1808 and subsequent revolts and wars of liberation throughout much of Spanish America.
1810	Pedro Ignacio Muiba, a Moxos chieftain, calls for the independence of Bolivia from Spain.
1821	The slave Atanásio, who had fled in government raids on fugitive slave communities on the Curuá River (western Pará) nine years earlier, heads a force of some forty slaves who found a new *quilombo* above the waterfalls on the Trombetas River.
1830	The Protocol Mosquera-Pedemonte establishes the Amazonian border between Peru and Gran Colombia only months after Ecuador declares its independence from the latter.
1835	The Prussian naturalist Robert Schomburgk voyages up the Amazon through the Rio Branco to the Guianas and Venezuela.
1835–39	An immense popular revolt known as the Cabanagem (from the word *cabano*, meaning hut or shack) sweeps much of the Portuguese-speaking Amazon, leaving thirty thousand people—approximately a quarter of the regional population—dead.
1839	Charles Goodyear sets the stage for the Amazonian Rubber Boom by perfecting the process of vulcanization.
1847	The American traveler William H. Edwards publishes his *Voyage up the River Amazon*. A heavily embellished popular piece, the book nonetheless does much to convince the British naturalists Henry Walter Bates and Alfred Russel Wallace to set out for the Amazon a year later.
1848	The Hakluyt Society reissues Ralegh's *Discoverie*, with a preface by Robert Schomburgk.
1852	Nine years after a steamboat navigates the Amazon for the first time, the Baron of Mauá founds the Amazon Steam Navigation Company.
1856	The Brazilian Empire establishes a directory of Indians for Amazonas, which includes 239 peoples, not all of whom are under official government control.
1858	Charles Darwin's publication of *The Origin of Species* intensifies popular and scientific interest in naturalist pursuits.
1862	Bates publishes his *Naturalist on the River Amazons* with publisher John Murray, who had already published both Edwards and Darwin. The book is a success, and a new, somewhat shorter version appears a year later.

1863	The foundation of the city of Iquitos in the Peruvian Amazon marks the growing financial importance of rubber, whose production triples in a single decade.
1866	In a journey through the Amazon, Aureliano Cândido Tavares Bastos transmits reports of commerce between the fugitive-slave communities on the Trombetas River and "the Dutch of Guyana" in which the blacks exchange tobacco, Brazil nuts, and sarsaparilla for guns and iron tools.
1872	Construction begins on the Madeira-Mamoré railroad, intended to link the rich rubber stands of the Purus and Juruá Rivers to the Bolivian coast. The initial engineer is an American, George Church, who describes the dense forests that will claim a human life for every railroad spike as "the garden of the Lord."
1876	The English traveler Henry Wickham transports Amazonian rubber tree seeds to the orchid houses of Kew Gardens, from which they are taken to Southeast Asia to serve as the basis for rubber plantations.
1877	Father José Nicolino Pereira de Souza makes his first of three journeys to the Trombetas region, where he encounters the slave descendants.
1880s	Amazonian rubber production doubles, following the invention of the pneumatic tire in 1877. In Brazil, rubber accounts for 10 percent of the nation's total exports.
1884	The founding of Riberalta marks the beginning of the neocolonial era of international capitalism in eastern Bolivia. Three years later, the native priest Andrés Guayocho leads an indigenous revolt against government authorities and new hordes of traders.
1888	The Golden Law abolishes slavery in Brazil. The newly free slaves in the Trombetas region respond by descending the area above the waterfalls and founding new communities more easily linked to commercial centers.
1889	Brazil ceases to be an empire and becomes a republic.
1896	Inauguration of the lavish Opera House in Manaus, which, in this same year, becomes the first large Brazilian city to introduce electric lighting.
1899	Henri and Otille Coudreau visit the Trombetas–Cuminá (Erepecuru) region. Their accounts mention slave descendants.
1900	Rubber becomes Brazil's second-leading export, after coffee, accounting for just under a quarter of the export total. A long-running boundary dispute between Brazil and French

	Guiana over the territory of Amapá is finally settled in Brazil's favor.
1902	Bolivia loses control over rubber-rich Acre to Brazil.
1904	Euclides da Cunha departs for the Amazon, where he will serve as head of a joint Brazilian-Peruvian Commission whose mission is to chart the boundaries of the rubber-rich Purus River region.
1907–9	Euclides publishes a series of essays about the Amazon in *Contrastes e confrontos, Peru versus Bolívia*, and *À margem da história*. The last of these volumes appears after his fatal confrontation with his wife's lover.
1908	With the publication of *Inferno verde*, a collection of short stories, Alberto Rangel popularizes the term *Green Hell*.
1909	Amazonian rubber prices double, only to collapse a year later as the entry of Asian plantation rubber onto the market destroys the Amazon's monopoly.
1912	An official report to the British government by Roger Casement documents shocking abuses of Indian laborers in rubber camps along the Putumayo River in Colombia and Peru. The Madeira-Mamoré railroad reaches completion after forty years of costly labor, just in time for the rubber bust.
1913	After visiting Argentina and the Brazilian south, Theodore Roosevelt joins the Brazilian colonel Cândido Mariano de Rondon in an expedition that successfully traces the course of the River of Doubt. Initially published in installments, his *Through the Brazilian Wilderness* appears in book form in the fall of 1914.
1913–21	The rubber merchant Tomás Funes seizes control of the provincial capital of San Fernando de Atabapo in Venezuela. He proceeds to enslave the Yekuana Indian population and rules the Territorio Amazonas as an independent fiefdom with no ties whatsoever to the central government in Caracas.
1922	Official inauguration of the important artistic and intellectual movement known as Brazilian Modernism. Three of the movement's most important works—Raul Bopp's long lyric poem *Cobra Norato*, Mário de Andrade's rhapsodic novel *Macunaíma*, and the composer Heitor Villa-Lobos' *Bachianas Brasileiras*—will draw directly on the Amazon for inspiration.
1924	The Colombian writer José Eustacio Rivera publishes what will become the most famous of all early jungle novels, *La vorágine* (The Vortex). The book does much to confirm

Amazonia's identity as a Green Hell among European and many Latin American readers.

1927   Henry Ford acquires land on the Tapajós River for a plantation called "Fordlândia," intended to supply his factories with rubber for tires. Microbes attack the rubber trees, which are planted too close together, forcing him to abandon the venture.

1930s   Long a staple of the regional economy, Brazil nuts become increasingly important in the Trombetas area as the century progresses. By the 1930s, members of the regional elite have acquired legal title to most of the lands that had long been worked by descendants of runaway slaves.

1937   The young Claude Lévi-Strauss, who is teaching at the University of São Paulo, makes a research trip into the Amazon.

1940   The Brazilian dictator Getúlio Vargas visits the Amazon and pronounces the region a keystone of his "Westward March," designed to integrate outlying regions of Brazil more fully into the nation. Twelve years later he will establish a separate administrative unit for the Amazon (SUDAM) and a national institute for research on the region.

1941   The Rio Protocol establishes the Amazonian borders between Peru and Ecuador.

1942   Brazil enters World War II on the side of the Allies. In the face of Axis control over the Malayan rubber plantations, a number of poor northeasterners enter national service as "rubber soldiers" in the Amazon. Some forty thousand of these forest conscripts will die of hunger and disease.

1955   Lévi-Strauss' *Tristes tropiques* marks a new vision of the Amazon as a precious, disappearing world.

1958   The Brazilian miner Nilson Pinheiro discovers gold on the Tapajós River, ushering in what will become the mammoth gold rush of the 1970s and 1980s. Pinheiro will be elected a state deputy in Pará twenty-four years later.

1960   President Juscelino Kubitschek moves the Brazilian capital inland to Brasília and initiates the "Highway of Jaguar" between Belém and Brasília. The opening of the Amazon to large-scale colonization finds echoes in the other Amazonian nations.

1964   A military coup in Brazil brings to power a group of development-minded generals.

1967   Military strategist General Golbery do Couto e Silva publishes a blueprint for Brazilian geopolitics in which the

Amazon plays an essential role. The American entrepreneur Daniel Ludwig acquires huge holdings in Jari, which will meet the same unhappy fate as Fordlândia. In this same year, enormous iron deposits are discovered in the Carajás mountains of southern Pará. In Bolivia, Che Guevara attempts to mobilize peasant resistance to the government in various areas of the interior, including the Amazon.

1968   The Brazilian dictatorship suspends habeas corpus. The center-right newsweekly *Veja* emerges and is soon publishing articles that mirror the nation's new sense of expectation about the development of the Amazon.

1969–76   The first stage of the vast Guri Dam in Venezuela begins. Stage II will begin in 1976 and go on for ten years.

1970   The Trans-Amazon highway, designed to link Brazil's "central platform" with the Amazon and the northeast, is initiated. In this same year, the American anthropologist Betty Meggers publishes *Amazonia: A Counterfeit Paradise,* which affirms the fragility of Amazonian soils and the region's ensuing unsuitability to all but small, nomadic populations. The first Earth Day is held in April of this year.

1970s   Increased coca growing, often with ties to guerrilla movements, becomes an issue, above all in the Colombian and Peruvian Amazon.

1972   The United Nations Conference on the Human Environment is held in Stockholm, marking the emergence of a globalist concern for the balance between development and environmental preservation. The Amazon and tropical rain forests emerge as a focus of international concern.

1972–74   The discovery of a small group of leftist guerrillas in the Araguaia River region confirms the Brazilian military's worst fears about the Amazon as a threat to national security and helps bolster ongoing colonization schemes designed to "stabilize" the region. Major Curió is one of the officers sent to oversee the "War of Araguaia."

1973   The Middle East oil crisis raises interest rates around the world. Brazil begins to eye the Amazon as an answer to its spiraling foreign debt, and the oil-rich Ecuadorean Amazon acquires new importance as multinational firms move to exploit its resources.

1975   Construction begins on Tucuruí, the world's fourth-largest dam, intended to provide the electric power for the mines of Carajás. The dam will flood vast areas of tropical forest on which many Indians, *caboclos,* and migrants depend for a livelihood. It also will destroy some 3 million trees and shrubs.

1976   The collection and republication of Euclides da Cunha's Amazonian essays in a single volume called *Um paraíso perdido* (A Lost Paradise) reflects the Amazon's growing visibility within Brazil.

1978   The Amazon Pact Treaty is signed by Venezuela, Colombia, Ecuador, Peru, Bolivia, Brazil, Guyana, and Suriname.

1979   Gold is discovered in Serra Pelada in the south of the state of Pará, a find that will be the single richest in Amazonian history. In the same year, the discovery of a 4-billion-ton bauxite deposit in the Trombetas region—a find that will make Brazil the world's third-largest supplier of the raw material for aluminum—leads a multinational partnership to construct a giant refinery at Porto Trombetas. In an attempt to mitigate the ensuing environmental destruction, the Brazilian federal environmental agency, IBAMA, sets aside 385,000 hectares along the Trombetas River, long inhabited and worked by slave descendants, as a biological reserve.

1980   Concerned about security in Serra Pelada, which borders the Carajás iron ore mine and whose location near the site of the Araguaia guerrilla movement prompts unhappy memories, the Brazilian military occupies Serra Pelada. The same Major Curió who had been involved in the repressive "War of Araguaia" resurfaces as the chief government official in the enormous mine.

1981   War breaks out between Ecuador and Peru over the Amazonian border.

1985   The ascension of a civilian government has little visible effect on developmentalist policies in the Brazilian Amazon. A year later, President José Sarney announces plans for a national security program in Amazonia called the Calha Norte, or the Northern Trench.

1986   Conservation biologist Edward O. Wilson coins the term *biodiversity.*

1987   The World Commission on Environment and Development's report *Our Common Future* makes *sustainable development* a buzzword and creates pressure on the governments of Amazonian nations to link preservation with development. In Parintins—a town of seventy-five thousand people that happens to be the second-largest city in the huge state of Amazonas—the inauguration of a new stadium for the once-modest Boi-Bumbá festival marks the transformation of local and regional folklore into a national and international tourist attraction.

1988   Article 68 of the new Brazilian constitution gives land rights to descendants of runaway slaves.

1989   The assassination of Chico Mendes, head of the Brazilian Rubber Tappers' Union, sends shock waves around the world. The government's new Nossa Natureza (Our Nature) program is a direct response to pressures from international agencies including the World Bank and Inter-American Development Bank. In the Trombetas region, the slave descendants create a grassroots political association known as ARQMO and the Brazilian national forestry division creates a national forest of more than 426,000 hectares directly across the river from the already existing biological reserve.

1990   The archaeological work of Anna Roosevelt, a direct descendant of Theodore, initiates a new wave of studies that definitively challenge ideas of Amazonian soils as fragile and unable to sustain large populations. In Bolivia, Moxo, Sirionó, Yuracaré, and Movima, Indians engage in a thirty-four-day march from Trinidad to La Paz to protest the usurpation of their lands.

1991   The formation of a Yanomami Park in Brazil and Venezuela recognizes the traditional homeland of this group of some twenty thousand indigenous peoples. In the same year, the new constitution of Colombia makes sustainable development mandatory. Although clearly unenforceable, this decree marks an important change in environmental thinking.

1992   The publication of a U.N. report on the Amazon titled *Amazonia without Myths* precedes the United Nations Conference on the Environment and Development, also known as "Eco 92," which convenes in Rio de Janeiro. The Kayapó leader Paiakan is effectively disgraced on the eve of the conference. A scientific expedition sets out to retrace the steps of the original Rondon-Roosevelt expedition to the River of Doubt. Gold prices, which had begun dropping toward the end of the 1980s, continue to slide. In Ecuador, several thousand Quichua, Achuar, and Shiwiar indigenous peoples march from Pastaza province to Quito seeking land rights in the Amazon.

1993   A new environmental law in Colombia establishes a fund to channel part of the profits from mining and petroleum extraction to provincial and municipal governments, with environmental projects slated to receive about a third of these funds. In the same year, Brazilian gold miners stage a much publicized massacre of Yanomami Indians in Haximu.

1994	Lévi-Strauss publishes his elegiac *Saudades do Brasil.*
1995	Boa Vista, just minutes by boat from the giant Porto Trombetas refinery, becomes the first *remanescente* community in Amazonia to gain collective title to its land. An ad for Simoniz car wax that focuses on an "Amazonian Indian" named Chief Tunabi underscores the growing appeal of both sustainable development and native peoples to an international public. New armed conflicts between Ecuador and Peru break out on the Amazonian border.
1996	On 17 April, police massacre twenty-eight landless peasants in Eldorado dos Carajás, in southern Pará.
1996–98	Sixteen more *remanescente* communities in the Trombetas-Erepecuru area gain legal title to their land.
1997–98	Devastating fires burn through northern Amazonia, destroying vast areas of brush land in Roraima and threatening Yanomami settlements in Brazil and Venezuela. A special supplement of *Veja* devoted to the Amazon touts the possibilities of scientific research (as opposed to earlier large-scale development initiatives) for the region.
1998	Signing of the Ecuador-Peru Peace Agreement.
1999	Suriname emerges as a new focus of an extended Amazonian gold rush. Fourteen thousand Brazilian miners cross the border into Suriname, creating conflicts with Indians and Suriname Maroons involved in mining. Colombia initiates a "Green Plan" to finance the reforestation of 160,000 hectares, and new fires break out in many parts of the Amazon.
2000	A march by the Indigenous Black and Popular Resistance movement in Brasília marks the five-hundred-year anniversary of Cabral's landing in Brazil. The march also signals a formal alliance of black, Amerindian, and other groups concerned with land rights in Brazil in general and in Amazonia in particular. In this same year, Brazil approves a $45 billion federal government program called "Advance Brazil" (Avança Brasil), intended to build more highways, hydroelectric dams, and railroads in the Amazon. In the United States, Congress gives final approval to Plan Colombia, a controversial $1.3 billion package of mostly military aid aimed at helping Colombia combat the flow of narcotics to the United States. Since much of the drug activity is in the Amazonian portion of the country, the plan is certain to affect the future of the Amazon.

Glossary of Selected Terms

The following glossary lists a number of recurring foreign-language terms, as well as key terms in English to which I have assigned a more specific meaning than customary.

Amazon	The entire area drained by the Amazon River and its tributaries. Some scholars limit their definition of the Amazon nations to Brazil, Bolivia, Peru, Ecuador, Colombia, and Venezuela; others include Suriname and the Guianas as well.
Amazonia	The term used in Latin America for the Amazon.
Amazons	The women warriors of Greek myth with whom Francisco de Orellana and his men claimed to have engaged in direct combat during their passage down what would become known as the Amazon River in 1542.
bamburrar	A gold miners' term that means "to strike it rich." The noun *bamburro* or *bamburra* refers to a lucky strike.
barranco	A gully or ravine where miners work.
blefar	To fail at gold mining, to be duped. The noun *blefe* carries similar connotations of a swindle or deception.
boto	(also spelled *bouto* or *boutu*) The popular name for the freshwater dolphin *Inia geof frensis geoffrensis,* found only in the Amazon basin. These animals are distinguished by their long snouts, the pronounced "melon" on top of their heads, and their often reddish color. The *boto* figures prominently in stories of enchantment.
caboclo	A Brazilian term for a person of mixed blood. Like *ribeirinho* (*ribereño* in Spanish), *caboclo* is often used for residents of the Amazonian interior. The term may also be used derogatorily to mean "hillbilly."
Cobra Norato	The protagonist of a story told throughout much of the Amazon region. The son of a human mother and a serpent

father, Cobra Norato does battle with his evil sister, then succeeds in transforming himself permanently into human form.

colono   Literally, "colonist." A term used for newcomers, usually small-scale agriculturalists, to the Amazon. Many of these people have settled along newly constructed roads.

dono   An owner, protector, or guardian of other natural entities. See also *mãe*.

drogas do sertão   Literally, "backlands drugs," the Portuguese term for the collection of products that Europeans sought in the Amazon.

El Dorado   A Spanish term that literally means "the Gilded One." It first described the fabled golden king, then quickly came to refer as well to this monarch's gleaming kingdom, often said to be situated beside a golden lake.

Encantado   An enchanted being capable of shape-shifting. Encantados often take the form of an aquatic animal (usually a snake or dolphin) who then transforms into human guise. The living Gold, which can take the form of a fearsome snake or caiman or a beautiful woman in white, is another kind of Encantado. Mother Waterfall, who wrapped runaway slaves in her misty embrace, thereby rendering them invisible to their pursuers, is another sort of enchanted being.

Encante   An enchanted place that appears and disappears to humans. The rich and beautiful city beneath the river that is home to the Encantados is the best-known of the Encantes. Other Encantes show up on the surface of the earth—storytellers may refer to the golden church that appears and disappears in the middle of the forest or the lake within a lake as "Encantes."

false fear   A term generally associated with eighteenth- and nineteenth-century theories of the sublime, but used here specifically to refer to the sorts of fear, awe, or horror focused on an object—in this case, a giant—that is not the true source of terror. The fear proves false because it can be allayed.

floresta   A term for *rain forest* widely used in Amazonia that has formal, literary connotations. Unlike the more ambiguous *selva* (forest or jungle), the *floresta* is usually a thoroughly attractive place.

garimpeiro   A term for *miner* that comes from a verb that means "to pick at," "to dig," or "to pick one's nose." Although a *garimpeiro* can work with diamonds, cassiterite, or bauxite, the term has become closely associated with gold. It appears

to have its origins in an eighteenth-century royal decree that
identified a group of diamond miners as "*grimpeiros*" who
live hidden away in the *grimpas*, or mountain peaks.

garimpo — The mine site where *garimpeiros* work. Because Amazonian
gold is alluvial in nature, *garimpos* are usually beside rivers.

giant — A term I borrow from Susan Stewart's *On Longing* to refer
to a fragment that comes to obscure, conceal, or skew the
reality of the larger whole to which it belongs. Giants serve
to contain far larger entities (such as all of Amazonian nature), whose immensity would otherwise inspire an overwhelming fear.

gigantification — The "giant-making" process whereby a selected fragment
comes not just to represent, but to erase the larger whole.
For example, the Amazon women whom Orellana and his
men defeated in battle stood in for a fierce yet alluring nature that in no way would admit defeat.

jungle — Today, a lush, wet tangle of vegetation with connotations of
excess and disorder. The original Hindi and Sanskrit roots
jangal or *jangala* actually mean "desert" or "dry place."

mãe — A protective entity charged with the care of a particular
geographic location or animal species. All living beings are
believed to have *mães*. Although *mãe* is a feminine noun
meaning "mother," the *mães* of Amazonian folk tradition
may be either male or female. See also *dono*.

mano (feminine mana) — A colloquial term that literally means "brother" or "sister,"
but which is used more broadly to indicate camaraderie.

Manoa — The capital of El Dorado. The name also applies to a group
of Amazonian natives—the Manoas or Manoaras, whose
name lives on in the present-day metropolis of Manaus.
The role of the Manoas—the dominant traders in the Rio
Branco–Rio Negro area—in supplying gold both to other
native groups and to the Portuguese provided the basis for
the identification of Manoa as the golden city by Sir Walter
Ralegh and others.

mata — The colloquial Amazonian term for the rain forest. Much
like its English equivalent, "the bush," the *mata* can be an
unknown and frightening territory. However, the word—
unlike the more formal and literary *floresta*—also suggests
a series of familiar, largely unsensational surroundings that
inspire a host of personal and collective memories. Although dictionaries often distinguish between the more extensive *mato* and the more local, less extensive *mata*, the
two terms are apt to be used interchangeably.

meeting of the waters	A geographic phenomenon that occurs when two or more rivers whose different colors reflect unequal temperature and diverse sediment loads flow side by side before they mingle. The single most famous confluence occurs at Manaus, where the "black" waters of the Negro join the "white" waters of the Solimões to form the Amazon. However, there are various other meetings of the waters in Amazonia.
mocambo	A settlement established by runaway African slaves. If anything, the term is even more derogatory than *quilombo*. See also *quilombo*.
muiraquitã	The frog-shaped nephrite talisman with which the Amazons are said to have presented their lovers during their periodic trysts.
Paititi	A legendary golden lake usually said to be in Bolivia or Peru.
panema	An incapacity with supernatural causes visited on human beings who do not exhibit the requisite respect for natural entities. A fisherman who becomes *panema* catches nothing. A gold miner who is *panema* can work day and night to no avail.
Parima (also *Parime, Paraima*)	A fabled golden lake or sea generally situated somewhere between the western Amazon and Orinoco river basins. The lake is often the site of the legendary city of Manoa.
peão rodado	A veteran of the gold camps. The term *peão* (whose literal meanings include "foot soldier," "pawn," and "farmhand") indicates lower social status.
quilombo	A settlement established by runaway African slaves. See also *mocambo*.
rain forest	Technically, any woodland with an annual rainfall of one hundred inches, marked by lofty, broad-leaved evergreen trees forming a continuous canopy. The English translation of a late-nineteenth-century German botanical word *(Regenwald)*, the term came into widespread popular use only in the early 1970s.
remanescente	Literally, a "remnant." The term, initially applied to Amazonian Indians, is presently used in Brazil to refer to the descendants of runaway African slaves.
ribeirinho (*ribereño* in Spanish)	A riverbank dweller. The term is used for nonelite residents of the Amazonian interior, the majority of whom are of mixed ethnic heritage. See also *caboclo*.
seepage	A term I use to refer to the contradictions that call attention to the larger whole that a particular giant is intended to

contain and obscure. Seepage occurs, for instance, when the authors of an ostensibly scientific study of the Amazonian rain forest employ terms with religious connotations to describe the trees ("the Green Cathedral").

Serra Pelada   The site of the biggest Amazonian gold strike in recorded history. The Serra Pelada mine, which still functions on a reduced basis, is in southern Pará. It is different from most gold mines because of its vast size, nonalluvial character, and direct government involvement.

Veja   A Brazilian newsweekly equivalent to the U.S. *Newsweek* or *Time*.

wilderness   Initially a place of wild beasts (from the Old English *wild-dëoren*), *wilderness* gradually came to mean a tract or region uncultivated and uninhabited by human beings. The U.S. Wilderness Act of 1964 speaks of "a place where man remains a visitor." The word has no direct equivalent in either Spanish or Portuguese.

Notes

Chapter 1. The Meeting of the Waters

1. The thirty-nine-minute IMAX movie *Amazon*, directed by Kieth Merrill and narrated by Linda Hunt, was released in 1997. I use it as one particularly vivid example of a whole genre of documentaries centered on Amazonian nature. Snippets of the film with corresponding text appear on the website www .amazonthefilm.com.

2. Mark Plotkin, a research associate at the Smithsonian's Museum of Natural History, is the author of various books and articles for a general audience, including *Tales of a Shaman's Apprentice*. The native healer is identified as Julio Mamani, a Bolivian Callawaya shaman.

3. The importance of Amazonian Indians as a cultural and political presence within the region would be difficult to underestimate. By centering this book's discussion on people of mixed blood (the great majority of whom are descended in part from Amerindian peoples), I by no means wish to minimize the Indians' significance. It is reflected in an explosion of scholarly literature on issues of indigenous representation in the Amazon, one of the most important areas of contemporary anthropology. See, for example, the work of Alcida Ramos, Terence Turner, Michael F. Brown, and Jean E. Jackson, cited in chapters 3 and 6. See too the individual contributions by these and other authors in important collections by Jonathan D. Hill *(Rethinking History and Myth)* and Greg Urban and Joel Sherzer *(Nation-States and Indians in Latin America)*. For representative essays by a number of primarily Brazilian scholars, see *Amazônia: Etnologia e história indígena,* ed. Eduardo Viveiros de Castro and Manuela Carneiro da Cunha.

4. Estimates of the Amazon's present population vary, depending in part on whether one is using the term *Amazon* as a geographical and botanical designation or as a political and administrative term, such as Brazil's "Legal Amazonia." The figure of 23 million, which includes Legal Amazonia (an administrative division that includes both forest and nonforest areas), appears in the 1992 U.N. report *Amazonia without Myths*. More recent estimates place as many as 30 million people in the Amazon as a whole.

5. Parintins is situated on the eastern border of Amazonas, a Brazilian state four times the size of California. Although its present population is only about

seventy-five thousand people, it is the second-largest city in the state. (The largest is the capital, Manaus, with a population of approximately 1.5 million.) Parintins would become my base of operations during my various subsequent trips to the Amazon.

6. An enormous amount of material has been written on what nature is and what it means to various social groups. Many of the more recent studies build on Raymond Williams' discussions of ideas of nature as cultural constructions. (See his essay "Ideas of Nature" and book *Keywords*.) For examples of this work from very different perspectives, see William Cronon's *Uncommon Ground*, Bruce Braun and Noel Castree's *Remaking Reality*, and Laura Rival's *The Social Life of Trees*. I have found direct implications for thinking about the representation of Amazonian nature in Robert Pogue Harrison's discussion of the relationship between nature and civilization in *Forests*, David Arnold's examination of the invention of tropicality in *The Problem of Nature*, and Catherine A. Lutz and Jane L. Collins' discussion of the marketing of nature in *Reading National Geographic*. I have also been interested in Bruno Latour's comments on the construction of the Amazon as a field of study in *Pandora's Hope* and in the application of Edward Said's notion of the Orient as a political and cultural creation to tropical nature in Larry Lohmann's "Green Orientalism" and Suzana Sawyer and Arun Agrawal's "Environmental Orientalisms."

Although it focuses on one particular Amazonian native group (the Achuar), Philippe Descola's *In the Society of Nature* offers a more general critique of customary Western distinctions between nature and culture in thinking about the relationships between Amazonian societies and their environments. (See also the essays in *Nature and Society*, edited by Descola and Gisli Pálsson.) Much practical information about these specific relationships appears in the essays in Darrel Posey and William Balée's *Resource Management in Amazonia*, and in Balée's later *Footprints of the Forest*. Antonello Gerbi provides a useful historical backdrop for conceptions of Latin America in *Nature in the New World*. Clarence J. Glacken's *Traces on the Rhodian Shore* provides a larger intellectual context.

7. The concern for how power interplays with the perception of particular landscapes and the allocation of specific natural resources is the basis for a number of new studies in political ecology. See, for example, James Fairhead and Melissa Leach's *Misreading the African Landscape* and Roderick Neumann's *Imposing Wilderness*. See also Mike Davis' discussion of Los Angeles as a locus for images of destruction in his *Ecology of Fear* and Bruce Willems-Braun's discussion of the politics of nature in postcolonial British Columbia in "Buried Epistemologies." I am grateful to U.C. Berkeley's Workshop in Environmental Politics for making me more aware of current writing in this vein.

8. These sorts of encounters are the subject of important studies such as Stephen Greenblatt's *Marvelous Possessions*, Mary Campbell's *The Witness and the Other World*, Beatriz Pastor Bodmer's *The Armature of Conquest*, Mary Louise Pratt's *Imperial Eyes*, and Neil Whitehead's excellent critical edition of Sir Walter Ralegh's *The Discoverie of the Large, Rich, and Bewtiful Empyre of Guiana*.

9. In so doing, I draw on a steadily growing body of work concerned with the imaginative construction of particular geographical spaces. For an introduction, see Alan R. H. Baker and Gideon Biger's *Ideology and Landscape in Historical Perspective,* Eric Hirsch and Michael O'Hanlon's *The Anthropology of Landscape,* Steven Feld and Keith Basso's *Senses of Place,* Roy Ellen and Katsuyoshi Fukui's *Redefining Nature,* and Christopher Tilley's *A Phenomenology of Landscape Places, Paths, and Monuments.* The preface to the Baker and Biger volume provides a useful historical perspective on ideology and landscape. Hirsch's discussion of the concept of landscape from an anthropological perspective in *The Anthropology of Landscape* (pp. 3–30), Edward S. Casey's musings on the intersection of space and time in the conception of specific localities in the Feld and Basso volume (pp. 13–52), Roy Ellen's introduction to the *Redefining Nature* essays (pp. 1–31), and Phil Macnaghten and John Urry's discussion of competing ideologies of nature in *Contested Natures* offer similarly useful, if conceptually different, overviews.

Among the studies of particular geographic places that I have found most useful are Peter Bishop's *The Myth of Shangri-La* and Patrick Vincent McGreevy's *Imagining Niagara.* See too the four articles on the iconology of space and place by Michael Taussig, Jonathan Bordo, Edward Said, and W. J. T. Mitchell in the winter 2000 issue of *Critical Inquiry* ("Geopoetics: Space, Place, and Landscape," p. 173). For a discussion of "place-making" in the specific context of the Amazon, see Hugh Raffles, " 'Local Theory': Nature and the Making of an Amazonian Place" and "Igarapé Guariba: Nature, Locality, and the Logic of Amazonian Anthropogenesis."

10. Largely discredited among scholars, the idea of the Amazon as "the lungs of the world" still has popular currency. It reflects the idea that the Amazon's many plants produce the oxygen we breathe.

11. The *Entangled* of my title is meant to echo both Darwin's "tangled bank" and Einstein's concept of "entanglement" in quantum mechanics, in which measuring one particle could instantly change the properties of another particle, no matter how far apart they were. *Edens* refers to a broader Amazonia-as-paradise theme that is ably discussed in Sérgio Buarque de Holanda's *Visão do paraíso,* Hugh Honour's *The New Golden Land,* Fredi Chiappelli's *First Images of America,* and E. M. P. Baudet's *Paradise on Earth.* I apply the theme especially to the Amazon in my essay "Amazonia as Edenic Narrative."

12. The theme of visions of the Amazon is the subject of Roger D. Stone's *Dreams of Amazonia,* and Neide Gondim's *A invenção da Amazônia.* See also Márcio Souza's *A expressão amazonense,* Pedro Maligo's *Land of Metaphorical Desires,* Ileana Rodríguez' "Naturaleza/nación," Lúcia de Sá Rego's "Reading the Rainforest," and the work of Jorge Marcone on early-twentieth-century "jungle novels" for analyses of literary images. For a broader Latin American context, see the selections in Susan E. Place's *Tropical Rainforests.* Julie Sloan Denslow and Christine Padoch's *People of the Tropical Rain Forest* is a pioneering study of rain forest imagery from different corners of the globe. See, in particular, Francis E. Putz and N. Michele Holbrook's "Tropical Rain Forest Images," pp. 37–52. Although Katherine Emma Manthorne's *Tropical Renais-*

sance deals specifically with North American artists' portrayals of Latin America in the middle of the nineteenth century, the section on "myths and mind sets" (pp. 9–30) provides a useful overview. See too Nancy Leys Stepan's *Picturing Tropical Nature* and the articles in the "Special Issue on Constructing the Tropics" of the *Singapore Journal of Tropical Geography,* pp. 1–98.

13. I take the term *Green Cathedral* from Juan de Onís' book of the same name. The term *Green Hell* was first popularized by the Brazilian writer Alberto Rangel, who refers to the Amazon as a hostile jungle in a 1908 collection of short stories, *Inferno verde.* The "Green Hell" image reappears in an influential book on conservation by R. J. A. Goodland and H. S. Irwin titled *Amazon Jungle: Green Hell to Red Desert,* published in 1975.

14. The three books I had written before arriving in the Amazon were all about traditions that were basically New World adaptations of Iberian forms. It was in the Amazon that I first began to study folk forms that were primarily, though not exclusively, Amerindian in origin.

15. A territorial size and population chart broken down by country appears in *Amazonia without Myths,* p. 9. The authors of the report discuss some of the varying bases for these calculations on pp. 9–13. Brazil is by far the largest single Amazonian nation in terms of both size (some 3.1 million square miles, or some two-thirds of the watershed) and population (some three-quarters of the total for the region, if one includes all of Legal Amazonia). Peru and Bolivia are the second-largest Amazonian countries in terms of size, and Peru is the second-largest in terms of population.

16. For a more detailed chronology, see appendix A. Significantly, there is presently no serious historical overview of the Amazon as a whole. One of the very few such attempts to describe the entire region, Caryl P. Haskins' *The Amazon,* is by now long outdated, and treatments of the region still tend to be part of larger national histories. Although Charles Wagley's *Man in the Amazon* acknowledges a larger Amazonian context, it too is dated and focuses heavily on Brazil. The *Amazonian Literary Review,* founded in 1998 by Nicomedes Suárez Araújo, represents an attempt to talk about the region as a whole from the standpoint of its literary production. *Terra das Águas,* a multidisciplinary journal of the Nucleus for Amazonian Studies at the Federal University of Brasília, also seeks to talk about the region as a whole.

17. See Nigel Smith, *The Amazon River Forest,* pp. 16–22, for an overview of Amazonian prehistory and suggestions for further reading. He notes that both genetic (DNA) and linguistic evidence supports the arrival of human beings in South America tens of thousands of years ago.

18. Anna Roosevelt and colleagues have found evidence of human presence at Pedra Pintada dating from 11,200 to 10,500 B.C. For further information, see A. C. Roosevelt et al., "Paleoindian Cave Dwellers in the Amazon: The Peopling of the Americas."

19. Estimates of the precontact population density of the Amazon Basin vary widely, with 15 million being on the high end. In *The Amazon River Forest,* Smith notes that Marajó Island, near Belém, may have had as many as a million inhabitants when the Marajoara culture flourished, from 400 to 1300 A.D. The

population of the Amazon floodplain and adjacent uplands probably had reached 10 million by the time the first Europeans made an appearance, and the population of Amazonia as a whole "was probably about fifteen million in 1500" (p. 28).

Donald Lathrap and William Denevan did important pioneering work on Amazonian demography in the 1960s and 1970s. For a fuller discussion of more recent population estimates, see Denevan's important essay "The Pristine Myth." For a discussion of the archaeological evidence, see Anna Roosevelt's *Moundbuilders of the Amazon.*

20. Smith, *Amazon River Forest,* p. 23. The village in question was one in a string of Tapajó settlements that have been excavated by present-day archaeologists.

21. For an initial overview, see Anthony Smith's *Explorers of the Amazon.* The long list of products that the Europeans were seeking are often described collectively in Portuguese as *drogas do sertão* (literally, "backlands drugs").

22. Gonzalo Pizarro was the actual head of the group. However, he sent ahead his captain, Francisco de Orellana, with a portion of the crew to look for food, and it was they who made their way down the length of the Amazon. I will have considerably more to say about this expedition in chapter 2.

23. Although the effects of disease on the Indian population would be felt somewhat later in the Amazon than in other, more urbanized, parts of the Americas, they nonetheless would prove catastrophic for many groups. For an overview, see John Hemming's *Red Gold.* For a much more recent account of the devastating effects of measles on the Yanomami Indians in the late 1960s, see Patrick Tierney's *Darkness in El Dorado,* a book whose charges of genocide by U.S. scientists have been hotly debated.

24. For an introduction to the Cabanagem, see Vicente Salles' *Memorial da Cabanagem.*

25. For more details, see Dauril Alden, "The Significance of Cacao Production in the Amazon Region in the Late Colonial Period," pp. 132–33.

26. Others who wrote about the Amazon were Father João Daniel (*Quinta parte do tesouro descoberto no Rio Maximo Amazonas* appeared in 1820); the Peruvians José Pavón, Hipólito Ruiz, and M. Dombey (1778); and the botanist Alexandre Rodrigues Ferreira, who led a Portuguese natural history commission into the Rio Negro (1783–93). A number of early chronicles appear in Antônio Porro's *As crônicas do Rio Amazonas.*

27. Mary L. Pratt makes this point in detail in the introduction to *Imperial Eyes.* See too the individual essays in David Philip Miller and Peter Hanns Reill's *Visions of Empire.* Scholars argue about the covert character of the removal of the rubber seeds.

28. By "the wild," I mean the relative wild, since Amazonian rubber trees are sometimes planted by humans on floodplains and in forests. For a detailed consideration of the environmental and economic aspects of rubber in the Brazilian Amazon, see Warren Dean's *Brazil and the Struggle for Rubber.*

29. For an excellent treatment of boom-and-bust cycles in the Amazon, see Stephen Bunker's *Underdeveloping the Amazon.* Jute was introduced into the

Amazon in 1931 by the Japanese entrepreneur Isukasa Uetsuka and remained the dominant cash crop along the middle stretch of the Amazon floodplain until the growing popularity of synthetic fibers caused it to crash in the 1980s.

30. Official rates of deforestation vary. The Brazilian government estimates that a total of 13 percent of the Brazilian Amazon has been deforested, but many individuals and organizations offer estimates that are sizably higher. Moreover, these figures do not reflect partial destruction of forests or the secondary and tertiary effects of environmental destruction on particular plant and animal species, or on rivers and lakes.

31. The assassination of Chico Mendes in 1989 caused a great stir in the international media and prompted a spurt of movies and TV documentaries, as well as a series of books, aimed at a popular audience. A number of them are reviewed in Kenneth Maxwell's article "The Mystery of Chico Mendes." The movies and books were intended to raise the general public's consciousness about rain forest destruction by giving the Amazon a human face. Although the majority of them idealized Mendes—who was indeed justly admirable—they did draw attention to at least one group of non-Indians in the Amazon, thereby broadening popular conceptions of the region.

32. The march in Bolivia was in 1990; in Ecuador, 1992. For a thorough discussion of Brazilian Indians' entry into national politics, see the chapter on legal weapons of conquest in Alcida Rita Ramos' *Indigenism*, pp. 243–66.

33. I build on Susan Stewart's ideas about "giants" here. For her, the gigantic is a key part of the Western tradition of "object-less desire." Desire, says Stewart, is object-less when it centers on something so immense as to defy effective description. The giant is an attempt to contain this immensity, while the miniature is an abbreviated version of a larger whole. Giants, for Stewart, are above all segments of an otherwise overpowering nonhuman nature. "Our most fundamental relation to the gigantic is articulated in our relation to landscape, our immediate and lived relation to nature as it 'surrounds' us," she explains. For a fuller discussion, see her book *On Longing*, pp. 70–131.

34. "False fear" is a concept often associated with eighteenth- and nineteenth-century notions of the sublime. It is terror, with a strong element of aesthetic pleasure, brought on by the sight of something that dwarfs the human observer. In this book, I use the term specifically to refer to the sorts of fears focused on an object that is not the true source of terror. The fear proves false because it can be allayed.

35. The term *lost world* as associated with the Amazon traces back to Sir Arthur Conan Doyle's 1912 novel, *The Lost World*, in which the intrepid scientist-explorer Challenger stumbles upon Amazonian dinosaurs in an early-twentieth-century version of Steven Spielberg's *Jurassic Park*.

36. The detail about the eating of shoe leather appears, among other places, in Gaspar de Carvajal's chronicle of the Amazon women, discussed in chapter 4.

37. I am thinking here specifically of the British rock star Sting and the Brazilian popular singer Milton Nascimento.

38. I use the term *landscape* here and throughout this book primarily as a synonym for *land*. However, the term has connotations of human domination

which various writers, including Simon Schama in his *Landscape and Memory*, have amply documented.

39. A deconstructionist would use the term *aporia*—that point where clear divisions unravel—for *seepage*. Since I am talking about giant containers, I prefer the more visual *seepage* here.

40. Catherine Caufield, *In the Rainforest*. The phrase "A strange, beautiful, imperiled world" is from the subtitle of the book.

41. The idea that the Amazon may have been home to complex civilizations reflects the presence of sophisticated artifacts such as the Marajoara pottery that Anna Roosevelt has studied. Although the notion that South American highland civilizations may actually have begun in, or been contemporaneous with human development in, the lowlands remains to be proved, it has new currency today among at least some archaeologists.

42. The Funk & Wagnalls *Standard Dictionary of Folklore and Legend* identifies a shape-shifter as "a creature or object which is able to change its shape either at will or under special circumstance" (p. 1004). Because shape-shifting is a common theme in many cultures, the particular definition and uses of these figures have prompted a large anthropological literature. Unlike some shape-shifters who are humans with special powers, the Amazonian Encantados are neither human nor animal. They are beings who usually dwell beneath the water in animal form and who have the ability to take on human appearance.

43. By the time I started the present book, I had already published a detailed overview of these narratives in *Dance of the Dolphin*. Although my own fieldwork has been primarily in Brazil, versions of these stories exist throughout the Amazon.

44. *Ribereño*, meaning "riverbank dweller," or the more general *mestizo*, is the Spanish term for a person of mixed blood, *caboclo* the Portuguese (*ribeirinho* is used in Portuguese as well). These terms are often used for residents of the Amazonian interior. In everyday usage within Amazonia, *caboclo* often has negative rural connotations—a little like the words *hillbilly* or *bumpkin*, with racial overtones. I use it strictly as a synonym for *mixed blood*—itself an ungainly and ambiguous term. While some Amazonian *caboclos* are primarily a mixture of white and Amerindian, there is often a strong African element as well in some parts of the Amazon (the Brazilian states of Pará and Maranhão, and the Colombian Chocó).

The term *colono* is used to refer to immigrants who came to the region after about 1960 from other parts of their respective countries, some of whom have intermarried with Amazonians. *Colonos* are usually poor.

The *colono, caboclo/ribereño*, and Amazonian Indian cultures have become mixed in many cases, adopting each other's stories, festivals, and beliefs. (The large Boi-Bumbá festival in Parintins, for example, is an Amazonian version of the northeastern Brazilian festival Bumba-meu-boi.) However, the groups have remained separate in other cases, and some *colonos* are very recent arrivals.

Many of the people who speak in this book are longtime residents of the Amazon, though a number of the gold miners resemble an uneasy blend of "tra-

ditional" settler and newcomer. Despite the rural connotations of all three
terms, the Amazonians who appear in these pages are often city dwellers.

Important exceptions to the general lack of scholarly interest in the Amazon's
mixed-blood population include the work of Charles Wagley, Eduardo Galvão,
Richard Pace (who revisits Wagley and Galvão's original field site of Gurupá a
half-century later in *The Struggle for Amazon Town*), Stephen Nugent, Peter
Gow, Hugh Raffles, Michael Chibnick, Nigel J. H. Smith, and Mark Harris. See
too the essays in *The Amazon Caboclo,* ed. Eugene Parker, and Binka Le Breton's more journalistic *Voices from the Amazon.* There are also a number of
studies of individual *caboclo* communities by Brazilian scholars. Particularly interesting in terms of the Encantado stories are Raymundo Maués' *A ilha encantada* and Violeta Loureiro's *Os parceiros do mar.* See also Deborah de Magalhães Lima Ayres' "The Social Category *Caboclo.*"

45. Ford acquired the two-and-a-half-million-acre property, which he baptized "Fordlândia," along seventy-five miles of the Tapajós River in 1927. He
shipped in houses, a school, a sawmill, a hospital, and other facilities from Dear-
born, Michigan, for a plantation that was to be a southern extension of his
Rouge Plant in Detroit. However, the enterprise failed miserably once the
canopies of the rubber trees he planted began to close in upon each other, allowing the microbe *microcyclus ulei* to strike and kill the trees.

46. This engagement has become a major topic for anthropologists. See, for
instance, the articles in Jean E. Jackson and Kay Warren's *Indigenous Movements, Self-Representation, and the State in Latin America* and in Frank A. Salamone's *The Yanomami and Their Interpreters.* See too Alcida Ramos' *Indigenism* and Sylvia Caiuby Novaes' *The Play of Mirrors.*

47. The "rubber soldiers" were conscripts who were given the choice of
working on Amazonian rubber plantations during World War II or going to the
front lines after Brazil joined the Allies. (Because the Axis had captured Malaya,
Brazilian rubber was once more in great demand.) Although these people were
promised pensions, few, if any, were ever able to collect remuneration for their
wartime services.

48. The "white" rivers are actually yellowish-white, the "black" rivers are
red-black, and the "clear" rivers are usually blue-green and even clearer than
their black counterparts. For striking photographs of the meeting of the waters,
see Tom Sterling, *The Amazon,* pp. 42–49. See also Harald Sioli's critical summary of Amazon River types in "The Amazon and Its Main Affluents," pp. 157–
62, in which he stresses the many transitions among these three water types.

49. It is not certain that the Manaus encounter is any more spectacular than
other such confluences at Santarém and in the Araguaia region, on the border
between the states of Pará and Tocantins. However, effective marketing has
made it, along with its Rubber Boom–era Opera House, one of the prime touris-
tic icons for the city.

50. The two principal rivers that meet at Santarém are the white-water Amazon and the clear-water Tapajós. It is the meeting of these two rivers that the
Elizabeth Bishop poem at the beginning of this book describes. The smaller,
clear-water Arapiuns also flows into the Tapajós around this point, merging its
blacker waters with the latter's bottle-green.

51. Jacques-Yves Cousteau and Mose Richards, *Jacques Cousteau's Amazon Journey,* p. 74. "Our conclusions are that a kind of aquatic alchemy takes place: when the waters mix, the white rivers add nutrients to the barren black rivers, while also neutralizing their acidity. At the same time, the black rivers dilute the turbidity of the white rivers, enabling sunlight to penetrate and photosynthesis to proceed. The answer is not a 'miracle of loaves and fishes' in the Amazon but pockets of vitality that nourish fish along the points of black- and white-water confluence." While not all limnologists would necessarily agree with this analysis, the idea of the meeting of the waters as a place of fertile intersections and ensuing transformations is what interests me here.

52. The fires returned with a vengeance during the drought-ridden summers of 1997–99. Reporters for international newspapers blamed colonists employing slash-and-burn agriculture, at the same time that accounts of similar fires in Florida were seen as an acts of nature. For an overview of the Amazonian fires, see Daniel C. Nepstad, Adriana G. Moreira, and Ane A. Alencar, *Flames in the Rain Forest.* The book includes a useful bibliography on pp. 141–50.

A TALE OF TWO CITIES

1. For an introduction to El Dorado, see Fernando Ainsa, *De la edad de oro a El Dorado;* Juan Gustavo Cobo Borda, ed., *Fábulas y leyendas de El Dorado;* John Hemming, *The Search for El Dorado;* and Demetrio Ramos Pérez, *El mito de El Dorado.* See too Constantino Bayle's *El Dorado fantasma,* Warwick Bray's *The Gold of El Dorado,* and Octavio Latorre's *La expedición a la Canela y el descubrimiento del Amazonas.* The first three books have excellent bibliographies. Enrique de Gandía gives a wealth of Spanish sources for El Dorado in *Historia crítica de los mitos de la conquista americana* (pp. 103–43), an essential source. John Silver examines the ideology underlying the golden city in "The Myth of El Dorado." Catherine Alès and Michel Pouyllau trace the idea of El Dorado over time in "La Conquête de l'inutile." For a broader, pictorial record of the New World as a source of ongoing treasure, see Hugh Honour's *The New Golden Land.* The Hemming volume includes a useful chronology of expeditions, and the Alès and Pouyllau article provides a detailed table of three centuries of maps.

2. Other, similarly resplendent mythical New World cities include the Seven Cities of Cíbola (usually located somewhere north of Mexico), the City of the Caesars (the southern latitudes of Patagonia), and the "fleece of Colclos," to which Columbus alluded. Often, El Dorado was said to sit on the margins of a lake, though the eighteenth-century friar Juan de Santa Gertrudis described it as a mountain that contained a vein of gold compressed with such force that it exploded like a volcano, spewing gold in all directions.

3. Roberto Levillier discussed this legendary lake in *El Patiti, El Dorado y las Amazonas.* For a reproduction of Joannes de Laet's 1630 map of Lake Parima, see Justin Winsor, "The Amazon and Eldorado," p. 588. *Parima* is sometimes spelled "Parime" or "Paraima." When pictured as a lake, El Dorado

often connects the Amazon with the Río de la Plata system. Other lakes associated with El Dorado at various times are the Xaraes and Titicaca.

Chapter 2. El Dorado and the Golden Legacy

1. The book, Patrick Tierney's *Darkness in El Dorado,* suggests that geneticist James Neel and anthropologist Napoleon Chagnon triggered an epidemic among the Yanomami Indians through their innoculation of the Yanomami with the Edmonston B measles vaccine. Although the film, *The Road to El Dorado,* released by Dreamworks in 2000, draws heavily on Mayan customs and archaeology, it is intentionally imprecise in terms of geography. The filmmakers make clear that it is the gold that initially interests the two fortune-hunting Spaniards, rather than the people or the place.

2. Pedro Cieza de León, *Guerras civiles del Perú,* vol. 3, and Juan de Castellanos, *Elegías de varones ilustres de Indias,* no. 9.12, p. 155. Relevant sections from these works appear in Cobo Borda, *Fábulas,* pp. 104–13 and 118–31.

3. Sir Walter Ralegh, *The Discoverie of the Large, Rich, and Bewtiful Empyre of Guiana,* transcribed, annotated, and introduced by Neil L. Whitehead. In his excellent critical introduction to this 1997 reissue of Ralegh's 1596 text—which ran through three editions in this same year and was rapidly translated into Latin, French, and German—Whitehead treats the text as a kind of proto-ethnography, as well as a literary creation. Other useful examinations of the *Discoverie* include David B. Quinn, *Raleigh and the British Empire* (good for straight historical information), Stephen J. Greenblatt's *Sir Walter Ralegh* (for its emphasis on cultural content; see pages 99–170 for the *Discoverie*), and Mary B. Campbell's chapter on Ralegh in *The Witness and the Other World* (it presents the *Discoverie* as an example of a new, more sober mode of travel writing). "Raleigh" is an alternate spelling of "Ralegh."

4. For a contemporary treatment of the mystical qualities of gold as a life force among particular indigenous cultures of Colombia, see Gerardo Reichel-Dolmatoff, *Amazonian Cosmos.*

A series of pictorial representations of native mining practices during the early colonial period appear in Cobo Borda, *Fábulas.* See also Whitehead's helpful discussion of golden metals as exchange medium and as symbol in Ralegh, *Discoverie,* pp. 75–91.

5. See Hemming, *The Search for El Dorado,* p. 10, for a more detailed account of Ordás' motives for his choice and his ensuing expeditions of 1530 and 1531.

6. Padre José de Acosta, *Historia natural y moral de las Indias,* p. 217.

7. The quote is from *Timon of Athens,* act 4, scene 3. For more on gold's ambiguous and shifting meanings, see Jenifer Marx, *The Magic of Gold,* and René Sédillot, *Histoire de l'or.*

8. For America as New World paradise, see Sérgio Buarque de Holanda, *Visão do paraíso.* For a direct comparison of one part of the Amazon (the Tapajós River region) to Eden, see Padre João Daniel, *Tesouro descoberto no Rio Amazonas,* vol. 1, p. 301. Although he dismissed as an exaggeration the belief

of some Amazonians that Adam lived along the Tapajós River in a still-existent palace, Father Daniel noted that "it is true that the whole region of the states of Amazonas and Grão Pará and all its accompanying rivers is like a great, well-cultivated garden, or a well-managed orchard, or a beautiful and abundant wood." Daniel, to be sure, had many predecessors. A full century earlier, for instance, his fellow Jesuit Simão de Vasconcellos had noted that "beside this river [the Maranhão] our Lord God had planted the terrestrial Paradise" (*Noticias curiosas e necessárias das coisas do Brasil,* vol. 1, pp. 31–32).

9. Cristóbal Colón, *Los cuatro viajes, Testamento,* p. 77. The italics are mine.

10. For these and other dazzling statistics, see Pierre Vilar, *A History of Gold and Money.* See too Alberto Miramón's *Realidad y quimera del oro de Indias.*

11. "All Europe was astounded by the gifts made by Montezuma to Cortés: the jewels and golden objects; the huge gold and silver wheels, as large as those of a cart, which caused Albrecht Dürer to exclaim, 'Never in my life did I see anything that moved me as much as these objects!' The treasure of Atahualpa likewise amazed the world, prompting pages of detailed and admiring description: life-size statues molded in gold, models of animals, birds, fish, and trees as well as everyday objects—all cast in the precious metal" (Fernando Ainsa, "The Myth, Marvel, and Adventure of El Dorado," pp. 17–18).

12. Padre Manuel da Nóbrega, *Cartas do Brasil,* p. 47.

13. Richard Grove makes this point in *Green Imperialism,* pp. 67–72, where it becomes an example of how early mistakes on the part of colonial powers forced them to adopt conservation measures in the Caribbean.

14. Gonzalo Jiménez de Quesada in Cobo Borda, *Fábulas,* pp. 78–79.

15. Juan Rodríguez Freyle, *El carnero.* The section on El Dorado is in chapter 5, pp. 44–56, and the reference to the golden caimans is on pp. 49–50.

16. One important effect of this sort of folklorization of the past, argues José Rabasa, is the vilification and concealment of contemporary Indians. Particularly evident in colonial writers, this dynamic lives on in "contemporary modernization programs that folklorize forms of life and deplore the old—thereby confining Indian cultures to the museum and the curio shop" (Rabasa, "Pre-Columbian Pasts," p. 246).

17. Fray Pedro Simón, *Noticias historiales de las conquistas de tierra firme en las Indias Occidentales,* vol. 2, p. 167. The entire story appears on pp. 166–76. It is reproduced in Cobo Borda, *Fábulas,* pp. 158–63. For a description of Father Simón's treatment of the Indians of his own era, which raises important larger questions about the place of native legends in his work, see Álvaro Félix Bolaños, *Barbarie y canibalismo en la retórica colonial.*

18. John Hemming quotes the German explorer Georg Hohermuth's description of how some of his men on a 1538 expedition "contrary to nature, ate human meat: one Christian was found cooking a quarter of a child together with some greens" (*The Search for El Dorado,* p. 63).

19. Ralegh, *Discoverie,* p. 196. This and all subsequent quotes are taken from the Whitehead edition.

20. Gonzalo Fernández de Oviedo y Valdés, *Historia General y natural de*

las Indias, book 49 (Seville 1535–47). Hemming in *The Search for El Dorado* quotes Fernández de Oviedo on pp. 97–99.

21. Ralegh, *Discoverie,* p. 141.

22. Ibid., pp. 139–40.

23. The holes in the giant container are still more poignant in light of Charles Nicholl's argument that Ralegh's search for Manoa was a spiritual and alchemical as much as a material pursuit (*The Creature in the Map,* pp. 319–329).

24. One skeptic was the anonymous chronicler of Juan Díaz de Solís' expeditions in the Río de la Plata region, who warned the Portuguese at various points throughout his narrative not to lose their time (or lives) looking for El Dorado in the midst of the "great swamps and marshes" that, he said, are all that the interior contains (*Conquista y colonización rioplatense,* vol. 1, p. 67).

25. Voltaire, *Candide,* chapters 17 and 18.

26. Ainsa, *De la edad de oro a El Dorado.*

27. For an introduction to the Land without Evil, see Hélène Clastres, *La terre sans mal.* For a discussion of contemporary messianic movements among Amazonian Indians, see Michael F. Brown and Eduardo Fernández, *War of Shadows.*

28. See Francisco Xavier Ribeiro de Sampaio's remarks in *Diário da viagem,* p. 100.

29. For a thorough discussion of Ralegh's Spanish sources, see the introduction to V. T. Harlow's 1928 edition of the *Discoverie.* These sources not only provide content, but also shape the conceptual outlines of his prose even as he rails against the barbarous Spaniards.

30. Sir Walter Ralegh, *The Discovery of the Large, Rich, and Beautiful Empire of Guiana,* ed. Robert H. Schomburgk. Since Schomburgk's preface is dated May 1848 and Bates and Wallace departed Liverpool on April 27, they almost certainly did not read the book before setting out for the Amazon. It is quite possible, however, that they read the book before writing their own accounts of travels in the Amazon—Wallace in 1853 and Bates some nine years later. The naturalists' accounts are Henry Walter Bates, *The Naturalist on the River Amazons;* Alfred Russel Wallace, *A Narrative of Travels on the Amazon and Rio Negro;* and Richard Spruce, *Notes of a Botanist on the Amazon and Andes.*

31. Edwards' book, *A Voyage up the River Amazon,* was first published in 1847. The book sold well enough to go through a new edition in 1855. Wallace refers to it on the first page of his own book.

32. H. M. Tomlinson, *The Sea and the Jungle,* p. 7.

33. "In this valley there is not a plain in the interior, not a hill, not a bank of a river, rivulet, lake, or *igarapé,* where we do not find the splendour and the superabundance of an extraordinary vegetation," Nery exclaimed effusively. "On all sides are exhaled the most varied perfumes" (*The Land of the Amazons,* p. 79).

34. See Humboldt's comments on El Dorado as a focus for geographic inquiry in the first chapter of volume 3 of his *Personal Narrative of Travels to the Equinoctial Regions of America, during the Years 1799–1804.* The fascination with El Dorado as a vast interior lake into which feed numerous waterways con-

tinues to surface on the eve of the twenty-first century in development proposals regarding an internal South American waterway. These proposals are the subject of Christian Brannstrom's "The River of Silver and the Island of Brazil."

35. The original publisher of Bates' *Naturalist,* John Murray, who also published Charles Darwin, insisted on a series of cuts in the second, 1864, edition that were restored in the subsequent 1892 commemorative edition. For a consideration of Bates in terms of the scientific imagery of the Amazon, see the section on the British naturalist in Hugh Raffles, "Igarapé Guariba," pp. 127–228. For basic biographical information, see George Woodcock, *Henry Walter Bates.* John Dickenson offers a useful summary in "Henry Walter Bates—The Naturalist of the River Amazons." Robert M. Stecher's "The Darwin-Bates Letters" provides a good sense of the relationship between the two men. For Bates' and Wallace's contributions to theories of evolution, see the essays in Barbara G. Eddall's *Wallace and Bates in the Tropics.*

36. Written in clear and vivid language, Bates' *Naturalist* remained popular longer than did the works of Spruce and Wallace, which offer an interesting complement and comparison. See Woodcock, *Henry Walter Bates,* p. 13, for the admiring comments of Darwin, D. H. Lawrence, George Orwell, and various other later writers. Capsule biographies of Bates and various other "scientific travelers" to Amazonia are contained in the *Dictionary of Scientific Biography,* editor-in-chief Charles Coulston Gillispie; compact listings of some of the most important of these are given in Márcio Souza's *Breve história da Amazônia,* pp. 77–78.

37. Mary Louise Pratt would almost certainly find Bates' work to be an excellent example of what she defines as the "anti-conquest," or those "strategies of representation whereby European bourgeois subjects seek to secure their innocence in the same moment as they assert European hegemony" (*Imperial Eyes,* p. 7). He reveals a much sharper sense of class consciousness and of the injustices of the social hierarchies that he encounters than do many of his contemporaries.

38. Much of Bates' scientific education took place at the Mechanics' Institutes, a kind of nineteenth-century adult school. Thanks in part to his association with Darwin, to whom he regularly furnished information, he was able to get a job as assistant secretary of the Royal Geographical Society, where he continued to edit transactions, reform the library, and organize expeditions for some twenty-seven years. While the job represented the lower echelons of respectability, and Bates was forced to sell off much of his field collection to support a growing family, it was nonetheless a big step up from his tradesman days.

39. See Charles Darwin, *Journal of Researches into the Natural History and Geology of the Countries Visited during the Voyage of the H. M. S.* Beagle *under the Command of Capt. Fitz Roy, R. N.,* pp. 185–209. The comments get more negative as the account progresses.

40. Bates, *Naturalist,* p. 3. Here, and throughout the following chapters, I provide page numbers for quotations that are a full sentence or more in length.

41. Bates' assertion that there is not a single word in Indian languages to signify a divine being appears in earlier works, including Alexandre Rodrigues Ferreira's *Viagem filosófica pelas Capitanias do Grão-Pará, Rio Negro, Mato*

Grosso e Cuiabá, p. 94. Bates, however, did not echo Ferreira's claim that "neither the wonder nor the beauty of the universe makes any impression upon [the Indians]." Indeed, his sympathy for individual Indians stems precisely from his sense of their intense feeling for the natural world.

42. Bates, *Naturalist,* p. 43.

43. Ibid., p. 376.

44. Henry Walter Bates, "A Pocket Diary Covering Parts of the Years 1848–1859." The small diary, with its fragile, pale blue pages, consists mostly of lists of supplies and specimens, interspersed with notations that serve as the seeds of passages in the *Naturalist.*

45. The fact that Roosevelt got the title wrong (he referred to Bates' book as *The Naturalist on the Amazon* on p. 357 of his own account) somewhat undercuts the glowing recommendation.

46. Theodore Roosevelt, *Through the Brazilian Wilderness.* The edition I have used, a reissue of the 1914 original that conserves the original page numbers, contains a foreword by the former president's great-grandson, Tweed Roosevelt, who was a member of the twenty-member group that retraced the expedition's original route in 1992. The *Scribner's* issues have a number of interesting photographs not included in the book. For a sense of how the book was received during the period, see "Through the Brazilian Wilderness" *(New York Times Literary Supplement),* "Mr. Roosevelt's New River" *(London Spectator),* and "Through the Brazilian Wilderness" *(Atheneum).* While judgments of the book are generally favorable, some reviewers scoffed at the idea that a river as big as (or bigger than) the Rhine could heretofore have escaped attention.

47. For an introduction to Roosevelt and his presidency, see Edmund Morris' *The Rise of Theodore Roosevelt.* John Milton Cooper Jr.'s *The Warrior and the Priest* compares the twenty-sixth president with his successor, Woodrow Wilson. Joseph Lawrence Gardner's *Departing Glory* is good on the years following Roosevelt's second term in office.

48. Joseph R. Ornig took this quote as the title for his book *My Last Chance to Be a Boy,* the only detailed account of Roosevelt's Amazonian expedition and an excellent source of background information. If the South American junket offered an adventurous escape from the maelstrom of politics, it also held out the prospect of money. Roosevelt went to the Amazon with a five-thousand-dollar advance from *Scribner's,* a promise of another ten thousand dollars for six to eight articles, and a 20 percent royalty agreement on an ensuing book (Ornig, p. 35). Financial backing for the expedition proper came from the American Museum of Natural History and the Brazilian government.

49. Roosevelt initially visited the urban centers of Argentina, Uruguay, Chile, and Brazil, where he spoke on the political reforms he had championed as a third-party candidate in the 1912 election. He then visited the Amazon between 27 February and 27 April 1914. Some riveting news clips of Roosevelt and the expedition appear in Sílvio Back's documentary movie *O Índio no Brasil* (1995). For one Brazilian perspective on Roosevelt's journey, see Luiz Cordeiro, *Roosevelt e a Amazônia.*

50. Rondon, whose mother was half Indian, is as complex a figure as Roosevelt. For an introduction, see Edilberto Coutinho's *Rondon* and Darcy Ri-

beiro's *O indigenista Rondon*. Rondon's own account of the expedition appears in Esther de Viveiros, *Rondon conta sua vida,* pp. 407–24. Since both men were extremely stubborn, and Roosevelt apparently knew only two words of Portuguese ("Mais canja," or "More chicken soup!"), the two attempted to communicate in French, with unquestionably interesting results.

51. For a consideration of the shifting meaning of the term *wilderness,* see William Cronon, "The Trouble with Wilderness." The junglelike wilderness was not peculiar to Roosevelt but lived on in later adventure travelogues such as Peter Grieve's *The Wilderness Voyage,* as well as present-day travel brochures that describe the Amazon as a "jungle wilderness."

52. For a discussion of Roosevelt as the president who helped to establish 150 national forests, five national parks, and more than fifty federal bird reservations, see Paul Russell Cutright, *Theodore Roosevelt, the Making of a Conservationist.* See too the section on Roosevelt in Ralph Lutts' *The Nature Fakers* and Donna Haraway's discussion of Roosevelt, in "Teddy Bear Patriarchy," as one of the American Museum of Natural History's guiding spirits in the emergence of a nature in which mystery and material resource mingle.

53. Roosevelt's attitudes toward race are the focus of Thomas G. Dyer's *Theodore Roosevelt and the Idea of Race.* See in particular the chapters on Roosevelt's "racial education" (pp. 1–44) and the chapter on his attitudes toward U.S. Indians (pp. 69–88).

54. Roosevelt, *Through the Brazilian Wilderness,* p. 145.

55. The adventure aspect of the travelogue, as well as Roosevelt's celebrity, explains its use as a prologue for a 1952 English-language translation of Jules Verne's 1883 novel *Eight Hundred Leagues on the Amazon.* And yet, if one compares *Through the Brazilian Wilderness* to other Amazon travelogues of the epoch, Roosevelt looks downright restrained. See, for instance, Algot Lange's 1912 *In the Amazon Jungle,* whose subtitle, *Adventures in the Remote Parts of the Upper Amazon River, Including a Sojourn among Cannibal Indians,* sets the stage for section headings such as "Horrible Slaughter," "Fevers," and "Poisoned Arrows." Even the toucan that appears as an illustration has a malevolent air. See also F. W. Up de Graf's *Head Hunters of the Amazon,* which appeared nine years after *Through the Brazilian Wilderness* with a foreword by Kermit Roosevelt.

56. William H. Fisher argues in "Native Amazonians and the Amazon Wilderness" that the end of the Rubber Boom changed the way the industrialized world imagined the Amazon. He contends that if Roosevelt had visited the region some three or four years earlier, his impressions and the sorts of tropes he used would probably have been very different. Although Roosevelt's fixation on the wilderness and his need to find a worthy competitor in nature cast doubt upon this argument, it is nonetheless intriguing.

57. Roosevelt, *Through the Brazilian Wilderness,* p. 324. The "absolutely unknown river" quote appears on p. 318.

58. Ibid., p. 108. The earlier *cajazeira* quote appears on p. 283.

59. Ibid., p. 290.

60. While fascination with the primitive would characterize the Surrealists and then burgeon once more after World War II, hints of it were already pres-

89

ent in the pragmatic Roosevelt. For a study of the concept of the primitive in the twentieth century, see Marianna Torgovnick, *Gone Primitive.*

61. Roosevelt, *Through the Brazilian Wilderness,* p. 217. For a suggestive comparison to this book, see Roosevelt's description of his African expedition of 1909 in *African Game Trails.* The ensuing quotes in this and the following paragraph are on pp. 218 and 219.

62. This same aura of mystery suffuses any number of later travel narratives—and, indeed, the IMAX movie, with its focus on the "timeless mystery" of the Amazon. See, among countless other travel accounts, Gordon Mac-Creagh's *White Waters and Black* (1926), which begins with an expression of the author's desire to record "all of the mysterious doings of all of the wild Indians" his expedition intends to confront in Amazonia; Jack White and Avril Grant White's *Jungle Down the Street* (1958), with its stress on "the cult of the macumba"; Brian Branstron's *The Last Great Journey on Earth* (1970), with its "interlude for mystery"; and Joe Kane's *Running the Amazon* (1989), which is at least as much about the "rapacious verdant chaos" that is the jungle as it is about the river he battles on a kayaking trip.

63. To cite just one of many examples, the eighteenth-century writer Father João Daniel noted that the Amazonian natives used no clothes, "as Adam and Eve in Paradise" (*Quinta parte do Tesouro descoberto no Rio Máximo Amazonas,* vol. 1, p. 301).

64. Roosevelt, *Through the Brazilian Wilderness,* p. 70.

65. The term *imperialist nostalgia* is Renato Rosaldo's. See the essay by the same name in his book *Culture and Truth,* pp. 68–87.

66. Frederick Jackson Turner, *The Frontier in American History.* For a series of discussions of changing perspectives on Turner's famous thesis, see Richard White and Patricia Nelson Limerick, *The Frontier in American Culture.*

67. "Roosevelt Now Homeward Bound," *New York Times,* 1 May 1914.

68. For an examination of Roosevelt as spokesperson for American imperialism, see David Henry Burton's *Theodore Roosevelt: Confident Imperialist* and Richard H. Collin's *Theodore Roosevelt, Culture, Diplomacy, and Expansion.*

69. Corinne Roosevelt Robinson asserted that the Amazonian venture cut short her brother's life in *My Brother, Theodore Roosevelt,* p. 278. Tweed Roosevelt expresses a similar opinion in his preface to the 1994 reissue of his great-grandfather's book (p. xiv).

70. For a good general introduction to the anthropologist and his work, see Marcel Hénaff's *Lévi-Strauss and the Making of Structural Anthropology.* Lévi-Strauss provides a revealing perspective on his own work in *Conversations with Claude Lévi-Strauss* and in Claude Lévi-Strauss and Diderot Eribon, *De prés et de loin.*

71. In its celebration of a remote, primordial past, the book has much in common with the Cuban novelist Alejo Carpentier's *The Lost Steps,* which appeared two years before it. For a discussion of textual similarities and contextual ties between these two major postwar works, see Mercedes López Barault, "Los pasos encontrados de Lévi-Strauss y Alejo Carpentier." See too John Incledon's "The Writing Lesson in *Los pasos perdidos.*"

The native groups that Lévi-Strauss describes—the Caduveo, the Bororo, the

Nambikwara, the Carajá, and the Tupi-Kawahib—are from different parts of the Brazilian interior. The Caduveo live on the Paraguay River. The other four groups are part of Legal Amazonia.

72. Clifford Geertz discusses the multiple literary genres within *Tristes tropiques* (travelogue, ethnography, meditation on the nature of anthropology, quest narrative, and symbolist text) in the chapter "The World in a Text," in *Works and Lives*. For other approaches to the book, see the various essays in Joel Askenazi et al., *Analyses et reflexions sur Lévi-Strauss, "Tristes tropiques,"* especially Alain Tissut's "L'Autre à la Croisée des Regards," pp. 91–95. Useful, more specialized considerations of the book include Cleo McNelly's "Natives, Women and Claude Lévi-Strauss," David Damrosch's "The Ethnic Ethnographer," and Christopher Johnson's "Cinna's Apotheosis." (The last article offers an intriguing examination of a classically structured play that Lévi-Strauss began to write in the middle of his fieldwork in the Amazon.) See too Sunpreet Arshi et al., "Why Travel?"

73. These impulses come under further scrutiny in John Avery Tallmadge's chapter on paradoxes of the exotic in his Ph.D. dissertation, "Narrative Artifice in the Literature of Exploration," and in the section on travel for science's sake in Dennis Porter's *Desire and Transgression in European Travel Writing* (pp. 246–84). See too Marianna Torgovnick's chapter "Remembering with Lévi-Strauss" in *Gone Primitive*, pp. 210–26.

74. Lévi-Strauss, *Tristes tropiques*, p. 37.

75. Ibid., p. 393.

76. Ibid., p. 330.

77. Ibid., p. 47.

78. This positive attitude toward the natives—hardly unusual for a twentieth-century social scientist—is not without precedent, however, and there is much in *Tristes tropiques* that recalls not just the eighteenth-century philosopher and writer Jean-Jacques Rousseau, but also the sixteenth-century philosopher Michel de Montaigne in "Of Cannibals."

79. Domingo de Vera's 1593 Guiana expedition supposedly got within a half league—a mere two miles—of El Dorado before staging an inexplicable retreat (Nicholl, *The Creature in the Map*, p. 11).

80. Lévi-Strauss, *Tristes tropiques*, p. 325. The italics are mine.

Chapter 3. The Encante as a World in Motion

1. I have changed all of the names of Amazonian storytellers to protect their privacy. For fuller descriptions of Tô Pereira and Gerineldo, see Candace Slater, *Dance of the Dolphin*, pp. 42–48.

2. For a comprehensive overview of the Encantado stories, see Slater, *Dance of the Dolphin*. For a pioneering study of the Encantado stories, see Eduardo Galvão, *Santos e visagens*. Raymundo Heraldo Maués' *A ilha encantada* examines the links between the Encantados and shamanism. Nigel J. H. Smith's *The Enchanted Amazon Rain Forest* offers another contemporary vision from the Brazilian Amazon. For examinations of the Encantado tradition in the Spanish-

speaking Amazon, see Fernando Madriz Galindo, "Los encantos, elementos del agua," and David Guss, "The Encantados." See too the section on the *yacuruna*, or water people, of the Peruvian Amazon in Jaime Regan, *Hacia la tierra sin mal*, pp. 173–85, and Regina Harrison's discussion of snake lovers in *Signs, Songs, and Memory in the Andes*, pp. 144–71.

3. The theme of an underwater city is common in many folk traditions, and some Amazonian storytellers actually compare the Encante to Ys (the subject of a television special) and, above all, Atlantis, with which some of them are familiar through books, movies, and a TV documentary about Colonel Percy Harrison Fawcett, who went looking for the residents of the lost continent of Atlantis in the area between the Xingu and das Mortes Rivers after he "saw" them during a London séance in the 1920s. See also the entries under Stith Thompson, *Motif-Index of Folk Literature*, motif F725.1, "submarine cities." For two early references to the Encante, see Francisco Bernardino de Sousa, *Lembranças e curiosidades do Valle do Amazonas*, p. 261, and Frederico José de Santa-Anna Nery, *Folk-lore brésilien*, p. 181. See also the chapter on submerged cities and marvelously powerful anacondas in Priscila Faulhaber's *O lago does espelhos*, pp. 151–99. Various Andean stories of underwater cities appear in Efraín Morote Best, *Aldeas sumergidas*, pp. 47–51, and Anne Marie Hocquengheim and Max Inga, *Los encantos de La Encantada*, pp. 47–51.

4. For a discussion of the relationship of this "water world" to other levels of the universe in indigenous thinking, see Peter Roe's *The Cosmic Zygote*, pp. 127–62. See too the references to watery domains and spirit beings in Gerardo Reichel-Dolmatoff's *Amazonian Cosmos*. For an Amazonian Indian parallel to the Encante, see Marc de Civrieux's "Medatia." An underwater city, sometimes known as "Temendauí," which is home to fair-haired immortals who "stage celebrations in the manner of the white man," appears in Curt Nimuendaju's *The Tükuna*, p. 138.

5. Henry Walter Bates mentions various folk beliefs about the particular freshwater dolphins known as the boto *(Inia geoffrensis geoffrensis)* in *The Naturalist on the River Amazons*. ("No animal in the Amazons region is the subject of so many fables as the Bouto," p. 291.) The dolphin who appears at country dances is a theme in Inglez de Souza's *Contos amazônicos*. For an introduction to the animal on whom these stories focus, see Robin C. Best and Vera M. F. da Silva's "Amazon River Dolphin."

6. See Seth Leacock and Ruth Leacock, *Spirits of the Deep*, and Napoleão Figueiredo and Anaíza Vergolino e Silva's *Festas de santo e encantados* for an introduction to the many African influences in these stories.

7. For more on these sources, see the chapter on dolphins as supernatural beings in Slater, *Dance of the Dolphin*, pp. 89–117.

8. In a random sample that Richard Pace conducted in the 1990s in the small town and surrounding interior of Gurupá, that area where Charles Wagley had done research in the 1950s, a full 74 percent of the respondents said that the boto could transform itself into human form (Pace, *The Struggle for Amazon Town*, p. 149).

9. For an overview of Amazonian urban centers, see John Browder and Brian Godfrey, *Rainforest Cities*.

10. For an introduction to the large body of work on post-1960s migration into Amazonia and its social and environmental consequences, see Marianne Schmink and Charles H. Wood, *Contested Frontiers in Amazonia,* together with their earlier *Frontier Expansion in Amazonia.* See too Judith Lisansky, *Migrants to Amazonia,* and Rolf Wesche and Thomas Bruneau, *Integration and Change in Brazil's Middle Amazon.*

11. For an introduction to the Boi-Bumbá, which came to Amazonia from the Brazilian northeast, see Simão Assayag, *Boi-Bumbá.* For a specific treatment of the Boi-Bumbá of Parintins, see Maria Laura Viveiros de Castro Cavalcanti, "O Boi-Bumbá de Parintins / Amazonas."

12. Probably the two most celebrated works in Brazil for which the Encantados have served as direct inspiration are Waldemar Henrique's 1933 musical composition "Foi Boto, Sinhá!" (words by Antonio Tavernard) and Raul Bopp's long lyric poem *Cobra Norato.*

The dolphin also has a kind of New Age appeal among today's urban middle classes, not only in Amazonia but also in other parts of the Amazonian nations and in the United States, Japan, and Europe. For a discussion of dolphins' particular symbolic appeal to the residents of industrial and postindustrial societies after the 1960s, see Mette Bryld, "Dialogues with Dolphins and Other Extraterrestrials." See too Mette Marie Bryld and Nina Lykke, *Cosmodolphins.*

13. Walter Lima Júnior's *The Dolphin* appeared in 1987. *Where the Water Runs Black,* directed by Christopher Kain and released by MGM in 1986, is based on David Kendall's novel *Lázaro.*

14. Woman, age twenty-two, born Zé Açu. Married ("but my husband is now working in Manaus"), housework, two years' schooling ("but I can do more than sign my name"). In the case of people whom I quote at length and who, unlike Tô Pereira and Gerineldo, do not reappear throughout the chapter, I have given the person's sex, age, place of birth, and place of residence if different from their birthplace. Marital status, occupation, and level of schooling follow. I do not give this information for the many short quotes that appear in this book. For the reader interested in learning more about the Encantado stories and individual storytellers, a wider selection of texts, together with the Portuguese originals, is available in Slater, *Dance of the Dolphin.*

15. Woman, age thirty-six, born Semeão (interior of Parintins), lives Porto Velho (four years). Separated, laundress, no formal education ("but next year, I'm going to see if I can't enroll in adult school").

16. Raimundo, age sixty-seven, born interior of Maués, lives Parintins. Married ("actually, she is my second wife; the first one died two days after the wedding"), fisherman and sometime carpenter, no formal education ("but my mother taught all of us children how to read").

17. Woman, age thirty-three, born Juruá River ("but I spent most of my childhood in the interior of Maués"), lives Maués. Single, sells perfume and makes crocheted goods, four years grade school.

18. John Hemming, *The Search for El Dorado,* pp. 97–99.

19. Woman, age eighty-four, born Mocambo, lives Manaus (two years). Widowed, no formal education ("but I can read and write more than some who say they've been to school").

20. The story is well known outside Amazonia as well because of Raul Bopp's poem. For a critical introduction to his particular use of this broader folk theme, see Lygia Morrone Averbuck, *Cobra Norato e a Revolução Caraíba* and Othon Moacyr Garcia's *Cobra Norato, o poema e o mito.*

21. Rosane, age seventeen, born interior of Santarém, lives Parintins (two years). Married, housework and coconut-sweet maker, two years high school.

22. *Regatões* have been essential commercial and social links throughout much of the history of the Amazon. For an introduction, see José Alípio Goulart, *O regatão.*

23. Charuto, age thirty-seven, born interior of Juriti Velho, lives Santarém (ten years). Married, dockworker and jack-of-all-trades ("life's more interesting that way"), "some" grade school.

24. For a good discussion of contemporary Amazonian folk healing and folk healers, see Maués, *A ilha encantada.* For an overview of the South American Indian shamanic tradition, which is one of the *caboclo* tradition's primary sources, see the section on "specialists" in Lawrence E. Sullivan's *Icanchu's Drum,* pp. 386–465.

25. Man, age eighteen, born Maués. Single, bicycle mechanic, two years high school.

26. For a native Amazonian (Yekuana) parallel to this story, see David M. Guss, trans., "Wiyu and the Man Who Liked to Shoot Dolphins." For a Portuguese-language version of the same story, see José Carvalho, *O matuto cearense e o caboclo do Pará,* pp. 22–24.

27. For a fuller explanation of Amazonian Aquatic Seducers, see Roe, *The Cosmic Zygote,* pp. 163–80. Gary Urton's *Animal Myths and Metaphors in South America* provides a useful broader context for the relationship between human and nonhuman entities in Amazonian Indian narratives.

28. I do not mean to suggest here that native myths do not reveal humor, but rather that they tend to be an open part of a cosmological vision often less directly apparent in the Encantado tales. Also, there may be striking differences among native groups, as well as between populations located in cities and others deep in the interior.

29. Peter Roe, "Anciently, There was a Woman who was always being molested by a Dolphin," *The Cosmic Zygote,* pp. 51–52.

30. The *mães* are also called *donos,* or owners. These two terms—the first feminine, the second masculine—are often used interchangeably. The *mãe* has similarities to the Master of Fish or Master of Game in a number of Amazonian Indian cultures. Whereas these Masters (called *Vai mahsë* by the Tukanoan people) are distinguished by their fluid, nonpersonifiable character, the *mães* are often more concrete, physical presences.

31. For one version of the Fish Woman story, see Michael F. Brown, *Tsewa's Gift,* p. 52. For a discussion of the World Tree, see Roe, *The Cosmic Zygote,* pp. 118–19.

32. Analyses of native Amazonian stories about whites include Júlio Cézar Melatti, "A origem dos brancos no mito de *Shoma Wetsa*"; Emilienne Ireland, "Cerebral Savage"; Peter Roe, "The Josho Nahuanbo Are All Wet and Undercooked"; and Charles R. Marsh Jr., "The Indians and the Whites." The tale of

Kwatïngï in Ellen B. Basso's *In Favor of Deceit,* pp. 29–83, explains how Europeans and Indians emerged as culturally distinct peoples.

33. For a fuller consideration of the Dolphin as gringo, see Slater, *Dance of the Dolphin,* pp. 202–32.

34. Janet M. Chernela, "Righting History in the Northwest Amazon," pp. 40–48. The story proper, narrated by Crispiniano Carvalho, appears on pp. 41–43. For further commentary on the narrative, see Janet M. Chernela and Eric J. Leed, "The Deficits of History." The Arapaço narrative actually turns out to be considerably more sanguine than a number of other native Amazonian tales in which white people's actions bring not just loss, but death. See, for instance, Thomas Gregor's "Dark Dreams about the White Man" for the Mehinaku, and Waud Kracke's "Death Comes as the White Man" for the Tupi-Kagwahiv. ("Kagwahiv" is an alternate spelling of "Kawahib.")

35. Edi Lopes, *É Cobra, é Grande!* This comic-book version, clearly influenced by the Japanese comics called *mangas,* presents a Mother of the Waters who recalls the warlike Amazons in her fierce power. She demands that a human couple choose to keep either Norato or his sister with them on earth, since one of the twins must remain with her beneath the waves. Although the idea of the power of nature is in no way foreign to either the Encantado stories or to indigenous myths, the plot, the language, and the conception of enchantment in *É cobra, é Grande!* are all very different. There is also a comic-book version about the Dolphin by the same author, called "A Lenda do Boto," which reveals the same sort of striking differences. I thank Stephen Nugent for a copy of these texts, both purchased in Santarém.

36. See the relevant listings in Johannes Wilbert, *Folk Literature of South American Indians: General Index.*

37. Gilberto Mestrinho, a former governor of Amazonas, served as the inspiration for Amazonian novelist Márcio Souza's highly satiric *A resistível asenção do Boto Tucuxi,* which portrayed Mestrinho as a salacious figure reminiscent of the Dolphin in various Encantado stories. Mestrinho later turned the tables on his critics by openly embracing the association with the Dolphin in his 1990 run for reelection. His opponents responded with the slogan "Vote for Gilberto—he may well be your father," a sardonic reference to the Dolphin's (and, apparently, the governor's) voracious libido, but Mestrinho still won the election.

38. The massacre of twenty-eight landless peasants, or *sem-terras,* took place in Eldorado dos Carajás on 17 April 1996.

39. For a useful comparison, see Charles Stewart, *Demons and the Devil,* in which the Greek *exotiká* often come to embody an embarrassingly backward past.

40. I was struck by the close similarities between a number of the stories I recorded in the 1990s and others carefully written down by Charles Wagley and Eduardo Galvão in the 1940s and early 1950s in Gurupá. Several dozen Encantado stories appear among the now-yellowed field notes in the Wagley archive in the University of Florida Special Collections Library at Gainesville. Unfortunately for present-day researchers, Wagley and Galvão concentrated on the story proper and rarely included the sorts of interjections, asides, and framing com-

mentary in which a good deal of the force and import of today's (and, almost certainly, yesterday's) stories lie.

41. These changes have been amply documented by scholars in a variety of disciplines. For an introduction to the ongoing transformation of the Amazon, see the ample bibliography in Susanna Hecht and Alexander Cockburn, *The Fate of the Forest,* pp. 319–43. For an overview of ongoing changes in the 1990s, see the essays in Charles Wood and Robert Porró, eds., *Patterns and Processes of Land Use and Deforestation in the Amazon.*

42. For references from various different cultures to an era in which birds and humans shared a common tongue, see David M. Guss, ed. and trans., *The Language of the Birds.*

43. For the importance of television as an agent of social transformation in contemporary Amazonia, see J. Timmons Roberts, "Expansion of Television in Eastern Amazonia."

44. Gerardo Reichel-Dolmatoff, "Cosmology as Ecological Analysis."

45. Eduardo Galvão discusses the complex of beliefs and prohibitions governing hunting and fishing known as *panema* in *Encontro de sociedades,* pp. 57–62. *Panema* is also used as an adjective in popular speech, as in, "That fisherman remained *panema* for many months after he killed the dolphin who had torn his net."

46. Fray Juan de Santa Gertrudis in Juan Cobo Borda, ed., *Fábulas,* p. 235. The phrase in Spanish is "De lejos lo verás, pero no podrás llegar allá, porque está encantado de los antiguos."

AMAZON WOMEN

1. For some other stiff competitors for gigantic status, see Luís Weckmann's section on monsters in *The Medieval Heritage of Mexico,* pp. 46–71. Weckmann's detail-packed bibliographic discussion of Amazons (pp. 46–60) is part of a chapter that also deals with giants (in the restricted sense of impossibly large beings) and pygmies.

2. The name Santa María del Mar Dulce (Saint Mary of the Freshwater Sea) is associated with Vicente Yáñez Pinzón, who entered the Amazon from the Atlantic Ocean in February 1500.

Chapter 4. Warrior Women, Virgin Forests, and Green Hells

1. Ralegh wrote that "these Amazones have likwise great store of these plates of golde, which they recover by exchange chiefly for a kinde of greene stones, which the Spaniards call Piedras Hijadas" (*Discoverie,* p. 146). The seventeenth-century Jesuit priest Cristóbal de Acuña and the eighteenth-century "scientific traveler" Charles de la Condamine also mention the stones. For a scholarly discussion of petrography, distribution, dating, and cultural affiliations of these animal-shaped pendants in the Caribbean and Amazonia, see Arie

Boomert, "Gifts of the Amazons." The type of jade used in these talismans is nephrite, also known as "kidney stone," which ranges in color from near-white to green.

2. The frog, according to Peter G. Roe, is related through analogy to the anaconda in that both swallow their food whole. The frog often fills in for the anaconda in places (within or outside the Amazon) where anacondas are not present—most notably, in the Caribbean. Both a male and a female symbol, the frog is often an important element in shamanism, hallucinogen use, and fire-bringing (personal communication, 3 April 1999). Although the frog is the most common animal depicted in the Amazon, historical sources also mention pendants in the shape of birds, lizards, fishes, and other animals. For a list of further sources on the *muiraquitã*, see Boomert, pp. 48–54. The article also includes useful maps and illustrations.

3. I rely heavily in my account of the classical Amazons on Josine H. Blok, *The Early Amazons*, which includes an ample bibliography, and on William Blake Tyrrell, *Amazons*, whose focus on the Amazon myth as part of a social dialogue concerning the Athenian marriage system represents a very different perspective. Other useful studies of the Amazon theme include Donald Sobol, *The Amazons of Greek Mythology* (see the section on the Amazons in literature and art, pp. 91–112); Page DuBois, *Centaurs and Amazons;* and Abby Wettan Kleinbaum, *The War against the Amazons*. The Kleinbaum book, which traces the Amazon theme over the centuries, includes some wonderful illustrations, such as a photograph of Katharine Hepburn as the Amazon princess Antiope.

Tyrrell says that the term *Amazons* comes from the Greek *a* (no) plus *mazos* (breast), but adds that the name preceded the phenomenon (p. 49). Blok, who asserts that the term is not Greek, gives various examples of spurious etymologies for the Amazons (including the "no breasts" derivation) on pp. 27–28.

4. Strabo placed the Amazons nearer to Greece, in Ephesus and Smyrna; Diodorus Siculus situated them in Libya or Atlantis. Herodotus placed them in Scythia in his history of the Greeks (see book 4, sections 110–17). He also described the war between Greeks and Amazons at the River Thermodon in book 9, section 27. These passages are easily accessible in Herodotus, *The History,* trans. David Grene, on pp. 320–22 and pp. 623–24.

5. For the emerging archaeological evidence along the present Russian-Kazakhstan border, see Jeannine Davis-Kimball and C. Scott Littleton, "Warrior Women of the Eurasian Steppes." For a brief summary of their preliminary findings, see David Perlmann, "New Evidence of Legendary Women Warriors."

6. Blok, *The Early Amazons*, p. 411. Female warriors in jackets, leather caps, and trousers and carrying Scythian bows begin appearing in Greek vase painting dating from 570 to ca. 540 B.C. This evidence bolsters suggestions of a society of northern origins present from the fifth century B.C. onward.

7. Penthesilea first appeared in an episode narrated by the Greek writer Arctinus. Quintus Smyrnaeus, a fourth-century A.D. author, described the beauty of Penthesilea's face as "awesome" and "radiant." Seeing her dead at his feet, Achilles is said to have "suffered greatly in his heart, that he slew her and did not bring her to Phthia as his shining wife, since in height and beauty she was blame-

less and like the immortals" (Tyrrell, *Amazons*, pp. 78–79). Penthesilea re-emerged as the heroine of a drama by the German poet and playwright Heinrich von Kleist in the early nineteenth century.

8. Blok describes early versions of the Penthesilea-Achilles story as presenting an "insoluble dilemma in terms of the heroic code of epic" (*The Early Amazons*, p. 281).

9. For a discussion of the Amazon theme in classical Greek art, see Dietrich von Bothmer, *Amazons in Greek Art*.

10. These authors include Iberian writers such as Isidro de Sevilla, Alfonso el Sabio, and Jorge Manrique. For a consideration of the Amazon theme in Spanish poetry of the Middle Ages, see Estelle Irizarry, "Echoes of the Amazon Myth in Medieval Spanish Poetry."

11. Mandeville, the first Spanish translation of whose book appeared in 1521, described the country of the Amazons, which he called the Maiden Land or Land of Women, as "an island, surrounded by water, except at two points where there are two ways in." His Amazons revealed notable class distinctions. Those "of great estate" cut off their left breast so as to carry their shields better, and ones "of low degree" cut off the right in order better to shoot arrows. See *The Travels of Sir John Mandeville*, translated with an introduction by C. W. R. D. Moseley, pp. 116–17. For a consideration of the book's place in the evolution of travel literature as a genre, see the section on Mandeville in Mary Campbell's *The Witness and the Other World*, pp. 122–61.

For a study of the role of the chivalric romances in *Don Quixote*, see Howard Mancing's *The Chivalric World of Don Quijote*.

12. I take this suggestion from Tyrrell, *Amazons*, p. 21. Even today, the Amazons are often associated with precious metals in popular iconography. See, for instance, Rui Mendes' photograph of a woman dressed as a latter-day Amazon in gold metallic bikini with gold chains, golden lace-up sandals, silver sword with gold hilt, and pink wings with gold trim. A cover illustration for the magazine *Paparazzi*, it is reproduced in Angela Magalhães and José Carlos Martins, eds., *Amazônia: Luz e reflexão*. For a fuller list of mythic figures associated with gold, see Dominic Janes, *God and Gold in Late Antiquity*, p. 20. Even Virgil's virgin warrior Camilla made her appearance in Book VII of the *Aeneid* with her hair "bound up in / gold, her quiver rattling death."

13. The wonderful detail of the silver tears appears in Weckmann, *Heritage*, p. 49. Weckmann notes that the legend of the Amazons' immense riches served to attract many volunteers to a 1530 expedition headed by Nuño de Guzmán, who set out that August "in search of Amazons" in the direction of the Mexican province of Astatlán.

14. Requisite sources for the New World Amazons include Weckmann's *Heritage* and the section on the Amazons in Enrique de Gandía's *Historia crítica de los mitos de la conquista americana*, pp. 71–101. Both of these works are dense compendia with many detailed references to the original primary and secondary colonial sources. See too Irving Leonard's examination of the Amazons in *Books of the Brave* (pp. 36–64), Alonso del Real's *Realidad y leyenda de las amazonas*, and Jean-Pierre Sánchez, *Le mythe des amazones du Nouveau Monde*, as well as the section on the Amazons in Roberto Levillier, *El Patiti, El*

Dorado y las Amazonas, pp. 115–59. Sharon W. Tiffany and Kathleen J. Adams examine gender issues associated with Amazons in various corners of the world in *The Wild Woman.* Batya Weinbaum's *Islands of Women and Amazons* offers an overview through time. For medieval European conceptions of the Amazons, see Vincent DiMarco's "The Amazons and the Ends of the World."

Columbus' *Diario* entry is 12 January 1493. The entry covers the events of that day and the next. He refers again to "una isla . . . poblada de mugeres sin hombre" ("an island populated by women without men") in the log entry of 16 January. Diego Álvarez Chanca, the physician who accompanied Columbus on his second voyage, mentions bow-and-arrow-wielding women in his letter to the mayor of Seville, which appears in Christopher Columbus, *Four Voyages,* pp. 18–68.

15. María Teresa Pérez summarizes some of the differences between Marco Polo's vision and that of Columbus in *El descubrimiento del Amazonas,* pp. 81–82. See too Miles H. Davidson's discussion of the influence of Marco Polo and Mandeville on Columbus in *Columbus Then and Now,* pp. 80–92.

16. Boomert, "Gifts of the Amazons," p. 34. Reports of these women often centered on key trade locations, which served as hubs of native-elite exchange networks. It appears likely that in the complex societies of the Amazonian and Orinocan floodplain, jade stones were primarily a form of diplomatic exchange coupled with marriage contracts. Elsewhere, in the tribal societies of the *terra firme* and the sea coasts, they were part of networks of formal, long-term gift and trading partnerships. For further details, see Boomert, pp. 37–38.

17. Whitehead offers this information in Ralegh, *Discoverie,* pp. 95–96.

18. See Robert F. Murphy and Yolanda Murphy, *Women of the Forest,* for an introduction to this widespread myth. See too Thomas Gregor, "A Mehinaku Myth of Matriarchy."

19. This back-and-forth movement, which suggests a kind of symbolic Ping-Pong played with multiple and differently weighted balls, offers a good example of the "transculturation" of which Mary Louise Pratt speaks in *Imperial Eyes.* For Pratt, transculturation is a phenomenon of the contact zone, which she defines as "the space of colonial encounters in which peoples geographically and historically separated come into contact with each other and establish ongoing relations, usually involving conditions of coercion, radical inequality, and intractable conflict" (p. 6). Here, not two but three principal players—the natives, the explorers, and the literary authors—were involved.

20. *Las sergas de Esplandián* is the fifth in a cycle of chivalric novels by Rodríguez de Montalvo known as "Amadís de Gaula," which encompasses ten books by different authors—including, besides Rodríguez de Montalvo, Pedro de Luján and Feliciano da Silva—who published their work over the course of four decades. After its initial publication, the *Sergas* book quickly went through at least four editions. For a feminist reading of Montalvo's *Sergas,* see Weinbaum's *Islands of Women,* pp. 128–51.

21. Pedro Mártir de Anglería is one of the authors to claim that the Amazons mutilated one breast. See Gandía, *Historia crítica,* p. 74.

22. Whitehead is one of the writers who argues for the Amazons as a primarily figurative device (Ralegh, *Discoverie,* p. 98).

23. Weckmann, *Heritage,* p. 51, citing Antonio de Herrera, 3 December, lib. 3, c.i and 4 December, lib.9, c.ix.

24. The Cortés quote appears in his *Cartas de relación de la conquista de México,* p. 202. Weckmann cites Antonio de Herrera's account of Cortés' naming of California on p. 65 of *Heritage.* A latter-day portrait of Queen Califia (sometimes "Calafia") appears in the magnificent gold-leafed Art Deco mural of Amazons and Spanish conquistadores in the Mark Hopkins Hotel in San Francisco. For photos and a description, see Zahid Sardar, "Play Back Time."

25. Gaspar de Carvajal, *Descubrimiento del Río de las Amazonas: Relación de fr. Gaspar de Carvajal,* edited and with an introduction by José Toribio Medina. The English translation of the Toribio Medina edition, from which I quote unless otherwise noted, is Carvajal, *The Discovery of the Amazon,* trans. Bertram E. Lee. Based on the manuscript version of the text belonging to the Duke of T'Serclaes de Tilly, the Toribio Medina edition (1894) remains the most authoritative edition of Carvajal's account. It is useful to compare it with the account that appears in the sixteenth-century historian Gonzalo Fernández de Oviedo's *Historia general de las Indias,* which Toribio Medina included as an appendix, as well as with the descriptions of the expedition by Garcilaso Inca de la Vega and Antonio de Herrera. An English translation of the latter two accounts appears in Clements R. Markham, trans., *Expeditions into the Valley of the Amazons,* pp. 1–20 and pp. 21–40. For a description of manuscript sources, see Carvajal, *Discovery,* pp. 7–10, and Jorge A. Garcés G.'s edition of the *Descubrimiento del Río Orellana,* pp. 6–8.

26. Ironically, given its influence on succeeding writers, including Ralegh, Carvajal's text, which has drawn the attention of historians, archaeologists, and demographers, has been almost ignored by literary critics. Three short articles on the text by literary critics—two of whom see it as an example of "magic realism"—do not do justice to its grounding in real people and places. (See Juan José Amate Blanco, "El realismo mágico en la expedición amazónica de Orellana"; Jorge H. Valdivieso, "Realismo mágico de la relación del *Nuevo descubrimiento* del famoso Rio Grande de las Amazonas de Fray Gaspar de Carvajal"; and Iber H. Verdugo, "La crónica de Gaspar de Carvajal.") The best treatments of the text that I have found to date are the brief but tantalizing comments of Beatriz Pastor Bodmer in *The Armature of Conquest* (pp. 165–68) and Ileana Rodríguez' brief discussion of Carvajal in "Naturaleza / nación."

27. Tyrrell, *Amazons,* p. 3.

28. The portrayal of the Amazon as simultaneously hostile and alluring is reminiscent in some ways of Christopher Miller's arguments in *Blank Darkness* about the juxtaposition of images of "Other-as-dream" and "Other-as-nightmare" in depictions of Africa going all the way back to the classical period. If, however, Africa appears as Miller's "ineffable dark continent, unknown and unknowable," the Americas, and the Amazon in particular, offer a mirror of that recast in a new form, and thus a portrait of at once frightening and marvelous potential.

29. Tyrrell, *Amazons,* p. 79.

30. For an introduction to the expedition, see Anthony Smith, *Explorers of the Amazon,* pp. 39–89. The large bibliography on Orellana consists of texts

mostly in the heroic mode ("Father of Ecuador," etc.). Toribio Medina offers a thumbnail biography of the captain (Carvajal, *Discovery*, pp. 36–44) and of Carvajal (pp. 12–22).

31. Toribio Medina defended Orellana, stressing the strength of the river currents, but there is no reason that the captain could not have been both unable and unwilling to return. The first three pages of Carvajal's account underscore the uneasy relationship between Orellana and an expedition leader who showed no particular consideration toward this worthy servant of the king.

32. One of the writers to draw most heavily on the Dominician friar's description of the Amazons was Ralegh, who actually learned Spanish in order to familiarize himself with existing accounts of El Dorado.

33. "The women bandage their legs from the calf to the knee with woven cotton to make them look thicker," explained the son. "The lady cacique who was made prisoner said the whole island belonged to women, and that the persons who had kept the armed boat from going ashore were also women, with the exception of 4 men who happened to be there because at a certain period of the year they come to lie with them. The same custom prevailed among the women of another island named Matininó, of whom they told what certain books tell of the Amazons. The Admiral believed it on account of what he had seen of those women and because of the energy and strength they displayed" (Fernando Colón, *The Life of the Admiral Christopher Columbus by his Son Ferdinand*, p. 170).

34. Cornelius O'Brien went on to meet on an island with their queen, who was called Cuna muchu, or "great woman" or lady. "Bernard O'Brien's Account of Irish Activities in the Amazon, 1621–4," in Joyce Lorimer, ed., *English and Irish Settlement on the River Amazon 1550–1646*, p. 266.

35. The comparison of tropical New World landscapes to temperate European ones is a common strategy in sixteenth-century travel narratives. Mary Campbell cites Ralegh's description of the exuberant Guianan countryside in terms that suggest an English woods in *The Witness and the Other World*, p. 245.

36. The class distinctions among the Amazons are foreshadowed in Mandeville. The gleaming flatware that Carvajal describes will reappear in a seventeenth-century description of the gigantic queen of the "island of California" cited by Weckmann in *Heritage*, p. 51.

37. The quote "they are rich and feared" ("son ricas y temidas") is from Nuño de Guzmán, who was one of various authors to foreshadow Carvajal in referring to the Amazons as "whiter than other women." Columbus had earlier described these women as "singularly bold and robust; extremely stout and yet very agile" ("de singular denuedo y robustez; gruesa por extremo y sin embargo agilísimas"). See Weckmann, *Heritage*, pp. 48 and 49 for these references. Other references to the Amazons appear in Nuño de Guzmán, *Memoria de los servicios*, pp. 116–17 and 157.

38. This comment appears in Fernández de Oviedo's version of Carvajal's manuscript, which is contained in Toribio Medina's edition of the narrative. See Carvajal, *Discovery*, p. 408.

39. For the full account, see Carvajal, *Discovery*, p. 214.

40. Other authors credit the Amazons with a more immaculate mode of conception. Antonio Pigafetta, for example, reports in his *First Voyage around the World* that these women were impregnated by the wind. For the classical sources that prefigure this sixteenth-century claim, see Gandía, "Historia crítica," p. 75.

41. Occasionally, the Amazons are depicted as actual cannibals. In the 1599 engraving *America* by Theodor Galle, the Amazon-like woman carrying a feathered spear in one hand and a man's severed head in the other is identified as a devourer of men. ("Estrix dira hominum," the caption reads.)

42. "They are said," Ralegh observed of the Ewaiponoma, "to be *the most mighty men* in the land and use bows, arrows and clubs *thrice as big as any* in Guiana" (*Discoverie*, p. 178, my italics). The Ewaiponoma sound a great deal like a cross between the giant known as the Juma and the hairy forest beings called Mapinguari, who have mouths in their stomachs—both common figures in folk stories told today throughout much of the Brazilian Amazon. Some storytellers do not believe in the literal existence of these beings; others claim to have caught glimpses of them or to have smelled their telltale odor. For useful comparative material, see the essays on the shifting figure of the Wild Man in Edward Dudley and Maximilian E. Novak, eds., *The Wild Man Within.*

43. Speaking of Ralegh's *Discoverie,* Louis Montrose argues that accounts of Amazons are more important than they might seem to modern readers, occupying an integral place in the narrative's "textual ideo-logic of gender and power." "The notion of a separatist and intensely territorial nation of women warriors," he says, "might be seen as a momentous transformation of the trope identifying the land with the female body. Implicit in the conceptual shift from the land as woman to a land of women is the possibility of representing women as collective social agents" (Montrose, "The Work of Gender in the Discourse of Discovery," p. 25). For another perspective of gender issues in Ralegh's narrative, see Mary C. Fuller, "Ralegh's Fugitive Gold."

44. This is the central argument of Alison Taufer in "The Only Good Amazon Is a Converted Amazon." The quote appears on p. 48.

45. Carvajal described how the Rio Negro flowed so abundantly, and with such violence, that it did not immediately mix with the Amazon but, instead, formed a streak for more than two leagues (*Discovery,* p. 204).

46. Carvajal, *Discovery,* p. 214.

47. Sometimes the friar's insistences bordered on the ridiculous, as when he explained to the natives at great length that the Spaniards were "servants and vassals of the Emperor of the Christians, the great King of Spain, and [that] he was called Don Carlos our master, to whom belonged the territory of all the Indies and many other dominions and kingdoms existing throughout the world, and that it was by his command that we were coming to that land, and that we were going to make a report to him on what he had seen in it" (Carvajal, *Discovery,* p. 182).

48. Stephen Greenblatt examines the European dream of encompassing alien others through linguistic understanding in *Marvelous Possessions.* See, in particular, the chapter "Kidnapping Language," pp. 86–118. Carvajal, I would ar-

gue, ostensibly rejected—or, more precisely, skirted and undercut—the marvelous in order better to control and possess.

49. Ironically, it is Carvajal's very focus on words that gives his text the wooden quality about which at least one of his translators complains. See C. de Melo Leitão's introduction to Carvajal, *Descobrimento do rio das Amazonas,* p. 5. The chronicle is full of verbs that describe linguistic actions such as "say," "repeat," "exclaim," "give to understand," "make understood," and so on.

50. Carvajal, *Discovery,* p. 214.

51. The feminization of the Indian is a common strategy in colonial writing. For one discussion, see Rolena Adorno, "El sujeto colonial y la construcción cultural de la alteridad." See too Álvaro Félix Bolaños, *Barbarie y canibalismo en la retórica colonial,* pp. 138–49, which discusses Father Pedro Simón's feminization of the Indian in his book *Noticias historiales* (the source of the *dragoncillo* legend discussed in chapter 2). Blanca Muratorio shows how the myth of the passive, easily dominated Indian has survived into the present and offers competing native versions of this officially sanctioned image in *The Life and Times of Grandfather Alonso.*

52. In assessing the role of the myth of the Amazons in the ideology of colonial occupation, Neil L. Whitehead states that while stories of the warrior women play a role in the ideology of colonial occupation by emphasizing the "exoticism, inversion and feminity" of Latin America, they lack the endurance of the El Dorado legend (Ralegh, *Discoverie,* p. 98). However, everything depends on what one means by "endurance."

53. Hernando de Ribeira, who explored the Paraguay region, describes the Amazons as living on the western side of a large lake known as "the Mansion of the Sun" (Ralegh, *Discovery,* ed. Robert H. Schomburgk, p. lvi). A decade earlier, in the 1530s, Gonzalo Jiménez de Quesada and Georg Hohermuth, governor of Venezuela during the time that Charles V granted the German house of Welser exploration rights, had heard similar tales on the existence of a "women-tribe" in the llanos, or lowland plains, of Venezuela and Colombia.

54. "Among the myths surrounding the conquest of the Americas, there is none so confused, so deformed, and so impenetrable as that of the myth of Amazons; none more despised, because misunderstood, nor more ignored, because impossible. And yet, it is the most authentic and the most luminous, not for what its name evoked—mere dream of the conquistadores—but because of what its illusion represented" (Gandía, *Historia crítica,* p. 72). Not surprisingly, Fernando Ainsa and Neil L. Whitehead, both of whom have written books about El Dorado, argue for the prominence of the golden king.

55. See Michael Taussig, *Shamanism, Colonialism, and the Wild Man.* The dialectic of terror and healing is much like that embodied by the Amazons. Although the warrior women were not curers, their vast treasures and their martial powers awakened a similar wonder mixed with intense fear.

56. Father Cristóbal de Acuña, "A New Discovery of the Great River of the Amazons," p. 122 (full discussion on pp. 41–142). The friar went on to associate the Amazons specifically with a peak called Yacamiaba, a name that would continue to appear in various guises over the centuries.

57. Charles de la Condamine, *Relation abrégée d'un voyage fait dans l'in-terieur de l'Amérique Méridionale*, pp. 125–26. David Cleary argues in his "Tristes Trope-iques" that la Condamine's fame is unmerited. However, he re-mains a central figure in discussions of the period.

58. Weckmann refers to these maps and cites Drouin de Bercy's *L'Europe et l'Amérique comparées* in *Heritage*, p. 40.

59. Ralegh, *Discovery*, ed. Robert H. Schomburgk, pp. lvi–lvii. Schom-burgk's purpose in citing these reports in his introduction to Ralegh's text was to play down its more seemingly fabulous aspects.

60. So does the search for the Amazons by travel writers such as Alex Shoumatoff, whose book *In Southern Light* chronicles his travels through the Brazilian Amazon in search of clues about the historical identity of the warrior women. See too Lyn Webster Wilde's *On the Trail of the Women Warriors*.

61. Theodore Roosevelt, *Through the Brazilian Wilderness*, p. 147. The ital-ics are mine.

62. For an introduction to the *novela de la selva* as a literary genre, see Jorge Marcone's "Jungle Fever" and "The Politics of Cultural Criticism and Sustain-able Development." Significantly, in terms of how the Amazon has been con-ceived by Brazilian intellectuals, there is no comparable designation for the *no-vela de la selva* in the Brazilian case, where critics often use terms such as "northern cycle" or "regional novel" to talk about these works. For a discussion of Brazilian novels specifically about the Amazon, see Pedro Maligo, *Land of Metaphorical Desires*.

Scholars disagree about the original date of publication for Alberto Rangel's *Inferno verde*. While many give a publication date of 1908, others cite a 1904 edition, privately printed in Rome. All, however, concur that Euclides da Cunha wrote his preface to the book in 1907. Although Rangel's book was important in its day, and is interesting in ideological terms, there is little critical writing on him. The sparse bibliography includes a biographical summary by Hélio Vianna ("Centenário de Alberto Rangel") and a brief section (pp. 51–54) in Maligo's *Land*.

63. The first quotation comes from Rangel, "Inferno verde," p. 181, the sec-ond from "O Tapará," p. 28, both of which appear in the collection *Inferno verde*.

64. José Eustacio Rivera goes on to refer to the jungle as "the wife of silence" and "mother of solitude and mist," as well as the "cathedral of nightmares" in *La vorágine* (The Vortex), p. 99.

65. Werner Herzog in *Burden of Dreams*, ed. Les Blank and James Bogan, p. 56. "And nature here is vile and base," says Herzog, whose *Aguirre, Wrath of God* (1972) and *Fitzcarraldo* (1982) both take place in the Amazon. "I wouldn't see anything erotical here. I would see fornication and asphyxiation and choking and fighting for survival and growing and just rotting away." Only a little later, however, he would speak of the jungle as something that he "loves." "It's not that I hate it," he says. "I love it. I love it very much. But I love it against my better judgment" (p. 57).

66. The reference to "um jogo fantástico e espectaculoso de sombras e cla-ridades," appears in Ferreira de Castro, *A selva*, p. 117.

67. "El rio es un ogre de mundos" ("The river is an ogre [devourer] of worlds"), says the narrator in Ciro Alegría's *La serpiente de oro* in mingled horror and admiration at the rushing water that gobbles up whole mountains (p. 12).

68. Rangel, "Inferno verde," in *Inferno verde* p. 281–82.

69. Rangel, "Maiby," in *Inferno verde,* p. 217.

70. These contradictions are the theme of Ileana Rodríguez' "Naturaleza/ nación."

71. Henry Walter Bates, *The Naturalist on the River Amazons,* p. 27.

72. The female quality of American nature has been pointed out frequently by authors as different in their aims and orientations as Carolyn Merchant (see the section "Nature as Female" in *The Death of Nature,* pp. 1–41) and Ileana Rodríguez ("Naturaleza / nación"). The varied forms that this femaleness often takes, however, and the political implications of particular portrayals, demand further analysis. For a start in this direction, see Suzana Sawyer and Arun Agrawal, "Environmental Orientalisms."

73. Bates, *Naturalist,* p. 240.

74. Ibid., p. 240. The reader is apt to be similarly cool about the prospect of "swimming to a tree and finding a nice snug place in the fork of some large bough where to pass the night" (p. 280).

75. Ibid., p. 248. (The italics are mine.)

76. This obsession with appearances and facades links Lévi-Strauss' work to the nineteenth-century symbolists. For more on this legacy, evident at various points throughout *Tristes tropiques,* see James Boon, *From Symbolism to Structuralism.* See too Clifford Geertz' comments on *Tristes tropiques* as symbolist poem in "The World in a Text" and José Guilherme Merquior, *L'esthetique de Lévi-Strauss.*

77. I take this pastiche of quotes from the first dozen entries under "Amazon Rain Forest" that I found on a random Internet search on 9 May 1999.

78. "¡Infelices, detrás de estas selvas está 'el más allá'!" exclaims the personage in Rivera's *La vorágine,* p. 36.

Chapter 5. Gold as a Woman

1. "The social relations in the mines, the hierarchy of values that exists there, are contradictory to the point of not permitting so much as a relative internal democracy. In gold mining, what holds is the 'law of the jungle' where 'everything is permitted' in the pursuit of fortune," says Argemiro Procópio Filho ("A miséria do colono e o ouro no Araguaia e Amazônia," p. 142). This "law of the jungle," however, has never been the whole story. Even today as the increasing imposition of hierarchy and technology in mining intensifies competitive pressures, miners tend to see themselves as both rivals and necessary allies. For an account of mining's rise as a clandestine activity that united the dispossessed in eighteenth-century Minas Gerais, Brazil, see Laura de Mello e Souza's *Desclassificados de ouro.*

2. The first *official* report of gold in the Brazilian Amazon appears to have been Estácio da Silveira's "Relações das coisas do Maranhão," published in Lisbon in 1624. In 1678, a group of Jesuits, acting on reports by Indian informants, began mining gold in northwest Maranhão, using African slaves. However, fears that mining might siphon off capital and labor from agriculture led to its official prohibition in Maranhão in 1730. For more details, see Ana Luiza Martins, "Breve história dos garimpeiros de ouro no Brasil," pp. 200–201.

3. Important historical sources for a more general history of gold in Brazil include Sérgio Buarque de Holanda's *Visão do paraíso* for the sixteenth and seventeenth centuries, and the ample body of work on the colonizers of the interior known as the *bandeirantes*. (See, for an introduction, Richard Morse's *The Bandeirantes*.) For the eighteenth century, see Charles Boxer's *The Golden Age in Brazil* and Virgílio Noya Pinto's *O ouro brasileiro e o comércio anglo-português*, along with Mello e Souza's *Desclassificados*. A. J. R. Russell-Wood's "The Gold Cycle, c1690–1750" offers a useful summary.

For a bibliography of works that deal with gold mining in Brazil during the nineteenth and twentieth centuries, see Ana Eugênia Gallo Cassini Cardillo, *Bibliografia sobre ouro no Brasil, 1840–1983*. For a historical summary, see Martins, "Breve história." Bernardino R. Figueiredo's "Garimpo e mineração no Brasil" links the past to the events of the 1970s and early 1980s. See too Antônio da Justa Feijão and José Armindo Pinto, "Amazônia e a saga aurífera do século XX."

4. The discovery of gold on the Tropas River, a tributary of the Tapajós, by the *garimpeiro* Nilson Pinheiro unleashed a gold rush fueled in part by an urbanization process that began after World War II. Between 1950 and 1970, some 18 million Brazilians moved from the countryside to cities, where only about a quarter of the migrants found a steady occupation. The colonization of Amazonia, which began in earnest in the 1960s, further fueled the gold rush, which reached its apex in the 1980s. For an introduction to the Tapajós region a century earlier, see the first section of João Barbosa Rodrigues' *Exploração e estudo do valle Amazonas: Rio Tapajós*.

5. In 1979, the Tapajós region was Brazil's largest gold producer, with an official yield of twenty tons of gold. Between 1980 and 1984, miners extracted more than three dozen tons of gold from Serra Pelada. For further statistics, see A. M. M. Souza and A. R. B. Silva, "Garimpo de Serra Pelada, Pará."

6. For an overview in English of miners in contemporary Brazil, see David Cleary, *Anatomy of the Amazon Gold Rush*. See too Gordon MacMillan, *At the End of the Rainbow?* and the section on Amazon gold in Marianne Schmink and Charles Wood, *Contested Frontiers* (pp. 219–49), as well as Schmink's earlier "Social Change in the *Garimpo*."

Among the most useful sources in Portuguese are the various essays in Bernardino R. Figueiredo et al., *Em busca do ouro*. For the eastern Amazon in particular, see A. D. Lestra and J. I. S. Nardi, *O ouro da Amazônia oriental*. The annual geological reports of the Brazilian Department of Mineral Production highlight particular gold-producing regions within the Amazon. See too the various articles on miners and gold mining from the 1970s and 1980s in the journal *Ciências da Terra*. Two more sociologically oriented reports specifically on the Tapajós region are Alberto Eduardo Carneiro da Paixão's *Trabalhadores rurais e garimpeiros no vale do Rio Tapajós* and Ireno José Santos de Lima's *Cantinas garimpeiras.*

7. For a comparative perspective, see W. W. Culver and T. C. Greaves, eds., *Miners and Mining in the Americas.* Nina S. de Friedemann, "'Troncos' among Black Miners in Colombia," pp. 204–25, is of particular interest. (The "troncos" are groups of families with rights to live, mine, and farm in a specific territory inherited from ancestors who took possession of the land more than 150 years ago.) David Hyndman's *Ancestral Rain Forests and the Mountain of Gold: Indigenous People and Mining in New Guinea* also provides a useful, more geographically distant, parallel to the Amazonian case.

8. Although the term *garimpo* and the related term *garimpeiro,* or miner, apply to any extractive site—diamonds, cassiterite, bauxite—these terms today are associated above all with gold. Their origins appear in a royal decree of 26 March 1731, which identifies the diamond miners in the Arraial de Tijuco (Minas Gerais) as "*grimpeiros,*" or men who live hidden away in the *grimpas,* or mountain peaks.

9. "We do not know an experience richer in variety of economic and social organization in Brazil," says Gabriel Guerreiro of the *garimpos* of Tapajós (Guerreiro, "Garimpagem de ouro na Amazônia," p. 102). "The particularities, differences, and similarities in mining communities found in over a hundred human agglomerations and around landing strips make the Tapajós an example without parallel." If the Tapajós, with its 250,000 square kilometers of gold-producing area, is varied in its own right, the differences between it and Rondônia, eastern Pará, Roraima, and gold-producing regions in other Amazonian countries are yet more pronounced.

10. In the widely used *chupadeira* system, a *jateiro* or *pistoleiro* uses a jet of water to dig while the individual known as the *maroqueiro* feeds a mixture of water, sediment, and gravel into a suction tube hooked up to a second water pump. There is also a *raleiro,* who oversees the entry of material into a metal drum that serves to slow down the flow of water, and an *embarcador,* who guides a slower stream of water over the rungs of a "long-ton" box.

11. See Brian J. Godfrey, "Migration to the Gold-Mining Frontier in Brazilian Amazonia," and Darrel Miller, "Highways and Gold."

12. See the photographs of gold miners in the initial section of Sebastião Salgado, *An Uncertain Grace,* pp. 10, 13, 17–22, and 24. Other striking portraits appear in Figueiredo's *Em busca do ouro* and in Ricardo Kotscho's *Serra Pelada.*

13. "What stands apart, above all else, is the appropriation of Serra Pelada by the mass media," says Elmer Prata Salomão succinctly in "Ofício e condição de garimpar," p. 58.

14. These statistics appear in Marianne Schmink and Charles H. Wood, *Contested Frontiers in Amazonia,* p. 225, and are based on regional newspaper reports of the period.

15. Although the number and status of women present in individual *garimpos* varies considerably, they remain an important part of the larger gold-mining venture. Some *garimpos* are home to wives and children, some prohibit prostitutes, some have a number of female shopkeepers (usually, but not always, with

husbands). For a discussion of women's labor in the gold camps, see Rita Maria Rodrigues, *Mulheres do Ouro*. Marieke Heemskerk looks at the role of Maroon women in the booming Suriname gold camps in "Gendered Responses to the Amazon Gold Mining Boom."

16. Population figures for the *garimpos* vary wildly. One way of ascertaining the number of miners in a particular moment might be to extrapolate from hospital records of malaria patients, the overwhelming majority of whom have some association with the *garimpos*. The hospital staff and the representatives of SUCAM, the Brazilian malaria control agency, with whom I spoke in both Santarém and Itaituba, estimate that at least 95 percent of all of the persons they see have either been in a *garimpo* or else have been in contact with *garimpeiros*.

17. For an interesting parallel to Amazonian women's place within the gold camps, see Jo Ann Levy's examination of women in the California gold rush, *They Saw the Elephant*. For a broader overview of the California gold rush that suggests many contrasts and comparisons with the Amazonian case, see Susan Lee Johnson's *Roaring Camp*.

18. The flat translation "gringo teacher" does not do justice to the mingling of genuine respect and equally genuine derision in this term. My identity as a professor, as well as an American and a Californian (few of the *garimpeiros* had not heard of Hollywood), gave me a certain social status. At the same time, I was an outsider who could be counted on to act in the bizarre ways that gringos inevitably do.

19. The mine folded in 1997 after almost forty years of operation—a good indication of gold's low price on the world market and of the insufficiency of traditional mining techniques. Although studies showed that a considerable amount of ore remained beneath the earth's surface, owner Seu Luiz could not find financing for the expensive machines required for its extraction.

20. Stories like these draw on a few real-life examples, such as that of Zé Arara ["Joe Macaw"], who became the owner of an important gold-buying enterprise in Itaituba that came to have branches in virtually all of the major *garimpos* before the price of gold fell, wiping out most of his gains.

21. *Porcentistas* earn a percentage of any strike. Day laborers usually earn only a token bonus. The most common system in the Tapajós, even today, remains the *meia-praça*, in which the owner of the camp or the *barranco* provides food, tools, and various other necessities, and the workers share with him in any profit. For a fuller explanation, see Cleary, *Anatomy*, pp. 104–32.

22. Marvelous details are in no way a peculiarity of twentieth-century Amazonian miners' tales. "The actions of the Crown in the cycle of gold and diamonds during the 1700s often reveal a strange similarity with contemporary thoughts and actions; so that today's Amazonia can be portrayed as a region 'of impenetrable mountain ranges, of enormous rivers, of mineral riches, of wild beasts and monsters,' a kind of ancient Hesperides guarded by dragons," says Bernardino Figueiredo ("Garimpo," p. 37). The quote is from Diogo de Vasconcelos' history of eighteenth-century Minas Gerais.

23. Man, age twenty-five, born interior of Imperatriz (Maranhão), has worked in gold camps on and off for the last seven years. Separated, works in construction when not prospecting, six years of schooling.

24. For the record, my hair is definitely brown by U.S. standards. "Blond" is a relative category in Brazil. "White" is again as much a category of social standing as it is of race. By using the diminutive *branquinha* instead of *branca*, the man softens the term and makes his statement more friendly.

25. Man, age fifteen ("really almost sixteen"), born interior of Gurupí (Maranhão), two years in gold camps. Single, one year high school ("not a lot, I guess; I didn't have a head for school").

26. These sorts of taboos are not limited to Amazonia. See Michael Taussig's *The Devil and Commodity Fetishism* for a description of similar beliefs in the mines of Bolivia.

27. Stories in which gold is allied with a snake appear not just in Brazil, but also in other parts of the Amazon, in the Orinoco, and in various parts of the Caribbean. See, for instance, Jean Petot, *L'or de Guyane*.

28. For a discussion of *panema* in mixed-blood Amazonian societies, see the chapter on it in Eduardo Galvão's "Panema." For a discussion of *panema* in a native Amazonian context, see Roberto da Matta, "Panema: Uma tentativa de análise estrutural." The kinds of prohibitions associated with *panema* regarding hunting and fishing practices as well as food preparation and consumption are laid out in detail in Raymundo Heraldo Maués' *A ilha encantada*.

29. Man, age twenty-three, born interior of Maranhão, has worked in the mines for seven months, worked as a taxicab driver before that ("and, I tell you, this is far less dangerous"). Single, "about eight" years of schooling.

30. Often a female symbol because of its association with menstruation and fertility, blood, in miners' stories, becomes a metaphor for the very essence of a man. Although miners had trouble explaining why Gold should be attracted to blood, my hunch is that there exists an implicit correlation between the shifting river of gold said to run beneath the earth and the river of blood that courses through a person's veins. The fact that the river of gold periodically changes course would help explain why a man who appears luckless may suddenly strike it rich, since the two streams have suddenly come into confluence.

31. Man, age sixty-four, born Tocantins, has been a miner off and on for thirty years. Married ("she's my third, maybe three's my lucky number"), no formal education "though I know how to read a bit and write my name."

32. The Suriname gold mines are presently drawing a large number of miners from outside the country, as well as from within. Not only is alluvial gold more readily accessible in many places there, but the national government has recently started selling small-scale mining licenses to Brazilian miners, giving them a legal status that Suriname Maroons and Amerindians do not enjoy. Officially, there were eight thousand Brazilian miners in Suriname in 1998, and Alfredo Wagner Berno de Almeida estimates that presently there are as many as fourteen thousand, most of them from the state of Maranhão (personal communication, 28 March 1999). Marieke Heemskerk looks at the Suriname miners, or "porkknockers," in "The Social Drivers of Small-Scale Gold Mining among the Maroons in Suriname."

33. Man, age forty, born São Joaquim, Amapá, five years in gold camps, works in construction when not mining. Married ("not in the church, but still I consider her to be my wife"), four years in grade school.

34. Man, age forty-four, born Maranhão, has been working on and off in gold mines for "about ten" years. "Shacked up," three years of schooling.

35. Man, age seventy-one, born Paraíba, twenty years in gold mines when not working as a carpenter. Widowed, no formal education, "but I've learned something on my own."

36. During the height of its economic importance, Serra Pelada produced a miners' cooperative. Newly politicized miners helped elect *garimpeiros* from Serra Pelada to public office, including a federal deputy, a state deputy, a mayor, and six assemblymen. For the effects of Serra Pelada on political mobilization, see Guerreiro, "Garimpagem de ouro," especially pp. 93–99. See too the more general treatment of the politics of gold mining in MacMillan, *Rainbow*, pp. 127–51.

37. Marlise Simons, "In the Gold Rush, Nature Is Viciously Trampled," in the *New York Times*. Other articles refer specifically to miners as "rapists of the land."

38. The ribbon is a token of a saint's vow, or *promessa*, a contract that a person makes with a Roman Catholic holy figure. The man will wear the ribbon until it falls off or until the Virgin responds positively to his request.

39. Man, age twenty-two, born interior of Maranhão, has been working off and on in gold mines for the past four years. Single, six years of schooling ("but I'm telling you, the school was bad, and I barely learned a thing").

40. Man, age fifty-four, born Itacoatiara (Amazonas), has worked as a shopkeeper and pinch-hit mechanic in *garimpos* for fifteen years. Married, two years in grade school.

41. "The *garimpeiro* became in many cases one who was obliged to expatriate or to pass a life of miseries, because with the prohibition of mining he lost his only means of subsistence. He had been set on exercising an office—clandestine mining—which he judged to be his right, and which had been unjustly usurped," says Joaquim Felício dos Santos in *Memórias do distrito diamantino*, p. 109. Published in 1868, the quote could apply to miners in many parts of Amazonia today.

42. The incidence and type of violent actions in the *garimpo* vary markedly depending on economic system, personalities, and the price and accessibility of alcohol, prostitutes, and drugs. It is possible, and even probable, that a statistical study would show *garimpos,* on the whole, to be less dangerous than a number of urban slums.

43. Man, age thirty-one, born Fordlândia, interviewed on boat to Itaituba, five years in gold mines. Married, previously barber ("sometimes I cut hair on the side in the *garimpo*"), grade school education.

44. Paulo insisted that the event had nothing to do with the abandonment of the shop. Seu Luiz, he asserted, had simply decided to move the support aspects of his operation closer to the actual work site. However, when some of the other miners learned where I had been, they joked about the shed's haunted character in a way that made me wonder if the move had been purely practical. "No way you'd get me in there!" exclaimed Carlinhos. "You gringos must like ghosts."

45. For one of the many accounts of Amazonian gold miners' environmen-

tally destructive activities, see Marcus Colchester, *Guyana: Fragile Frontier*. Discussions of miners' attacks on native people appear in Alcida Rita Ramos, *Sanumá Memories*, pp. 271–312; in MacMillan, *Rainbow*, pp. 24–54; and in Jan Rocha's *Murder in the Rainforest*. See too the various essays in Lívia Barbosa, Ana Lúcia Lobato, and José Augusto Drummond, eds., *Garimpo, meio ambiente e sociedades indígenas* and the chapter on gold mining in Argemiro Procópio, *Amazônia: Ecologia e degradação social*, pp. 72–100.

46. "A nova febre dourada," *Veja*, 18 January 1989, pp. 74–76.

47. James Brooke, "Gold's Lure versus Indian Rights"; Thomas Kamm, "Amazon Tragedy"; Cynthia Gorney, "The Last Frontier," Part V.

48. Lúcio Flávio Pinto describes this scapegoating of the miner within and outside Brazil in "Garimpeiro serve de bode expiatório."

49. Conveniently distant from newspaper readers in terms of both geography and social class, these "environmental outlaws" appear enmeshed in clandestine (in the sense of unregulated) economic activities that, as one writer for the influential Brazilian newsweekly *Veja* notes sourly, "do absolutely nothing for the nation" ("A nova febre dourada," *Veja*, 18 January 1989). This attitude on the part of the contemporary Brazilian elite can be traced back to the early eighteenth century, when officials denounced the clandestine miners as outlaws and bandits.

50. Gilberto Dimenstein, *Meninas da noite*.

51. This is a pastiche composed from multiple articles.

52. Julia Preston, "Brazil Frees Minors in Brothels."

53. The most infamous attack on the Yanomami occurred in Haximu in 1993, where gold miners murdered sixteen villagers. Earlier atrocities had taken place in Paapiú and Olomai.

54. Gorney, "Feverish Dreams of Fast Fortune Infect Amazonian Gold Camps," in the series "The Last Frontier," Part V.

55. Jan Knippers Black, "Limits of Boom-and-Bust Development: Challenge of the Amazon."

56. The detrimental effects of mercury pollution on plants, animals, and humans are, unfortunately, well documented. See, for example, Jed Greer, "The Price of Gold," and Leslie E. Sponsel, "The Master Thief."

57. Education campaigns are making inroads in the way miners use mercury. *As Aventuras de Zé de Ouro e Faguio* (The Adventures of Joe Gold and Flash) is a comic-book-like information pamphlet produced by the Gold Miners' Association of Tapajós, underwritten by the European Commission, and disseminated by the government of the state of Pará. The antics of the hero bring home daily problems and possible practical solutions. I thank David Cleary for copies of these publications.

58. The miner's position is very close to that of the Indian environmental activist and scholar Ramachandra Guha, who depicts preservation as an obsession of rich northerners with too much time on their hands. See the discussion "Radical American Environmentalism and Wilderness Preservation" in Guha and Juan Martínez-Alier's *Varieties of Environmentalism*, pp. 92–108, for a fuller expression of this point of view.

Chapter 6. Roots of the Rain Forest

1. There are rain forests on all continents today except Europe and Antarctica. For a scholarly introduction, see Paul Westamacott Richards, *The Tropical Rain Forest*. For more journalistic treatments with stunning photographs, see Arnold Newman, *Tropical Rainforest*, and Lisa Silcock, ed., *The Rainforests*.

2. As Anna Tsing and others have been quick to point out, "the environmental movement" is actually an umbrella term for many different sorts of groups with different definitions of the natural world and different political objectives. For an introduction to the diversity in the movement, see Ramachandra Guha and Juan Martínez Alier, *Varieties of Environmentalism*.

3. For an overview, see Nigel J. H. Smith, *The Amazon River Forest*. See too David Cleary's capsule summary in "Towards an Environmental History of the Amazon." Hugh Raffles describes ongoing human manipulation of Amazonian watercourses in "Igarapé Guariba."

4. This sort of native manipulation of the land has been amply documented. See William Balée's *Footprints of the Forest* for one of many examples.

5. Cattle probably reached the Amazon basin by 1644. Ranches were established on the seasonally wet grasslands of Marajó Island in 1680. By 1806, 226 ranches were in operation. For more on cattle in the Amazon, see Smith, *The Amazon River Forest*, pp. 84–87.

6. David Sweet, "A Rich Realm of Nature Destroyed," deals with the period between 1640 and 1750. For other perspectives on this period, see the essays in Dauril Alden, ed., *The Colonial Roots of Modern Brazil*.

7. "Cosmopolitan" does not necessarily mean "big." Manaus, which today has more than 1.5 million people, had a population of approximately six thousand inhabitants in 1867 and no more than twenty thousand in 1893.

8. J. Valerie Fifer, *Bolivia: Land, Location, and Politics since 1825*, pp. 137–38.

9. As Barbara Weinstein notes in *The Amazon Rubber Boom*, the treatment of rubber tappers varied widely depending on place and time. Nonetheless, the labor practices to which both natives and immigrants were subjected were often abusive in the extreme.

10. Henry Walter Bates, *The Naturalist on the River Amazons*, p. 376.

11. These transformations have been well documented, and there is a massive amount of documentation on the complex events I sketch here. For a starting point, see the ample list of references in Susanna Hecht and Alexander Cockburn's *Fate of the Forest*, pp. 319–43. For a follow-up, see later work by Anthony Hall, Nigel J. H. Smith, William Balée, Anthony Anderson, and Emilio Moran.

12. For a discussion of Vargas' concept of Brazilian manifest destiny as exemplified in the Westward March (Marcha para o Oeste), see William Raymond Steiger, "What Was Once Desert Shall Be a World."

13. The Alliance for Progress was an international development program established by the United States and twenty-two Latin American countries in the Charter of Punta del Este in August 1961. Its stated objectives were sustained growth in per capita income, a more just distribution of income, development of

industry and agriculture, agrarian reform, improvements in health and welfare, and stabilization in the prices of both domestic and export goods.

14. The emphasis on national security was particularly strong in Brazil following the military coup of 1964. For introductory discussions of migration into the Amazon, see Marianne Schmink and Charles H. Wood, *Contested Frontiers*. The ensuing urbanization in the region is the subject of John Browder and Brian Godfrey's *Rainforest Cities*.

15. Not surprisingly, some areas show a greater rate of environmental disturbance than others. In Brazil, deforestation was particularly severe in Mato Grosso and southern Pará during the 1960s, and later in Rondônia and Roraima. Stimulated in large part by clearing for coca production, forest loss has been similarly intense in the upper Putumayo and Caquetá River areas of Colombia, in the Ecuadorean province of Napo, and in the Tingo Maria-Pucallpa region of Peru.

16. The body of work on the effects of these policies is immense. See, for a beginning, Shelton H. Davis' *Victims of the Miracle* and Nigel J. H. Smith's *Rainforest Corridors*. For more recent follow-ups, see the essays in Marianne Schmink and Charles H. Wood's *Frontier Expansion in Amazonia,* and in Charles H. Wood and Roberto Porro's *Land Use and Deforestation in the Amazon.*

17. Different scholars date the movement differently. See, for example, the discussions in Allan Schnaiberg's *The Environment*, pp. 362–411, and Donald Worster's discussion of "the age of ecology" in *Nature's Economy,* pp. 339–48. For a discussion of the importance of these and other key events in the formation of a new globally oriented environmentalism, see "The Culture of Global Environmentalist Discourse," pp. 172–212, in Kay Milton, *Environmentalism and Cultural Theory.* For a general history of the international environmental movement, see John McCormick, *Reclaiming Paradise.* See too Stephen Yearley's "Environmentalism."

18. For a detailed discussion of the terms *rain forest, wilderness,* and *jungle,* see Candace Slater, "Amazonia as Edenic Narrative." *Jungle* has much older Sanskrit roots. For a useful parallel involving terms in Spanish, see Ileana Rodríguez' "Naturaleza/nación." See also Francis E. Putz and N. Michele Holbrook's "Tropical Rain Forest Images."

19. The term *rain forest* (or *rainforest,* a botanical term that emerged at the end of the nineteenth century) does not even appear in a number of the standard dictionaries that gather dust in used bookstores. Moreover, even those dictionaries in which the term appears may define rain forests as "normally temperate woodlands." Only in the 1970s did *rain forest* begin making a regular appearance in general-use dictionaries, and only then did rain forests become customarily tropical landscapes in the popular imagination, as opposed to temperate ones.

20. A. F. S. Schimper, *Plant-geography upon a Physiological Basis,* as quoted in the *Oxford English Dictionary,* 2nd ed., vol. 13, i.iii., p. 260.

21. This definition appears in the on-line version of *Merriam-Webster's Collegiate Dictionary* (www.m-w com/cgi-bin/dictionary), which I selected because of its easy availability and, therefore, wide use. Note that the first definition the

dictionary offers is for tropical areas; *temperate rain forest* (as opposed to the unmodified *rain forest*) is listed as a separate entry.

Not all scholars agree on the hundred-inch criterion. See, for a more detailed treatment, L. R. Holdridge's classic six-zone classificatory model for tropical forests in his *Forest Environments in Tropical Life Zones* and the discussion of rain forests in Martin Kellman and Rosanne Tackaberry's *Tropical Environments,* pp. 132–43. Botanists are less concerned about strict distinctions among forest areas today than they were in the past.

22. The maximum height of rain forest trees varies from forest to forest. Some botanists give an average height of thirty to fifty meters, with some individual trees reaching as high as sixty.

23. There is a copious amount of information on wilderness, a term that has had distinctly different meanings over time. For an introduction, see J. Baird Callicot and Michael P. Nelson's *The Great New Wilderness Debate,* which includes classic texts by Frederick Jackson Turner, William Cronon, Roderick Nash, and others.

24. The sobriquet "heart of darkness" for the (African) jungle comes, of course, from Joseph Conrad's celebrated novella. For an introduction to the jungle as literary landscape, see Zohreh T. Sullivan, "Enclosure, Darkness, and the Body: Conrad's Landscape."

25. The button was for sale during the summer of 1996 in Toby's Feed Barn, in Point Reyes, California, which sells seed to local farmers and fancy soap to tourists. The woman whom it pictures looks much like a modern-day descendant of Rima, the ethereal heroine of W. H. Hudson's early-twentieth-century novel *Green Mansions.*

26. There is also a Spanish-language version of *Amazonia without Myths,* which has gone through at least two editions.

27. For documents relating to "Eco 92," see *UNCED: The Earth Summit.* Held in Rio in June 1992, the conference attracted 117 heads of states and representatives of 178 nations. The main documents it produced include the Convention on Biological Diversity, the Framework Convention on Climate Change (also known as the Global Warming Convention), the Declaration on Environment and Development (a list of twenty-seven broad, nonbinding principles for environmentally sound development), Agenda 21 (global strategies for cleaning up the environment and encouraging environmentally sound development), and the Statement of Principles on Forests, which calls on nations to monitor and assess the impact of development on forest resources.

28. The term *sustainable development* became popular in 1987 with the publication of the World Commission on Environment and Development's report *Our Common Future,* intended to identify strategies that would find common ground between environmentalists and "Third World" groups. For an early critical review of sustainable development as a concept, see S. N. Lélé, "Sustainable Development." For a description of the tensions between proponents of biodiversity and proponents of sustainable development, see Kent H. Redford and Steven E. Sanderson, "The Brief, Barren Marriage of Biodiversity and Sustainability." For an excellent history of the relatively recent idea of biological diversity, see David Takacs, *The Idea of Biodiversity.*

29. Both forest and Indian possess what Pierre Bourdieu has referred to as "symbolic capital"—a value that can be transferred through association to other objects, people, and ideas. For a fuller explanation, see Bourdieu, *Outline of a Theory of Practice,* pp. 171–83. For a discussion of environmental images in the media (particularly television), see James Shanahan and Katherine Mc-Comas, *Nature Stories.*

30. According to David R. Berlin, group product manager for Simoniz, at that time a division of First Brands, the "chief" ad was designed for media use during 1995 only (personal communication, 19 July 1995).

31. Arturo Escobar examines these sorts of contradictions in his discussion of the redefinition of nature under sustainable development in *Encountering Development,* pp. 203–11.

32. The carnauba, whose scientific name is *Copernicia prunifera,* does not even appear in Andrew Henderson's encyclopedic *Palms of the Amazon,* which lists 151 types of Amazonian palm. For a botanical description of the palm, see Andrew Henderson, Gloria Galeano, and Rodrigo Bernal, *The Palms of the Americas,* pp. 60–61. A photograph and maps of its distribution area appear in plate 8 and figure 65. See too the section on harvesting carnauba in Francisco Barboza Leite, *Tipos e aspectos do Brasil,* pp. 143–45.

33. This figure is even more impressive given the small population of the Brazilian Amazon at this time—only a little over three hundred thousand for the entire region in 1870.

34. See Smith, *The Amazon River Forest,* p. 44.

35. The alleged "Hamburger Connection," which generated considerable negative publicity for McDonald's, turned out to have little basis in fact in the case of specifically Amazonian rain forests. See Susanna Hecht's responses to Alexander Cockburn in his article "Trees, Cows and Cocaine."

36. I picked up flyers in 1998 in Buellton and Arroyo Grande, California. For an introduction to the growing scholarly bibliography on the McDonald's Corporation, see John F. Love's *McDonalds: Behind the Arches.* Sidney W. Mintz' "Swallowing Modernity" underscores the corporation's larger goals in its public relations campaigns.

37. McDonald's is by no means alone in this sort of rhetoric. "We must conduct all aspects of business as responsible stewards of the environment by operating in a manner that protects the Earth," declares Horst Rechelbacher, founder and CEO of the Aveda Corporation, in a statement that appears on the company's website (www.aveda.com).

38. When I wrote to the McDonald's Corporation to ask where this first picture was taken, Jerry Horn of the Customer Satisfaction Department wrote back that "the photo on the 'Did You Know?' No. 5 leaflet is a tropical forest in South America" (personal correspondence, 14 June 1994). I called Mr. Horn on 28 June to ask about the exact location of this rain forest, and he informed me that an outside firm "scoured all over in the Amazon for it." Asked who could give me the precise location, he replied that the photo was a stock shot from the Leo Burnett archives and that no one could say "where in the world it came from, except that it is definitely a tropical rain forest in South America."

39. I thank Professor Joe Antos of the University of Victoria, a specialist in

plant ecology of the Pacific Northwest, for his professional evaluation of this photo (telephone conversation, 2 June 1994).

40. I am grateful to Professor Ignacio Chapela of U.C. Berkeley's College of Natural Resources and to Professor Francis E. Putz of the University of Florida for their assessment of this second photograph (personal communications, 31 May 1996 and 19 May 2000). Professor Chapela suggested that the forest might be located near a road; Professor Putz did not share this opinion.

41. For a discussion of nature as oasis, see Tanya M. Luhrmann, "The Resurgence of Romanticism," and Marianna Torgovnick's chapters on the New American Indian and New American White, pp. 135–55, in her book *Primitive Passions*. For a discussion of the nineteenth-century American roots of the neopastoral movement that resurfaced in a more global form in the 1960s, see Peter Schmitt, *Back to Nature*.

42. "The Environmental Lifestyle Store is the ultimate showcase of Aveda," says Rechelbacher on the company's website, "because Aveda is a lifestyle product and service company committed to supporting two ecosystems: the planet and the human body. *Each thrives on harmony and balance and is vitally interconnected*." (The italics are mine.)

43. For a useful general context for these ongoing changes within Latin America, see Susan E. Place's *Tropical Rainforests*.

44. "The fresh organic power of the rainforest captured in a fragrance for men," reads the text on the box of this cologne spray. "Rich vanilla, crisp leaves, teak and bamboo create a unique environment of natural warmth and pure masculinity."

45. Peter de Jonge, "Riding the Wild, Perilous Waters of Amazon.com."

46. This shift toward the inclusion of humans is nowhere more obvious than in books, games, and computer products aimed at children. For a good example of the Rain Forest as it is presented today to a younger audience, see the "Amazon rain forest" issue of *Kids Discover* (vol. 6, no. 8, 1996) and its accompanying video package.

47. Beth A. Conklin and Laura Graham discuss this article and the larger trajectory of Paiakan in "The Shifting Middle Ground."

48. This importance is nothing new. Alcida Ramos does an excellent job of showing how Brazilian Indians have been essential to Brazil's definition of itself for centuries in *Indigenism*. "The country would be unthinkable without its constructed Indian," she says flatly (p. 292).

49. For a good example of these articles, see "Os Gigantes, Finalmente," 14 February 1973, which describes in great detail the first encounter between the Kranhacarore and the anthropologists Cláudio and Orlando Villas Boas. The description of the encounter is arranged in lines on the left side of a page full of photographs of solitary woods and a gleaming river, so that the text reads read almost like a poem.

50. See, for instance, the breathless description of how progress is affecting the lives of some fifteen thousand previously uncontacted Indians in "Os índios sem história," 19 May 1976.

51. See the withering attack on the associations between the British rock star Sting and the Txucarramáe Indian chief Raoni, who is pictured in an audience

with the pope, in "Todos no Morumbi," 5 July 1989, pp. 80–84. See also Laurentino Gomes and Paulo Silber, "Gigolôs de índios," 1 July 1992, pp. 36–38.

52. Laurentino Gomes and Paulo Silber, "A explosão do instinto selvagem: Paiakán, o cacique-símbolo da pureza ecológica, estupra e tortura uma adolescente," 10 June 1992, pp. 68–73. The article was accompanied by a cover photograph of Paiakan in full Kayapó regalia. A rough translation of its title is "The Explosion of Savage Instinct: Paiakan, the Chief-Symbol of Ecological Purity, Rapes and Tortures an Adolescent Girl." For an analysis of the motives underlying the article's vitriolic attack, see Cecilia McCallum, "The *Veja* Payakan." See also Zanoni Neves' "Os índios na mídia." Although a number of other well-respected Brazilian news publications, including the *Folha de São Paulo,* followed *Veja*'s lead in denouncing Paiakan, the accusation was never proved in court. Paiakan's lawyers claimed that the young woman had been attacked by his wife, Irekan, who, as a "primitive" could not be held accountable for what she did, and the case was eventually dismissed.

53. "The ecological sermonizing of the rich countries is capable of concealing objectives considerably more tempting than the golden tamarin monkey," one writer observes tartly (if not necessarily incorrectly) in one such article before going on to lambaste Amazonian Indians for their willingness to serve as international poster children ("Índios, fantasmas, e grandes interesses," 25 August 1993). For a discussion of larger shifts in environmental thinking in Brazil, see José Augusto Pádua's *Ecologia e política no Brasil* and the articles in Eduardo J. Viola's *Ecologia, ciência, política* and his later *Meio ambiente, desenvolvimento e cidadania.*

54. For a good overview of emerging movements, see the section "Environmental Destruction, Social Conflict, and Popular Resistance," pp. 179–308, in David Goodman and Anthony Hall's *The Future of Amazonia.*

55. The idea of an Amazon that hides its fragility behind a facade of exuberant vegetation, of which there were already hints in Lévi-Strauss, found its way into scholarly studies of the 1970s such as Betty Meggers' influential *Amazonia: Man and Culture in a Counterfeit Paradise.* Donald Lathrap challenged Meggers' thesis of a thinly populated (and therefore pristine) Amazon in work published as early as 1970, such as *The Upper Amazon,* and more recent research by scholars such as Anna Roosevelt *(Moundbuilders of the Amazon)* and William Denevan ("The Pristine Myth") definitively debunk Meggers' idea. So does current archaeological research on the *terra firme* by Michael Heckenberger, which suggests that the southern Amazonian plateau was colonized by 10,000 B.C., if not earlier. Nonetheless, this notion retains considerable popular appeal.

56. James Brooke, "Brazil Creates Reserve for Imperiled Amazon Tribe."

57. Jack Epstein, "Battle over Rich Brazilian Lands."

58. This is the subtitle of Epstein's "Battle over Rich Brazilian Lands."

59. There is an important and growing body of work on Amazonians' ability to manipulate this new vocabulary, as well as the visual signs used to invoke Western notions of the exotic Other (feather headdresses, body paint, body ornamentation)—a more general phenomenon that Gayatri Spivak has labeled "strategic essentialism." For some of the most important and provocative analy-

ses of this deployment of symbols, see Margaret E. Keck's "Social Equity and Environmental Politics in Brazil," Beth A. Conklin's "Body Pain, Feathers and VCRs," Jean Jackson's "Culture, Genuine and Spurious," and Sylvia Caiuby Novaes' *The Play of Mirrors.*

For a sampling of discussions specifically of the Kayapó and the Yanomami, see Alcida Ramos' *Indigenism,* Terence Turner's "Representing, Resisting, Rethinking" and "History, Myth, and Social Consciousness among the Kayapó of Central Brazil," William H. Fisher's "Megadevelopment, Environmentalism, and Resistance," and Laura R. Graham's "Brazilian Indians and the Symbolic Politics of Language in the Global Public Sphere." Both groups have been extensively studied. More than sixty anthropologists have written on the Yanomami alone.

Linda Rabben's *Unnatural Selection* is also useful for its many examples of journalistic writing. Geoffrey O'Connell's *Amazon Journal* chronicles the struggle of one U.S. journalist to come to terms with an ongoing symbolic interplay.

60. Among the names most often associated with these positions are that of the conservation biologist John Terborgh, the anthropologist John F. Oates, and the primatologist Thomas Struhsaker. Their perspective is particularly clear in Terborgh's *Requiem for Nature,* Oates' *Myth and Reality in the Rain Forest,* and Struhsaker's *Ecology of an African Rain Forest,* whose subtitle speaks of the conflict between "conservation" and "exploitation," as opposed to "use" or "development." The economist Richard Rice of Conservation International, whose article on the problems of sustainable management appeared on the cover of *Scientific American* under the title "The Hoax of Sustainable Forest Development," would be a good example of a social scientist who has championed this position in a popular arena. See too R. E. Rice, R. E. Gullison, and J. W. Reid, "Can Sustainable Management Save Tropical Forests?" For an overview of the more general position that underlies many of these articles, see William K. Stevens, "Conservationists Win Battles but Fear War Is Lost." The debate continues in the articles included in the October 2000 issue of *Conservation Biology* (vol. 14, no. 5), which contains a special "Conservation Forum" section that includes a half dozen articles on the theme (pp. 1351–74).

61. The three quotes are from John F. Oates, "Why a Prime Model for Saving Rain Forests Is a Failure."

62. The parameters of the debate become clear if one reads Oates' *Myth and Reality in the Rain Forest* as a rebuttal to *The Myth of Wild Africa,* by Jonathan S. Adams and Thomas O. McShane. See James Fairhead and Melissa Leach's ensuing criticisms of Oates' book in the *Times Literary Supplement* a year later. The tendency to force Amazonians into narrow categories as environmental defenders has been discussed by various anthropologists, as well as by the zoologist Kent Redford in his article "The Ecologically Noble Savage." See also Douglas J. Buege's "The Ecologically Noble Savage Revisited."

63. John Terborgh, "A Dying World," p. 40. The reference to "football" is a mistranslation of *futebol,* or soccer. Latin Americans have little interest in North American football. Terborgh takes a somewhat more moderate position on people in "The Fate of Tropical Forests," one of the articles in the Octo-

ber 2000 issue of *Conservation Biology* (pp. 1358–61). Here, he claims that the debate "is not over goals but process, in particular the role to be played by rural and indigenous people as stewards of the land and its natural resources" (p. 1358).

64. Terborgh, "A Dying World," p. 40.

65. These are amply documented by natural scientists and social scientists alike in Wood and Porro, *Land Use and Deforestation in the Amazon.*

66. Claude Lévi-Strauss, "Photographs and Memories from the Lost World of Brazil."

67. Claude Lévi-Strauss, *Saudades do Brasil,* p. 18.

68. Ibid., pp. 18–19.

69. John Terborgh, *Requiem for Nature.* I take the quotes from the book jacket. The book begins with a description of how a childhood full of summer days spent roaming the woods and streams ends when development causes the forest to vanish. (*"Those were idyllic times,* brought to a harsh and abrupt end after the close of World War II, when the bucolic tranquility of our neighborhood was shattered by an onslaught of bulldozers, trucks, and construction workers. Seemingly overnight, the forest vanished. Broad red scars in the earth, the future streets and lanes of middle-class suburbs bespoke the agony of the land," p. ix. The italics are mine.) James Fairhead and Melissa Leach point out a similarly nostalgic undercurrent in "The Nature Lords," their review in the *Times Literary Supplement* of John F. Oates' seemingly objective *Myth and Reality in the Rainforest.*

70. The cover of *Requiem for Nature* pictures Rousseau's *La Cascade* (The Waterfall), in which two human and two animal figures are dwarfed by the trees with heart-shaped leaves that rise up all around them.

Chapter 7. Lakes within Lakes

1. There is a growing body of work on *quilombos* and ex-*quilombos* in Brazil. For a useful review of some of the most recent work, see Alfredo Wagner Berno de Almeida, "Quilombos: Repertório bibliográfico." The two most important overviews of African slavery in the Amazon are Vicente Salles, *O negro no Pará,* and Napoleão Figueiredo and Anaíza Vergolino-Henry, *A presença africana na Amazônia colonial.*

2. Richard Price provides a useful summary of recent writing on the Brazilian *remanescentes* in "Scrapping Maroon History." Price's long-standing focus on Suriname gives him a provocative perspective on the Brazilian case, in which protest was generally more muted than among other fugitive black communities in Latin America. The term *maroon* comes from the Spanish word *cimarrón,* which means "wild" or "unruly."

3. Arturo Escobar invites comparisons with other Maroon communities in his discussion of biodiversity as a new repertory of images of nature and culture for slave descendants on Colombia's Pacific coast in his "Cultural Politics and Biological Diversity." See too the articles on the Chocó region in Juana Camacho and Eduardo Restrepo's *De montes, ríos, y ciudades,* especially Restrepo's

"Territorios e identidades híbridas," pp. 245–62. David Guss' "The Selling of San Juan" and "Hidden Histories" (both about Venezuela) provide a useful contrast to the Brazilian Amazon. For a broader discussion of what "maroonness" means today, see Kenneth Bilby and Diana Baird N'Diaye's "Creativity and Resistance," Richard Price's *First-Time* and *Alabi's World,* and Norman Whitten's "Blackness in the Americas."

4. For a detailed study, see Rosa Acevedo and Edna Castro, *Negros do Trombetas,* a significant omission from Richard Price's otherwise representative list of studies in "Scrapping Maroon History." For a summary, see Lúcia M. M. de Andrade, "Os quilombos da bacia do Rio Trombetas." See also Eliane Cantarino O'Dwyer's "Remanescentes de quilombos na fronteira amazônica" and *Terra de Quilombos,* José Luís Ruiz-Peinado Alonso's "Hijos del río," and Eurípedes A. Funes' "Nasci nas Matas, nunca tive senhor." (The last work deals primarily with the community of Pacoval, near Alenquer.) The primary historical sources for the decades immediately preceding the abolition of slavery are A. C. Tavares Bastos, *O Valle do Amazonas* (1866); Domingos Soares Ferreira Penna, *Obras Completas* (1867); and the third section of João Barbosa Rodrigues' *Exploração e Estado do Vale Amazonas,* titled "Rio Trombetas" (1875). For a general overview of Maroon communities in Brazil, see the essays in João José Reis and Flávio dos Santos Gomes, *Liberdade por um fio.* For the New World in general, see Richard Price, *Maroon Societies.*

5. The growing list of scholarly publications on the Brazilian ex-*quilombos* parallels this growth in national and international attention. Between 1995 and 1997, seventy-three new books, theses and dissertations, monographs, and articles appeared on the theme. As a further indicator of the range of this interest, the authors include anthropologists, historians, legal specialists, archaeologists, agronomists, and cartographers (Almeida, "Quilombos: Repertório," pp. 51–70).

6. For one attempt to think through some of the features that distinguish Brazilian *remanescentes* from their counterparts in other locations, see Flávio dos Santos, "Ainda sobre os quilombos."

7. Article 68 asserts, "Definitive property rights are given to the descendants of the communities of quilombos who are occupying their lands, the State to issue to them respective titles." (My translation.) See *Informe revisão constitutional,* nos. 2, 3 and 4.

8. Provisory Measure 1911, issued in October 1999, for instance, blocked the passage of title scheduled for the *remanescente* communities of Castanhanduba, Apuí, Cuecé, Silêncio, Matá, São José (Óbidos), and Curiaú (Amapá), by transferring authority for the granting of legal title from the INCRA (the National Institute for Colonization and Agrarian Reform) to the Ministry of Culture, forcing these communities to petition the executive branch for a solution to the impasse. In July 2000, eleven *remanescente* communities in the Palmares district (in the Brazilian northeast) received collective title to their lands without the accompanying appropriation of private ranches within them, making the title worthless. Some states have refused to register collective titles, further complicating the *remanescentes'* legal claims to these lands.

9. Although African slavery in the Amazon is certainly older than Pombal, it

is he who greatly increased the slave traffic. For an account of the Companhia Geral, which transformed the eastern Amazon's place in an international economy, see A. Carreira's *A Companhia Geral do Grão-Pará e Maranhão*. For an introduction to Pombal (Sebastião José de Carvalho e Mello), who exercised enormous power in Portugal from 1750 to 1777, see Kenneth Maxwell's *Pombal, Paradox of the Enlightenment*. The book includes a useful discussion of an extensive bibliography (pp. 167–74).

10. For more facts and figures on cacao during this period, see Nigel J. H. Smith, *The Amazon River Forest*, pp. 36–43.

11. *Wild* here is a relative term. The cacao trees along the floodplains of the western Amazon that the Europeans encountered were almost certainly planted in part by native peoples. In the eighteenth century, the itinerant judge Francisco Xavier Ribeirode Sampaio remarked on their great abundance along portions of the river between Manacapuru and Coarí.

12. These numbers were small in absolute terms—between 30,000 and 50,000. However, given the reduced population of the Amazon in general, and the Óbidos–Monte Alegre area in particular, at the time the numbers were highly significant. In 1800, there were only 90,000 people recorded in all of Amazonia. By 1840, there were still fewer than 130,000.

13. The Brazilian Amazon never rivaled Venezuela or Guayaquil (Ecuador) in terms of cacao production. And yet, although it remained a distant fifth among the administrative units of Brazil most actively engaged in trade with Portugal by the end of the eighteenth century, cacao changed what had been an overwhelmingly extractive economy into one in which plantation agriculture played an increasingly significant role. For more on cacao and its importance to the Amazonian economy, see Dauril Alden, "The Significance of Cacao Production in the Amazon Region." For a striking engraving of cacao in the wild, see Paul Marcoy, *A Journey across South America*, half-vol. 4, p. 453. An illustration of a cacao orchard in cleared forest near Santarém in the mid-1870s and another illustration of laborers drying the fruit on the floodplain appear in Herbert Huntington Smith, *Brazil, the Amazons and the Coast*, pp. 113 and 260.

14. Rubber took off with the inauguration of regular steamship services along the main course of the Amazon in 1853. For a discussion of rubber, see Barbara Weinstein's *The Amazon Rubber Boom* and Warren Dean's *Brazil and the Struggle for Rubber*. Rubber production tripled in the 1860s, increasing another 800 percent by the 1880s. By 1900, rubber accounted for a full quarter of all Brazilian exports, making it the nation's most important export after coffee. Rubber prices doubled in 1909, a year before the entry of Malayan plantation rubber onto the world market brought on a dramatic bust.

15. Rubber was associated above all with the headwaters of the Madeira, Purus, and Juruá Rivers in the western Amazon, and, to a somewhat lesser degree, with the Xingu and Tapajós regions. According to Nigel Smith, cacao towns, such as Alenquer and Monte Alegre, "became depressed communities during the rubber boom" (*The Amazon River Forest*, p. 44).

16. For a comparative perspective on the brutal treatment that inspired slaves to flee, see John Hope Franklin and Loren Schweninger's discussion of the southern United States in *Runaway Slaves*.

17. Vicente Salles' *Memorial da Cabanagem* remains the single best account of this popular rebellion—one of the biggest and most important in all of Latin America. For an overview of the Cabanagem and its effect on conceptions of race and race relations, see David Cleary, "'Lost Altogether to the Civilised World.'" Slaves were particularly likely to flee during the holiday periods of the rainy season, which stretches from December to June (Funes, "Nasci nas matas," p. 473).

18. Reports of commercial ties between the *mocambos* and Suriname appear in Tavares Bastos, *Valle do Amazonas*, which in 1866 cited reports that the escaped slaves traded their produce with "the Dutch" primarily for iron tools and weapons (p. 202).

19. João Barbosa Rodrigues refers to Atanásio, who officially belonged to Major Martinho da Fonseca Seixa, in his *Exploração e estudo do valle do Amazonas*, p. 25. José Alípio Goulart also mentions Atanásio in his section on river merchants and black slaves in *O regatão*, pp. 156–58. For a good general introduction to the period, see Vicente Salles' *O negro no Pará*.

20. "It was Maravilha in which resided the great-great-grandfathers and great-grandfathers of the old people who presently inhabit the remanescente communities within this area," affirms Lúcia de Andrade in "Os Quilombos."

21. Some *quilombos* were a more openly guarded secret than others. While the Trombetas communities were tucked away high above waterfalls, the *quilombo* of Arapemã was situated very close to Óbidos. Likewise, various other *quilombos* grew up not far from Belém, where the city and its numerous small ports served as hiding places for the slaves who arrived there to buy and sell.

22. Ferreira Penna offered this description in 1867 (see Acevedo and Castro, *Negros*, p. 79, for details). In 1870, the acting president of Pará, Manuel José de Siqueira Mendes, signed an order authorizing the destruction of all of the *quilombos*. The last expedition of which there is a record targeted a *quilombo* in the Curuá in 1876. See Orville Derby, "O Rio Trombetas," p. 369, for documentation of this mission. Acevedo and Castro in *Negros* provide a useful table of travelers—mostly priests or scientists—who visited (and often wrote about) the greater Trombetas region and its *quilombos* between 1725 and 1899 on pp. 91–92.

23. See the section on the Brazil-nut economy and accompanying patronage system in Acevedo and Castro, *Negros*, pp. 140–49. For a useful parallel, see Marília Emmi's *A oligarquia do Tocantins e o domínio dos castanhais*.

24. The original members of the Porto Trombetas venture were the Companhia Vale do Rio Doce of Brazil together with Alcan of Canada, the Brazilian Companhia de Alumínio, the Dutch Billiton, the Norwegian Norsk Hydro, and the U.S. Reynolds, with Rio Doce as the controlling member.

25. C. Pedroso Filho, "Trombetas, nasce uma cidade." For a stinging contrast, see Lúcio Flávio Pinto's "Trombetas: Os desafios de um projeto concebido por multinacionais na Amazônia."

26. IBAMA is an acronym for Instituto Brasileiro do Meio Ambiente e dos Recursos Naturais Renováveis (Brazilian Institute for the Environment and Renewable Natural Resources). For an introduction to Brazilian environmental institutions, see Ronald Foresta, *Amazon Conservation in the Age of Develop-*

ment. Foresta, unfortunately, appears wholly unaware of the existence of the *remanescentes.* In his account of the establishment of the national forest of Sacara Taquera by the Brazilian Institute for Forest Development, pp. 198–205, he notes simply that "neighboring *caboclos* protest that IBDF guards threaten their livelihood." (The italics are mine.)

27. The Trombetas biological reserve, 385,000 hectares, was created by Decree 84.018/79 on 21 September 1979. The Sacará–Taquera national forest, with 426,600 hectares, followed on 27 December 1989 with Decree 98.707/89. Under Brazilian law, biological reserves cannot have inhabitants, and they restrict activities to scientific research. Similar, though slightly less stringent, restrictions apply to national forests.

28. ARQMO now has its own website. See "Projeto Manejo dos Territórios Quilombolas" at www.quilombo.org.br.

29. The names of these organizations in Portuguese are the Associação dos Povos contra a Barragem and the Comissão pró-Índio. For more information on the former, consult the website of the International Rivers Network, www.irn .org/programs/latamerica.

30. For an introduction to the larger black-rights movement in Brazil that provides a partial context for the Amazonian *remanescentes,* see Michael George Hanchard, *Orpheus and Power,* and Henrique Cunha Júnior, *Textos para o movimento negro.*

31. For a clear summary of the complicated seven-step entitulation process, see Lúcia de Andrade and Girolamo Treccani, "Terras de Quilombo." The additional communities are Água Fria (1996); Bacabal, Aracuan de Cima, Aracuan do Meio, Aracuan de Baixo, Serrinha, Terra Preta II, and Jaraucacá (1997); and Pancada, Araçá, Espírito Santo, Jauari, Boa Vista do Cuminã, Varre Vento, Jarauacá, and Acapu (1998).

32. The *remanescentes* are not the only ones trying to puzzle out the various meanings of *remanescente* and *quilombo.* For a few of a growing number of discussions of the movement from a legal-historical definition to a more sociological, community-involved interpretation of these terms, see Andrade, "Terras de Quilombo"; Alfred Wagner Berno de Almeida, "Quilombos: Sematologia face a novas identidades"; and Eliane Cantarino O'Dwyer, "Terra de quilombos."

33. Michael Astor, "Hope for the Amazon Jungle." "In an area replanted in 1982, the forest is so tall and thick it's hard to distinguish it from the original," Astor reports enthusiastically. He goes on to note that Rio do Norte invests 10 percent of its dividends—about $2.2 million a year—in reforestation.

34. The nineteenth-century "scientific travelers" James C. Fletcher and Daniel Parish Kidder provide illustrations of some of the instruments of torture routinely used on runaway black slaves throughout much of Brazil. These include a heavy iron collar and something called "the log and chain." There is also a tin mask used to keep urban slaves from drinking sugar-rum and their country cousins from eating clay, both "bad customs" to be discouraged. See *Brazil and the Brazilians,* pp. 131–32.

35. Tavares Bastos, for instance, spoke disparagingly (if with marvelous irony) of the "despotic elected government" of the runaway slave communities in *Valle do Amazonas* (pp. 119–20). Henri Anatole Coudreau expresses irrita-

tion at various points in his *Voyage au Trombetas* with how the *remanescentes* fail to share information about the watercourses.

36. Since 1988, *remanescentes* throughout Brazil have had a greater presence in the international press, which featured various articles about ex-*quilombos* as part of ceremonies in 1995 commemorating the three hundredth anniversary of the violent death of Zumbi, leader of the large and particularly militant northeast Brazilian *quilombo* of Palmares. Robert Stam's discussion of cinematic representations of *quilombos* in *Tropical Multiculturalism*, pp. 41–44 and 310–16, provides a useful context. The Amazonian *remanescentes*, however, have received relatively little media attention.

37. The involvement of blacks in gold mining has a historical basis. David Cleary relates a contemporary oral history about how nineteenth-century black *quilombo* residents taught the Indians of Maranhão the techniques of gold mining. The narrative offers a wonderful affront to stereotypes not only because native peoples are usually portrayed as victims of the mixed-blood (and thus, "nonnative") miners, but also because most depictions of black Amazonians present them as students of the Indians (which they probably were in various other cases). For the details, see Cleary, *Anatomy of the Amazon Gold Rush*, pp. 40–44. An early-nineteenth-century association between fugitive blacks and gold mining in Colombia appears in the writings of Humboldt, who mentions how black women set a heavy stone on the nape of their neck so as to duck more deeply under the gold-rich Andágueda River. The description appears together with a striking photograph of present-day blacks extracting gold in the Chocó in Benjamín Villegas, ed., *The Route to Humboldt*, vol. 2, p. 131. See also Nina S. De Friedemann's "'Troncos' among Black Miners in Colombia" for a discussion of contemporary miners who trace back their ancestry to runaway slaves.

38. I focus on the gold miners because the reader is already familiar with them. However, I just as easily could have compared the *remanescentes* to rubber tappers or to native peoples—both groups with which they have much in common through their political activism.

39. In theory, the hunting and consumption of river turtles is either prohibited or highly regulated. In practice, turtles—once abundant but now an endangered species—continue to be consumed in many parts of the Amazon.

40. Woman, age nineteen, Boa Vista. Single, four years of school.

41. For further discussion of the customary division between saints and Encantados, see Candace Slater, *Dance of the Dolphin*, pp. 138–65.

42. Woman, age forty-two, born Silêncio do Matá, lives in Óbidos. Separated, laundress, "little" formal education.

43. There is a large body of work on the black folk-saints Anthony, Thomas, and above all, Benedict in Brazil. For more on this particular narrative, see Candace Slater, "Breaking the Spell."

44. Woman, age twenty-two, born Boa Vista, lives in Oriximiná. Single, works in clinic, eight years of schooling.

45. Although *azinhavre* literally means "verdigris," the Portuguese word possesses connotations that the English term does not. The speakers regard this substance as a kind of congealed sweat, a bad-smelling and potentially lethal proof of gold's living nature.

46. Seu Tico, age seventy-three, Lago de Abuí, interviewed in Boa Vista. Married, no formal education.

47. Father Nicolino published a description of his first trip up the Cuminá–Erepecuru River in 1876, which Lúcia de Andrade cites in "Os Quilombos da Bacia do Rio Trombetas," p. 91. The diary of his three expeditions appeared in the *Revista de Estudos Paraenses* in 1894. I have not been able to locate either reference.

48. Fray Juan de Santa Gertrudis, "El hedor pestífero del oro," p. 234.

49. Man, age thirty-three, born Erepecuru River, now spends most of his time in Oriximiná. Married, carpenter and sometime healer, "some" formal education.

50. Woman, age sixty-eight ("or maybe sixty-seven"), born Abuí, interviewed in Boa Vista. Married, does "a little bit of everything," no formal education.

51. Woman, age thirty-six, born on Trombetas River, has lived in Oriximiná on and off for the last ten years. Separated, works as laundress, two years' formal education.

52. For a consideration of native groups' attempts to speak to a national and international public, see Alcida Rita Ramos' "From Eden to Limbo" and "Indian Voices"; Beth A. Conklin and Laura Graham's "The Shifting Middle Ground"; and Sylvia Caiuby Novaes, *The Play of Mirrors*. For a consideration of the rubber tappers, see Margaret E. Keck, "Social Equity and Environmental Politics in Brazil," and the useful overview in Anthony Hall's *Sustaining Amazonia*, pp. 91–133.

53. For an excellent discussion of the use of "borrowed words," see Laura R. Graham, "Brazilian Indians and the Symbolic Politics of Language in the Global Public Sphere." See also the chapter on Indian voices in Alcida Rita Ramos' *Indigenism*, pp. 119–44.

54. The *remanescentes* are by no means the only people to have suppressed painful memories of brutal treatment. "It's a part of history that as a black I wasn't familiar with myself," says Mary Young, the editor of two books of U.S. slave narratives, whose family "just didn't talk about slavery." She is quoted in Doreen Carvajal, "Slavery's Truths (and Tales) Come Flocking Home."

55. There is a large and growing body of work on what is often called "the selective uses of the past." For a useful overview, see the introduction to the essays in *History and Ethnicity*, ed. Elizabeth Tonkin, Maryon McDonald, and Malcolm Chapman. Among the large number of books and articles on the relationship between memory and the present that best illumine the *remanescentes*' situation are Joanne Rappaport's *The Politics of Memory* (about native historical interpretation in the Andes) and Elizabeth Tonkin's "Narrating Our Pasts" (about the construction of oral histories in Africa).

56. Nené, age thirty-eight, Espírito Santo. Married, "some" schooling "and all of my children have learned how to read and write."

57. See, by way of comparison, the accounts of the African past in Tamara Giles-Vernick's "*Doli:* Translating an African Environmental History of Loss in the Sangha River Basin of Equatorial Africa." In her similarly useful "Na lege ti guiriri" (On the Road of History), Giles-Vernick discusses the shifting meanings

of roads as expressions of connections to past people, practices, knowledge, and spaces.

58. Woman, age seventy-eight, Água Fria. Widowed, "almost no" schooling.

59. See Alfredo Wagner B. de Almeida, "Terras de preto, terra de santo, terras de índio," for tensions among different ethnic groups within the Amazon. Emblematic of the intricately intertwining history of Amerindians and African slave descendants in the Amazon, the word *remanescente* was first applied to indigenous—not runaway slave—groups during the early twentieth century. See José Maurício Andion Arruti, "A emergência dos remanescentes."

60. The *remanescentes'* stories of sufferings endured during the time of the candles find a counterpart in accounts of barbarities inflicted on Amazonian native peoples during the same era. David Sweet cites accusations by Jesuit priests that an Indian found slacking off in the cacao groves would be hung by the neck so that his feet barely touched the ground. Forced to stick his tongue into the matchlock of a musket that dangled there, he would then be whipped to death (Sweet, "'A Rich Realm of Nature Destroyed,'" p. 160).

61. Dona Lia, age sixty-three, Espírito Santo. Married, no formal schooling.

62. Acevedo and Castro, *Negros,* p. 165. The full title of the book in Portuguese is *Negros do Trombetas: Guardiães das matas e rios* (Blacks of the Trombetas: Guardians of the Forests and Rivers).

63. Chicão, age fifty, born Tapagem. Married, fisherman and farmer, no formal education "but my mother taught us all to read." For a description, and photos, of the actual side-necked (podocnemid) turtles, see R. C. Best, "The Aquatic Mammals and Reptiles of the Amazon," pp. 386–94.

64. "A landscape," says Keith Basso, "has ontological import because it is lived in and through, mediated, worked on and altered, replete with cultural meaning and symbolism—and not just something looked at or thought about, an object merely for contemplation, depiction, representation and aestheticization" ("Stalking with Stories," p. 19). Steven Feld refers to "the constant play between specific and general, personal and social, momentary and historical resonances" for local place names, "along with the time-space connections they consummate in place" ("Waterfalls of Song," p. 109).

65. Christopher Tilley speaks about this kind of inscription of human activities within a landscape through which daily passages become biographic encounters in *A Phenomenology of Landscape Places, Paths, and Monuments.* "Memories of previous moves in a landscape are as essential to understanding as they are in playing a game of chess," he says (p. 27).

66. Zé Cândido, age fifty-four, Boa Vista. Married, carpenter, no formal education.

67. Among the *remanescentes,* goods are always shared. Although one can hope that another will refuse the invitation, it must be made. "Why do you keep offering me cigarettes when you know that I don't smoke?" I once asked Manuel Pedro. "Because I cannot smoke myself if I don't include you," he responded. "Besides, who knows if one day you won't change your mind?"

68. "For native people," says Peter Gow, "'being civilized' is not opposed to an idyllic 'traditional' culture which has been lost, but to the ignorance and helplessness of the forest-dwelling ancestors. To be 'civilized' is to be au-

tonomous, to be able to live in villages rather than in accordance with native people's own values, rather than the capricious wishes of a boss" (*Of Mixed Blood*, p. 2). Although Gow is speaking here not of African Amazonians, but of Peruvian peoples of mixed ethnic heritage, his point sheds light on Benedita's aversion to what looks to her like the exoticization of a past to which few *remanescentes*, despite their sometimes nostalgic rhetoric, would like to return.

Chapter 8. Beyond Eden

1. See Pennie L. Magee, " 'The Water Is Our Land.' "

2. Peter Gow makes the point beautifully of how forests divide human settlements in his "Land, People and Paper in Western Amazonia." "In the forest," he says, "sight penetrates only a short distance into the mass of trees. Along the big rivers, you can see further, but even here there is no distant blue horizon. The sky starts abruptly from behind the screen of forest. Sight is hemmed in, and you would succumb to claustrophobia had not a plane journey or many days of travel let you know the scale of this land of big rivers and unending forests" (p. 60). The idea of the immense Rain Forest depends on an aerial view that few Amazonians can claim. Ironically, it is deforestation that makes possible a wider forest view.

3. For a discussion of the Greek and Latin roots that have given us present-day words, including both *savage* and *sylvan*, see Robert Harrison, *Forests*, pp. 27–28.

4. "Sounds Like Science Quiz," National Public Radio, 12 June 1999.

5. Here, I refer above all to popular imagery. Certainly, scholars such as Nigel J. H. Smith *(The Amazon River Forest),* Michael Goulding *(The Fishes and the Forest),* and Hugh Raffles ("Igarapé Guariba") have emphasized with great effectiveness the interplay of land and water in Amazonia. This book purposefully begins with a U.S. poet's evocation of the meeting of the waters, coupled with an Amazonian storyteller's reference to trees. However, even in scholarly circles, discussions of the land, and of terrestrial flora and fauna, have often overshadowed treatments of the water and its symbolic, as well as material, importance.

6. See Hugh Raffles' nuanced discussion of anthropogenic waterways in "Igarapé Guariba." Although human beings have long directly intervened in the waterways as well as the land in the Amazon, their control has never been complete.

7. In its fundamental instability, the Encante recalls the wondrous chaos that Ovid describes in the beginning of *Metamorphoses:* "What was land, sea, sky, was / Unstable, swimless, unlit; nothing kept shape, / Everything against everything" (p. 3).

8. Amazonians are by no means the only people to whom water, and the interweavings of land and water, is essential. Speaking of Bosavi, New Guinea, for instance, Edward L. Schieffelin in *The Sorrow of the Lonely and the Burning of the Dancers* notes that most places in the forest are named after the stream that gives the land its contours in that vicinity. "The name of a locality carries, in ef-

fect," he says, "its own geographical coordinates, which place it in determinate relation to the brooks and streams that flow through the forest" (p. 30). He later goes on to note that the rivers of the Bosavi area appear to Kaluli mediums as broad roads all leading downstream till they converge in a single road of the dead (p. 106). Likewise, in the section of his article titled "Land as Water as Land," Steven Feld notes the Bosavi practice of attaching land-form descriptive modifiers to specific water names and water-form modifiers to specific land names (Feld, "Waterfalls of Song," p. 109).

9. For more on the time in which humans and animals spoke to each other as portrayed in various cultures, including the native Amazonian, see the selections in David M. Guss' *The Language of Birds.*

10. *Anaconda,* directed by Luís Llosa, is a 1997 thriller about a group of documentary filmmakers who run into a series of monstrous river snakes.

11. The idea of the boto as a "pink" dolphin appears to have originated with Jacques Cousteau, who identified it as such in his documentary *Amazon: Journey to a Thousand Rivers.* The "pink" dolphin has become a fixture on TV documentaries and eco-tours. There have even been Elderhostel educational programs for senior citizens focused on these animals.

12. For a discussion of (tropical) nature as a present-day variant on the English Commons, see the chapter "Nature: A Global Commons" in John Terborgh's *Requiem for Nature,* pp. 187–208.

13. There is a large body of work in Portuguese on Euclides da Cunha, but still relatively little in English on this major figure—in part because he is so exceedingly difficult to translate. What is genuinely grand in Portuguese sounds grandiose in English; what is moving in the original sounds wooden in translation. For a general introduction to Euclides, see Walnice Nogueira Galvão, ed., *Euclides da Cunha,* as well as Galvão's excellent introduction to the Spanish-language translation of Euclides' *Os sertões.* Leopoldo Bernucci's *A imitação dos sentidos* documents Euclides' sources and his continuing influence on Brazilian letters. See too Nicolau Sevcenko's *Literatura como missão,* Abguar Bastos' *A visão histórico-sociológico de Euclides da Cunha,* and Clóvis Moura's *Introdução ao pensamento de Euclides da Cunha.*

14. Because of his family's relatively precarious economic situation, Euclides was in a different position from those with greater immediate access to both wealth and power. Though he was extremely well read, the constant need to worry about money set him apart from a number of his intellectual peers. For a biographical introduction to Euclides, see Sylvio Rabello's *Euclides da Cunha.* Also extremely useful in this respect is Francisco Venâncio's *Euclydes da Cunha a seus amigos* and the wealth of letters contained in Walnice N. Galvão and Oswaldo Galotti's *Correspondência de Euclides da Cunha (ativa).*

15. For a detailed introduction to *Os sertões,* see Olímpio de Souza Andrade, *História e interpretação de "Os sertões."* For an English-language introduction to the messianic community of Canudos, see Robert Levine's *Vale of Tears.*

16. For a chronology of Euclides' stay in Amazonia, see da Cunha, *Um paraíso perdido,* xxxiv–xxxvi. The charge to the joint commission appears on pp. 270–71.

17. Euclides actually had evinced interest in the Amazon as early as 1898. See his article "Fronteira sul do Amazonas—questões de limites" in *Estado de São Paulo*, 4 November 1898.

18. Euclides identified this book's purpose as to avenge "all of the barbarities" that had besmirched "the marvelous Hiléia [Humboldt's term for the Amazon] since the seventeenth century." The essays that he saw as preliminary sketches for it appear in *Contrastes e confrontos* (1907), *Peru versus Bolívia*, and *À margem da história* (1909). The first book contains twenty-eight articles (not all about the Amazon), most previously published in southern newspapers. The second consists of articles originally published in the *Jornal do Comércio*. The third is divided into four parts, the first of which, "Terra sem história" (Land without History), deals with the Amazon. *Um paraíso perdido* finally did appear almost eighty years after Euclides' death in a commemorative volume titled *Um paraíso perdido, Reunião dos ensaios amazônicos*. I have used another posthumous collection, titled *Um paraíso perdido (Ensaio, Estudos e Pronunciamentos sobre a Amazônia)*, edited by Leandro Tocantins, which appeared in 1986. This edition includes not only the previously published essays, but also various newspaper articles, prefaces, personal correspondence, and notes.

19. The astonishing details of the affair between Euclides' wife, Anna, and the army officer (and future general) Dilermando de Assis are the stuff of novels. So is the later death of Euclides' second son and namesake at the hands of Dilermando, who had become his stepfather following the elder Euclides' death. For a dramatic account of the events, and of the relationship between Euclides and his two eldest children (the firstborn, Solon, would die in Amazonia), see Francisco Foot Hardman, "Pai, Filho: Caligrafias de afeto."

20. In part because of the essays' unfinished nature, in part because of the continuing distance of the Amazon from the centers of Brazilian political and intellectual power, the body of work on them—as opposed to that on *Rebellion in the Backlands*—remains painfully small. The handful of books and articles about Euclides' Amazonian writings include Leandro Tocantins, *Euclides da Cunha e o "Um paraíso perdido,"* and Velloso Leão's *Euclides da Cunha na Amazônia*. See also chapters 8–10 in Sylvio Rabello's *Euclides da Cunha* and Tocantins' preface to *Um paraíso perdido*. Francisco Venâncio Filho's *Euclides da Cunha* includes an interesting collection of remarks that Alberto Rangel and other notable contemporaries made about Euclides in newspapers of the time. For newer and very promising work on the Amazonian essays, see Francisco Foot Hardman's "Brutalidade antiga: Sobre história e ruína em Euclides" and the section on Euclides in Fadel David Antonio Filho's "A visão da Amazônia brasileira." In English, see the section on the literature of the Rubber Boom in Pedro Maligo's *Land of Metaphorical Desires*, pp. 49–95.

21. In this encapsulation of oppositions, Euclides would appear to be a case study of what Homi Bhabha has called the "Janus-faced" creole intellectual who continually fluctuates between being complicit with and resistant to the nation. The difference, once again, is that Euclides was so clearly aware of his own contradictions, and actively played with them. (See Bhabha, *Nation and Narration*, p. 294.)

22. "He doesn't combine these opposing states to create an activity that,

while hybrid, is, nonetheless, more defined and stable. They [these oppositions] merely come together without ever fusing," says Euclides in reference to the conflicting tendencies he sees among the Peruvian *caucheros,* or rubber tappers ("Os Caucheros," *Um paraíso perdido,* p. 71). This phrase could be an epithet for the Amazonian essays and for himself. All translations here are my own.

23. "Brasileiros," *Um paraíso perdido,* p. 86.

24. "Terra sem história," *À margem da história,* p. 50.

25. "Impressões Gerais," *Um paraíso perdido,* p. 26.

26. He does refer to them in essays such as "Caucheros." Moreover, while they occupied relatively little space in the essays, Euclides was considerably more interested in both the Indian and mixed-blood populations than were the vast majority of the nineteenth-century European scientific travelers.

27. "Um clima caluniado," *Um paraíso perdido,* p. 61.

28. "O inferno verde," *Um paraíso perdido,* p. 203.

29. "Um clima caluniado," *Um paraíso perdido,* p. 52.

30. Ibid.

31. "Impressões Gerais," *Um paraíso perdido,* p. 19.

32. Ibid., p. 31.

33. The language of the nation as family recalls Homi Bhabha's comments about the cultural construction of nationness as a form of "social and textual *affiliation*" (*Nation and Narration,* p. 292; my italics). Doris Sommer's *Foundational Fictions* also stresses the importance of the metaphor of the nation as a family.

34. "Entre o Madeira e o Javari," *Um paraíso perdido,* p. 19. ("A Amazônia, mais cedo ou mais tarde, se destacará do Brasil, naturalmente e irresistívelmente, como se despega um mundo de uma nebulosa—pela expansão centrífuga do seu próprio movimento.")

35. "A Transacreana," *Um paraíso perdido,* p. 105.

36. "Amazônia: A gestação de um mundo," *Um paraíso perdido,* p. 4.

37. "O inferno verde," *Um paraíso perdido,* p. 207.

38. The phrase in Portuguese is "um idioma estranho gravado do áspero dos dizeres técnicos" ("Amazônia: A gestação de um mundo," *Um paraíso perdido,* p. 4). Luiz Costa Lima's discussion in *Terra ignota* of what he feels to be Euclides' misreadings of European scientists in *Rebellion in the Backlands,* and the implications of these misreadings for the ongoing relationship between science and literature in Brazil, raises questions equally relevant to the Amazonian essays. Lima asserts that Euclides often misunderstood the European writers, or read them carelessly; however, one could as easily argue that he purposefully misread them in order to bolster his own aims.

39. "Um clima caluniado," *Um paraíso perdido,* p. 59.

40. Ratzel, although influenced by the evolutionary theories of Darwin and of the German zoologist Ernst Heinrich Haeckel, became increasingly critical of what he came to see as the mechanistic quality of their writings. In his later writings, he drew as much on philosophy as he did on biology. Published in 1902, his essay "Lebensraum" (Living Space), which relates human groups to the spatial units where they develop, is often cited as a starting point in geopolitics. The actual term *geopolitics* was coined some fifteen years later by the Swedish polit-

ical scientist and conservative politician Rudolf Kjellén to describe the problems and conditions within a state that arise from its geographic features.

41. Golbery's most important book in terms of policy for the Amazon was *Geopolítica do Brasil,* which appeared two years after the military coup of 1964. A professor at the National War College (a kind of Brazilian West Point), he believed that Brazil's geopolitical imperative was the establishment of a strong nation that had, through internal expansion, gained complete control of its own national territory.

42. *Geopolítica,* p. 124. The term is "uma ilha vasta e despovoada" in Portuguese.

43. Golbery saw the Amazon as the only one of Brazil's major regions to actively resist unification. "Only Hiléia [among all the regions of Brazil] tableland, truly evades its [proper] unifying role within the tableland, resisting cohesive and agglutinative action, not simply through the irregularity of the Amazonian river valley, but also, and above all, through the discontinuity which separates the eastern tributaries from the southern margin of the great river, and through the powerful tropical jungle which perpetually resists connections along its low and badly defined divisions" (*Geopolítica,* p. 39).

44. The immense Calha Norte project was the first Amazon program of the new civilian government that replaced the military dictatorship in 1985. The package included the development of the Northern Perimeter Highway, agricultural projects and colonization on the southeastern zone of the Yanomami territory, and the development of the São Paradão hydroelectric plant. The area under its control stretched all the way from Tabatinga at the Peruvian border to Oiapoque, at the border of French Guiana, a total of four thousand miles.

45. Tânia Varella, "Ciência na mata," *Veja* on-line, www2.uol.com.br/veja/.

46. "Judas-Asvero," *Um paraíso perdido,* pp. 76–81.

47. The first quotation appears on page 80, the second on page 76.

48. "Amazônia: A gestação de um mundo," p. 28. In its ensuing invitation to new modes of organization and expression, the Amazon helped Brazilians to create the sorts of imaginative bonds about which Benedict Anderson speaks in *Imagined Communities.*

49. "O inferno verde," *Um paraíso perdido,* p. 201.

50. "Um clima caluniado," *Um paraíso perdido,* p. 53.

51. "O inferno verde," *Um paraíso perdido,* p. 200.

52. Ibid., p. 201. ("Para vê-la deve renunciar-se ao próposito de descortiná-la," wrote Euclides in one of the essays' most beautiful passages.)

53. The relationship between Euclides and Rangel merits detailed study. While most literary critics have assumed that Rangel, a younger man and far less talented writer, borrowed heavily from Euclides in his short stories, it turns out that Euclides took at least as much as he gave. Many of the actual phrases in the essays have parallels in earlier writings by Rangel. The latter's long description of scarecrows in the story "Inferno verde," for instance, found echoes in the searing image of the effigy upon whom the rubber tappers fired during its unhappy voyage down the river during Holy Week in Euclides' unforgettable "Judas-Asvero." Rangel's reference to Amazonia as "a slandered land" reverberated in Euclides' "A Slandered Climate," and his Orestes-like *caboclo* bears a

decided resemblance to Euclides' "Titanic caboclos" who engage in the Sisyphean task of rubber tapping. Euclides' description of the winter floods as "a wet sponge that rubs out a badly made design" likewise recalled Rangel's earlier comparison of these floods to "a great sponge" that wipes out familiar landmarks.

54. Euclides' vision of the Amazon as the last page of Genesis, in which writing equals knowledge, recalls Michel Foucault's definition of "the dream of natural science" as the reuniting of words with things.

55. "Brasileiros," *Um paraíso perdido,* p. 86.

56. For an English-language introduction to Brazilian Modernism, which bears scant relation to the Spanish American and U.S. movements of the same name, see Roberto Schwarz' *Misplaced Ideas* and Randal Johnson's "Tupy or not Tupy." For an introduction in Portuguese, see the essays by Antonio Candido, "Literatura e cultura de 1900 a 1945" (pp. 139–67) and "A literatura na evolução de uma comunidade" (pp. 109–38) in his *Literatura e sociedade.* See too Mário da Silva Brito's *História do modernismo no Brasil.*

57. The full title of Mário de Andrade's book is *Macunaíma: O herói sem caráter (rapsódia).* The author's choice of the term *rhapsody* is meant to underscore the novel's improvisational quality. Villa-Lobos openly "Brazilianized" Bach in the title of his work, which draws on folk themes from the Amazon as well as other parts of Brazil. The fight among literary critics as to whether *Cobra Norato* is lyric poetry or an epic has raged since its initial publication in 1929. Carlos Drummond de Andrade, almost certainly Brazil's greatest twentieth-century poet, referred on one occasion to this work as "the most Brazilian of all Brazilian poems."

58. *Cobra Norato* is based directly on the Encantado story discussed in chapter 3. *Macunaíma* draws on a series of Indian transformation myths, collected by the German ethnographer Theodor Koch-Grünberg in Roraima, to create a fiction full of metamorphoses. The *Bachianas Brasileiras* is a cycle of nine movements written between 1930 and 1945, each of which has a Brazilian and a European title. In them, as well as in Villa-Lobos' ballet *Amazonas,* the composer makes particular use of the songs of Amazonian birds, including *uirapuru,* which Amazonians often describe as an Encantado.

References

Acevedo, Rosa Elizabeth, and Edna Castro. *Negros do Trombetas: Guardiães de matas e rios.* 2nd rev. ed. Belém, Brazil: Editora Cejup, 1998.

Acosta, Padre José de. *Historia natural y moral de las Indias.* Ed. José Alcina Franch. 1st ed. Crónicas de América 34. Madrid: Historia 16, 1987.

Acuña, Cristóbal de. "A New Discovery of the Great River of the Amazons." Madrid: Royal Press, 1641. Reprinted in *Expeditions into the Valley of the Amazons.* Trans. and ed. Clements R. Markham. Vol. 24. London: Hakluyt Society, 1859.

Adams, Jonathan S., and Thomas O. McShane. *The Myth of Wild Africa: Conservation without Illusion.* Berkeley: University of California Press, 1996.

Adorno, Rolena. "El sujeto colonial y la construcción cultural de la alteridad." *Revista de crítica literaria latinoamericana* 14, no. 28 (1988): 55–68.

Ainsa, Fernando. *De la edad de oro a El Dorado: Génesis del discurso utópico americano.* Mexico City: Fondo de Cultura Económica, 1992.

———. "The Myth, Marvel, and Adventure of El Dorado: Semantic Mutations of a Legend." *Diogenes* 412 / 4, no. 164 (1993): 13–26.

Alden, Dauril. "The Significance of Cacao Production in the Amazon Region in the Late Colonial Period: An Essay in Comparative Economic History." *Proceedings of the American Philosophical Society* 120 / 2 (April 1976): 103–35.

———, ed. *Colonial Roots of Modern Brazil: Papers of the Newberry Library Conference.* Berkeley and Los Angeles: University of California Press, 1973.

Alegría, Ciro. *La serpiente de oro.* 1935. Bogotá: Editorial La Oveja Negra, 1980. (Translated by Harriet de Onís as *The Golden Serpent.* New York: New American Library, 1963.)

Alès, Catherine, and Michel Pouyllau. "La conquête de l'inutile. Les geographies imaginaries de l'Eldorado." *L'Homme* 122–124, vol. 22 (2–3–4) (1992): 271–308.

Almeida, Alfredo Wagner Berno de. "Quilombos: Repertório bibliográfico de uma questão redefinida (1995–1997)." *BIB* 45 (1998): 51–70.

———. "Quilombos: Sematologia face a novas identidades." In *Frechal: Terra de preto-Quilombo reconhecido como reserva extrativista*, pp. 11–19. Org. Projeto Vida de Negro. São Luís, Brazil: SMDDH / CCN-PVN, 1996.

———. "Terras de preto, terras de santo, terras de índios: Uso comum e conflito." *Cadernos do NAEA* 10 (1989): 163–96.

Alonso, José Luís Ruiz-Peinado. "Hijos del río: Negros del Trombetas." In *Memoria, creación e historia: Luchar contra el olvido / Memòria, creació i història: Lluitar contra l'oblit*, ed. Pilar García Jordán, Miquel Izard, and Javier Laviña, pp. 349–57. Barcelona: Generalitat de Catalunya et. al., 1994.

Álvarez Chanca, Diego. "Carta del físico Diego Álvarez Chanca al cabildo de Sevilla dándo le cuenta del segundo viaje de Cristóbal Colón." In Christopher Columbus, *Four Voyages to the New World: Letters and Selected Documents*. Ed. and trans. R. H. Major, pp. 18–68. New York: Corinth Books, 1961.

Amate Blanco, Juan José. "El realismo mágico en la expedición de Orellana." *Cuadernos Hispanoamericanos* 510 (1992): 61–72.

Amazonia without Myths. Washington, D.C.: Inter-American Development Bank, 1992.

Anderson, Benedict. *Imagined Communities: Reflections on the Origin and Spread of Nationalism*. Rev. and extended ed. London: Verso, 1991.

Andrade, Lúcia M. M. de. "Os quilombos da bacia do Rio Trombetas: Breve histórico." *Revista de Antropologia* 38, no. 1 (1995): 79–99.

Andrade, Lúcia de, and Girolamo Treccani. "Terras de quilombo." In *Direito Agrário Brasileiro*, ed. Raimundo Laranjeira, pp. 593–656. São Paulo: LTR 2000.

Andrade, Mário de. *Macunaíma*. Trans. E. A. Goodland. 1st ed. New York: Random House, 1984.

"A nova febre dourada." *Veja*, 18 January 1989, pp. 74–76.

Antonio Filho, Fadel David. "A visão da Amazônia brasileira: Uma avaliação do pensamento geográfico entre 1900 e 1940." Ph.D. diss., Universidade Estadual Paulista, 1995.

Arnold, David. *The Problem of Nature: Environment, Culture, and European Expansion. New Perspectives on the Past*. Oxford, England, and Cambridge, Mass.: Blackwell, 1996.

Arruti, José Maurício Andion. "A emergência dos 'remanescentes': Notas para o diálogo entre indígenas e quilombolas." *Mana* 3, no. 2 (1997): 7–38.

Arshi, Sunpreet, et. al. "Why Travel? Tropics, En-tropics and Apo-tropaics" In *Travellers' Tales: Narratives of Home and Displacement*, ed. George Robertson et. al., pp. 225–41. London and New York: Routledge, 1994.

Askenazi, Joel, et al. *Analyses et reflexions sur Lévi-Strauss, "Tristes tropiques": L'autre et l'ailleurs*. Paris: Ellipses, 1992.

Assayag, Simão. *Boi-Bumbá: Festas, andanças, luz e pajelanças*. Rio de Janeiro: INL, MEC, 1961.

Astor, Michael. "Hope for the Amazon Jungle." *San Francisco Chronicle*, 21 August 1999.

Averbuck, Lygia Morrone. *Cobra Norato e a revolução caraíba*. Rio de Janeiro: José Olympio; Brasília: INL, 1985.

Ayres, Deborah de Magalhães Lima. "The Social Category Caboclo: History, Social Organisation, Identity and Outsiders; Social Classification of the Rural Population of an Amazonian Region." Ph.D. diss., Cambridge University, 1992.

Baker, Alan R. H., and Gideon Biger, eds. *Ideology and Landscape in Histori-cal Perspective: Essays on the Meanings of Some Places in the Past.* Cam-bridge: Cambridge University Press, 1992.

Balée, William L. *Footprints of the Forest: Ka'apor Ethnobotany—The Histor-ical Ecology of Plant Utilization by an Amazonian People.* Biology and Re-source Management in the Tropics (series). New York: Columbia University Press, 1994.

Barbosa, Lívia, Ana Lúcia Lobato, and José Augusto Drummond, eds. *Ga-rimpo, meio ambiente e sociedades indígenas.* Niterói, Brazil: EDUFF, 1992.

Basso, Ellen B. *In Favor of Deceit: A Study of Tricksters in an Amazonian Soci-ety.* Tucson: University of Arizona Press, 1987.

Basso, Keith. "'Stalking with Stories': Names, Places, and Moral Narratives among the Western Apache." In *Text, Play, and Story: The Construction and Reconstruction of Self and Society,* ed. Edward Bruner, pp. 19–55. 1983 Proceedings of the American Ethnological Society. Washington, D.C.: 1984.

Bastos, Abguar. *A visão histórico-sociológico de Euclides da Cunha.* São Paulo: Companhia Editora Nacional, 1986.

Bates, Henry Walter. *The Naturalist on the River Amazons: A Record of Ad-ventures, Habits of Animals, Sketches of Brazilian and Indian Life, and As-pects of Nature under the Equator, during Eleven Years of Travel.* With an introduction by Alex Shoumatoff. 3rd ed. (Originally published in 1863.) New York: Penguin, 1989.

———. "A Pocket Diary Covering Parts of the Years 1848–1859." Documents Section, British Museum of Natural History.

Baudet, E. H. P. *Paradise on Earth: Some Thoughts on European Images of Non-European Man.* Trans. Elizabeth Wentholt. New Haven: Yale Univer-sity Press, 1965.

Bayle, Constantino. *El Dorado fantasma.* 2nd ed. Madrid: Publicaciones del Consejo de la Hispanidad, 1943.

Bercy, Drouin de. *L'Europe et l'Amérique comparées.* 1818. Reprint, Upper Saddle River, N.J.: Gregg, 1968.

Bernucci, Leopoldo. *A imitaçao dos sentidos: Prógonos, contemporâneos e epí-gonos de Euclides da Cunha.* São Paulo: Edusp; Boulder: University of Col-orado Press, 1995.

Best, Robin. "The Aquatic Mammals and Reptiles of the Amazon." In *The Amazon: Limnology and Landscape Ecology of a Mighty Tropical River and Its Basin,* ed. Harald Sioli, pp. 371–412. Monographiae Biologicae 52. Dor-drecht (Netherlands): Dr W. Junk Publishers, 1984.

Best, Robin C., and Vera M. F. da Silva. "Amazon River Dolphin, Boto Inia ge-offrensis (de Blainville, 1817)." In *Handbook of Marine Mammals,* ed. S. H. Ridgway and R. Harrison. Vol. 4, *River Dolphins and the Larger Toothed Whales,* pp. 1–23. San Diego: Academic Press, 1989.

Bhabha, Homi K., ed. *Nation and Narration.* London and New York: Rout-ledge, 1990.

Bilby, Kenneth, and Diana Baird N'Diaye. "'Creativity and Resistance': Maroon Culture in the Americas." In *1992 Festival of American Folklife,* ed. Peter Seitel.Washington, D.C.: Smithsonian Institution, 1992.

Bishop, Elizabeth. "Santarém." In *The Complete Poems, 1927–1979*, pp. 185–87. New York: Farrar, Straus, Giroux, 1983.

Bishop, Peter. *The Myth of Shangri-La: Travel Writing and the Western Creation of Sacred Landscape*. Berkeley: University of California Press, 1989.

Black, Jan Knippers. "Limits of Boom-and-Bust Development: Challenge of the Amazon." *USA Today,* 8 March 1993.

Blank, Les, and James Bogan, eds. *Burden of Dreams: Screenplay, Journals, Reviews, Photographs*. Io 32. Berkeley, Calif.: North Atlantic Books, 1984.

Blok, Josine, ed. *The Early Amazons: Modern and Ancient Perspectives on a Persistent Myth*. Religions in the Graeco-Roman World 120. Leiden and New York: E. J. Brill, 1995.

Bodmer, Beatriz Pastor. *The Armature of Conquest: Spanish Accounts of the Discovery of America, 1492–1589*. Trans. Lydia Longstreth Hunt. Stanford: Stanford University Press, 1992.

Bolaños, Álvaro Félix. *Barbarie y canibalismo en la retórica colonial: Los indios pijaos de Fray Pedro Simón*. Bogotá: CEREC, 1994.

Boomert, Arie. "Gifts of the Amazons: 'Green Stone' Pendants and Beads as Items of Ceremonial Exchange in Amazonia and the Caribbean." *Antropologica* 67 (1987): 33–54.

Boon, James. *From Symbolism to Structuralism: Lévi-Strauss in a Literary Tradition*. Oxford: Blackwell, 1972.

Bopp, Raul. *Cobra Norato e outros poemas*. 16th ed. Coleção Vera Cruz 168. Rio de Janeiro: Civilização Brasileira, 1988.

Bourdieu, Pierre. *Outline of a Theory of Practice*. Translated by Richard Nice. Cambridge: Cambridge University Press, 1993.

Boxer, Charles. *The Golden Age in Brazil: Growing Pains of a Colonial Society, 1695–1750*. New York: St. Martin's Press, 1995.

Brannstrom, Christian. "The River of Silver and the Island of Brazil." *Terrae Incognitae* 27 (1995): 1–14.

Branstron, Brian. *The Last Great Journey on Earth*. London: Hodder and Stoughton, 1970.

Braun, Bruce, and Noel Castree, eds. *Remaking Reality: Nature at the Millennium*. London and New York: Routledge, 1998.

Bray, Warwick. *The Gold of El Dorado*. From the exhibition "Gold of El Dorado, the Heritage of Colombia." New York: American Museum of Natural History, 1979.

Brito, Mário da Silva. *História do modernismo no Brasil*. 5th ed. Coleção Vera Cruz 63. Rio de Janeiro: Civilização Brasileira, 1978.

Brooke, James. "Brazil Creates Reserve for Imperiled Amazon Tribe." *New York Times,* 19 November 1991.

———. "Gold's Lure versus Indians' Rights: A Brazilian Conflict Sets the Amazon Aflame." *New York Times,* 21 January 1990.

———. "In T. R.'s Footsteps, Scientists Embark on Amazonian Expedition." *New York Times,* 25 February 1992.

Browder, John O., and Brian J. Godfrey. *Rainforest Cities: Urbanization, Development, and Globalization of the Brazilian Amazon*. New York: Columbia University Press, 1997.

Brown, Michael F. *Tsewa's Gift: Magic and Meaning in an Amazonian Society.* Washington, D.C.: Smithsonian Institution Press, 1986.

Brown, Michael F., and Eduardo Fernández. *War of Shadows: The Struggle for Utopia in the Peruvian Amazon.* Berkeley: University of California Press, 1991.

Bryld, Mette. "Dialogues with Dolphins and Other Extraterrestrials: Displacements in Gendered Space." In *Between Monsters, Goddesses, and Cyborgs: Feminist Confrontations with Science, Medicine, and Cyberspace,* ed. Nina Lykke and Rosi Braidotti, pp. 47–21. London and New York: Zed Books, 1996.

Bryld, Mette, and Nina Lykke. *Cosmodolphins: Feminist Cultural Studies of Technology, Animals, and the Sacred.* London and New York: Zed Books, 1999; distributed in the United States by St. Martin's Press.

Buarque de Holanda, Sérgio. *Visão do paraíso: Os motivos edênicos no descobrimento e colonização do Brasil.* 2nd rev. ed. São Paulo: Cia. Ed. Nacional / Editora da Universidade de São Paulo, 1969.

Buege, Douglas J. "The Ecologically Noble Savage Revisited." *Environmental Ethics* 18, no. 1 (1996): 71–88.

Bunker, Stephen. *Underdeveloping the Amazon: Extraction, Unequal Exchange, and the Failure of the Modern State.* Chicago: University of Chicago Press, 1988.

Burke, Edmund. *A Philosophical Enquiry into the Origin of Our Ideas of the Sublime and the Beautiful.* Edited and with an introduction and notes by J. T. Boulton. 1757. London: Routledge and Paul; New York: Columbia University Press, 1958.

Burton, David Henry. *Theodore Roosevelt: Confident Imperialist.* Philadelphia: University of Pennsylvania Press, 1969.

Callicot, J. Baird, and Michael P. Nelson. *The Great New Wilderness Debate.* Athens: University of Georgia Press, 1998.

Camacho, Juana, and Eduardo Restrepo, eds. *De montes, ríos, y ciudades: Territorios e identidades de la gente negra en Colombia.* Bogotá: Fundación Natura / Ecofondo / Instituto Colombiano de Antropología, 1998.

Campbell, Mary B. *The Witness and the Other World: Exotic European Travel Writing, 400–1600.* Ithaca, N.Y., and London: Cornell University Press, 1988.

Candido, Antonio. "Literatura e Cultura de 1900 a 1945." In *Literatura e sociedade: Estudos de teoria e história literária,* pp. 109–38. São Paulo: Companhia Editora Nacional, 1980.

———. "A literatura na evolução de uma comunidade." In *Literatura e sociedade: Estudos de teoria e história literária,* pp. 139–67. 1965. Rev. ed., São Paulo: Companhia Editora Nacional, 1980.

Cardillo, Ana Eugênia Gallo Cassini. *Bibliografia sobre ouro no Brasil, 1840–1983.* Brasília, D. F.: Ministério das Minas e Energia, Departamento Nacional da Produção Mineral, 1983.

Carpentier, Alejo. *The Lost Steps.* Trans. Harriet de Onís. 1st ed. New York: Knopf, 1956.

Carreira, A. *A Companhia Geral do Grão-Pará e Maranhão.* São Paulo: Editora Nacional, 1988.

Carvajal, Doreen. "Slavery's Truths (and Tales) Come Flocking Home." *New York Times,* 28 March 1999, Week in Review section.

Carvajal, Gaspar de. *Descobrimento do rio das Amazonas.* Trans. and annotated by C. de Melo Leitão. Bibliografia pedagógica brasileira, Serie 5a, Brasiliana, vol. 203. São Paulo: Companhia Editora Nacional, 1941.

———. *Descubrimientos del Río de las Amazonas: Relación de fr. Gaspar de Carvajal.* With a historical introduction by José Toribio Medina. Seville: E. Rasco, 1894.

———. *Descubrimiento del Río de Orellana.* Versión de Jorge A. Garcés G., prologue by J. Roberto Páez. Archivo Municipal Publicaciones 28. Quito: Impr. Municipal, 1958.

———. *The Discovery of the Amazon, According to the Account of Friar Gaspar de Carvajal and Other Documents,* as published with an introduction by José Toribio Medina. Trans. Bertram E. Lee, ed. H. C. Heaton. New York: American Geographical Society, 1934.

Carvalho, José. *O matuto cearense e o caboclo do Pará: Contribuição ao Folclore Nacional.* 2nd. ed. Fortaleza. Imprensa Universitária da Universidade Federal do Ceará, 1973.

Casey, Edward S. "How to Get from Space to Place in a Fairly Short Stretch of Time: Phenomenological Prolegomena." In *Senses of Place,* ed. Steven Feld and Keith H. Basso, pp. 13–52. Santa Fe, N.M.: School of American Research Press, 1996.

Castree, Noel, and Bruce Willems-Braun, eds. *Remaking Reality: Nature at the Millennium.* London: Routledge, in press.

Castro, Eduardo Viveiros de, and Manuel a Carneiro da Cunha. *Amazônica: Etnologia e história indígena.* São Paulo: Núcleo de História Indígena e do Indigenismo; Fundação Amparo à Pesquisa do Estado de São Paulo, 1993.

Castro, Ferreira de. *A selva: Romance.* 21st ed. Lisbon: Guimarães, n.d. (Translated by Charles Duff as *The Jungle: A Tale of the Amazon Rubber-Tappers.* New York: The Viking Press, 1935.)

Caufield, Catherine. *In the Rainforest: Report from a Strange, Beautiful, Imperiled World,* with a new afterword. Chicago: University of Chicago Press, 1991.

Chernela, Janet M. "Righting History in the Northwest Amazon." In *Rethinking History and Myth: Indigenous South American Perspectives on the Past,* ed. Jonathan D. Hill, pp. 35–49. Urbana: University of Illinois Press, 1988.

Chiappelli, Fredi, with Michael J. B. Allen and Robert L. Benson. *First Images of America: The Impact of the New World on the Old.* 2 vols. Berkeley: University of California Press, 1976.

Chibnick, Michael. *Risky Rivers.* Tucson: University of Arizona Press, 1994.

Civrieux, Marc de. "Medatia: A Makiritare Shaman's Tale." Trans. David M. Guss. In *The Language of the Birds: Tales, Texts and Poems of Interspecies Communication,* ed. David M. Guss, pp. 55–78. San Francisco: North Point Press, 1985.

Clastres, Hélène. *La terre sans mal: Le prophetisme tupi-guarani*. Paris: Éditions du Seuil, 1975.

Cleary, David. "After the Frontier: Problems with Political Economy in the Modern Brazilian Amazon." *Journal of Latin American Studies* 25 (1993): 331–49.

———. *Anatomy of the Amazon Gold Rush*. Iowa City: University of Iowa Press, 1990.

———. "'Lost Altogether to the Civilised World': Race and the Cabanagem in Northern Brazil, 1750 to 1850." *Comparative Studies in Society and History* 40, no. 1 (1998): 109–35.

———. "Towards an Environmental History of the Amazon: Prehistory to the Nineteenth Century." Unpublished ms.

———. "Tristes Trope-iques: Science and the Representation of Nature in Amazonia since the Early Eighteenth Century." Unpublished ms.

Cobo Borda, Juan Gustavo, ed. *Fábulas y leyendas de El Dorado*. Barcelona: Tusquets Editores, 1987.

Cockburn, Alexander. "Trees, Cows and Cocaine: An Interview with Susanna Hecht." *New Left Review* 173 (1989): 34–45.

Colchester, Marcus. *Guyana: Fragile Frontier. Loggers, Miners and Forest Peoples*. London and Gloucestershire: Latin American Bureau, World Rainforest Movement, 1997.

Collin, Richard H. *Theodore Roosevelt, Culture, Diplomacy, and Expansion: A New View of American Imperialism*. Baton Rouge: Louisiana State University Press, 1985.

Colón, Cristóbal (Christopher Columbus). *Los cuatro viajes, testamento*. Ed. Consuelo Varela. Madrid: Alianza, 1986.

Colón, Fernando. *The Life of the Admiral Christopher Columbus by His Son Ferdinand*. Trans. and annotated by Benjamin Keen. New Brunswick, N.J.: Rutgers University Press, 1959.

Columbus, Christopher. *Four Voyages to the New World,* letters and selected documents. Ed. and trans. R. H. Major. The American Experience Series. New York: Corinth Books, 1961.

Condamine, Charles de la. *Relation abrégée d'un voyage fait dans l'interieur de l'Amérique méridionale*. Paris: Pissot, 1745.

Conklin, Beth A. "Body Paint, Feathers and VCRs: Aesthetics and Authenticity in Amazonian Activism." *American Ethnologist* 24, no. 4 (1997): 711–37.

Conklin, Beth A., and Laura Graham. "The Shifting Middle Ground: Amazonian Indians and Eco-Politics." *American Anthropologist* 97, no. 4 (1995): 695–710.

Conquista y colonización rioplatense. Vol. 1. Buenos Aires: Jacobo Peuser, 1941.

Conrad, Joseph. *Heart of Darkness: An Authoritative Text, Backgrounds and Sources, Criticism*. 3rd ed. Ed. Robert Kimbrough. New York: Norton, 1988.

Cooper, John Milton, Jr. *The Warrior and the Priest: Woodrow Wilson and Theodore Roosevelt*. Cambridge: Belknap Press of Harvard University Press, 1983.

Cordeiro, Luiz. *Roosevelt e a Amazônia (Ementas, traços e rabiscos)*. Rio de Janeiro: Canton e Beyer, 1914.

Cortés, Hernán. *Cartas de relación de la conquista de México*. Madrid: España-
Calpe, 1970.

Costa Lima, Luiz. *Terra ignota*. Rio de Janeiro: Civilização Brasileira, 1997.

Coudreau, Henri Anatole. *Voyage au Trombetas, 7 août 1899–25 novembre
1899*. Paris: A. Lahure, 1900.

Cousteau, Jacques-Yves. *Journey to a Thousand Rivers*. Time-Life Video, the
Cousteau Society. Atlanta: Turner Home Entertainment, 1990. Videocassette.

Cousteau, Jacques-Yves, and Mose Richards. *Jacques Cousteau's Amazon Journey*. New York: Harry N. Abrams, 1984.

Coutinho, Edilberto. *Rondon: O salto para o desconhecido*. São Paulo: Editora
Nacional, 1987.

Couto e Silva, Golbery do. *Geopolítica do Brasil*. Rio de Janeiro: J. Olympio,
1967.

Cowell, Adrian. *The Decade of Destruction: The Crusade to Save the Amazon
Rain Forest*. New York: Henry Holt & Co., 1990.

Cronon, William. "The Trouble with Wilderness." In *Uncommon Ground: Rethinking the Human Place in Nature*, ed. William Cronon, pp. 69–90. New
York: Norton, 1996.

Culver, W. W., and T. C. Greaves, eds. *Miners and Mining in the Americas*.
Manchester, England: Manchester University Press, 1985.

Cunha Júnior, Henrique. *Textos para o movimento negro*. São Paulo: Edicon,
1992.

Curtis, Helena, and N. Sue Barnes. *Invitation to Biology*. 3rd ed. New York:
Worth Publishers, 1982.

Cutright, Paul Russell. *Theodore Roosevelt: The Making of a Conservationist*.
Urbana: University of Illinois Press, 1985.

da Cunha, Euclides. "Fronteira Sul do Amazonas—Questões de Limites." *Estado de São Paulo*, 4 November 1898.

———. *Los sertones*. Trans. Estela dos Santos. Prologue, notes, and chronology
by Walnice Nogueira Galvão. Caracas: Biblioteca Ayacucho, 1980.

———. *Um paraíso perdido: Ensaios, estudos, e pronunciamentos sobre a
Amazônia*. Ed. with notes and introduction by Leandro Tocantins. Rio de Janeiro: José Olympio, 1986.

———. *Um paraíso perdido: Reunião dos ensaios amazônicos, seleção e coor-
denação de Hildon Rocha*. Introduction by Arthur Cézar Ferreira Reis.
Petrópolis: Editora Vozes, 1976.

Damrosch, David. "The Ethnic Ethnographer: Judaism in *Tristes tropiques*."
Representations 50 (1995): 1–13.

Daniel, João Padre. *Quinta parte do tesouro descoberto no Rio Máximo Amazonas*. 2 vols. 1820. Anais da Biblioteca Nacional 95. Rio de Janeiro: Biblioteca Nacional, 1975.

Darwin, Charles. *Journal of Researches into the Natural History and Geology of the Countries Visited during the Voyage of the* H. M. S. Beagle *under the Command of Capt. Fitz Roy, R. N.* New York: The Heritage Press,
1957.

Davidson, Miles H. *Columbus Then and Now: A Life Reexamined.* Norman: University of Oklahoma Press, 1997.

Davis, Mike. *Ecology of Fear: Los Angeles and the Imagination of Disaster.* 1st ed. New York: Metropolitan Books, 1998.

Davis, Shelton H. *Victims of the Miracle: Development and the Indians of Brazil.* 1977. Cambridge: Cambridge University Press, 1988.

Davis-Kimball, Jeannine, and C. Scott Littleton. "Warrior Women of the Eurasian Steppes: New Evidence Suggests that Tales of Amazon Warriors May Be More Than Mere Legend." *Archaeology* 50, no. 1 (1997): 44–49.

Dean, Warren. *Brazil and the Struggle for Rubber: A Study in Environmental History.* Cambridge and New York: Cambridge University Press, 1987.

Denevan, William M. "The Pristine Myth: The Landscape of the Americas in 1492." *Annals of the Association of American Geographers* 82, 3 (1992): 369–85.

Denslow, Julie Sloan, and Christine Padoch, eds. *People of the Tropical Rain Forest.* Berkeley: University of California Press; Washington, D.C.: Smithsonian Institution Traveling Exhibition Service, 1988.

Derby, Orville. "O rio Trombetas." *Boletim do Museu Paraense de Historia Natural e Etnografia* 2, nos. 1–4 (1898): 366–82.

Descola, Philippe. *In the Society of Nature: A Native Ecology in Amazonia.* Cambridge: Cambridge University Press, 1994.

Descola, Philippe, and Gisli Pálsson, eds. *Nature and Society: Anthropological Perspectives.* London and New York: Routledge, 1996.

Dickenson, John. "Henry Walter Bates—The Naturalist of the River Amazons." *Archives of Natural History* 19, no. 2 (1992): 209–18.

Dictionary of Scientific Biography. Editor-in-chief Charles Coulston Gillespie. 16 vols. New York: Scribner, 1970–1980.

DiMarco, Vincent. "The Amazons and the End of the World." In *Discovering New Worlds: Essays on Medieval Exploration and Imagination,* ed. Scott D. Westrem, pp. 69–90. New York: Garland, 1991.

Dimenstein, Gilberto. *Meninas da noite: A prostituição de meninas-escravas no Brasil.* 2nd ed. São Paulo: Atica, 1992.

Doyle, Sir Arthur Conan. *The Lost World.* New York: The Review of Reviews Company, 1912.

DuBois, Page. *Centaurs and Amazons: Women in the Pre-History of the Great Chain of Being.* Ann Arbor: University of Michigan Press, 1982.

Dudley, Edward J., and Maximilian E. Novak, eds. *The Wild Man Within: An Image in Western Thought from the Renaissance to Romanticism.* Pittsburgh: University of Pittsburgh Press, 1972.

Dyer, Thomas G. *Theodore Roosevelt and the Idea of Race.* Baton Rouge: Louisiana State University Press, 1980.

Eddall, Barbara G., ed. *Wallace and Bates in the Tropics: An Introduction to the Theory of Natural Selection.* London: Macmillan, 1969.

Edwards, William H. *A Voyage Up the River Amazon, Including a Residence at Pará.* Rev. ed. London: John Murray, 1855.

Ellen, Roy, and Katsuyoshi Fukui, eds. *Redefining Nature: Ecology, Culture, and Domestication.* Oxford and Washington, D.C.: Berg, 1996.

Emmi, Marília. *A oligarquia do Tocantins e o domínio dos castanhais*. Belém, Brazil: NAEA / CFCH, 1988.

Epstein, Jack. "Battle over Rich Brazilian Lands." *San Francisco Chronicle*, 29 December 1993.

Escobar, Arturo. "Cultural Politics and Biological Diversity: State, Capital, and Social Movements in the Pacific Coast of Colombia." In *The Politics of Culture in the Shadow of Capital*, ed. Lisa Lowe and David Lloyd, pp. 201–26. Durham, N.C.: Duke University Press, 1997.

———. *Encountering Development: The Making and Unmaking of the Third World*. Princeton, N.J.: Princeton University Press, 1995.

Fairhead, James, and Melissa Leach. *Misreading the African Landscape: Society and Ecology in a Forest-Savanna Mosaic*. African Studies Series 90. Cambridge: Cambridge University Press, 1996.

———. "The Nature Lords." *Times Literary Supplement,* no. 5066, 5 May 2000.

Faulhaber, Priscila. *O lago dos espelhos: Etnografia do saber sobre a fronteira em Tefé/Amazonas*. Belém: Museu Paraense Emílio Goeldi, 1998.

Feijão, Antônio da Justa, and José Armindo Pinto. "Amazônia e a saga aurífera do século XX." In *Garimpo, meio ambiente e sociedades indígenas,* ed. Lívia Barbosa, Ana Lúcia Lobato, and José Augusto Drummond, pp. 18–36. Niterói: EDUFF, 1992.

Feld, Steven. "Waterfalls of Song: An Acoustemology of Place Resounding in Bosavi, Papua New Guinea." In *Senses of Place*, ed. Steven Feld and Keith H. Basso, pp. 91–135. Santa Fe, N.M.: School of American Research Press, 1996.

Feld, Steven, and Keith Basso, eds. *Senses of Place*. Santa Fe: School of American Research Press, 1996.

Fernández de Oviedo y Valdés, Gonzalo. *Historia general y natural de las Indias*. Book 49. Seville: 1535–47.

Ferreira, Alexandre Rodrigues. *Viagem filosófica pelas capitanias do Grão-Pará, Rio Negro, Mato Grosso e Cuiabá: 1783–1792. Memórias: Zoologia e Botánica*. Rio de Janeiro: Conselho Federal de Cultura, 1973.

Figueiredo, Bernardino R. "Garimpo e mineração no Brasil." In *Em busca do ouro: Garimpos e garimpeiros no Brasil*, organized by Gerôncio Albuquerque Rocha, pp. 11–34. São Paulo: Marco Zero, 1984.

Figueiredo, Bernardino R., et al. *Em busca do ouro: Garimpos e garimpeiros no Brasil*. Organized by Gerônico Albuquerque Rocha. São Paulo: Marco Zero, 1984.

Figueiredo, Napoleão, and Anaíza Vergolino e Silva. *Festas de santo e encantados*. Belém, Brazil: Academia Paraense de Letras, 1972.

Figueiredo, Napoleão, and Anaíza Vergolino-Henry. *A presença africana na Amazônia colonial: Uma notícia histórica*. Série de Documentos Históricos, vol. 1. Belém: Arquivo Público, 1990.

Fisher, William H. "Megadevelopment, Environmentalism, and Resistance: The Institutional Context of Kayapó Indigenous Politics in Central Brazil." *Human Organization* 53, no. 3 (1995): 220–32.

————. "Native Amazonians and the Amazon Wilderness." In *Creating the Countryside: The Politics of Rural and Environmental Discourse,* ed. E. Melanie DuPuis and Peter Vandergeest, pp. 166–203. Philadelphia: Temple University Press, 1996.

Fletcher, James C., and D. P. Kidder. *Brazil and the Brazilians, Portrayed in Historical and Descriptive Sketches.* New edition, revised and enlarged. London: Sampson, Low, Son and Marston; Boston: Little, Brown and Co., 1866.

"Floresta de incertezas." *Veja,* 17 May 1989, p. 73.

Foresta, Ronald A. *Amazon Conservation in the Age of Development: The Limits of Providence.* Gainesville: University of Florida Press, Center for Latin American Studies, 1991.

Franklin, John Hope, and Loren Schweninger. *Runaway Slaves: Rebels on the Plantation.* New York: Oxford University Press, 1999.

Fuller, Mary C. "Ralegh's Fugitive Gold." In *New World Encounters,* ed. Stephen J. Greenblatt, pp. 218–40. Berkeley: University of California Press, 1993.

Funes, Eurípedes A. "Nasci nas matas, nunca tive senhor: História e memória dos mocambos do baixo Amazonas." In *Liberdade por um fio: História dos quilombos no Brasil,* ed. João José Reis and Flávio dos Santos Gomes, pp. 467–97. São Paulo: Companhia das Letras, 1996.

Galvão, Eduardo Enéas. "Panema: Uma crença do caboclo amazônico." In *Encontro de sociedades: Índios e brancos no Brasil,* pp. 57–62. Coleção Estudos Brasileiros 29. Rio de Janeiro: Paz e Terra, 1979.

————. *Santos e visagens: Um estudo da vida religiosa de Itá, Amazonas.* Brasiliana 284. São Paulo: Cia. Ed. Nacional, 1955.

Galvão, Walnice Nogueira, ed. *Euclides da Cunha.* São Paulo: Atica, 1984.

Galvão, Walnice Nogueira, and Oswaldo Galotti. *Correspondência de Euclides da Cunha.* São Paulo: Edusp, 1997.

Gandía, Enrique de. *Historia crítica de los mitos de la conquista americana.* Madrid: Juan Roldán y Compañía, 1929.

Garcia, Othon Moacyr. *Cobra Norato, o poema e o mito.* Rio de Janeiro: São José, 1962.

————. "Raul Bopp." In *Poetas do modernismo: Antologia crítica.* Vol. 3, ed. Leodegário A. de Azevedo Filho, pp. 15–57. Brasília: INL, 1972.

Gardner, Joseph Lawrence. *Departing Glory: Theodore Roosevelt as Ex-President.* New York: Scribner, 1973.

Geertz, Clifford. "The World in a Text." In *Works and Lives: The Anthropologist as Author,* pp. 25–48. Stanford: Stanford University Press, 1988.

"Geopoetics: Space, Place and Landscape." *Critical Inquiry* 26, no. 2 (2000): 173–42.

Gerbi, Antonello. *Nature in the New World: From Christopher Columbus to Gonzalo Fernández de Oviedo.* Trans. Jeremy Moyle. Pittsburgh: University of Pittsburgh Press, 1985.

Giles-Vernick, Tamara. "*Doli:* Translating an African Environmental History of Loss in the Sangha River Basin of Equatorial Africa." *Journal of African History* 41, no. 3 (2000): 373–94.

————. "Na lege guiriri (On the Road of History): Mapping Out the Past and Present in M'Bres Region, Central African Republic." *Ethnohistory* 43, no. 2 (1996): 247–75.

Glacken, Clarence J. *Traces on the Rhodian Shore: Nature and Culture in Western Thought from Ancient Times to the End of the Eighteenth Century.* Berkeley: University of California Press, 1967.

Godfrey, Brian J. "Migration to the Gold-Mining Frontier in Brazilian Amazonia." *Geographical Review* 82, no. 4 (1992): 458–69.

Gomes, Laurentino, and Paulo Silber. "'A explosão do instinto selvagem' Paiakan, o cacique símbolo da pureza ecológica, estupra e tortura uma adolescente." *Veja,* 10 June 1992, pp. 68–73.

————. "Gigolôs de índios." *Veja,* 1 July 1992, pp. 36–38.

Gondim, Neide. *A invenção da Amazônia.* São Paulo: Marco Zero, 1994.

Goodland, R. J. A., and H. S. Irwin. *Amazon Jungle: Green Hell to Red Desert; an Ecological Discussion of the Environmental Impact of the Highway Construction Program in the Amazon Basin.* Developments in Landscape Management and Urban Planning 1. Amsterdam and New York: Elsevier Scientific Publications, 1975.

Goodman, David, and Anthony Hall, eds. *The Future of Amazonia: Destruction or Sustainable Development?* New York: Macmillan, 1990.

Gorney, Cynthia. "The Last Frontier." Part 5. *Washington Post,* 17 December 1991.

Goulart, José Alípio. *O regatão (mascate fluvial da Amazônia).* Rio de Janeiro: Conquista, 1968.

Goulding, Michael. *The Fishes and the Forest: Explorations in Amazonian Natural History.* Berkeley: University of California Press, 1980.

Gow, Peter. "Land, People and Paper in Western Amazonia." In *The Anthropology of Landscape: Perspectives on Place and Space,* ed. Eric Hirsch and Michael O'Hanlon, pp. 43–62. Oxford: Clarendon Press, 1995.

————. *Of Mixed Blood: Kinship and History in Peruvian Amazonia.* Oxford: Clarendon Press; New York: Oxford University Press, 1991.

Graham, Laura R. "Brazilian Indians and the Symbolic Politics of Language in the Global Public Sphere." In *Indigenous Movements, Self-Representation, and the State in Latin America,* ed. Jean Jackson and Kay Warren. Austin: University of Texas Press, forthcoming.

Greenblatt, Stephen J. *Marvelous Possessions: The Wonder of the New World.* Chicago: University of Chicago Press, 1991.

————. *Sir Walter Ralegh: The Renaissance Man and His Roles.* New Haven: Yale University Press, 1973.

Greer, Jed. "The Price of Gold: Environmental Costs of the New Gold Rush." *The Ecologist* 23, no. 3 (1993): 91–96.

Gregor, Thomas. "Dark Dreams about the White Man." *Natural History* 92, no. 1 (1983): 8–14.

————. "A Mehinaku Myth of Matriarchy." In *Working Papers on South American Indians,* pp. 24–32. Bennington, Vt.: Bennington College, 1984.

Grieve, Peter. *The Wilderness Voyage.* London: Jonathan Cape, 1952.

Grove, Richard. *Green Imperialism: Colonial Expansion, Tropical Island Edens, and the Origins of Environmentalism, 1600–1860.* Studies in Environment and History. Cambridge and New York: Cambridge University Press, 1995.

Guerreiro, Gabriel. "Garimpagem de ouro na Amazônia: Reflexos econômicos, sociais e políticos." In Bernardino R. Figueiredo et al., *Em busca do ouro: Garimpos e garimpeiros no Brasil,* organized by Gerôncio Albuquerque Rocha, pp. 87–106. São Paulo: Marco Zero, 1984.

Guha, Ramachandra, and Juan Martínez-Alier. *Varieties of Environmentalism: Essays North and South.* London: Earthscan, 1997.

Guss, David M. "The Encantados: Venezuela's Invisible Kingdom." *Journal of Latin American Lore* 8, no. 2 (1982): 223–72.

———. "Hidden Histories: African-American Tales of Resistance and Arrival." *Journal of Latin American Lore* 20, no. 1 (1997): 161–72.

———. "The Selling of San Juan: The Performance of History in an Afro-Venezuelan Community." *American Ethnologist* 30, no. 3 (1993): 451–73.

———, ed. and trans. *The Language of the Birds: Tales, Texts, and Poems of Interspecies Communication.* San Francisco: North Point Press, 1985.

———, trans. "Wiyu and the Man Who Liked to Shoot Dolphins." *Archive Newsletter* (University of California, San Diego) 44 (1990): 15–16.

Guzmán, Nuño de. *Memoria de los servicios que había hecho Nuño de Guzmán, desde que fue nombrado Gobernador de Panuco en 1525.* Ed. Manuel Carrera Stammpa. Mexico City: José Porrua e Hijos, 1955.

Hall, Anthony. *Sustaining Amazonia: Grassroots Action for Productive Conservation.* Manchester, England, and New York: Manchester University Press, 1997.

Hanchard, Michael George. *Orpheus and Power: The Movimento Negro of Rio de Janeiro and São Paulo, Brazil, 1945–1988.* Princeton, N.J.: Princeton University Press, 1994.

Haraway, Donna. "Teddy Bear Patriarchy." In *Primate Visions: Gender, Race, and Nature in the World of Modern Science,* pp. 26–58. New York: Routledge, 1989.

Hardman, Francisco Foot. "Brutalidade antiga: Sobre história e ruína em Euclides." *Revista Estudos Avançados* 26 (January–April 1996): 293–310.

———. "Pai, Filho: Caligrafias do afeto." *Revista USP,* no. 23 (September–November 1994): 92–101.

Harris, Mark. "People of the Amazon Floodplain: Kinship, Work and Sharing in a Caboclo Community near Óbidos, Pará, Brazil." Ph.D. diss., University of London, 1996.

Harrison, Regina. *Signs, Songs, and Memory in the Andes: Translating Quechua Language and Culture.* Austin: University of Texas Press, 1989.

Harrison, Robert Pogue. *Forests: The Shadow of Civilization.* Chicago and London: University of Chicago Press, 1992.

Haskins, Caryl P. *The Amazon: The Life History of a Mighty River.* Garden City, N.Y.: Doubleday, Doran and Co., 1943.

Hecht, Susanna, and Alexander Cockburn. *The Fate of the Forest: Developers, Destroyers, and Defenders of the Amazon.* 2nd ed. New York: Harper Perennial, 1990.

Heckenberger, Michael. "War and Peace in the Shadow of Empire: Sociopoliti-
cal Change in the Upper Xingú of Southeastern Amazonia, A.D. 1400–
2000." Ph.D diss., University of Pittsburgh, 1996.

Heckenberger, M. J., J. B. Petersen, and E. B. Neves. "Village Size and Permanence in Amazonia: Two Archaeological Examples from Brazil." *Latin
American Antiquity* 10, no. 4 (1999): 353–76.

Heemskerk, Marieke. "Gendered Responses to the Amazon Gold Mining
Boom: The Case of Suriname's Maroons." Unpublished ms.

———. "The Social Drivers of Small-Scale Gold Mining among the Maroons in
Suriname." Unpublished ms.

Hemming, John H. *Red Gold: The Conquest of the Brazilian Indians.* Cambridge: Harvard University Press, 1978.

———. *The Search for El Dorado.* London: Joseph, 1978.

Hénaff, Marcel. *Lévi-Strauss and the Making of Structural Anthropology.*
Trans. Mary Baker. Minneapolis: University of Minnesota Press, 1998.

Henderson, Andrew. *The Palms of the Amazon.* Oxford: Oxford University
Press, 1955.

Henderson, Andrew, Gloria Galeano, and Rodrigo Bernal. *The Palms of the
Americas.* Princeton, N.J.: Princeton University Press, 1995.

Herodotus. *The History.* Trans. David Grene. Chicago and London: University
of Chicago Press, 1987.

Herzog, Werner. *Burden of Dreams: Screenplay, Journals, Reviews, Photographs.* Ed. Les Blank and James Bogan. Berkeley: North Atlantic Books,
1984.

Hill, Jonathan D., ed. *Rethinking History and Myth: Indigenous South American Perspectives on the Past.* Urbana: University of Illinois Press, 1988.

Hirsch, Eric, and Michael O'Hanlon, eds. *The Anthropology of Landscape: Perspectives on Place and Space.* Oxford: Clarendon Press, 1995.

Hocquengheim, Anne Marie, and Max Inga. *Los encantos de La Encantada.*
Biblioteca Campesina 7. Piura, Peru: Centro de Investigación y Promoción
del Campesinado, 1989.

Holdridge, L. R. *Forest Environments in Tropical Life Zones: A Pilot Study, by
L. R. Holdridge and Others.* 1st ed. Oxford and New York: Pergamon Press,
1971.

Honour, Hugh. *The New Golden Land: European Images of America from the
Discoveries to the Present Time.* New York: Pantheon Books, 1975.

Hudson, W. H. *Green Mansions: A Romance of the Tropical Forest.* London:
Duckworth & Co., 1904.

Humboldt, Alexander von. *The Route of Humboldt: Colombia and Venezuela.*
2 vols. Directed, designed, and edited by Benjamin Villegas. Translated by
Allan S. Trueblood. Bogotá: Villegas Editores, 1994.

Humboldt, Alexander von, and Aimé Bonpland. *Personal Narrative of Travels
to the Equinoctial Regions of America, during the Years 1799–1804.* Vol. 3.
Trans. and ed. Thomasina Ross. London: Henry G. Bohn, 1852.

Hyndman, David. *Ancestral Rain Forests and the Mountain of Gold: Indigenous People and Mining in New Guinea.* Boulder, San Francisco, and Oxford: Westview Press, 1994.

Incledon, John. "The Writing Lesson in *Los pasos perdidos.*" *Siglo XX / 20th Century* 8, nos. 1–2 (1991): 55–68.

"Índios, fantasmas, e grandes interesses." *Veja,* 25 August 1993, p. 73.

Informe revisão constitutional—Os direitos dos remanescentes de quilombo. Nos. 2, 3, and 4. São Paulo: Comissão Pró-Índio de São Paulo, 12, 17, and 27 January 1994.

Inglez de Souza [Herculano Marcos]. *Contos amazônicos.* Rio de Janeiro: Laemmert, 1893.

Ireland, Emilienne. "Cerebral Savage: The Whiteman as Symbol of Cleverness and Savagery in Waurá Myth." In *Rethinking History and Myth: Indigenous South American Perspectives on the Past,* ed. Jonathan D. Hill, pp. 157–73. Urbana: University of Illinois Press, 1988.

Irizarry, Estelle. "Echoes of the Amazon Myth in Medieval Spanish Poetry." In *Women in Hispanic Literature: Icons and Fallen Angels,* ed. Beth Miller, pp. 53–66. Berkeley: University of California Press, 1983.

Jackson, Jean E. "Culture, Genuine and Spurious: The Politics of Indianness in the Vaupés, Colombia." *American Ethnologist* 22, no. 1 (1995): 3–27.

Jackson, Jean E., and Kay Warren, eds. *Indigenous Movements, Self-Representation, and the State in Latin America.* Austin: University of Texas Press.

Janes, Dominic. *God and Gold in Late Antiquity.* Cambridge and New York: Cambridge University Press, 1998.

Johnson, Christopher. "Cinna's Apotheosis: *Tristes tropiques* and the Structure of Redemption." *French Studies* 48, no. 3 (1994): 299–309.

Johnson, Randal. "Tupy or not Tupy." In *On Modern Latin American Fiction,* ed. John King, pp. 41–59. New York: Farrar, Straus, Giroux, 1987.

Johnson, Susan Lee. *Roaring Camp: The Social World of the California Gold Rush.* New York and London: W. W. Norton, 2000.

Jonge, Peter de. "Riding the Wild, Perilous Waters of Amazon.com." *New York Times Magazine,* 14 March 1999, pp. 36–41.

Kamm, Thomas. "Amazon Tragedy." *Wall Street Journal,* 21 March 1990.

Kane, Joe. *Running the Amazon.* 2nd ed. New York: Vintage, 1990.

Keck, Margaret E. "Social Equity and Environmental Politics in Brazil: Lessons from the Rubber Tappers of Acre." *Comparative Politics* (July 1995): 409–24.

Kellman, Martin, and Rosanne Tackabery. *Tropical Environments: The Functioning and Management of Tropical Ecosystems.* New York: Routledge, 1997.

Kendall, David. *Lázaro.* Toronto: McClelland and Stewart, 1983.

Kleinbaum, Abby Wettan. *The War against the Amazons.* New York: McGraw-Hill, 1983.

Kotscho, Ricardo. *Serra Pelada: Uma ferida aberta na selva.* São Paulo: Editora Brasiliense, 1984.

Kracke, Waud. "Death Comes as the White Man: The Conqueror in Kagwahiv Cosmology." Paper presented at the Symposium on Myth Values and Contact in Indigenous South America, American Anthropological Association, Philadelphia, 5 December 1986.

Lange, Algot. *In the Amazon Jungle: Adventures in the Remote Parts of the*

Upper Amazon River, Including a Sojourn among Cannibal Indians, edited in part by J. Odell Hauser. New York and London: G. P. Putnam's Sons, 1912.

Lathrap, Donald W. *The Upper Amazon.* New York: Praeger Publishers, 1970.

Latorre, Octavio. *La expedición a la Canela y el descubrimiento del Amazonas.* Quito: Artes Gráficas Señal Impreseñal Cia., 1995

Latour, Bruno. *Pandora's Hope: Essays on the Reality of Science Studies.* Cambridge: Harvard University Press, 1999.

Leacock, Seth, and Ruth Leacock. *Spirits of the Deep: A Study of an Afro-Brazilian Cult.* Garden City, N.Y.: Doubleday, 1972.

Le Breton, Binka. *Voices from the Amazon.* West Hartford, Conn.: Kumarian Press, 1993.

Leite, Francisco Barboza. *Tipos e aspectos do Brasil: Excertos da revista brasileira de geografia.* 10th rev. ed. Rio de Janeiro: Departamento de Documentação e Geográfica e Cartográfica, 1975.

Lélé, S. N. "Sustainable Development: A Critical Review." *World Development* 19 (1991): 607–21.

Leonard, Irving Albert. *Books of the Brave; Being an Account of Books and of Men in the Spanish Conquest and Settlement of the Sixteenth-Century New World.* 1949. Berkeley: University of California Press, 1992.

Lestra, A. D., and J. I. S. Nardi. *O Ouro da Amazônia oriental; O mito e a realidade.* Belém, Brazil: Grafisa, 1982.

Levillier, Roberto. *El Patiti, El Dorado y las Amazonas.* Buenos Aires: Emecé Editores, 1976.

Levine, Robert M. *Vale of Tears: Revisiting the Canudos Massacre in Northeastern Brazil, 1893–1897.* Berkeley and Los Angeles: University of California Press, 1991.

Lévi-Strauss, Claude. *Conversations with Claude Lévi-Strauss.* Ed. G. Charbonnier, trans. John and Doreen Weightman. London: Cape, 1969.

———. "Photographs and Memories from the Lost World of Brazil." *New York Review of Books* 2, no. 20 (21 December 1995).

———. *Saudades de São Paulo.* São Paulo: Companhia das Letras, 1996.

———. *Saudades do Brasil: A Photographic Memoir.* Trans. Sylvia Modelski. Seattle: University of Washington Press, 1995.

———. *Tristes tropiques.* Trans. John and Doreen Weightman. 1973. Reprint, New York: Modern Library, 1997.

Lévi-Strauss, Claude, and Diderot Eribon. *De prés et de loin; Suivi de "Deux ans aprés."* 2nd ed. Paris: Editions O. Jacob, 1996.

Levy, Jo Ann. *They Saw the Elephant: Women in the California Gold Rush.* Norman: University of Oklahoma Press, 1992.

Lima, Ireno José Santos de. *Cantinas garimpeiras: Um estudo das relações sociais nos garimpos de ouro do Tapajós.* Belém, Brazil: Governo do Estado de Pará / SEICOM, 1994.

Lima Júnior, Walter. *The Dolphin (Ele, o boto).* Cinematográficas L. C. Barreto. Fox Lorber Home Video, 1991. Videocassette.

Lisansky, Judith. *Migrants to Amazonia: Spontaneous Colonization in the Brazilian Frontier.* Boulder, Colo.: Westview Press, 1990.

Lohmann, Larry. "Green Orientalism." *The Ecologist* 23, no. 6 (1993): 202–4.

Lopes, Edi. "A Lenda do Boto." *Caleidoscópio*. N.p, n.d.

———. "É Cobra, é Grande!" *Caleidoscópio*. N.p., n.d.

López-Barault, Mercedes. "Los pasos encontrados de Lévi-Strauss y Alejo Carpentier: Literatura y antropología en el siglo veinte." *La revista del Centro de Estudios Avanzados de Puerto Rico y el Caribe* 7 (1988): 81–92.

López de Gómara, Francisco. *Historia general de las Indias y vida de Hernán Cortés*. Prologue and chronology by Jorge Gurría Lacroix. Biblioteca Ayacucho 64–65. 1552. Reprint, Caracas: Biblioteca Ayacucho, 1979.

Lorimer, Joyce, ed. "Bernard O'Brien's Account of Irish Activities in the Amazon, 1621–4." In *English and Irish Settlement on the River Amazon 1550–1646*, pp. 263–68. Hakluyt Society second series 171. London: Hakluyt Society, 1989.

Loureiro, Violeta Refkalefsky. *Os parceiros do mar: Natureza e conflito social na pesca da Amazônia*. Brasília: CNPq; Belém: Museu Paraense Emílio Goeldi, 1985.

Love, John F. *McDonald's: Behind the Arches*. Rev. ed. New York: Bantam Books, 1995.

Luhrmann, Tanya M. "The Resurgence of Romanticism: Contemporary Neopaganism, Feminist Spirituality, and the Divinity of Nature." In *Environmentalism: The View from Anthropology*, ed. Kay Milton, pp. 219–32. New York: Routledge, 1993.

Lutts, Ralph H. *The Nature Fakers: Wildlife, Science, and Sentiment*. Golden, Colo.: Fulcrum, 1990.

Lutz, Catherine A., and Jane L. Collins. *Reading National Geographic*. Chicago: University of Chicago Press, 1993.

MacCreagh, Gordon. *White Waters and Black*. New York and London: The Century Company, 1926.

MacMillan, Gordon. *At the End of the Rainbow? Gold, Land, and People in the Brazilian Amazon*. New York: Columbia University Press, 1995.

Macnaghten, Phil, and John Urry. *Contested Natures*. London and Thousand Oaks, Calif.: Sage Publications, 1998.

Madriz Galindo, Fernando. "Los encantos, elementos del agua." *Boletín del Instituto de Folklore* 2, no. 2 (1955): 61–65.

Magalhães, Angela, and José Carlos Martins, eds. *Amazônia: Luz e reflexão*. Rio de Janeiro, Funarte, and Caracas: Conac, 1997.

Magalhães, Marco. "A energia da floresta." *Veja*, 19 October 1984, p. 48.

Magalhães Lima Ayres, Deborah de. "The Social Category *Caboclo*: History, Social, Organisation, Identity and Outsiders; Social Classification of the Rural Population of an Amazonian Region." Ph.D. diss., Cambridge University, 1992.

Magee, Pennie L. "'The Water Is Our Land': Peasants of the River Tocantins, Brazilian Amazonia." Ph.D. diss., University of Florida, Gainesville, 1990.

Mahar, Dennis J. *Frontier Development Policy in Brazil: A Study of Amazonia*. New York: Praeger Publishers, 1979.

———. *Government Policies and Deforestation in Brazil's Amazon Region*. Washington, D.C.: World Bank, 1989.

Maligo, Pedro. *Land of Metaphorical Desires: The Representation of Amazonia in Brazilian Literature.* New York: Peter Lang Publishing, 1998.

Mancing, Howard. *The Chivalric World of Don Quijote: Style, Structure, and Narrative Technique.* Columbia: University of Missouri Press, 1982.

Mandeville, Sir John. *The Travels of Sir John Mandeville.* Trans. C. W. R. D. Moseley. Harmondsworth, England, and New York: Penguin, 1985.

Manthorne, Katherine Emma. *Tropical Renaissance: North American Artists Exploring Latin America, 1839–1879.* Washington, D.C.: Smithsonian Institution Press, 1989.

Marcone, Jorge. "Jungle Fever: Primitivism in Environmentalism, Rómulo Gallegos' Canaima, and the Romance of the Jungle." In *Primitivism and Identity in Latin America: Essays on Art, Literature, and Culture,* ed. Erik Camayd-Freixas and José Eduardo González, pp. 157–72. Tucson: University of Arizona Press, in press.

———. "The Politics of Cultural Criticism and Sustainable Development in Amazonia: A Reading from the Spanish American Romance of the Jungle." *Hispanic Journal* 19, no. 2 (fall 1998): 281–94. (Special issue: "Ecology and Latin American and Caribbean Literatures," ed. Patrick Murphy and Roberto Forns-Broggi.)

Marcoy, Paul [Laurent Saint-Cricq]. *A Journey across South America from the Pacific Ocean to the Atlantic Ocean,* half-vol. 4. London: Blackie and Son, 1874.

Markham, Sir Clements R. *Expeditions into the Valley of the Amazons, 1539, 1540, 1639.* Translated and edited, with notes, by Clements R. Markham. London: Hakluyt Society, 1859.

Marsh, Charles R., Jr. "The Indians and the Whites: Two Bororo Texts." *Latin American Indian Literatures* 1, no. 1 (1977): 34–36.

Martins, Ana Luiza. "Breve história dos garimpos de ouro do Brasil." In *Em busca do ouro: Garimpos e garimpeiros no Brasil,* organized by Gerôncio Albuquerque Rocha, pp. 177–222. São Paulo: Marco Zero, 1984.

Marx, Jenifer. *The Magic of Gold.* Garden City, N.Y: Doubleday, 1978.

Matta, Roberto da. "Panema: Uma tentativa de análise estrutural." In *Ensaios de antropologia estrutural,* pp. 202–8. Petrópolis, Brazil: Vozes, 1973.

Maués, Raymundo Heraldo. *A ilha encantada: Medicina e xamanismo numa comunidade de pescadores.* Coleção Igarapé. Belém, Brazil: Universidade Federal do Pará, 1990.

Maxwell, Kenneth. "The Mystery of Chico Mendes." *New York Review of Books,* 28 March 1991, pp. 39–48.

———. *Pombal, Paradox of the Enlightenment.* Cambridge and New York: Cambridge University Press, 1995.

McCallum, Cecilia. "The *Veja* Payakan: The Media, Modernism, and the Image of the Indian in Brazil." *Commission on Visual Anthropology Newsletter* 2, no. 94 (1994): 2–8.

McCormick, John. *Reclaiming Paradise: The Global Environmental Movement.* Bloomington: Indiana University Press, 1989.

McGreevy, Patrick Vincent. *Imagining Niagara: The Meaning and Making of Niagara Falls.* Amherst: University of Massachusetts Press, 1994.

McNelly, Cleo. "Natives, Women and Claude Lévi-Strauss." *The Massachusetts Review* (winter 1975): 7–29.

Meggers, Betty. *Amazonia: Man and Culture in a Counterfeit Paradise.* Chicago: Aldine, 1971.

Melatti, Júlio Cézar. "A origem dos brancos no mito de *Shoma Wetsa.*" *Anuário antropológico* 84 (1985): 109–73.

Mello e Souza, Laura de. *Desclassificados de ouro.* Rio de Janeiro: Graal, 1982.

Merchant, Carolyn. *The Death of Nature: Women, Ecology, and the Scientific Revolution.* San Francisco: Harper and Row, 1980.

Merquior, José Guilherme. *L'esthetique de Lévi-Strauss.* Paris: PUF, 1977.

Miller, Christopher. *Blank Darkness: Africanist Discourse in French.* Chicago: University of Chicago Press, 1985.

Miller, Darrel. "Highways and Gold: Change in a Caboclo Community." In *The Amazon Caboclo,* ed. Eugene Parker. Studies in Third World Societies 32, pp. 167–98. Williamsburg, Va.: Department of Anthropology, College of William and Mary, 1985.

Miller, David Philip, and Peter Hanns Reill, eds. *Visions of Empire: Voyages, Botany, and Representations of Nature.* Cambridge, New York, and Melbourne: Cambridge University Press, 1996.

Milton, Kay. *Environmentalism and Cultural Theory: Exploring the Role of Anthropology in Environmental Discourse.* London and New York: Routledge, 1996.

Mintz, Sidney W. "Swallowing Modernity." In *Golden Arches East: McDonald's in East Asia,* ed. James L. Watson, pp. 183–200. Stanford: Stanford University Press, 1997.

Miramón, Alberto. *Realidad y quimera del oro de Índias.* Bogotá: Valencia Eds., 1978.

Montaigne, Michel de. "Of Cannibals." In *The Complete Essays of Montaigne.* Trans. Donald M. Frame, pp. 150–59. Stanford: Stanford University Press, 1958.

Montrose, Louis. "The Work of Gender in the Discourse of Discovery." In *New World Encounters,* ed. Stephen J. Greenblatt, pp. 1–41. Berkeley: University of California Press, 1993.

Moran, Emilio F. *Through Amazonian Eyes: The Human Ecology of Amazonian Populations.* Iowa City: University of Iowa Press, 1993.

Morote Best, Efraín. *Aldeas sumergidas: Cultura popular y sociedad en los Andes.* Biblioteca de la Tradición Andina 9. Cuzco, Peru: Centro de Estudios Rurales Andinos Bartolomé de las Casas, 1988.

Morris, Edmund. *The Rise of Theodore Roosevelt.* New York: Coward, McCann, and Geoghegan, 1979.

Morse, Richard M. *The Bandeirantes.* New York: Knopf, 1965.

Moura, Clóvis. *Introduçao ao pensamento de Euclides da Cunha.* Rio de Janeiro: Civilização Brasileira, 1964.

Muratorio, Blanca. *The Life and Times of Grandfather Alonso: Culture and History in the Upper Amazon.* New Brunswick, N.J.: Rutgers University Press, 1991.

Murphy, Robert F., and Yolanda Murphy. *Women of the Forest*. New York: Columbia University Press, 1974.

Nepstad, Daniel C., Adriana G. Moreira, and Ane A. Alencar. *Flames in the
Rain Forest: Origins, Impacts, and Alternatives to Amazonian Fire*. Brasília:
The Pilot Program to Conserve the Brazilian Rain Forest, 1999.

Nery, Frederico José de Santa-Anna. *Folk-lore brésilien: Poésie populaire.—con-
tes et légendes.—fables et mythes.—poésie, musique, danses et croyances des
Indiens*. Preface by Prince Roland Bonaparte. Paris: Perrin, 1889.

———. *The Land of the Amazons*. Trans. George Humphery. 1884. Reprint,
London: Sands & Co, 1901.

Neumann, Roderick P. *Imposing Wilderness: Struggles over Livelihood and Nature Preservation in Africa*. Berkeley: University of California Press, 1998.

Neves, Zanoni. "Os índios na mídia." *Boletim da Associação Brasileira de
Antropologia* 22 (1994): 16.

Newman, Arnold. *Tropical Rainforest: A World Survey of Our Most Valuable
and Endangered Habitat with a Blueprint for Survival*. New York: Facts on
File, 1990.

Nicholl, Charles. *The Creature in the Map: A Journey to El Dorado*. New York:
William Morrow and Company, 1995.

Nimuendaju, Curt. *The Tükuna*. Ed. Robert H. Lowie, trans. William D. Ho-
henthal. Publications in American Archaeology and Ethnology 45. Berkeley:
University of California Press, 1952.

Nóbrega, Padre Manuel da. *Cartas do Brasil e mais escritos (opera omnia)*. Ed.
Serafim Leite. Coimbra, Portugal: Universidade de Coimbra, 1955.

Novaes, Sylvia Caiuby. *The Play of Mirrors: The Representation of Self as Mirrored in the Other*. Trans. Izabel Murat Burbridge. Austin: University of
Texas Press, 1997.

Nugent, Stephen. *Amazonian Caboclo Society: An Essay on Invisibility and
Peasant Economy*. Providence, R.I.: Berg Publishers, 1993.

———. "The Coordinates of Identity in Amazonia: At Play in the Fields of Culture." *Critique of Anthropology* 17, no. 1 (1997): 33–51.

Oates, John F. *Myth and Reality in the Rain Forest: How Conservation Strategies Are Failing in West Africa*. Berkeley: University of California Press,
1999.

———. "Why a Prime Model for Saving Rain Forests Is a Failure." *Chronicle
of Higher Education*, 14 January 2000.

O'Connell, Geoffrey. *Amazon Journal: Dispatches from a Vanishing Frontier*.
New York: Dutton, 1997.

O'Dwyer, Eliane Cantarino. " 'Remanescentes de quilombos' na fronteira amazônica: A etnicidade como instrumento de luta pela terra." In *Terra de quilombos*, ed. Eliane Cantarino O'Dwyer, pp. 121–39. Rio de Janeiro: Associação Brasileira de Antropologia, 1995.

Onís, Juan de. *The Green Cathedral: Sustainable Development of Amazonia*.
Oxford: Oxford University Press, 1992.

Ornig, Joseph R. *My Last Chance to Be a Boy: Theodore Roosevelt's South
American Expedition of 1913–14*. Mechanicsburg, Penn.: Stackpole Books,
1994.

"Os Gigantes, Finalmente." *Veja,* 14 February 1973.

"Os índios sem história." *Veja,* 19 May 1976.

Ovid's Metamorphoses. Trans. Charles Boer. Dallas: Spring Publications, Inc., 1989.

Pace, Richard. *The Struggle for Amazon Town: Gurupá Revisited.* Boulder, Colo.: Lynne Rienner, 1998.

Pádua, José Augusto. *Ecologia e política no Brasil.* Rio de Janeiro: Espaço e Tempo, 1987.

Paixão, Alberto Eduardo Carneira da. *Trabalhadores rurais e garimpeiros no vale do rio Tapajós.* Belém, Brazil: Governo do Estado do Pará / SEICOM, 1994.

Parker, Eugene, ed. *The Amazon Caboclo: Historical and Contemporary Perspectives.* Studies in Third World Societies 32. Williamsburg, Va.: Department of Anthropology, College of William and Mary, 1985.

Pedroso Filho, C. "Trombetas, nasce uma cidade." *Manchete* (1978): 68–78.

Penna, Domingos Soares Ferreira. *Obras Completas de Domingos Soares Ferreira Penna.* Vols. 1 and 2. 1867. Reprint, Belém, Brazil: Conselho Estadual de Cultura, 1973.

Pérez, María Teresa. *El descubrimiento del Amazonas: Historia y mito.* Seville: Ediciones Alfar, 1989.

Perlmann, David. "New Evidence of Legendary Women Warriors." *San Francisco Chronicle,* 28 January 1997.

Petot, Jean. *L'or de Guyane: Son historie, ses hommes.* Paris: Editions Caribéenes, 1986.

Pigafetta, Antonio. *The First Voyage around the World (1519–1522): An Account of Magellan's Expedition.* Ed. Theodore J. Cachey, Jr. New York: Marsilio Publishers, 1995.

Pinto, Lúcio Flávio. "Garimpeiro serve de bode expiatório." *Jornal Pessoal,* 3 December 1989.

———. "Trombetas: Os desafios de um projeto concebido por multinacionais na Amazônia." *TDI,* no. 5. (August 1985): 23–44.

Pinto, Virgílio Noya. *O ouro brasileiro e o comércio anglo-português: Uma contribuição aos estudos da economia atlântica no século XVIII.* São Paulo: Companhia Editora Nacional, 1979.

Place, Susan E. *Tropical Rainforests: Latin American Nature and Society in Transition.* Jaguar Books on Latin America 2. Wilmington, Del: Scholarly Resources, 1993.

Plotkin, Mark J. *Tales of a Shaman's Apprentice: An Ethnobotanist Searches for New Medicines in the Amazon Rain Forest.* 2nd ed. New York: Penguin Books, 1994.

Porro, Antônio. *As crônicas do Rio Amazonas.* Petrópolis, Brazil: Vozes, 1993.

Porter, Dennis. *Desire and Transgression in European Travel Writing.* Princeton, N.J.: Princeton University Press, 1991.

Posey, Darrel, and William Balée, eds. *Resource Management in Amazonia: Indigenous and Folk Strategies.* Advances in Economic Botany 7. New York: New York Botanical Garden, 1989.

Pratt, Mary Louise. *Imperial Eyes: Travel Writing and Transculturation.* New York: Routledge, 1991.

Preston, Julia. "Brazil Frees Minors in Brothels." *Washington Post,* 27 January 1992.

Price, Richard. *Alabi's World.* Baltimore: The Johns Hopkins University Press, 1983.

————. *First-Time: The Historical Vision of an Afro-American People.* Baltimore: The Johns Hopkins University Press, 1983.

————. *Maroon Societies: Rebel Slave Communities in the Americas.* 2nd. ed. Baltimore and London: The Johns Hopkins University Press, 1996.

————. "Scrapping Maroon History: Brazil's Promise, Suriname's Shame." *New West Indian Guide / Nieuwe West-Indische Gid* 72, nos. 3 and 4 (1998): 233–55.

Procópio, Argemiro. *Amazônia: Ecologia e degradação social.* São Paulo: Editora Alfa-Omega, 1992.

Procópio Filho, Argemiro. "A miséria do colono e o ouro no Araguaia e Amazônia." In *Em busca do ouro: Garimpos e garimpeiros no Brasil,* organized by Gerôncio Albuquerque Rocha, pp. 121–44. São Paulo: Marco Zero, 1984.

Quinn, David B. *Raleigh and the British Empire.* London: Hodder and Stoughton Ltd., 1947.

Rabasa, José. "Pre-Columbian Pasts and Indian Presents in Mexican History." *Disposition* 19, no. 46 (1994): 245–70.

Rabben, Linda. *Unnatural Selection: The Yanomami, the Kayapó, and the Onslaught of Civilization.* Seattle: University of Washington Press, 1998.

Rabello, Sylvio. *Euclides da Cunha.* 2nd ed. Coleção Vera Cruz 103. Rio de Janeiro: Civilização Brasileira, 1966.

Raffles, Hugh. "Igarapé Guariba: Nature, Locality, and the Logic of Amazonian Anthropogenesis." Ph.D. diss., Yale University, 1998.

————. "'Local Theory': Nature and the Making of an Amazonian Place." *Cultural Anthropology* 14, no. 3 (1999): 323–60.

Ralegh, Sir Walter. *The Discoverie of Guiana, by Sir Walter Ralegh.* Edited from the original text, with introduction, notes, and appendixes of hitherto unpublished documents, by V. T. Harlow. London: Argonaut Press, 1928.

————. *The Discoverie of the Large, Rich, and Bewtiful Empyre of Guiana.* Transcribed, annotated, and introduced by Neil L. Whitehead. Norman: University of Oklahoma Press, 1997.

————. *The Discovery of the Large, Rich, and Beautiful Empire of Guiana.* Ed. Robert H. Schomburgk. London: Hakluyt Society, 1848.

Ramos, Alcida Rita. "From Eden to Limbo: The Construction of Indigenism in Brazil." In *Social Constructions of the Past: Representation as Power,* ed. George C. Bond and Angela Gilliam, pp. 74–88. London: Routledge, 1994.

————. "Indian Voices: Contact Experienced and Expressed." In *Rethinking History and Myth: Indigenous South American Perspectives on the Past,* ed. Jonathan D. Hill, pp. 214–34. Urbana: University of Illinois Press, 1988.

————. *Indigenism: Ethnic Politics in Brazil.* Madison: University of Wisconsin Press, 1998.

————. *Sanumá Memories: Yanomami Ethnography in Times of Crisis*. Madison: University of Wisconsin Press, 1995.

Ramos Pérez, Demetrio. *El mito de El Dorado: Su génesis y proceso*. 2nd ed. Mundus novus 6. Madrid: Ediciones Istmo, 1988.

Rangel, Alberto. *Inferno verde*. 3rd. ed. Tours, France: Typ. E. Arrault, 1920.

Rappaport, Joanne. *The Politics of Memory: Native Historical Interpretation in the Colombian Andes*. Cambridge Latin American Studies 70. Cambridge and New York: Cambridge University Press, 1990.

Real, Alonso del. *Realidad y leyenda de las amazonas*. Colección Austral. Madrid: Espasa-Calpe, 1967.

Redford, Kent H. "The Ecologically Noble Savage." *Orion Nature Quarterly* 9, no. 3 (1990): 25–29.

Redford, Kent H., and Steven E. Sanderson. "The Brief, Barren Marriage of Biodiversity and Sustainability." *Bulletin of the Ecological Society of America* 73 (1992): 36–39.

Regan, Jaime. *Hacia la tierra sin mal: La religión del pueblo de la Amazonia*. 2nd rev. ed. Iquitos, Peru: CETA, 1993.

Reichel-Dolmatoff, Gerardo. *Amazonian Cosmos: The Sexual and Religious Symbolism of the Tukano Indians*. Chicago: University of Chicago Press, 1971.

————. "Cosmology as Ecological Analysis: A View from the Rain Forest." *Man* 11 (1976): 307–18.

Reis, João José, and Flávio dos Santos Gomes, eds. *Liberdade por um fio: História dos quilombos no Brasil*. São Paulo: Companhia das Letras, 1996.

Ribeiro, Berta G. *Amazônia urgente*. Belo Horizonte, Brazil: Editora Itatiaia, 1990.

Ribeiro, Darcy. *O indigenista Rondon*. Rio de Janeiro: Ministério da Educação e Cultura, 1959.

Ribeiro de Sampaio, Francisco Xavier. *Diário da viagem que em visita, e correição das povoações da capitania de S. Joze do Rio Negro fez o ouvidor, e intendente geral da mesma*. Lisbon: Tipografia da Academia, 1825.

Rice, Richard E., Raymond E. Gullison, and John W. Reid. "Can Sustainable Management Save Tropical Forests?" *Scientific American* 276, no. 4 (April 1997): 44–50.

Richards, Paul Westamacott. *The Tropical Rain Forest: An Ecological Study*. Cambridge: Cambridge University Press, 1966.

Rival, Laura, ed. *The Social Life of Trees: From Symbols of Regeneration to Political Artifacts*. Oxford: Berg, in press.

Rivera, José Eustacio. *La vorágine*. 3rd ed. Buenos Aires: Losada, 1953. (*The Vortex*. Trans. Earle K. James. New York: G. P. Putnam's Sons, 1935.)

Roberts, J. Timmons. "Expansion of Television in Eastern Amazonia." *Geographical Review* 85, no. 1 (1995): 41–49.

Robinson, Corinne Roosevelt. *My Brother, Theodore Roosevelt*. New York: Charles Scribner's Sons, 1921.

Rocha, Jan. *Murder in the Rainforest: The Yanomami, the Gold Miners, and the Amazon*. London: Latin American Bureau, 1999.

Rodrigues, João Barbosa. "Exploração e estudo do valle do Amazonas: Rio Tapajos." In *Rios de Amazonas,* five pamphlets in one volume, no.1. Rio de Janeiro: Typographia Nacional, 1875.

———. "Exploração e estudo do valle do Amazonas: Rio Trombetas." In *Rios de Amazonas,* five pamphlets in one volume, no.3. Rio de Janeiro: Typographia Nacional, 1875.

Rodrigues, Rita Maria. *Mulheres do Ouro: O trabalho feminino nos garimpos do Tabajós.* Belém, Brazil: Governo do Estado do Pará and Secretaria do Estado de Indústria, Comércio e Mineração-SEICOM, 1994.

Rodríguez, Ileana. "Naturaleza / nación: Lo salvaje-civil escribiendo Amazonia." *Revista de crítica literaria latinoamericana* 23, no. 45 (1997): 26–42.

Rodríguez de Montalvo, Garci. *Las Sergas de Esplandián. Libros de Caballerías.* Vol. 40. Ed. D. Pascual de Gayangos. Madrid: Biblioteca de Autores Españoles, 1857.

Rodríguez Freyle, Juan. *El carnero.* Bogotá: Ministerio de Educación Nacional, Ediciones de la Revista Bolívar, 1955.

Roe, Peter G. *The Cosmic Zygote: Cosmology in the Amazon Basin.* New Brunswick, N.J.: Rutgers University Press, 1982.

———. "The Josho Nahuanbo Are All Wet and Undercooked: Shipibo Views of the Whiteman and the Incas in Myth, Legend, and History." In *Rethinking History and Myth: Indigenous South American Perspectives on the Past,* ed. Jonathan D. Hill, pp. 106–35. Urbana: University of Illinois Press, 1988.

"Roosevelt Now Homeward Bound." *New York Times,* 1 May 1914.

Roosevelt, A. C., et al. "Paleoindian Cave Dwellers in the Amazon: The Peopling of the Americas." *Science* 272 (1996): 373–84.

Roosevelt, Anna Curtenius. *Moundbuilders of the Amazon: Geophysical Archaeology on Marajó Island, Brazil.* San Diego: Academic Press, 1991.

Roosevelt, Theodore. *African Game Trails, An Account of the African Wanderings of an American Hunter-Naturalist, by Theodore Roosevelt.* New York: Scribner, 1910.

———. *Through the Brazilian Wilderness.* 1914. Reprint, with a foreword by Tweed Roosevelt. Mechanicsburg, Pa.: Stackpole Books, 1994.

Rosaldo, Renato. *Culture and Truth: The Remaking of Social Analysis.* 2nd ed., with a new introduction. Boston: Beacon Press, 1993.

Russell-Wood, A. J. R. "The Gold Cycle, c1690–1750." In *Colonial Brazil,* ed. Leslie Bethell, pp. 190–243. Cambridge and New York: Cambridge University Press, 1987.

Salamone, Frank A. *The Yanomami and Their Interpreters.* Lanham, Md.: University Press of America, 1997.

Salgado, Sebastião. *An Uncertain Grace.* Photographs by Sebastião Salgado. Essays by Eduardo Galeano and Fred Tichin. New York: Aperture Foundation, 1990.

Salles, Vicente. *Memorial da Cabanagem: Esboço do pensamento político-revolucionário no Grão-Pará.* Belém, Brazil: Edições CEJUP, 1992.

———. *O negro no Pará sob o regime da escravidão.* 2nd ed. Belém, Brazil: Ministério da Cultura e Secretaria de Estado de Cultura, 1988.

Salomão, Elmer Prata. "Ofícios e condição de garimpar." In Bernardino R.

Figueiredo et al., *Em busca do ouro: Garimpos e garimpeiros no Brasil,* organized by Gerôncio Albuquerque Rocha, pp. 35–87. São Paulo: Marco Zero, 1984.

Sánchez, Jean-Pierre. *Le mythe des amazones du Nouveau Monde.* Acta columbinae 12. Kassell, Germany: Edition Reichenberger, 1991.

Santa Gertrudis, Fray Juan de. "El hedor pestífero del oro." In *Fábulas y leyendas de El Dorado,* ed. Juan Cobo Borda, pp. 232–35. Barcelona: Tusquets Editores, 1987.

Santos, Flávio dos. "Ainda sobre os quilombos: Repensando a construção de símbolos de identidade étnica no Brasil." In *Política e Cultura: Visões do passado e perspectivas contemporâneas,* ed. Maria Hermínia Tavares de Almeida, Peter Fry, and Elisa Reis, pp. 197–222. São Paulo: ANPOCS / HUCITEC, 1996.

Santos, Joaquim Felício dos. *Memórias do distrito diamantino.* 5th ed. Petrópolis, Brazil: Vozes / INL / MEC, 1958.

Sardar, Zahid. "Play Back Time." *San Francisco Examiner Magazine,* 30 April 1995.

Sá Rego, Lúcia de. "Reading the Rainforest." Ph.D. diss., Indiana University, 1997.

Sawyer, Suzana, and Arun Agrawal. "Environmental Orientalisms." *Cultural Critique* 45, in press.

Schama, Simon. *Landscape and Memory.* New York: Knopf, 1995.

Schieffelin, Edward L. *The Sorrow of the Lonely and the Burning of the Dancers.* New York: Saint Martin's Press, 1976.

Schimper, Andreas Franz Wilhelm. *Plant-geography upon a Physiological Basis.* Rev. ed. Trans. William R. Fisher. Oxford: Clarendon Press, 1903.

Schmink, Marianne. "Social Change in the *Garimpo.*" In *Changes in the Amazon Basin,* vol. 2, ed. John Hemming, pp. 185–99. Manchester, England; Manchester University Press, 1985.

Schmink, Marianne, and Charles H. Wood. *Contested Frontiers in Amazonia.* New York: Columbia University Press, 1992.

———, eds. *Frontier Expansion in Amazonia.* Foreword by Charles Wagley. Gainesville: University of Florida Press, 1984.

Schmitt, Peter J. *Back to Nature: The Arcadian Myth in Urban America.* New York: Oxford University Press, 1969.

Schnaiberg, Allan. *The Environment: From Surplus to Scarcity.* New York and Oxford: Oxford University Press, 1980.

Schwarz, Roberto. *Misplaced Ideas: Essays on Brazilian Culture.* Edited with an introduction by John Gledson. London and New York: Verso, 1992.

Sédillot, René. *Histoire de l'or.* Paris: Fayard, 1972.

Sevcenko, Nicolau. *Literatura como missão: Tensões sociais e criação cultural na Primeira República.* São Paulo: Brasiliense, 1983.

Shanahan, James, and Katherine McComas. *Nature Stories: Depictions of the Environment and Their Effects.* Cresskill, N.J.: Hampton Press, Inc., 1999.

Shoumatoff, Alex. *In Southern Light: Trekking through Zaire and the Amazon.* New York: Simon and Schuster, 1986.

Silcock, Lisa, ed. *The Rainforests: A Celebration.* Compiled by the Living Earth Foundation. San Francisco: Chronicle Books, 1990.

Silver, John. "The Myth of El Dorado." *History Workshop* 34 (1992): 1–15.

Simón, Pedro. *Noticias historiales de las conquistas de tierra firme en las Indias occidentales.* Vol. 2. Ed. Manuel José Forero. Bogotá: Biblioteca de Autores Colombianos, 1953.

Simons, Marlise. "In the Gold Rush, Nature Is Viciously Trampled." *New York Times,* 17 May 1989.

Sioli, Harald. "The Amazon and Its Main Affluents: Hydrography, Morphology of the River Courses, and River Types." In *The Amazon: Limnology and Landscape Ecology of a Mighty Tropical River and Its Basin,* ed. Harald Sioli, pp. 127–65. Monographiae Biologicae 56. Dordrecht (Netherlands): Dr W. Junk Publishers, 1984.

Slater, Candace. "Amazonia as Edenic Narrative." In *Uncommon Ground: Rethinking the Human Place in Nature,* ed. William Cronon, pp. 114–31. New York: Norton, 1996.

———. "Breaking the Spell: Accounts of *Encantados* by Descendants of Runaway Slaves." In *Monsters, Tricksters, and Sacred Cows: Animal Tales and American Identities,* ed. A. James Arnold with an afterword by Derek Walcott, pp.157–84. Charlottesville: University of Virginia Press, 1996.

———. *Dance of the Dolphin: Transformation and Disenchantment in the Amazonian Imagination.* Chicago: University of Chicago Press, 1994.

Smith, Anthony. *Explorers of the Amazon.* London: Viking, 1990.

Smith, Herbert Huntington. *Brazil, the Amazons and the Coast.* New York: Charles Scribner's Sons, 1879.

Smith, Nigel J. H. *The Amazon River Forest: A Natural History of Plants, Animals, and People.* New York: Oxford University Press, 1999.

———. *The Enchanted Amazon Rain Forest: Stories from a Vanishing World.* Gainesville: University of Florida Press, 1996.

———. *Rainforest Corridors: The Transamazon Colonization Scheme.* Berkeley: University of California Press, 1982.

Sobol, Donald. *The Amazons of Greek Mythology.* New York: Barnes and Co., 1972.

Sommer, Doris. *Foundational Fictions: The National Romances of Latin America.* Berkeley: University of California Press, 1991.

Sousa, Francisco Bernardino de. *Lembranças e curiosidades do Valle do Amazonas.* Belém, Brazil: Typographia do Futuro, 1873.

Souza, A. M. M., and A. R. B. Silva. *Garimpo de Serra Pelada, Pará.* Garimpos do Brasil: DNPM, 1983.

Souza, Márcio. *Breve história da Amazônia.* São Paulo: Marco Zero, 1994.

———. *A expressão amazonense: Do colonialismo ao neocolonialismo.* Esta América 5. São Paulo: Alfa-Omega, 1968.

———. *A resistível asenção do boto tucuxi: Folhetim.* Rio de Janeiro: Marco Zero, 1982.

Souza Andrade, Olímpio de. *História e interpretação de "Os sertões."* 3rd. ed. São Paulo: Edart., 1966.

"Special Issue on Constructing the Tropics." *Singapore Journal of Tropical Geography* 21, no. 1 (March 2000).

Sponsel, Leslie E. "The Master Thief: Gold Mining and Mercury Contamination in the Amazon." In *Life and Death Matters*, ed. B. R. Johnson, pp. 99–127. Walnut Creek, Calif.: Alta Mira Press, 1997.

Spruce, Richard. *Notes of a Botanist on the Amazon and Andes, Being Records of Travel on the Amazon and Its Tributaries*. Ed. and condensed by Alfred Russel Wallace. London: Macmillan and Co., 1908.

Stam, Robert. *Tropical Multiculturalism: A Comparative History of Race in Brazilian Cinema and Culture*. Durham, N.C., and London: Duke University Press, 1997.

Stecher, Robert. "The Darwin-Bates Letters: Correspondences between Two Nineteenth-Century Travellers and Naturalists." *Annals of Science* 23, no. 1 (1969): 1–47, and 25, no. 2 (1969): 95–125.

Steiger, William Raymond. "What Was Once Desert Shall Be a World: Getúlio Vargas and Westward Expansion in Brazil, 1930–1945." Ph.D. diss., UCLA, 1995.

Stepan, Nancy Leys. *Picturing Tropical Nature*. London and Ithaca, N.Y.: Reaktion Books and Cornell University Press, 2001.

Sterling, Tom. *The Amazon*. Amsterdam: Time-Life Books, 1973.

Stevens, William K. "Conservationists Win Battles but Fear War Is Lost." *New York Times,* 11 January 2000.

Stewart, Charles. *Demons and the Devil: Moral Imagination in Modern Greek Culture*. Princeton: Princeton University Press, 1991.

Stewart, Susan. *On Longing: Narratives of the Miniature, the Gigantic, the Souvenir, the Collection*. Baltimore: Johns Hopkins University Press, 1984.

Stone, Roger D. *Dreams of Amazonia*. 2nd ed. New York: Penguin, 1993.

Struhsaker, Thomas T. *Ecology of an African Rain Forest: Logging in Kibale and the Conflict between Conservation and Exploitation*. Gainesville: University of Florida Press, 1997.

Sullivan, Lawrence E. *Icanchu's Drum: An Orientation to Meaning in South American Religions*. New York: Macmillan, 1988.

Sullivan, Zohreh T. "Enclosure, Darkness, and the Body: Conrad's Landscape." *The Centennial Review* 25, no. 1 (1981): 59–79.

Sweet, David. "A Rich Realm of Nature Destroyed: The Middle Amazon Valley 1640–1750." 2 vols. Ph.D. diss., University of Wisconsin, 1974.

Takacs, David. *The Idea of Biodiversity: Philosophies of Paradise*. Baltimore: Johns Hopkins Press, 1996.

Tallmadge, John Avery. "Narrative Artifice in the Literature of Exploration." Ph.D. diss., Yale University, 1977.

Taufer, Alison. "The Only Good Amazon Is a Converted Amazon: The Woman Warrior and Christianity in the Amadís Cycle." In *Playing with Gender: A Renaissance Pursuit,* ed. Jean R. Brink, Maryanne C. Horowitz, and Allison P. Coudert, pp. 35–51. Urbana: University of Illinois Press, 1991.

Taussig, Michael T. *The Devil and Commodity Fetishism in South America*. Chapel Hill: University of North Carolina Press, 1980.

———. *Shamanism, Colonialism and the Wild Man: A Study in Terror and Healing*. Chicago: University of Chicago Press, 1987.

Tavares Bastos, A. C. *O vale do Amazonas: A livre navegação do Amazonas, estatística, produção, comércio, questões fiscais do vale do Amazonas.* 3rd ed. São Paulo and Brasília: Editora Nacional / INL, 1975.

Teixeira, Hélio. "A década da conquista." *Veja,* 18 August 1982, pp. 90–103.

Terborgh, John. "A Dying World." *New York Review of Books* 48, no. 1 (20 January 2000): 38–40.

———. "The Fate of Tropical Forests: A Matter of Stewardship." *Conservation Biology* 14, no. 5 (2000): 1358–61.

———. *Requiem for Nature.* Washington, D.C.: Island Press, 1999.

Thompson, Stith. *Motif-Index of Folk Literature: A Classification of Narrative Elements in Folk-tales, Ballads, Myths, Fables, Medieval Romances, Exempla, Fabliaux, Jest-books, and Local Legends.* Rev. ed. 6 vols. Bloomington: Indiana University Press, 1955–58.

"Through the Brazilian Wilderness." *The Athenaeum* 4548 (26 December 1914): 664–65.

"Through the Brazilian Wilderness." *New York Times Literary Supplement,* 15 November 1914.

Tierney, Patrick. *Darkness in El Dorado: How Scientists and Journalists Devastated the Amazon.* New York and London: W. W. Norton, 2000.

Tiffany, Sharon W., and Kathleen J. Adams. *The Wild Woman: An Inquiry into the Anthropology of an Idea.* Cambridge, Mass.: Schenkman Publishing Company, 1985.

Tilley, Christopher. *A Phenomenology of Landscape Places, Paths, and Monuments.* Oxford and Providence, R.I.: Berg, 1994.

Tissut, Alain. "L'autre a la croisée des regards." In *Analyses et reflexions sur Lévi-Strauss, "Tristes tropiques": L'autre et l'ailleurs,* Joel Askenazi et. al., pp. 91–95. Paris: Ellipses, 1992.

Tocantins, Leandro. *Euclides da Cunha e o paraíso perdido.* Manaus: Edições Governo do Estado do Amazonas, 1966.

"Todos no Morumbi." *Veja,* 5 July 1989, pp. 80–84.

Tomlinson, H. M. *The Sea and the Jungle.* New York: E. P. Dutton, 1920.

Tonkin, Elizabeth. *Narrating Our Pasts: The Social Construction of Oral History.* Cambridge: Cambridge University Press, 1992.

Tonkin, Elizabeth, Maryon McDonald, and Malcolm Chapman, eds. *History and Ethnicity.* A. S. A. Monographs 27. London and New York: Routledge, 1989.

Torgovnick, Marianna. *Gone Primitive: Savage Intellects, Modern Lives.* Chicago: University of Chicago Press, 1990.

———. *Primitive Passions: Men, Women, and the Quest for Ecstasy.* New York: Knopf, 1997.

Turner, Frederick Jackson. *The Frontier in American History.* 1894. Reprint, Tucson: University of Arizona Press, 1986.

Turner, Terence. "History, Myth, and Social Consciousness among the Kayapó of Central Brazil." In *Rethinking History and Myth: Indigenous South American Perspectives on the Past,* ed. Jonathan D. Hill, pp. 195–213. Urbana: University of Illinois Press, 1988.

———. "Representing, Resisting, Rethinking: Historical Transformations of Kayapó Culture and Anthropological Consciousness in Colonial Situations." In *Essays on the Contextualization of Ethnographic Knowledge,* ed. George Stocking, pp. 285–313. Madison: University of Wisconsin Press, 1991.

Tyrrell, William Blake. *Amazons: A Study in Athenian Mythmaking.* Baltimore: Johns Hopkins University Press, 1984.

UNCED. *The Earth Summit.* London: Graham and Trotman, 1993.

Up de Graf, F. W. *Head Hunters of the Amazon: Seven Years of Exploration and Adventure.* With a foreword by Kermit Roosevelt. Garden City, N.Y.: Duffield and Co., 1923.

Urban, Greg, and Joel Sherzer, eds. *Nation-States and Indians in Latin America.* 1st ed. Symposia on Latin America (series). Austin: University of Texas Press, 1991.

Urton, Gary, ed. *Animal Myths and Metaphors in South America.* Salt Lake City: University of Utah Press, 1985.

Valdivieso, Jorge H. "Realismo mágico en la relación del *Nuevo descubrimiento* del famoso Río Grande de las Amazonas de Fray Gaspar de Carvajal." *Letras de Deusto,* no. 44 (May–August 1989): 327–34.

Varella, Flávia. "Ciência na mata: Biólogos se embrenham nas matas para conhecer o que pretendem preservar." In *Amazônia: Suplemento especial, Veja.* December 1997. Veja on-line, www2.uol.com.br/veja/.

Vasconcellos, Simão de. *Notícias curiosas e necessárias das coisas do Brasil,* vol. 1. Lisbon: João da Costa, 1668.

Velloso Leão. *Euclides da Cunha na Amazônia.* Rio de Janeiro: Livraria São José, 1966.

Venâncio Filho, Francisco. *Euclides da Cunha: Ensaio bio-bibliográfico.* Rio de Janeiro: Oficina Industrial Gráfica, 1931.

———. *Euclydes da Cunha a seus amigos.* São Paulo: Companhia Editora Nacional, 1938.

Verdugo, Iber H. "La crónica de Gaspar de Carvajal." *Mundi* 2, no. 4 (1988): 73–89.

Verne, Jules. *Eight Hundred Leagues on the Amazon.* 2 vols. in 1, with notes on the Amazon by Theodore Roosevelt. 1883. Reprint, New York: Didier, 1952.

Vianna, Hélio. "Centenário de Alberto Rangel." *Revista do Instituto Histórico e Geográfico Brasileiro* 294 (January–March 1972): 237–54.

Vilar, Pierre. *A History of Gold and Money, 1450–1920.* 2nd ed. Trans. Judith White. London and New York: Verso, 1991.

Viola, Eduardo J., et al. *Ecologia, ciência, e política.* Ed. Mirian Goldenberg. Rio de Janeiro: Editora Revan, 1992.

———. *Meio ambiente, desenvolvimento e cidadania: Desafios para as ciências sociais.* São Paulo: Cortez Editora and Florianópolis: Editora da UFSC, 1995.

Viveiros, Esther de. *Rondon conta sua vida.* Rio de Janeiro: Livraria São José, 1958.

Viveiros de Castro Cavalcanti, Maria Laura. "O Boi-Bumbá de Parintins / Amazonas: Breve história e etnografia da festa." *Visões da Amazônia: História, ciência e saúde.* Vol. 6, Suplemento especial. Rio de Janeiro: Casa Oswaldo Cruz / Fiocruz, 1999.

von Bothmer, Dietrich. *Amazons in Greek Art.* Oxford: Clarendon Press, 1957.

Wagley, Charles. *Amazon Town: A Study of Man in the Tropics.* New York: Macmillan, 1953.

———, ed. *Man in the Amazon.* Twenty-third Latin American Conference, University of Florida, 1973. Gainesville: University Press of Florida, 1974.

Wallace, Alfred Russel. *A Narrative of Travels on the Amazon and Rio Negro, with an account of native tribes, and observations on the climate, geology, and natural history of the Amazon Valley.* 4th ed. (originally published in 1853). London and New York: Ward, Lock, Bowden and Co., 1892.

Weckmann, Luis. *The Medieval Heritage of Mexico.* Trans. Frances M. López-Morillas. 1983. New York: Fordham University Press, 1992.

Weinbaum, Batya. *Islands of Women and Amazons: Representations and Realities.* Austin: University of Texas Press, 1999.

Weinstein, Barbara. *The Amazon Rubber Boom, 1850–1920.* Stanford: Stanford University Press, 1983.

Wesche, Rolf, and Thomas Bruneau. *Integration and Change in Brazil's Middle Amazon.* Ottawa: University of Ottawa Press, 1990.

White, Jack, and Avril Grant White. *Jungle Down the Street.* London: Phoenix House, 1958.

White, Richard, and Patricia Nelson Limerick. *The Frontier in American Culture: An Exhibition at the Newberry Library, August 26, 1994–January 7, 1995.* Ed. James R. Grossman. Chicago: The Library; Berkeley: University of California Press, 1994.

Whitten, Norman E., Jr., and Arlene Torres. "Blackness in the Americas." *NACLA,* Report on the Americas 25, no. 4 (1992): 16–22.

Wilbert, Johannes. *Folk Literature of South American Indians: General Index.* Los Angeles: UCLA Latin American Center Publications, 1992.

Wilde, Lyn Webster. *On the Trail of the Women Warriors.* London: Constable, 1999.

Willems-Braun, Bruce. "Buried Epistemologies: The Politics of Nature in (Post)colonial British Columbia." *Annals of the Association of American Geographers* 87, no. 1 (1997): 3–31.

Williams, Raymond J. "Ideas of Nature." In *Ecology: The Shaping Enquiry,* ed. Jonathan Benthall, pp. 146–66. London: Longman, 1972.

———. *Keywords: A Vocabulary of Culture and Society.* London: Fontana, 1976.

Winsor, Justin. "The Amazon and Eldorado." In *History of America,* vol. 1, ed. Justin Winsor, pp. 579–90. Boston and New York: Houghton, Mifflin and Company, 1886.

Wood, Charles H., and Roberto Porro, eds. *Land Use and Deforestation in the Amazon.* Gainesville: University of Florida Press, in press.

Woodcock, George. *Henry Walter Bates: Naturalist of the Amazons*. London: Faber and Faber, 1969.

World Commission on Environment and Development. *Our Common Future*. Oxford and New York: Oxford University Press, 1987.

Worster, Donald. *Nature's Economy: A History of Ecological Ideas*. 2nd ed. Cambridge and New York: Cambridge University Press, 1994.

Yearley, Stephen. "Environmentalism: Science and a Social Movement." *Social Studies of Science* 19 (1989): 343–55.

Acknowledgments

The search for initial answers to the Amazon-size questions of how we and others, including those within Amazonia, view a region long equated with "pure nature" has left me with a series of Amazon-size debts. I am grateful to my students in a seminar on Brazilian civilization at U.C. Berkeley who, one bright November day in 1987, sent me to the library with their casual request for "something about the ways that different people have thought about the Amazon." Though I didn't know it then, my inability to locate a convincing overview of the Amazon as symbol would be the first step on a long, winding road. I also thank the participants in a variety of subsequent graduate and undergraduate classes on whom I tried out my emerging ideas. The members of the two National Endowment for the Humanities Summer Seminars that I directed in 1992 and 1995 were similarly helpful in establishing the framework for this book.

The ideas in *Entangled Edens,* as well as my decision to write for an audience not limited to specialists on the Amazon, owe much to my involvement in two residential research seminars at the nine-campus Humanities Research Institute, headquartered at the University of California, Irvine. Extended conversations with the environmental historians, biologists, and landscape architects in the first of these two seminars, William Cronon's "Reinventing Nature" group, revealed unexpected ties between portrayals of the Amazon and other representations of national parks, urban gardens, and toxic dumps. The sorts of interchanges that produced our collective volume, *Uncommon Ground,* led me to think more deeply about the particular sort of nature—so different from the austere grandeur of Yosemite or from a city park with chubby pigeons—that today's rain forests represent.

A second research seminar at Irvine—this one on the practical implications of rain forest representations, which I went on to convene six years later—helped shape the final version of this book. I thank Scott Fedick, Alex Greene, Paul Greenough, Nancy Peluso, Suzana Sawyer, and Charles Zerner for their part in the conversations that helped me think once more about how particular images of the Amazon collide and intertwine.

Conversations with a wide variety of Amazonians also left a deep and obvious mark upon this book. Had I not spent a total of some twenty-six months (spread over twelve years) in Amazonia's tiny hamlets and big cities, I would have had little idea of the native roots of many of our own most common images of the Amazon. It was the miners whom I met in a string of gold camps, the Brazil-nut gatherers deep within the forest, and the taxi drivers in the steamy bustle of Manaus who truly forced me to reexamine my own ideas about the human relationship to nature. Likewise, the Indian and mixed-blood storytellers whom I recorded on a trip to the Rio Negro just as this book entered production reminded me how much the individual narratives I examine have to do with larger questions of justice. I thank Victor Leonardi and Cezar Martins de Sá, the leaders of the commemorative Humboldt Expedition, for their invitation to join what turned out to be a genuine voyage of discovery.

Among the many persons in the Amazon to whom I owe special thanks are Lucila Campos and her family, Padre Benito di Pietro, Sylvia Amaral and Nilton Rodrigues, Aracélia Farias, Marlicy Bemerguy and family, Patrícia Coelho, Zé Brasil, Rosângela Azevedo, Isabel Vieira, and Milton Hatoum. Although there are a multitude of others whom I do not name here, my enduring debts to them are clear. Each time that I listen to their voices on recordings, and my dog yelps back at the dogs who bark in the background, I find myself reentering another world. Full of dazzling light, this world also has its sudden shadows, whose existence only the speakers on these tapes could have helped a stranger to perceive.

These experiences in the Amazon would have been impossible without financial support. This support—which also helped to finance my earlier book *Dance of the Dolphin*—includes research monies tied to a Chancellor's Professorship at U.C. Berkeley and yearlong research grants from the National Endowment for the Humanities. It also includes the University of California President's Research Fellowship in the Humanities, which I was fortunate enough to hold on two separate occasions. I am similarly grateful to the Rockefeller Foundation for a month's stay in its study center in Bellagio, and to the Stanford Humanities Center, which made available a summer office where I could work on the notes to this book. Warm thanks also to the American Philosophical Society, and to U.C. Berkeley's Committee on Research and Humanities Research Program for summer research monies and sabbatical supplements.

Gwen Kirkpatrick, Donald Moore, and, above all, Richard White made the time to help me when I needed help the most. I have a special debt to students and colleagues at the University of Florida, where, as the Bacardi Eminent Visiting Scholar, I was able to complete the body of this book. There, Nigel Smith, Felix Bolaños, Jeffrey Needell, Marianne Schmink, Richard Bodmer, Charles Wood, Amanda Stronza, and Laura Ogden were particularly generous with their time and knowledge.

I am grateful as well to a long list of other friends and colleagues, including Mark Rose, Charles Halpern, Robert Harrison, David Baron, Hugh Raffles, Robert Hass, José Rabasa, Luiza Moreira, Agnes Robinson, Lola Haskins, and Jenny Price. Francisco Foot Hardman, Leopoldo Bernucci, José Carlos Barreto, William Denevan, Robert Stam, Dain Borges, Joseph Ornig, Nicomedes Suárez-Araúz, and Rolena Adorno provided me with useful research references. The particularly able group of students who assisted me at Berkeley includes Nicole Caso, who helped whip into shape a daunting bibliography, Alessandra Santos, Amy Myers, Vivaldo Santos, Kirsten Ernst, Allison Eymil, Carrie McKellogg, Shon Smith, Pedro Coelho, and Gail Solomon. Laura de la Cruz and Lyman Hong played a similarly helpful role at Florida and Irvine. Special thanks go to my editor, Monica McCormick, for her unwavering enthusiasm and good counsel to me. I thank the expert reviewers in literature, geography, environmental history, and anthropology, who gave me the benefit of insights and practical knowledge drawn from their own disciplines. I also warmly thank Jacqueline Volin for her insightful copyediting, and project editors Jan Spauschus Johnson and Mary Severance, designer Nicole Hayward, and cartographer Bill Nelson for their part in seeing this book into print.

I owe much to my parents, Adelaide Nielsen Slater and the late Frank J. Slater, whose drawers full of wonderfully strange objects acquired during World War II Air Force missions to Egypt, India, and China made me, since early childhood, want to see the world. My family's outings to Theodore Roosevelt's estate at Sagamore Hill, where mammoth elk and buffalo gazed down upon us in the parlor and the pantry dwarfed our kitchen, filled me with an abiding fascination for the man who had once lived there.

My debts to my husband, Paul Zingg, are similarly numerous and enduring. Not only has he sat through countless movies that happen to have the words *rain forest, Amazon,* or *jungle* in the title, but his voice on the other end of the telephone has given me new courage in muddy gold camps and on sunstruck docks in moments when it seemed that I would remain stranded there for years.

Finally, I thankfully remember the poet Elizabeth Bishop, whom I trudged through the snow to see one frosty day in Boston. Still a student with relatively little knowledge of Brazil, I had trouble imagining the Amazon that she began describing halfway through a conversation about her own poetry. "You really ought to go there," she declared as I later wrapped myself in a thick scarf and pulled on a pair of woolly mittens. "The people are remarkable. So full of life and stories. And the river! No one who sees it can forget the meeting of the waters."

Index

Acevedo, Rosa, 177
Achilles, 82, 83, 245n7, 246n8
Achuar peoples, 216
Acosta, José de, Fr., 30–31
Acuña, Cristóbal de, Fr., 12, 95, 207, 244n1 (chap. 1), 251n56
"Advance Brazil" (Avança Brasil), 217
Africa, 248n28
Agenda 21, 262n27
Aguirre, Lope de, 206–7, 208
Aguirre, Wrath of God (Herzog), 252n65
Aikeam-Benano, 84
Ainsa, Fernando, 38
Alcan of Canada, 270n24
Alcoa, 162
Aldeias, 11, 208
Alenquer, 161, 269n15
Alexandros, 83
Alfonso X, el Sabio, 246n10
Alliance for Progress, 136, 260–61n13
Almeida, Alfredo Wagner Berno de, 257n32
Alvares Cabral, Pedro, 206
Álvarez Chanca, Diego, 247n14
"Amadís de Gaula," 85, 206, 247n20
Amapá, 212
Amazon. *See also* Amazons; Rain Forest:
colonization of, 160, 208, 209, 269n9;
commerce in, 11–12; da Cunha on,
190–203; definition of, 9, 218; devel-
opment programs in, 12–13; earliest
inhabitants of, 265n55; female personification of, 79, 99–100, 253n72;
highways in, 135, 136; history of,
10–11, 134–35, 226n16; history of,
chronological, 205–17; modern travel
narratives about, 238n62; opening up
of, 135–36; original name of, 22; po-

litical symbolism of, 194; populist or-
ganizations in, 13, 19; products of (*see
specific commodities*); size of, 2; urban
expansion in, 136
Amazon: Journey to a Thousand Rivers
(documentary by Cousteau), 276n11
Amazonas (Villa-Lobos), 280n58
Amazon.com, 147–48
Amazon Cooperation Treaty, 139
The Amazon (Haskins), 226n16
Amazonia: A Counterfeit Paradise (Meg-
gers), 214
Amazon (IMAX film), 2–4, 7, 9, 20,
186, 187, 200, 223n1
Amazonian Literary Review, 226n16
Amazonian peoples. *See also* Indigenous
peoples; Miners, gold; *Remanescentes
de quilombo: Amazonia without
Myths* on, 150; concept of Amazon of,
73, 75; in new representations of Rain
Forest, 148; as shape-shifters, 9; vo-
cabulary and, 265n59
Amazonia without Myths, 192, 216; on
Amazonians, 150; impact of, 139–41;
population estimates in, 223n4,
226n15; Simoniz car wax ad and, 142;
Spanish-language version, 262n26
Amazon Pact Treaty, 215
The Amazon River Forest (Smith), 151
The Amazon Rubber Boom (Weinstein),
260n9
Amazons: barbaric traits of, 89–90,
250n41; classical and Old World, 15,
82–83, 245–46n7, 245nn3,4,6;
Columbus on, 84, 205; definition of,
94, 218; difference between Green Hell
and, 98; difference between New
World and classical, 85; dominance

317

(*See also* Giants: process of making);
seepage and, 36
Global Warming Convention, 262n27
Gold (Encantado). *See also Garimpos*
(mining camps); Miners, gold: female
characteristics of, 103, 109, 112,
257n30; as giant, 104; human blood
and, 114–15, 116, 123, 257n30;
metamorphosis and, 170–71; miners
and, 18, 102–3, 109, 114, 115–18,
127; reptilian manifestations of, 113–
14; stories about, 110–15, 123; taboos
associated with, 113, 257n26
Golden church story, 170–72
Golden Law, 211
Gold (metal), 12; Amazons associated
with, 83, 84; *chupadeira* system in
mining of, 255n10; discovery of, 105,
106–7, 215, 217, 254nn2,4,5, 255n9,
256n19; European views of, 30–31,
32; history of mining of, 104–5,
257n32, 272n37; influx into Europe,
32; quote about, 77; stories about indigenous, 33–34
Goodyear, Charles, 210
Gow, Peter, 274–75n68, 275n2
Grão Pará, 207
Great Mistresses. *See* Amazons
Green Cathedral: images and meaning of,
8, 226n13; Rain Forest as, 139
Green Cathedral (Onís), 226n13
Green Hell: Amazon as, 95–99; differ-
ence between Amazons and, 98; im-
ages and meaning of, 8, 44; popular-
ization of term, 212, 213, 226n13
Green Imperialism (Grove), 233n13
Green Mansions (Hudson), 44
"Green Plan," 217
Grieve, Peter, 237n51
Gringos, 69, 70, 71, 256n18
Grove, Richard, 233n13
Guadalupe, 84
Guerreiro, Gabriel, 255n9
Guerrillas, 214
Guevara, Ernesto "Che," 214
Guha, Ramachandra, 259n58
Guri Dam, 214
Guyana, 215
Guzman, Nuño de, 89, 246n13, 249n37

Haeckel, Ernst Heinrich, 278n40
Hakluyt Society, 210

"Hamburger Connection," 263n35. *See
also* McDonald's Corporation
Haskins, Caryl P., 226n16
Haximu, 216, 259n53
"Heart of darkness," 262n24
Hellanicus, 83
Hemming, John, 233n18
Henrique, Waldemar, 241n12
Heredia, Pedro de, 206
Herodotus, 83, 245n4
Herrera, Antonio de, 248n25
Herzog, Werner, 97, 252n65
"Highway of the Jaguar," 213
Higino's Lake, 179–81, 183, 186, 203
Hiléia, 277n18, 279n43
Historia general de las Indias (Fernández
de Oviedo), 248n25
Hog plum (*cajazeira*), 46
Hohermuth, Georg, 233n18, 251n53
Homer, *Iliad* of, 82
Horn, Jerry, 263n38
Hortus amoenus, 31, 97
Hudson, W. H., 44
Humboldt, Alexander von, 12, 40, 184,
209, 272n37
Hunt, Linda, 223n1

IBAMA (Instituto Brasileiro do Meio
Ambiente e dos Recursos Naturais
Renováveis), 162, 175, 176, 215,
270n26
Iliad (Homer), 82
Imaginative communities, 279n48
IMAX, film made by, 2–4, 7, 9, 20, 186,
200, 223n1
Imperial Eyes (Pratt), 247n19
Imperialist nostalgia, 238n65
INCRA (National Institute for Colonization and Agrarian Reform), 268n8
Indian Support Commission, 163
Indigenous Black and Popular Resistance
movement, 217
Indigenous peoples. *See also names of
specific groups:* being "civilized" and,
274–75n68; diseases and, 11, 43, 208,
227n23, 232n1; feminization of by
Europeans, 251n51; folklorization of,
233n16; giant-making process and,
15–16; gold miners and, 122; gold stories and, 33–34; Lévi-Strauss on, 154–
55, 238–39n71; massacres of, 217,
243n38; media portrayal of, 148–49,

Raimundo (informant) (*continued*)
62, 64; personal experience with Encantados, 60–61; on rejection of Encantado stories, 75; on shamans, 66
Rain Forest: connotations of term for,
137–38; contrast of 1970s Rain Forest and present-day, 148; definition
of, 138, 275n2; as giant, 15, 16, 49,
137–39, 153; as giant, examples of,
139–46; gold miners and, 125–26; as
Green Cathedral, 139; as iconic forest,
6; idealization of Amazon and, 101;
indigenous groups and, 148–50; marketing of products from, 147–48,
264nn44,46; media version of, 186–
87 (*see also* Media); parrots as symbolic of, 17–18; pessimism about,
150–53; as portrayed by McDonald's,
144–46, 147; as portrayed in *Amazonia without Myths*, 139–41, 142, 150;
as portrayed in Simoniz car wax ad,
141–44, 148; present-day representations and, 146–53; *Saudades do Brasil*
on, 153–57, 217; as symbol of Amazon, 133–36; wilderness and, 49
Rain forest, 221, 261n19, 262n22
Ralegh, Walter, 29; on Amazons, 90,
244n1 (chap. 4); on Ewaiponoma,
250n42; expedition of, 207; on
Guiana/El Dorado, 34, 35, 36, 38;
influences on, 248n26, 249n32; name
spelling of, 232n3; nature of search
for Manoa, 234n23; quote from,
23; retelling of Juan Martínez story,
36–37
Ramos, Alcida, 264n48
Rangel, Alberto, 96–98, 199, 212,
226n13, 252n62, 279–80n53
Ratzel, Friedrich, 278–79n40
Rebellion in the Backlands (da Cunha).
See Os sertões (da Cunha)
Rechelbacher, Horst, 263n37, 264n42
Reducciones, 11, 208
Reforestation, 271n33. *See also* De-
forestation
Regatões, 242n22
Regenwald, 138, 221
Remanescentes de quilombo: animals in
stories of, 167; ARQMO and, 162–
63, 164, 216, 271n28; attitude toward
garimpos, 165–66; Brazil-nut trade

and, 175–76, 213; characteristics of
stories of, 166; as children of the river,
18–19, 159–63, 173–81; definition
of, 159, 221, 271n32, 274n59; Encantados in stories of, 168–70, 177;
golden church story, 170–72; gold
miners and, 165–66, 173; goods sharing, 274n67; Higino's lake story of,
179–81, 183, 186, 203; history of,
160–62; IBAMA and, 162, 175, 176;
impact of environmental policies on,
162; individual and community in stories of, 166–67; lake within a lake
story (*see* Lake-within-a-lake stories);
land battles of, 160, 162–63, 217,
268nn7,8; location of, 159, 270n21;
media stories about, 272n36; nature as
hostile in stories of, 169–70; outsiders
and, 164–65, 174–75, 180–81, 204,
270n22; recording stories of, 163–65;
relations with indigenous peoples,
176–77; saints in stories of, 167–68,
272n43; scholarly studies of, 268n5;
self-identity of, 160; slave memories of,
173–74, 176, 273n54; time of the candles story, 173–74; violence in stories
of, 166; vocabulary shifts of, 173,
178–79
Requiem for Nature (Terborgh), 155,
156, 266n60, 267nn69,70
A resistível asenção do Boto Tucuxi
(Souza), 243n37
Reynolds Aluminum, 162, 270n24
Ribeira, Hernando de, 251n53
Ribeirinhos, 17, 221, 229n44
Ribeiro de Sampaio, Francisco Xavier,
209, 269n11
Riberalta, 211
Rice, Richard, 266n60
Richards, Mose, 1, 231n51
"A Rich Realm of Nature Destroyed"
(Sweet), 134
Rio do Norte, 271n33
Rio Dúvida, 44, 45, 47–48
Rio Earth Summit, 139, 262n27
Rio Negro, 20, 91, 250n45
Rio Protocol, 213
Rivera, José Eustacio, 212
River of Doubt, 44, 45, 47–48
"The River of Silver and the Island of
Brazil" (Brannstrom), 235n34

Text: 10/13 Sabon
Display: Sabon
Compositor: G & S Typesetters, Inc.
Printer & binder: Edwards Brothers, Inc.